D1546890

COMMITTED TO CLASSICISM
THE BUILDING OF DOWNING COLLEGE
CAMBRIDGE

THEOLOGIA
MEDICINA
LEX
MAG CHARTA

COMMITTED TO CLASSICISM
THE BUILDING OF DOWNING COLLEGE CAMBRIDGE

CINZIA MARIA SICCA

with contributions by
CHARLES HARPUM & EDWARD POWELL

Photography, Design and Production by
TIM RAWLE

Foreword by H.R.H. The Duchess of Kent

Published by Downing College, Cambridge
First published in 1987
Copyright © Cinzia Maria Sicca
Copyright © Tim Rawle: location photographs and Figure 4

All rights reserved. No part of this publication may be reproduced, stored in any retrieval system, or transmitted in any form or by any means, without the prior permission in writing of the publishers.

British Library Cataloguing in Publication Data:

Sicca, Cinzia Maria
Committed to Classicism: The Building of Downing College, Cambridge
1. Downing College – Buildings – History
2. Architecture – England – Cambridge – History
3. Cambridge (Cambridgeshire) – Buildings, structures, etc.
I. Title II. Harpum, Charles III. Powell, Edward
IV. Rawle, Tim
727'.3'0942659 LF176

ISBN 0 9511620 1 2 (cased)
ISBN 0 9511620 0 4 (paperback)

Photography, design and production by Tim Rawle
Set in Linotron 202 Palatino by Goodfellow & Egan, Cambridge
Origination by Repro (Cambridge) Limited
Printed by Labute Limited, Cambridge
Bound by Cambridge University Press

Front cover illustrations
JAMES WYATT (1746–1813): Perspective of the courtyard looking south, 1804.
LEWIS WILLIAM WYATT (1777–1853): Elevation of the south block, 1805.
WILLIAM WILKINS (1778–1839): Elevation of the south block, after 1812.
Rear cover
View of the west range as executed
Frontispiece
THE FLAXMAN SEAL. *J.Flaxman delin., J.Heath sculpt., 21.6×17.8 cm. Engraving.* John Flaxman (1755–1826), the most celebrated British Neo-Classical sculptor, presented the design for a College seal to the first Master, Dr Francis Annesley, in 1802. The Governing Body ordered it to be engraved in the same year but sadly never adopted it as the College's official emblem.
Dedication
View of the east range as executed

To Past and Present Members of
Downing College

Contents

List of Illustrations
with Photographic Acknowledgements

Colour Plates:

Black & White:

Acknowledgements

Amongst Cambridge colleges, Downing has one of the richest but least known collections of architectural drawings documenting the various phases of its building history. Some of these drawings were exhibited in 1977 at the Fitzwilliam Museum in an important exhibition organized by Dr David Watkin, devoted to Classicism in nineteenth century Cambridge. The exhibition, however, did not prompt any detailed study of either the drawings or the actual buildings, and in his useful 1980 monograph on William Wilkins, R.W. Liscombe could devote only a limited space to the study of Downing.

During the tenure of my Research Fellowship at Downing, I came to love the drawings and appreciate the influence that they exerted over generations of Fellows. Their unpublished state appeared regrettable, particularly at a time of lively architectural debate on the long-lasting values of Classicism and of rediscovered interest in architectural drawings. This book originated from the desire to publish the drawings in the collection and to tell the story of the building of the college, as revealed by these graphic materials, and by the historical documents in the college's possession.

It is always a pleasure to reach the point where one can express both personal and professional gratitude to the many people and institutions who have helped in the preparation of a book. The Master and Fellows of Downing College granted me absolute freedom in their muniment room and enthusiastically supported the idea of the book. Their confidence in the project, their generosity and their continuous encouragement has made the whole enterprise a sheer pleasure. Amongst them I would like to single out some colleagues and friends who have been particularly helpful: Stephen Fleet and John Treherne, without whom the book would have not come to life; David Blackadder, who patiently agreed to a number of extravagant requests and cheerfully answered innumerable questions; Stanley French, who opened up the archives and shared his deep knowledge of them with me; Ted Powell, who helped in drafting chapter I; Charles Harpum, who contributed his legal knowledge to the first chapter of the book, as well as his loyal friendship throughout.

I am grateful to John Newman, who allowed me to present an abridged version of chapters two and three at the Annual Conference of the Society of Architectural Historians, which took place in London in March 1986. Useful comments were then provided by Howard Colvin, J. Mordaunt Crook and David Watkin. Robin Middleton has answered some of my questions on eighteenth and nineteenth century architecture. Christopher Pickford has provided important information on George Byfield.

I would like to express my gratitude to Jill Lever and the staff of the RIBA Drawings Collection; Margaret Richardson and the staff of Sir John Soane's Museum; the National Portrait Gallery; the Public Record Office at Chancery Lane; the Library of the University of Cambridge and its Photographic Unit, particularly Gerry Bye, possibly the most patient and punctual photographer in the world; and Alan Farrant, of the University Library Conservation Unit, who prepared Wilkins' architectural drawings for photography.

Geoffrey Bursill-Hall, John Harris and Tim Rawle read the manuscript and saved me from many mistakes. Above all I wish to thank my husband, Piers Bursill-Hall, who endured my preoccupied presence and frequent absence with great cheerfulness, and in addition helped with objective criticism and unstinted encouragement.

Cinzia Maria Sicca — Downing College
June 1986

Foreword by H.R.H. The Duchess of Kent

York House
St. James's Palace
London S.W.1

As a kinswoman of the College's third Master, the Rev. Thomas Worsley; the mother of a Downing man, and the Patron of the College, I am especially pleased to write a preface to this first, comprehensive architectural history of Downing.

Generations of undergraduates and members of the public have grown to love the unique and dramatic setting of Downing. Secluded from the excited activity of Regent Street, with its ever increasing number of offices and shops, the College buildings are arranged to form an open quadrangle in which the harmonious proportions of the architecture combine with the serene landscaping to create a haven of beauty and peace. Yet behind the tranquillity and elegance of those Ionic porticoes lies a history of battles, legal and intellectual, far more complex than one could possibly imagine. The book unravels the history of the troubled beginnings of the College and throws new, definitive light on the events leading to the choice of William Wilkins as the architect of the original buildings.

This book, however, does more than just tell the history of the 19th century core of college buildings: it also deals with the present century, showing that the collective architectural taste expressed by members of the college from 1929 onwards has been powerfully moulded by Wilkins' pre-existent neo-classical architecture. Although Wilkins' original design was never completed his drawings have been lovingly preserved in the College. They have acted as a constant reminder of the aims to which the founders aspired, and as a relentless source of inspiration.

These drawings are fully reproduced and catalogued for the first time, and I trust the readers will find their interest and beauty challenging. It is hoped that the catalogue of the drawings will mark the first step in a more extensive programme of restoration and preservation of this uniquely complete collection, which will eventually make them more accessible to both the Downing community and the general public.

Katharine

PATRON

Autumn 1986

I

The Architecture of Downing College: an historical introduction

The controversy over the choice of an architect for Downing College became in 1804 a *cause célèbre* of British architecture and has long been recognized as a major turning point in the history of the Greek Revival, the style based on Greek classical precedents which became fashionable during the first two decades of the nineteenth century. When considered in detail, the history of the building of Downing College assumes an even greater importance: it is the history of the way in which a powerful intellectual group of the early nineteenth century – which shall for convenience be called the Graecophils – established themselves as arbiters of taste, acted as a pressure group and thus forced a weak corporate client (a young, incohesive college community) to respond to public pressures. Until that moment the college had been acting in a very private and traditional way, and when the public pressure exercised by the Graecophils was relieved, the fractured 'corporate' client found itself divided into factions which led to building in a most un-college-like and un-corporate-like manner, producing the skeleton of the college buildings we have today. In practice the relationship with the architect proceeded along the conventional lines of a number of single private patrons with their chosen architect.

The early history of the building of Downing College exemplifies with unusual clarity the changes in the relationship between architect and patron which marked the passage from the eighteenth to the nineteenth century. The new century saw the introduction of new technologies and with them came social and cultural changes which, inevitably, were reflected in and affected the organization of the architectural profession and practice.

The history of Downing also draws attention to several other issues of interest, all connected with the history of nineteenth century architecture at large rather than with the history of collegiate building alone. The major ones can be outlined here, dividing them for convenience into problems related to the 'patron' and problems related to the architect. On the patron's side one of the crucial questions seems to be the following: when dealing with a corporate patron – in this case the Fellowship of a college – to what extent does the prior existence of a building functioning as a communal base help to determine the patron's identity as a community? In other words, was the Downing client so weak simply because it did not physically exist as a community? This lack of identity and protracted 'non-existence' as a community was certainly the cause of the subsequent fragmentation and division when dealing in 1807–1820 with Wilkins, the architect eventually appointed, but may also have been ultimately responsible for the rejection of one of the designs, namely the one by George Byfield. Furthermore, one of the questions raised is: how clear was the layout of the proposed college in the minds of its earliest members? Did they provide the architect (or architects) with a detailed brief or did the architect devise his own brief?

Seen from the point of view of the architect, Downing's history provides answers to questions such as: how did early nineteenth century architects address a corporate patron? How did they present their ideas? Can we detect an increasing degree of sophistication in the presentation of drawings, estimates and specifications? Confronted with a unique opportunity such as building an entirely new college, to what extent did these architects attempt to produce designs reflecting new ideas on education? Another important question concerns the extent to which the architects taking part in the competition attempted to integrate the new college with the town. The range of problems raised by the study of Downing's architecture is indeed vast and, as it can be easily gauged, goes well beyond strict architectural history. Some of them are representative of the nineteenth century at large, others are peculiar to the college and its troubled beginnings. It is necessary to give here a brief outline of the dispute over the legitimacy of the foundation, since it so much affected the actual building of the college.

Downing College owes its foundation to Sir George Downing, the third baronet and grandson of the founder of the Downing fortune.[1] Born in 1685, Downing was married at the age of fifteen to his cousin Mary Forester. The marriage was never consummated, and in 1715 Mary petitioned the House of Lords – unsuccessfully – for the annulment of the marriage by Act of Parliament. The best that she could obtain was a legal separation, which undid the effects of the marriage on the property rights of the parties.[2] This received the sanction of Parliament in 1717. Later that year, on 20 December, Downing made his will. It was a complex document which created a strict settlement.[3] By it, he bequeathed his estates to his cousin Jacob Garrett Downing (son of his uncle Charles) for life, thereafter to his cousin's eldest and other sons successively in tail male.[4] If Jacob and his sons died without issue, the property was to pass to Thomas Barnardiston[5] (son of Downing's maternal aunt, Mary) for life, thereafter to his eldest and other sons successively in tail male. If Barnardiston or his sons died without issue, there were similar provisions successively for Charles and John Peters (sons of the first baronet's youngest sister, Martha).[6] If all of these persons or their sons were to die without issue, the property was to pass to five named trustees to purchase land in Cambridge on which to build and seek a charter for a college, to be called Downing's College. The will also appointed advisers to the trustees in founding a college – the Masters of Clare Hall (now Clare College) and St. John's College, and the Archbishops of York and Canterbury.

Sir George Downing's estates were extensive and valuable. They were subsequently valued at £4,200 per annum, and were spread across Cambridgeshire, Bedfordshire and Suffolk. In Cambridgeshire, there were estates in East Hatley, Tadlow, Croydon, Clopton and Bottisham, as well as fee farm rents in Bourn, Denny Abbey, Histon, Girton, Ditton, Horningsea and Waterbeach, and rights of common and view of frankpledge in the Hatleys, Croydon, Tadlow, Gamlingay (Fig.1), the Swaffhams, Bottisham, Reach, Stow-cum-Quy and Little Wilbraham. In Bedfordshire there were lands in Wrestlingworth and Cockayne Hatley, and in Suffolk at Cowlinge and Dunwich.

Sir George died in 1749 and his estates passed under his will to Sir Jacob Downing. All the trustees named in Sir George's will predeceased him. By the time Sir Jacob died childless in 1764, both the Peters brothers and Thomas Barnardiston had died without issue. Sir Jacob left all his property, including the estates inherited from Sir George Downing, to his wife, Lady Margaret Downing (Pl.I), though under Sir George's will, Sir Jacob had only a life interest. If, however, the limitations contained in Sir George's will were void, then Jacob was entitled to the Downing estates absolutely because he was, in the eyes of the law, Sir George's heir. Lady Downing's entitlement therefore depended on the validity of the trust to create Downing College.

The University of Cambridge was, of course, extremely interested in acquiring a new foundation which, on paper, appeared to be well endowed. Thus, on 1 May 1764, a few months after Sir Jacob's death, the Hon. Charles Yorke – son of Lord Chancellor Hardwicke and brother of the Visitor of St. John's (the college which had its Master named as a trustee in Sir George Downing's will) – in his role as University Counsel, caused the Attorney-General to file an information in the Court of Chancery on the relation of the University of Cambridge against Lady Downing. This was done in order to have Sir George's will established, the trusts carried out, an account of profits from the date of Sir Jacob's death drawn up, and to appoint a receiver.

The court case *Attorney General* v. *Downing* was heard in two parts.[7] The first, which is of some legal interest, came before Lord Chancellor Camden, assisted by Sir Thomas Sewell, Master of the Rolls, and Sir John Wilmot, Chief Justice of the Common Pleas. Judgment was given in June 1768. The court had to consider three questions. The first was whether the trusts to create a college were illegal and void on grounds of 'mortmain',[8] that is to say because the trusts took effect as a gift to a corporation. Because a corporation never dies, such gifts were considered objectionable.[9] That contention was rejected. The gift operated as a bequest to Sir George's heirs, subject to a trust to found and endow the college. That trust was charitable, within the Charitable Uses Act 1601,[10] and as such was exempted from the effect of the mortmain legislation.[11] Secondly, it was said that the trust was not of such a nature that the court ought to enforce it. This argument failed, partly because 'trusts are always imperative and are obligations upon the conscience of the party intrusted', and partly because the foundation of a college was (despite arguments to the contrary) a useful and meritorious object. The third point did not strictly arise in these immediate circumstances, but the court nevertheless expressed an opinion on it. If the trusts had been void or unenforceable, would the estate have been applied to an analogous charitable purpose by a doctrine known as *cy-pres*?[12] The court held, on the basis of precedents (though with no great enthusiasm), that it would. On that basis therefore, even if the trusts had been void, Lady Downing's claim would have failed. In the second part of the action, heard by Lord Camden alone, a number of very technical points failed to be considered. Judgment was given in July 1769. The outcome of the case was that the court ordered the execution of the trusts provided that a royal charter could be obtained. Those persons who at law were Sir George's heirs were to be the trustees and it fell to them to obtain the charter, apply for a licence to purchase an appropriate piece of land in Cambridge and become the Visitors of the new college. All costs were to be paid out of the testator's estate. No order was made, however, for the transfer of the estates from Lady Downing to the heirs-at-law or for the appointment of a receiver. The heirs-at-law happened to be ladies[13] who must have found very little appeal in the tasks which would fall upon them as a

1 Jenkinson and Lovell, Plan of Sir George Downing's estate at Gamlingay, Cambridgeshire, 1801

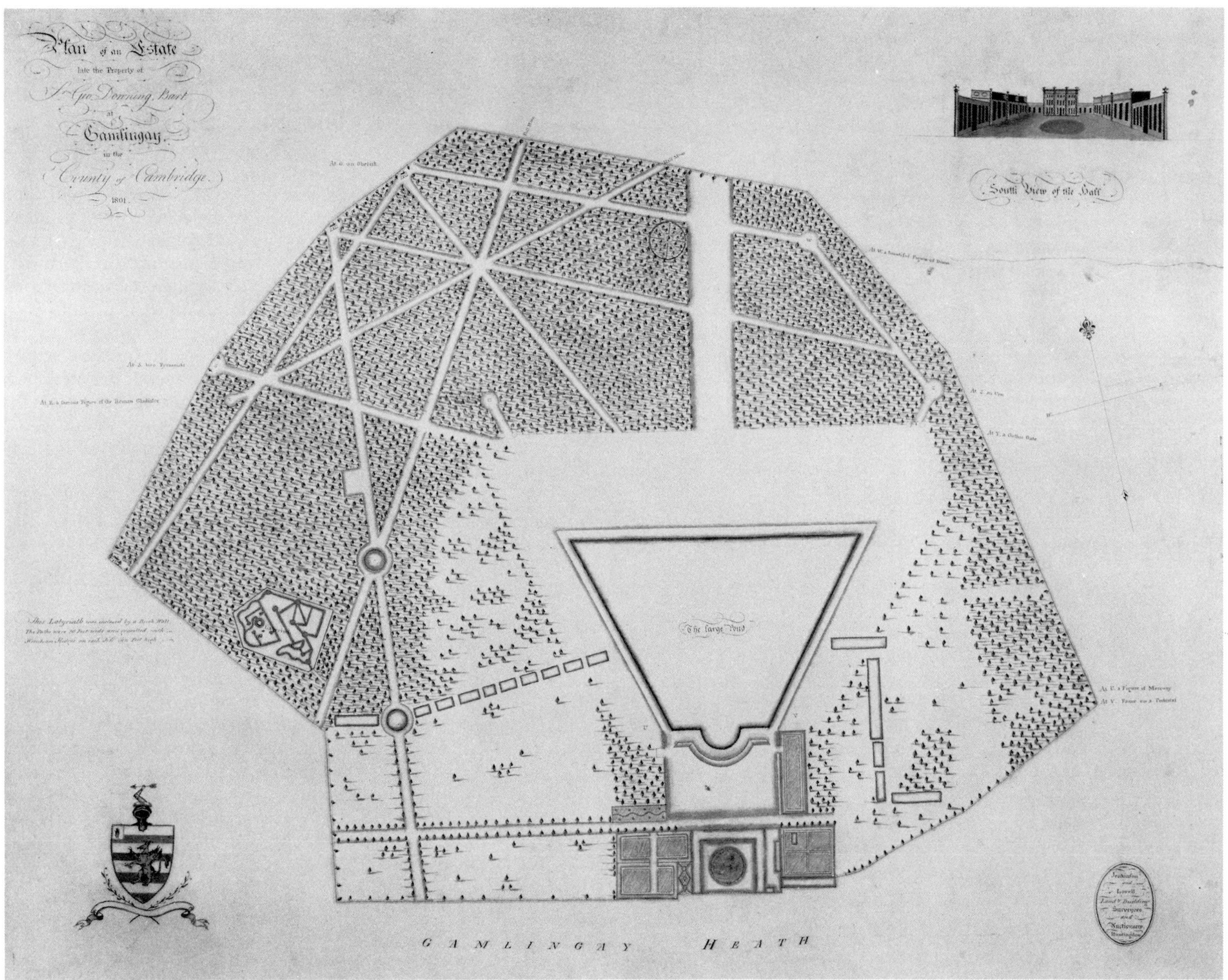

1

consequence of the Court's judgment. A letter from Wilmot to Elizabeth Ewer's husband, the Bishop of Bangor, vividly describes the type of considerations which eventually made them accept their fate and highlights the system of patronage which later on played such an important part in the choice of an architect:

> I have no doubt of advising the Heirs at Law to accept it [the Court's order], in case Lord Chancellor continues in the same opinion to give it. It is an honour in a family to be Visitors of such a College as this, and their petitioning the King to carry this bequest into execution, will give them power and credit, and profit too, for they will then have considerable sway in the disposition of fellowships and other profitable emoluments that may be in future a considerable benefit to the family. And I see no reason why your Lordship may not be the first Master of Downing College. Therefore think it should be accepted, and I dare say there are many great familys [sic] who would give many £1000's for such an honour.[14]

In 1770 the heirs-at-law petitioned for a Royal Charter of foundation. The petition was referred to the Attorney-General and the Solicitor-General, but no action was taken upon it throughout the 1770s, perhaps as a result of the hostility of the incumbent Attorney-General, Edward Thurlow, towards the university from which he had been sent down as an undergraduate. This period of inactivity is perhaps also explained by the death of Charles Yorke in 1770.[15] The Downing cause was not to find another active champion until the choice of Francis Annesley (Fig.2), son of one of the heirs-at-law, as the first Master of Downing. There is no precise record documenting the date and circumstances of Annesley's appointment, but it is possible that after the death of John Ewer, the Bishop of Bangor, in 1774, and in the absence of any other charismatic figure amongst them, Annesley became the obvious candidate of the heirs-at-law. The members of the various families had by now clearly realized that Wilmot's advice of 1768 was correct and that great power and influence was to be gained by associating their names with a Cambridge college. In 1778/79 Annesley's name begins to appear with regularity in a bill of costs, as being in frequent consultation with the solicitors of the heirs-at-law.

Lady Margaret Downing died in 1778, but her claims to Sir George Downing's estates did not die with her. She passed them to the two principal beneficiaries of her will, her second husband George Bowyer and her nephew Jacob John Whittington, who continued to oppose the college's foundation.

With Annesley's appearance on the scene the inertia of the 1770s seems to have ended. In 1781 a petition was again submitted to the king for a royal charter of foundation. Once more it was referred to the Law Officers, who expressed themselves in favour of the petition but were unable to make any recommendations for a scheme to found a college because none had been appended to the petition. A year later Cambridge University established a Syndicate to look after its interests in the Downing cause. Various schemes for a charter were prepared using as models the charters of Sidney Sussex, St. John's, Pembroke, Caius, Trinity and Emmanuel, as well as that of Wadham College, Oxford. Initially it was envisaged that three professorships would be established, in medicine, the laws of England and practical astronomy. This latter discipline was desirable for its practical applications to navigation, perhaps in memory of the founder's connection with the United States of America. The Professor of Astronomy was, according to an early draft of the charter, to be given an assistant, and the heirs-at-law undertook to build an observatory on the grounds of the college. In subsequent drafts astronomy was replaced by natural philosophy, but eventually this subject too was dropped. In all the surviving drafts[16] the heirs-at-law petitioned the king for permission to appoint a foreigner to the professorship of medicine showing that they were aware of the advancement of medical studies in the four great continental centres of Montpellier, Paris, Leyden and Vienna.

In 1783, Jacob Whittington appealed to Chancery to review the 1769 decree authorising the heirs-at-law to apply for a charter, but his appeal was dismissed by the Lords Commissioners.[17] Two years later, the heirs-at-law submitted a fresh petition for a charter to the king, with a scheme attached: this time the Law Officers felt unable to proceed until they had received a valuation of the lands bequeathed by Sir George Downing. Attention now focussed on the establishment of control by the heirs-at-law, represented by Annesley, over the Downing estates, which were still in the hands of Lady Margaret's heirs, Bowyer and Whittington. The University strengthened Annesley's hand by making him its Syndic in the matter, although he was not a member of the university. Annesley still lacked formal standing

2 after A.Hikel, Portrait of Francis Annesley, Master 1800–1812

in the eyes of the Court of Chancery, however, and in order to obtain it he lodged a suit, in 1788, in the Prerogative Court of the Province of Canterbury, which had jurisdiction in testamentary cases, to be appointed administrator of Sir George Downing's estate. The purpose of this was, it seems, to give him the right to sue for the income from the estates which had accrued since the death of Lady Downing. In 1792, after years of tortuous litigation, during which the case was fiercely fought by George Bowyer, Annesley was granted letters of administration.

Armed with this authority, Annesley returned to Chancery. Litigation was delayed by Bowyer's absence at sea, but in 1795 the court confirmed the 1769 decree, and in the following year it received a report on the value of the Downing estates, which was set at £4,200 per annum, clearly sufficient for the establishment of a college. A final attempt to block the foundation of the college by Bowyer and Whittington failed.[18] The final stumbling-block before a royal charter could be granted was the acquisition of land on which to build the college. Sir George Downing's will had established that the heirs-at-law should purchase land for the college before applying for a royal charter, and the Chancery decree of 1769 apparently ordered that a conditional contract be made for such a purchase, although this carried obvious risks for the vendor should the petition for a charter subsequently be refused. The purchase, in 1798, of a quarter-acre plot of land, near Midsummer Common, called Doll's Close, satisfied the legal requirement, although it was clearly far too small for collegiate purposes.

Chancery gave leave for the heirs-at-law to petition anew for the royal charter, which they promptly did. The petition was referred to a sub-committee of the Privy Council which conducted a detailed inquiry into the funds which would be available to the college. This involved a settlement between the university and the petitioners, on the one side, and Bowyer and Whittington, the heirs of Lady Downing, on the other, over the income which had been received from the estates since Sir Jacob Downing's death in 1764. Theoretically, with an annual value of £4,200, this amounted to over £100,000. Any attempt to secure such a large sum might, however, have involved protracted litigation which would have further delayed the college's foundation. A compromise was reached, by which Lady Downing's heirs agreed to pay the income from the estates over the previous six years only – approximately £24,000. The legal costs of all parties were deducted from this figure, leaving to the heirs-at-law, and thus the new college, only £9,780. 18s. 1d. The compromise was reported to the Lord Chancellor on 5 March 1800.[19] The Privy Council established to its own satisfaction that a start could be made on the college buildings from the existing resources, and advised the king to grant the charter.

The Royal Charter for Downing College was issued on 22 September 1800. This was followed, on 23 July 1805, by the publication of detailed statutes for the regulation of the college. The statutes were published by the heirs-at-law, as trustees, with the approval of the Archbishops of Canterbury and York and the Master of St. John's College, in their capacity as advisers to the trustees under the terms of Sir George Downing's will.[20] Under these statutes Downing was far from being an autonomous, self-governing institution administered by its governing body. In financial matters, in particular, it remained within the tutelage of the Court of Chancery. A building fund was set up, controlled by Chancery, which had first claim on the college's income, and the court appropriated to it £3,000 per annum. The building schemes, and all payments for building costs, had to be approved by the Master in Chancery.[21]

II

Early Projects for the College 1771–1805

Unlike the other Cambridge colleges, most of which had grown around an original medieval nucleus, Downing was a new foundation. In 1717 the founder, Sir George Downing, had bequeathed estates in Cambridgeshire, Bedfordshire and Suffolk to certain trustees, in trust for his cousin Jacob Garret Downing. In case of the extinction of the male line, the trustees, named in the will as the holders of the Masterships of Clare Hall and St. John's College and of the Archbishoprics of Canterbury and York, were directed to purchase a piece of ground in Cambridge on which they should build all the edifices necessary for an educational institution which would be known by the name of its founder.

The peculiar and entangled legal situation that ensued, and which has been outlined in the previous chapter, had certain crucial repercussions on the history of the building: it meant *inter alia* that from the Lord Chancellor's judgment in 1769, until the time when the royal charter was granted in 1800, there was a problematic relationship between the client and the architect. This was largely determined by the fact that the client had no real identity, since the Fellowship was only established in 1800, and also by the fact that the ultimate decision in all matters rested with the Master in Chancery. The Court of Chancery also held complete control over the college finances, including the building fund, until the middle of the nineteenth century. Any architect trying to build Downing College was thus dealing, not just with one committee, but with several at once. Admittedly, having a committee as a client was not a great novelty: in Cambridge and Oxford most college and university buildings had in the past been placed under the supervision of either the governing body or of smaller *ad hoc* committees. In Cambridge in the seventeenth and eighteenth centuries this had certainly been the case for the new Fellows' building at King's (known as the Gibbs' building), for Wren's Library at Trinity, for the Senate House and for the new east frontage of the Old Schools (just to mention a few examples). Both in London and in provincial towns, contemporary public buildings were decided upon by committees: examples include the Mansion House in London, the York Assembly Rooms, St. George's Hospital in London or the New Dormitory at Westminster School.

The fact that the Downing client was a group of individuals did not make the commission either more difficult or anomalous, the real anomaly was that as a corporate body or entity the client initially did not really exist. The very group of people who should have decided what they wanted and how they wanted did not exist until 1800. At that point, when the college consisted of a Master (Dr Francis Annesley), two Professors (Sir Busick Harwood and Edward Christian) and three Fellows (John Lens, William Meek and William Frere), the committee still lacked a sense of identity and cohesion. Most of its members lived outside Cambridge (Annesley in London, Christian spent most of his time in Hertfordshire where he was from 1790 Professor of law at the East India College, Frere had been called to the bar and joined the Norfolk circuit) or in other Cambridge colleges, so they had not had the opportunity to develop, over a period of time, a sense of belonging to an institution, a communion of intents, or any other sense of corporate identity within Cambridge. This latter factor was especially important in Cambridge, where the sense of belonging to a college can be precisely identified with a building or group of buildings.

The very peculiar situation in which the members of the newly established college found themselves largely explains the way in which the client proceeded, in the selection of an architect first and, later on, in the erection of the building. In this respect, the history of Downing College turns out to be in one way peculiarly Cantabrigian and in another not. It vacillated between being treated as a local affair, in which local friendships and traditional allegiances were at work, and being very much a public business, run from London by certain intellectual groups. Because of the pressure imposed on the clients by external forces, namely the supporters of the Greek Revival, the nature of the commission was transformed. By 1804 it had been turned into a competition, although it was never advertised as such.

Let us go back to the pre-1800 story, when the first architect to be connected with the scheme for the new college was James Essex. In a letter to the Secretary of the Society of Antiquaries, Richard Gough, dated 21 November 1771, Michael Tyson, a Fellow of Corpus Christi College and a popular amateur artist, wrote: 'Essex is come down from London with a commission to purchase, at any rate, Pembroke Leas, to build Downing College upon, and immediately to draw a plan and elevation of the new College. The charter is to be framed out of hand, and the foundation laid as soon as possible.' The choice of an architect at this point in time was the immediate consequence of the 1769 judgment, ordering the execution of the trusts, provided that a royal charter could be obtained, and of the 1770 petition for a royal charter.

Essex was very much a local man. Born in Cambridge in 1722, he was the son of James Essex, a carpenter and joiner of Cambridge who had been extensively employed by the university and colleges throughout the first half of the eighteenth century. The younger James was educated at the grammar school attached to King's College, and subsequently studied architecture under the guidance of the amateur architect Sir James Burrough (1691–1764), the Master of Caius. Essex collaborated with Burrough on several Cambridge commissions and, after Burrough's death, took over from him the design and building of the chapel at Clare. Despite his semi-academic education and his determination to establish himself as an architect, Essex did not sever his ties with the practical side of the building trade. He kept practising in his father's business and after the latter's death in 1749 he built the famous wooden 'mathematical' bridge at Queens' College, to the designs of William Etheridge. A brief survey of Essex's activity in Cambridge up to 1771 immediately reveals his popularity with the colleges. In 1749–1750 he built the wooden bridge at Queen's; in 1750 he equipped the so-called Dome Room in the University Library (now the antechamber to the Council Room and Vice-Chancellor's Office); in 1755–1758 he supervised the reconstruction of the north and south sides of Nevile's Court at Trinity College; in 1757 he built the Ramsden Building at St. Catharine's College; in 1758–1769 he ashlared the interior of the quadrangle at Christ's College; in 1760–1764 he repaired and refitted the Hall at Emmanuel; in 1762 he refitted the Combination Room of Jesus College; in 1766–1768 he completed the west end of the Senate House; in 1760–1775 he rebuilt the street front of Emmanuel College; in 1770–1774 he designed and built the new building at the south end of the west range of Trinity's Great Court, including the Combination Room; in 1770–1775 he designed and installed the new reredos in the chapel at King's College. It is thus not at all surprising to find Essex entrusted with the choice of a site for Downing and with the design of the buildings themselves. His name might have been put forward by either the Master of St. John's or the Master of Clare, both appointed trustees of Sir George Downing's will and both of whom would have known Essex through his direct involvement with the building activities of their respective colleges.

As a local architect Essex had a lot to commend himself in the eyes of the heirs-at-law and of the trustees of Sir George Downing's estates. Unlike Oxford, Cambridge colleges had traditionally favoured the employment of local craftsmen and builders. There had, of course, been a few exceptions in the seventeenth century with Wren's Library at Trinity and the Chapels at Pembroke and Emmanuel, and in the earlier part of the eighteenth century, notably when the university had turned to James Gibbs for the design of the Senate House and when Gibbs – the last in a series of renowned London architects approached by the college – designed and built the Fellows' Building at King's. On the whole, however, local talent had been preferred to the more glittering, considerably more expensive, and more volatile London architects. Furthermore, Essex had the additional appeal of being an architect – hence something of an intellectual – as well as a trusted local craftsman. His training under Sir James Burrough had made him perfectly conversant and versatile in the Neo-Palladian idiom so fashionable in the eighteenth century, but had not diminished his natural interest in the Gothic. Unlike his contemporaries, who treated Gothic as a decorative style, appealing principally because of its romantic associations, Essex admired Gothic buildings because of their structural and tectonic qualities. His unique understanding of medieval architecture was acquired through painstaking antiquarian research which extended far beyond East Anglia and which gained him, in 1762–1765, the surveyorship of Lincoln cathedral, and, in January 1772, membership of the Society of Antiquaries. Essex's capacity to switch from a classical to a Gothic style was an additional element in his favour, particularly in the early stage of the Downing commission when no aesthetic faction appears to have been pressing in favour of any given style. Indeed, had Essex lived longer and the litigation proceeded more speedily, the buildings of Downing College might have presented a very different aspect.

No drawing by Essex for the college appears to have survived amongst his papers now preserved in the British Museum, so it is impossible to ascertain how far he had gone in his designs by the time of his death on 14 September 1784. The only evidence contained amongst the British Museum papers of Essex's connection with the Downing project is a manuscript copy of Sir George Downing's will (an unusual document for an architect to peruse) which Essex had presumably treated as a brief, in the absence of any more precise document concerning the size and scope of the projected college.[1] Essex died of a stroke following a protracted period of ill-health which began in the late 1770s. This slow decline must have alerted the various people involved in the establishment of the college and prompted them to search for a new architect, since in 1783 we find James Wyatt sketching a design for the building in an album, now in the collection of the Vicomte de Noailles (Paris).

A little more than a month after Essex's death, James Wyatt was being mentioned as 'the architect' of the college. Writing on 27 October 1784 to the Rev. Mr Ashby at Barrow, near Newmarket, Michael Lort, Fellow of Trinity College, reported that:

> Mr Ainsly the new Mr of Downing has been here to fix on a site for his new College, for, though many has been proposed to him, yet objections are made to all – Mr Wyatt the architect wishes much that it should be opposite to some of the colleges on the River, for then he thinks he shall not be crampt for Room, & may make four fine facades; but how will they here get an access to, & communication with, the Town? The most promising spot seems to be that between Bp Watsons house and the Tennis Court, but here tis said they cannot dig cellars, a material object, I presume, to such a college.- The King has recommended two particulars – that it may not be a Gothic building, & that the Professors be obliged to publish their lectures – to this latter, I do not assent, Lectures thus published will do little credit to the author or his college.[2]

Lort's reference to the king's opposition to a Gothic building for the new college may suggest that Essex's design was indeed in this very style. Although a large proportion of James Wyatt's ecclesiastical as well as private commissions were Gothic too, his professional breakthrough had come in 1769–1772 with what made him fashionable in the eyes of the large public, namely his successful Neo-Palladian design for the Pantheon in Oxford Street. This was a building for entertainments, almost a covered winter version of the famous Ranelagh Gardens. It was built in a basically classical style which, however, departed from the archaeological interest underlining the work of contemporary architects such as Robert Adam, or the Earl of Burlington in the earlier part of the century. Rather than being based on the Pantheon in Rome, after which it was named, Wyatt's building was modelled on Santa Sophia, Constantinople, then a little known and little admired Byzantine church. But, the success of the Pantheon was tremendous and in 1772 Wyatt was elected Associate Member of the Royal Academy. This was just the beginning of his career which led to his occupying key positions of increasing prestige: in 1782 he was appointed Architect to the Board of Ordnance, in 1796 Surveyor General and Comptroller of the Office of Works, and in 1805 President of the Royal Academy.

No document survives fully accounting for the trustees' choice of Wyatt as the new architect for Downing College, but it is possible to provide interpretations for this move. With the death of James Essex Cambridge was deprived of that particular type of local craftsman-turned-architect that the university and colleges (the town's major patrons) had so favoured for centuries. Essex's death created a real gap: William Wilkins senior (1715–1815), the father of Downing's future architect and a plasterer/architect himself, had not yet moved to Cambridge and there was no other man in the town competent enough to handle the design of a whole new college. This shortage of local talent presented itself at a time when the whole structure of the building profession was undergoing a drastic transformation. These changes had been brought about by the slow but steady emergence, since the middle of the eighteenth century, of properly trained architects who, by the time of the accession of George III, constituted the nucleus of what today we would call a profession. The figure of the aristocratic amateur architect which had loomed so large over the architectural achievements of the earlier part of the century was swept away, and the practice, common in the provinces during the previous three hundred years, of turning to a local craftsman or master mason, with a pattern book or a model to copy or adapt, was no longer acceptable. In the specific case of the new college the scale and importance of the commission required the employment of a professional of the highest calibre. Since such a person was not available in Cambridge itself, it was necessary to turn elsewhere, and London was the obvious place. Still, this does not answer the question of why the choice fell on Wyatt in particular. At the time London offered a number of excellent architects in their professional prime: Robert Adam (1728–1792), Sir William Chambers (1723–1796), George Dance the younger (1741–1825), Henry Holland (1745–1806), Robert Mylne (1733–1811), Sir John Soane (1753–1853) and James Stuart (1713–1788), to mention but a few. Yet Wyatt had achieved sudden fame with the Oxford Street Pantheon and he quickly eclipsed architects like Adams and Chambers. He was certainly well known to London residents, such as Francis Annesley. His name was not unknown in the academic circles of Cambridge either, partly because his buildings were mentioned in newspapers and journals such as *The Gentleman's Magazine*, and through his extensive work in Oxford in the years before his rise to fame and the death of Essex. Between 1773 and 1783 Wyatt worked at Christ Church (1773–1783), Worcester College (1776), New College (1778), Brasenose College (1779–1780), the Radcliffe Observatory (1776–1794) and the Music School (1780). A direct knowledge of college buildings and some experience in dealing with committees of dons might have been regarded by the heirs-at-law, the trustees and the Court of Chancery as a further point in Wyatt's favour. Finally, it should be remembered that his position in the Board of Ordnance coupled with the patronage he received from the king, made Wyatt, if not the only choice, certainly a very difficult one to match.

From the very start of his involvement with the college, in c.1783, Wyatt appears to have realized that this was not only an extraordinary architectural commission but that it also might afford him the opportunity to leave his imprint over the town at large. Michael Lort's letter, quoted above, refers, in fact, to Wyatt's wish that the site chosen for the buildings should be 'opposite to some of the colleges on the River', in other words on The Backs opposite the great colleges. This marked a rather neat departure from the line of thinking pursued by Essex and prejudiced the suitability of the Pembroke Leys. In 1784 the land across the river, from Queens' to St. John's, was not built on; the bridges were few and private (with the only exception of Garret Hostel Bridge) since they belonged to the colleges (Queens', King's, Clare, Trinity and St. John's) and led into gardens, orchards and fields belonging to the colleges. The town had expanded south and eastwards, leaving the area to the west very much untouched. Wyatt's preference for a site across the river betrays the urban scale of his conception. Had it been possible to acquire a site across The Backs, Wyatt would have had to solve the problem of access to and from the town, as well as that of tidying up the appearance of The Backs generally in order to open up vistas towards his new buildings. These, if sited according to his wish, would have created a powerful architectural focus on the opposite side of the river, but only provided that the thick and old fashioned plantations belonging to the five major colleges along The Backs could be reshaped or even completely removed.

Wyatt was not the first in the eighteenth century to turn his attention to this part of the town: in 1725, Charles Bridgeman had devised a scheme for new walks and plantations at King's (which were never implemented), and then in 1779 Lancelot 'Capability' Brown had presented the Senate of Cambridge University with a plan for extensive alterations to The Backs. This plan, which survives in the University Library, presupposed that the individual colleges would renounce their ancient boundaries in order to create a typically Brownian wide, open park, with an encircling thickly planted walk and clumps of trees scattered around the lawns. The river was to be widened and its natural course altered by the introduction of a great single bend. Brown's plan was not executed because of its cost and because it impinged too drastically on the privileges of the individual colleges. When Wyatt seized upon the idea of a site on the west bank of the river he must have been aware of Brown's plan and he must have believed that he stood a better chance of bringing it into execution, at least to some extent, because, unlike Brown, he was proposing the erection of a major building for a new college which was favoured by the university.

Wyatt's grand scheme to erect the college along The Backs never materialized; indeed it is not known whether the heirs-at-law ever made any serious attempt to acquire land in that area. The Pembroke Leys, contained within Pembroke College, the Old Addenbrooke's site and St. Andrew's Street, would have been a very good alternative but turned out to be an inpractical proposition since they were fragmented into too many occupancies and ownerships, several with common rights extinguishable only by Act of Parliament. By 1796, when the Crown was petitioned for a charter of incorporation, the heirs-at-law needed to find a piece of land which could be easily acquired and would satisfy the Court as a suitable site, even though there was probably no real intention to build on it. The City Corporation offered two sites: fifteen acres of pasture land at Parker's Piece, and a smaller plot of one acre and twenty-three poles known as Pound Hill, near Castle Hill. Francis Annesley, acting as agent for the heirs-at-law, provisionally agreed to take both sites on a 999 years lease, subject to the condition that if the charter were not granted within one year the agreement should be void. Since the condition was not met the agreements became null, and two years later, in 1798, the heirs-at-law acquired from the Cambridge Corporation an acre of land called Doll's Close, facing the open common called Butt Green, south-east of Jesus College (Fig.3). The site was hardly suitable but it appeared to satisfy the Court and enabled the cause to proceed in its course. The charter was granted in June 1800 and passed the Great Seal on 22 September 1800. It was at this time that James Wyatt was officially appointed 'Architect of the College'.[3]

June 1800 marks the official birth of Downing College in more than one way; not only was the charter granted, the first Master, Professors and Fellows nominated and the architect officially appointed, but the designs for the college were also becoming more concrete, accompanied by estimates and calculations. Slowly but steadily the project was growing from what may have been little more than a doodle in a sketchbook, with no particular reference to any specific site, to being a proper project, with a brief as well as specific practical requirements to fulfil.

The charter itself acted as brief, for it established the number of Senior Members to be part of the institution, apart from the Master and the two Professors, and, under Statute XVII (*Of Rooms*), it set out certain conditions which – as we shall see – were to determine the plan of the building. Statute XVII ruled that 'There shall be a Lodge built and set apart for the Master; and one for each of the Professors; which, as well as the apartments of Fellows and Scholars, shall be enjoyed by them rent free'.

Provisions for the Master's Lodge are neither unusual nor surprising; since the Reformation the limited space previously assigned to the Head of a college had been found to be too small for the requirements of hospitality and entertainment; in addition Heads of Houses were granted the liberty of marriage, so it had become necessary to provide proper accommodation for a family and its household. It became customary, in both Cambridge and Oxford, to build lodges for the Masters and their families which stood separate or isolated from the main body of the college. However, the statutes for Downing College extended this privilege to the Professor of Law and the Professor of Medicine who, unlike any other Fellow of the college, were also free to marry. This was an unprecedented step since no other Professor in the university was entitled to accommodation for himself and his family within college precincts. The Regius Professors were all entitled to rooms in Trinity, but this did not extend to their families.

This departure from the established Oxford and Cambridge tradition was important on two counts: firstly, from a purely educational point of view because it introduced the idea of resident professors which was then to become characteristic of American universities. When designing the University of Virginia, in 1817, Thomas Jefferson introduced ten lodges for the professors, and although there is no evidence of Jefferson's direct knowledge of what was going on at Downing – of which a section was being built in those years – he is likely to have known the college's statutes. The change introduced by the new statutes had the effect, from the strictly architectural point of view, of raising the problem of designing an institutional building which, at the same time, needed to provide private housing of appropriately high standards. The problem was an interesting and challenging one because private accommodation (with its special requirements and established typological solutions) had to be fitted into the complex scheme of an institutional building, like a college, without breaking – in either plan or elevation – the hierarchical principles underlying the actual building.

The charter did not determine the number of undergraduates the college should admit, and James Wyatt seems to have been little bothered by this crucial omission in the brief. He chose to provide for a notional number of sixteen to twenty undergraduates. It was only in May 1805, and possibly at the request of one of the other architects then submitting designs, that the Master in Chancery pronounced that it would be '. . . proper to provide in the Buildings for the said College accommodation for twenty Undergraduates and Members.'[4]

On 2 June 1800 Wyatt produced a first rough estimate of the costs for building the college. As this is the architect's only surviving written description of the buildings and their functions, it is worth quoting at length. He wrote:

> The space required to accommodate a Master, two Professors, Sixteen Fellows & from Sixteen to Twenty Undergraduates; with a Chapel, Library & Hall; Bursery, Muniment Room, Common Room &c. &c., will be about two hundred and fifty feet square. The expence of which according to the first Idea drawn cannot be less than £60,000. The Ornamental parts will be near £10,000 of that sum, but may be executed at leisure without any impediment to the habitation of the building. The habitable part may be executed without difficulty in four or five Years as the money may be advanced. To erect one Wing of this building and part of the front including the Gateway which will contain the Masters Lodgings, the two Professors & those of the three fellows and the Porters will

3 Plan of the town of Cambridge showing Doll's Close

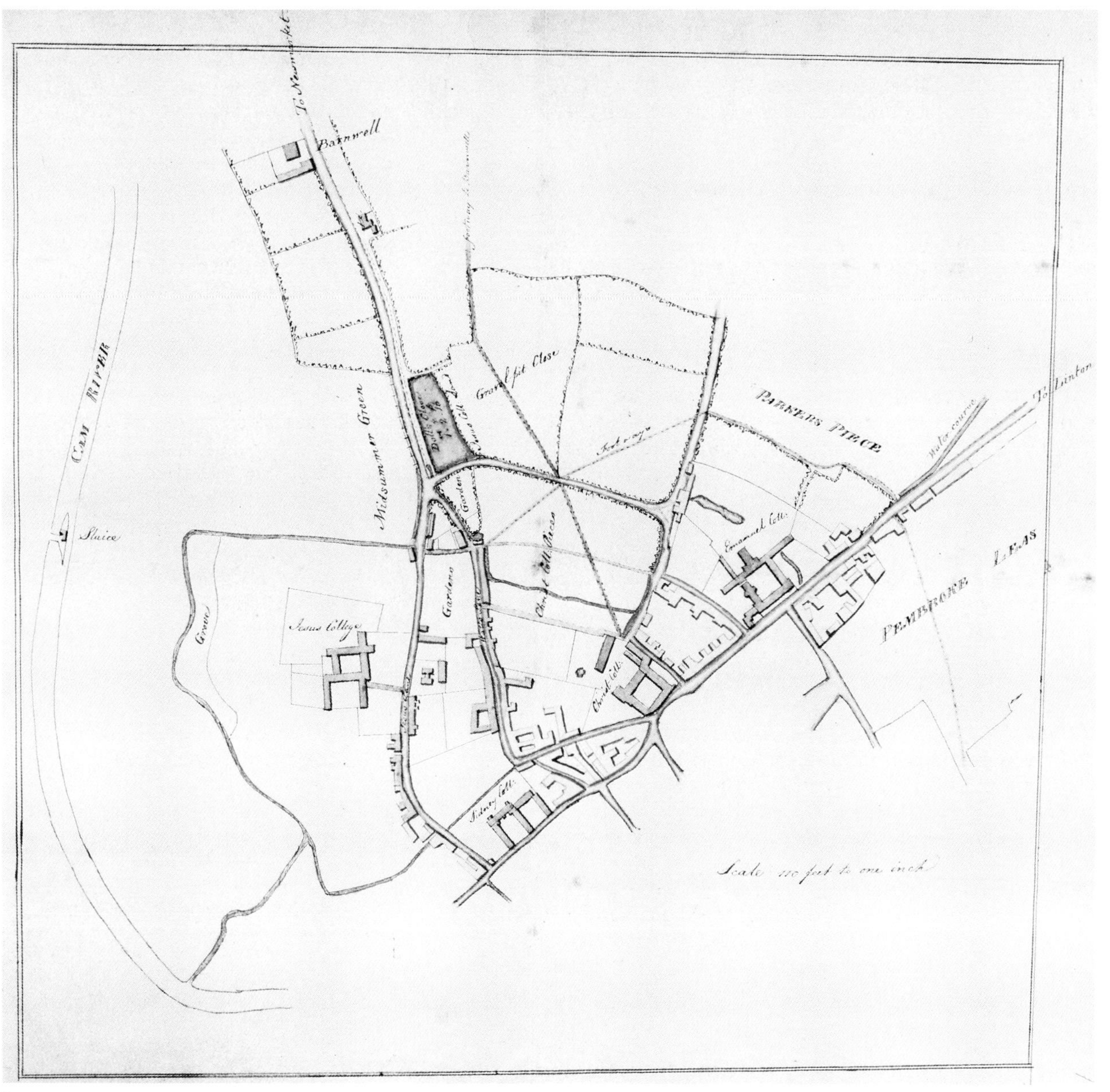

3

> cost about £20,000 & might be finished if great exertion was used in about 3 Years.[5]

Wyatt's reference to 'the first Idea drawn' suggests that he was presenting two alternative designs, one of which was more elaborate, thus more expensive than the other. The text of his estimate, however, does not seem to imply the existence of any considerable difference in either size or layout between these two designs. Only three drawings by Wyatt survive in the British Architectural Library,[6] all clearly belonging to the same set, although one shows a simplified treatment of the chapel. This confirms the existence of an alternative design in which the ornaments were considerably reduced. All three drawings are beautifully finished perspectival views of the college from various points of view.

The college was to have a quadrangular shape (Fig.4) with the south range extended to the east and west so as to stretch beyond the quadrangle proper. The court thus created was to be completely enclosed, with the principal access into it being provided by a triumphal arch in the middle of the north range (Fig.5). There were additional side entrances in the middle of the east and west ranges, which were understated inside the court itself but marked out on the exterior where they coincided with a central projecting block of three bays with a recessed portico framed by Doric columns supporting an entablature and attic (Fig.6). All these elements – that is, the columns, the entablature

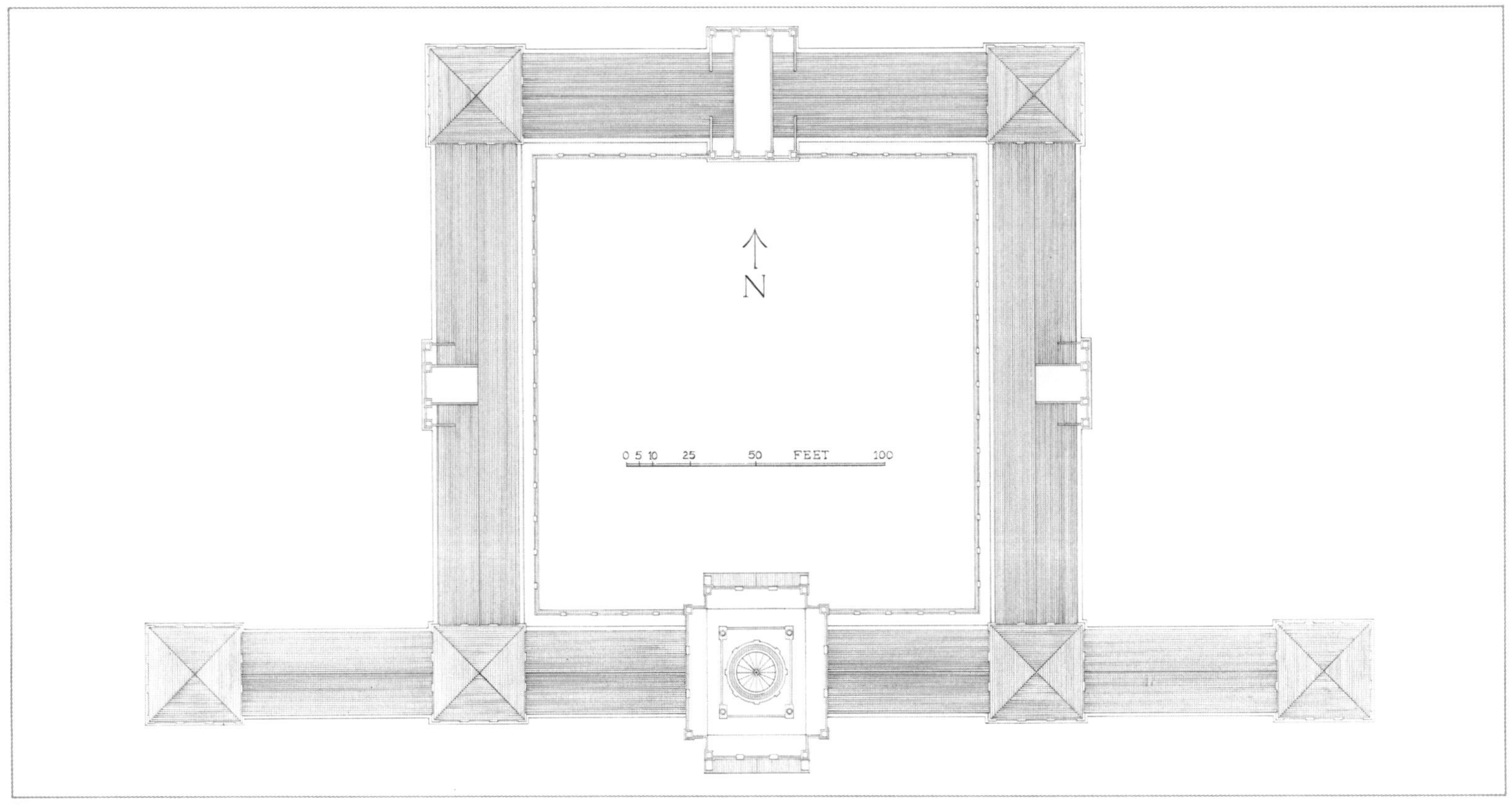

4

4 Reconstruction of James Wyatt's plan for Downing College

5 James Wyatt (1746–1813), Perspective from north-west, c.1804

6 James Wyatt, Perspective from south-west, c.1804

5

6

and the attic with small pilasters corresponding to the columns – were combined together as in a Roman triumphal arch thus repeating, in a subdued tone, the motif of the principal entrance to the court. The courtyard was surrounded by a continuous Roman Doric colonnade spanning two storeys (Pl.II). The columns, resting on bases, were raised over two steps and supported an entablature with triglyphs (the rectangular blocks subdividing the Doric frieze) surmounted by a balustrade. There was no break in the entablature nor in the colonnade which simply turned round to form the projecting portico of the chapel in the middle of the south range. This portico, as well as its mirror image on the outer southern elevation, had four columns and was crowned by a triangular pediment behind which rose an elaborate square tower. This has been described as the most interesting feature in the whole design[7] although it has not previously been noticed that it was precisely in the tower that Wyatt was prepared to compromise and envisaged alternative solutions. A comparison of the perspective from the north-west (Fig.5) with the perspective from the south-west (Fig.6) will reveal Wyatt's proposed alternative handling of the chapel tower. In the first of these drawings, the perspective from the north-west, the tower is square in plan with pilasters marking its outer corners, exactly as in the perspective from the south-west, although without the decorative urns; the space between the columns is also considerably smaller and the distance of the pair of columns from the wall behind is reduced too. The columns here do not frame a round-headed window, as in the perspective from the south-west, but a Vitruvian opening which appears to be convex – thus following the cylindrical shape of the drum on which the dome rests. The dome is less shallow than in the other design, and crowns a drum void of decorations. Indeed, in the perspective from the north-west, the dome was definitely inspired by Donato Bramante's dome for the little temple of S.Pietro in Montorio, Rome (1502–1506).

Wyatt's design distinguishes between the treatment of the courtyard and that of the outer elevations of the buildings, in other words the college is given an outer and an inner skin. The west and east elevations were identical but the north and south were not, and they also differed from the other two. Certain elements were repeated throughout, such as the corner units (presumably meant to house the Master's and Professors' Lodges, and the Fellows' and Chaplains' accommodation), the triumphal arch motif adopted for the main and side entrances, and the portico of the chapel which is repeated on the south elevation of the south range. The exterior of Wyatt's college is not as unified and coherent as his courtyard. The courtyard presents the viewer with a continuum of columns which completely hide the facades behind; the exterior, on the other hand, is highly fragmented and syncopated, alternating small cubical shapes (the corner units) with lower, elongated ones acting as links. As well as contraposing geometrical shapes, on the exterior Wyatt plays with the contraposition of stylar and astylar surfaces, that is the use of columns in contrast with plain surfaces. The different treatment of the courtyard and of the external elevations betrays different architectural sources: the Roman Doric colonnade is reminiscent of Christopher Wren's work at the Royal Hospital, Chelsea (1682–1692) and at the Royal Hospital for Seamen in Greenwich (1696–1716), whilst the articulation of the exterior is definitely inspired by British Neo-Palladian examples from the middle to the latter part of the eighteenth century.

Wyatt's design for the college implies a large increase in the land available and the possibility of viewing all four elevations freely. This would have been possible only on a river site or on the Pembroke Leys. Certainly the design documented by the surviving drawings was not conceived with Doll's Close, the site acquired in 1798, in mind. The design appears not to have been significantly altered because the 1803 revised estimate mentions no substantial change to be introduced. On 23 July 1803 Wyatt submitted a revised estimate according to which the overall expense would have amounted to £54,000; he envisaged starting with the north side of the quadrangle which by this time had been extended to an overall length of 300 feet.[8] Indeed it is likely that Wyatt kept pressing for a change of site in order to implement his scheme in full. This was finally agreed upon on 31 January 1804 when the Master in Chancery granted permission to acquire the Pembroke Leys (Fig.7), the site originally mooted as far back as 1771.[9] This was, of course, an extremely important decision and one which, in theory, had the funds been available, should have been followed by the beginning of the building work. The college now had the site it thought most appropriate and it had a project from one of the leading London architects, nothing else seemed to be wanting. It is thus with surprise that we find the first Master, Dr Annesley, requesting in early 1804 Thomas Hope's opinion on Wyatt's drawings for the college.

7 Plan of Pembroke Leys, 1803

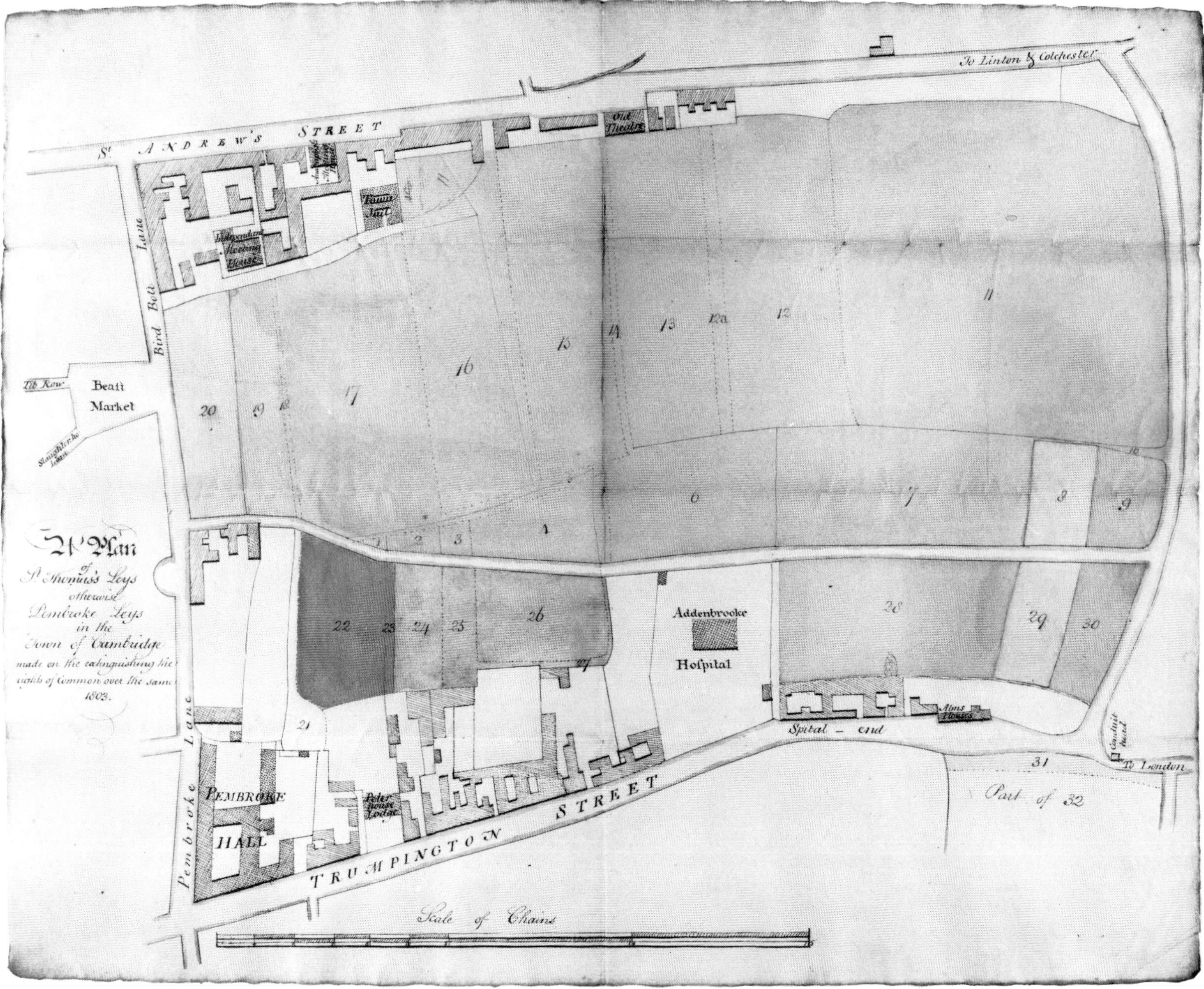

7

Thomas Hope (1769–1831) was the eldest son of a wealthy Scottish merchant family which had been established in Amsterdam for several generations. In 1795, the death of his parents and the French occupation of Holland forced him to abandon his adopted country and he came to England where he established himself as a connoisseur and patron of the arts. Hope's education had fostered this love for the arts; between 1787 and 1795 he had completed the grandest of Grand Tours, travelling extensively in Europe and in Asia Minor, and acquiring a considerable knowledge of the architecture, sculpture and painting of these countries. His interests focussed in particular on the artistic productions of these ancient civilizations which he believed had attained the highest aesthetic purity, unparalleled by the moderns. Hope, who was a competent draughtsman himself, was accompanied in his travels by the painter George Wallis (1792) and by the French artist Preault (1799); they recorded in some five hundred and twenty-five drawings the landscape, life and art of Turkey, Asia Minor, Syria, Egypt and Greece.[10] During the course of his travels, Hope developed and cultivated an ever increasing interest in antique sculpture and applied arts, and began collecting statues and vases which formed the basis of his collection. This was also increased by the works he commissioned of contemporary artists of international standing, such as Flaxman, Canova, Thorwaldsen, Haydon, Westall and West. They were favoured by Hope because they were all inspired by ancient Greek examples, of which they sought to reproduce the spirit as well as the forms.

Nevertheless, by 1804, the year in which Francis Annesley requested his opinion on Wyatt's designs for Downing College, Hope's claims to fame were still limited. None of his highly influential books and articles had yet appeared in print,[11] his collection had not yet been seen by the public of fellow connoisseurs and artists,[12] and indeed Hope himself had not yet attained official recognition for his scholarship since he had not yet been elected a member of the major learned societies with which he was later to be associated. In 1800 he had been made a member of the Society of Dilettanti, but that was all.

Why, then, was Hope invited to comment on the designs for Downing? The question has long puzzled architectural historians who, because of the lack of surviving personal papers of either Hope or Annesley, have been left to speculate. A personal contact has been presumed between the man who was to become the pundit of Neo-Classicism in this country and the Master of Downing.[13] The possibility has also been suggested that the two men shared the same aesthetic views and enthusiasm for Greek architecture, such hypothesis being based on the fact that Annesley was an hereditary trustee of the British Museum and, we are asked to assume, a lover of the arts. Too little is known about Annesley's intellectual and artistic pursuits to express any definitive opinion; indeed it is questionable whether Annesley was solely responsible for calling upon Hope as an arbiter of taste. Other members of the college might have prompted that suggestion, and they in turn might have voiced the opinions of members of the university at large. In the history of the aesthetic controversy over the design for Downing College the Cambridge Graecophils, present within the university and the colleges at large, must have played a very important role, though one that is difficult to pinpoint with absolute precision.

Even assuming that he ever held such strong convictions, Annesley was not the only member of the college likely to oppose Wyatt's designs on purely aesthetic grounds. The Downing Professor of Medicine, Sir Busick Harwood (1745–1814), had an impeccable pedigree as an antiquarian and connoisseur. In 1783 he had been elected a fellow of the Society of Antiquaries and he was a well known member of that group of Cambridge scholars referred to as the Cambridge Hellenists or Graecophils. The supposition that Harwood might have been at the centre of a 'conspiracy' which aimed at replacing the more traditional James Wyatt with an innovative Greek revivalist architect such as William Wilkins is strengthened by the fact that in 1800 Harwood had been one of the three sponsors (the others being the Reverend Thomas Kerrich, University Librarian, and Craven Ord, Vice-President of the Society of Antiquaries) who had introduced Wilkins, the future architect of the College and the leading Greek revivalist architect in the country, into the Society of Antiquaries.[14]

The Graecophils were not a particularly homogeneous group in so far as they were not organized in a society or club exclusively devoted to the revival of Greek art. They were scholars of various disciplines, united by their common interest in Greek classical culture. A large part of their understanding of the various expressions of such culture was based on their philological researches; indeed philology appears to have preceded archaeological investigation amongst the Cambridge scholars[15]. They included men of such diverse academic specialization as Edward

Blomfield (1788–1816), Thomas Briggs (1767–1831), Jacob Bryant (1715–1804), the Reverend E.D.Clarke (1769–1822), J.M.Cripps (1780–1853), E.Dodwell (1767–1832), the Reverend J.C. Eustace (1762?-1815), Sir William Gell (1777–1836), George Gordon 4th Earl of Aberdeen (1784–1860), Charles Kelsall (1782–1857), Henry Gally Knight (1786–1846), John Bacon Sawrey Morritt (1772–1843), John Tweddell (1769–1799), Robert Walpole (1781–1856), William Wilkins (1788–1839), and George Downing Whittington (1781–1807), to mention just a few. The most famous one, however, was Lord Byron (1788–1824). All of them had been Cambridge undergraduates and almost all had become Fellows in their own or in other colleges. Graecophils could be found in all the colleges, but there seems to have been a special concentration at St. John's and Trinity. Their conspicuous presence at St. John's is of particular interest to the history of Downing because of the special ties between St. John's and the new college. As it will be remembered, the Master of St.John's was one of the four trustees named by Sir George Downing in his will, and a large proportion of the first Fellows came from St. John's.[16]

The Cambridge Graecophils travelled to Greece earlier and more extensively than their Oxford counterparts, and soon established Greece as the new goal of the British 'grand tourist'. Although the Graecophils did not necessarily travel with the aim of collecting ancient works of art, inevitably their trips produced some extraordinarily valuable acquisitions. Such was the depredation of Greece and the ignorance of its inhabitants that anybody could pick up an inscription or a statue with the aid of a little persuasion and a modest bribe. The Reverend E.D. Clarke, for instance, recounts how he found the colossal Cistophorous of Eleusis, formerly known as the Ceres, and now in the Fitzwilliam Museum, Cambridge, 'in a dunghill, buried to her ears'.[17] Their early contacts with Greek art made the Cambridge Graecophils appreciate its beauty, and its diversity from Roman classical art. This, coupled with their natural academicism, ensured their adhesion to the aesthetic principles of Neo-Classicism expounded in other quarters in England – particularly by the Society of Dilettanti – and in Europe at large.

There is no room here to describe the genesis and evolution of Neo-Classicism[18] but it is necessary to explain, even briefly, why Neo-Classicism in architecture was so successfully accepted. With its return to the roots of Greek classical architecture and its emphasis on archaeological accuracy, Neo-Classicism abolished the theoretical mediation of the Renaissance and its concentration on classical Roman sources. Post-medieval architecture in Europe had been largely modelled on the classical buildings of Rome and from the fifteenth century onwards its theoretical basis had been provided by the rediscovered writings of Vitruvius and Frontinus. Roman classical buildings were better known and studied than any other building from the classical past on account of their accessibility. Renaissance architects abstracted from the manuscripts and from the surviving ruins the rules of 'Classical' architecture. These rules adapted and reinterpreted according to need, grew to form the common architectural language which spread throughout Europe from the Italian Renaissance towns and courts. The passage from Gothic architecture to the Italianate style was to become an obligatory one for any country claiming to be Renaissance-enlightened, progressive and civilized. The architecture of the Italian Renaissance provided images of order, symmetry, elegance and grandeur, and it soon became the symbol of civilization, of the direct cultural and political links between modern Europe and the Roman republic. Throughout the sixteenth, seventeenth and early eighteenth centuries the architectural language established by the Italian Renaissance architects and based on Roman classical architecture remained the current architectural form of expression. Architects who could not travel to Italy learnt it from the numerous illustrated treatises which had been produced by Italian architects such as Andrea Palladio, Vincenzo Scamozzi and Jacopo Barozzi da Vignola. This of course meant that the original sources became more remote and the principles they embodied were understood through the filter of the Renaissance architects' *own* interpretation. Until the middle of the eighteenth century, archaeological investigation was not actively pursued by English architects, who appear to have been satisfied with an increasingly rarified language derived from Palladio.

Paradoxically, it was the Neo-Palladians' quest for rigour and simplicity, coupled with their all-encompassing antiquarian interests, that started off a new interest in empirical observation and precise scholarship based on a literal rendering of the monuments, unclouded by attention to the rules imposed by more recent tradition. One of the consequences of this approach was to re-evaluate the undeveloped character, lack of monumentality and primitiveness of Greek architecture in particular. The archaic quality of Greek architecture appealed to the architects of the second half of the eighteenth century, who were struggling to free themselves from the excesses of the Baroque and Rococo phases. Greek architecture provided historical precedents for their functionalist and rationalist goals, it also answered the need for a return to the origins of architecture which was being advocated by the architectural writers of the time.[19]

In this country great impetus and support was given, during the second half of the eighteenth century, to the archaeological investigation of architectural monuments by the learned societies such as the Society of Antiquaries and, more particularly, the Society of Dilettanti. They not only fostered debate on the subject, but also promoted archaeological research by sponsoring expeditions to the classical sites and financing the publication of the results of these researches. In so doing, the societies soon became important instruments in the formulation of taste and, given the powerful social position of many of their members, they could ensure the successful implementation of their aesthetic doctrines.[20]

Seen against this background, common to the intellectual circles of Cambridge and London, the existence of a 'faction' opposed to James Wyatt's tired Classicism is no longer surprising. The choice of Thomas Hope as a judge of Wyatt's designs for Downing College begins to make sense if it is read as a symptom of a diffuse unease and dissatisfaction with an architectural style which has lost its incisiveness. In 1804, Hope was one of the few Graecophils and influential members of the Society of Dilettanti who could have been consulted and, as it happened, the only one present in England.[21] He may also have been one of the very few who would have dared publicly to oppose Wyatt, a royal protégé, the Surveyor of the Office of Works, and already an aspirant to the Presidency of the Royal Academy of Arts.

Hope's reply to Annesley took the unusual shape of a printed pamphlet dated 22 February 1804 and entitled *Observations on the Plans and Elevations designed by James Wyatt, Architect, for Downing College, Cambridge; in a Letter to Francis Annesley, Esq. M.P.*. The 'Letter' was written in a pompous style and a large part of it was actually devoted to establishing Hope's own credentials as an unimpeachable architectural critic. His stinging comments concentrated on the proposed elevations, glossing over the ground plans and the relationship between interior and exterior on account of the fact that: 'The destination of a college admits of no great fancy in the internal distribution; though I think a little more elegance and variety might have been introduced in this latter, without any diminution of convenience.'[22]

The elevations, however, had little to recommend themselves in the eyes of Hope. Their major, unforgivable fault was the fact that they sported a Roman Doric order rather than a Greek one. Hope's argument was that '. . . in a building which, from the immensity of the sum allotted to its construction, is enabled, as well as intended, to become one of the first ornaments to the country . . .' it was to be wished that '. . . instead of the degraded architecture of the Romans, the purest style of the Greeks had been exclusively adhibited.' Greek architecture was to be preferred because of its greater closeness to the archetype of the wooden hut, 'the original type of the subsequent stone edifices of Greece and Rome.' More specifically, Greek Doric, with its simplicity of line, better proportions and greater strength, produced a more lasting and powerful effect on the viewer. Wyatt's fault, Hope implied, was not to have travelled, thus restricting his knowledge of architecture to the examples provided by Rome via the Renaissance architects. But not all contemporary architects had such limited horizons; indeed a few had already shown their better judgment, and here Hope proceeded to name William Wilkins, who had recently (in the summer of 1803) returned from a three-year long journey through southern Italy and the Peloponnese, bringing back accurate records of Greek temples in which the archaic Doric order was variously used.

William Wilkins (1778–1839), was the eldest son of a Norwich plasterer and self-taught architect. He was first educated at Norwich Grammar School, then in 1796 won a scholarship to Gonville and Caius College, Cambridge to read mathematics. He received his B.A. as sixth wrangler in 1800. While still an undergraduate he began to cultivate an interest in architecture, classical, and antiquarian studies. It was in these years that he made measured drawings of King's College Chapel (now at Columbia University) and exhibited at the Royal Academy for the first time. In 1800 Wilkins was introduced into the Society of Antiquaries in recognition of his knowledge of 'the History of the Antiquities of Great Britain' and 'ancient architecture of this Kingdom'. This honour was followed in 1801 by the award of the Worts Travelling Bachelorship which enabled Wilkins to undertake an extensive tour of Magna Graecia, Greece and Asia Minor. During the three years of the Travelling Bachelorship, Wilkins gathered the material for the majority of his publications and the inspiration for his architectural designs. Immediately after his return to Cambridge, in the summer of 1803, he was elected to a fellowship at Gonville and Caius and began work on the publication of *Magna Graecia* (Cambridge 1807), a study of the Greek antiquities in Sicily and Italy. Wilkins' return to Cambridge marked the resumption of his contacts with the Cambridge Graecophils and the start of his friendship with the fourth Earl of Aberdeen.

Wyatt's designs attracted Hope's criticism on other counts too: the colonnade surrounding the courtyard was blamed for not being raised on a higher stylobate as in Greek temples (cf. Pl.II); the portico in the centre of the south range should have been given six instead of four columns, and the architect was accused of having given the entablature 'almost burlesque' proportions. The gateway on the centre of the north range was criticized for its proportions and Hope advocated instead something along the lines of a town gate he had seen in Berlin (Langhans' Brandenburg Gate of 1789–93), 'imitated from the Propylaea'; the windows should have been oblong instead of square. The tower above the chapel was referred to as 'non-descript'. Not content with his harsh, though often correct, criticisms, Hope concluded his reply stating that in Wyatt's designs he could not see 'one striking feature, one eminent beauty. Neither elevations nor sections display a single instance of fancy, a single spark of genius, to make up for their many faults. Everything alike in them is trite, common place, nay, often vulgar.'

It is hard to imagine a more unconditional condemnation of Wyatt on the one hand, and on the other a more precise description of the fundamental characteristics of Wilkins' winning design for the college. This, however, does not mean that Hope wrote his reply with a set of drawings by Wilkins in front of him. It is doubtful that Wilkins had had enough time to even start thinking about the possibility of a design for Downing, and his supporters may not have envisaged the need for an immediate alternative scheme. Hope's 'Letter' should be read as a programmatic statement of intentions on the part of the Graecophils and their faction, whose principal aim was that of undermining Wyatt's scheme on aesthetic and theoretical grounds. Although the 'Letter' may have been meant to suggest Wilkins as the only possible alternative to Wyatt, it failed to do so forcefully enough, since he was only mentioned (p.22) as somebody who had 'lately brought home, and soon intends to publish, designs of a Greek temple, in the cella of which Doric columns rise on distinct bases.' The new college outside the medieval centre was, in the eyes of the Graecophils, a golden opportunity for they could get a whole college in the style they favoured and ensure a striking monument to their new taste. By making his reply available to the public in print Hope sought to open up the debate on the architectural style of the first new large educational building in Cambridge, and to establish Greek architecture as the style of the new century. He must also have been conscious that a public reply would change the nature of the commission, snatching it from the secluded world of Cambridge combination rooms and bringing it into the public domain. He must have foreseen the possibility of an open competition, or at any rate the chance of forcing both the college and the Court of Chancery to reconsider their course of action, thus gaining time to rally further support around Wilkins.

The events of 1804 are summed up in the college's Minutes Book as follows:

> In the Year 1804, A Plan for the Buildings by Mr James Wyatt being laid before the Master in Chancery with an Estimate he required a second to be submitted to him in consequence of which a second plan and estimate were made by Mr James [sic] Byfield Architect and other plans and estimates were afterwards voluntarily made and offered to the College by Mr William Wilkins, Junior Fellow of Caius College and Architect and by Mr Francis Sandys and Mr Lewis Wyatt Architects. These plans and estimates being submitted to the College at different Meetings and to the Master in Chancery that of Mr Wilkins was ultimately approved and ordered by the Court to be carried into execution.[23]

Clearly the minutes of the Governing Body's meetings were written some years later and somewhat regardless of the correct sequence of events. In this particular entry, for instance, the developments which took place over 1804 and 1805 are all compressed into the same year. The Court Decisions, however, help to unravel the story, which seems to have unfolded along the following lines. James Wyatt's designs, possibly accompanied by Hope's unflattering criticism, were submitted by the college solicitors to the Court of Chancery whose Master, Francis Paul Stratford, found himself forced to accept the consequences entailed in Hope's pamphlet: he had to 'request' a new design. The documents indicate that Master Stratford did not suggest the name of the new architect; this appearing to have been entirely the Governing Body's free choice. We can only speculate about the events leading to the choice of George Byfield as the author of a new scheme for the college. The Graecophils' aim, as we have seen, was that of ousting Wyatt and establishing the validity of the Greek alternative. If, as it would seem, the whole ploy had been staged for the benefit of their champion, William Wilkins, they needed to gain time since their architect had just returned from his travels abroad and had no previous experience of designing a complex building such as a college. This very time lag, as well as their victory in effectively re-opening the commission, provided an unexpected, but welcome opportunity for other 'factions' to start meddling in the whole affair. In a society which was still dominated by a system of patronage, it was inevitable that more than one power group wanted to secure such an important commission for their protégés; this is probably how Byfield came to be chosen.

George Byfield (c.1756–1813) was described at his death as 'an eminent architect, who has built several Gaols, and for many years has made this branch of his profession his particular study.'[24] In fact the number of gaols designed and built by Byfield is much smaller than the obituary would suggest[25] and was largely outnumbered by his designs for domestic architecture and public buildings. Despite the obvious success that Byfield enjoyed, illustrated by his activity in London as well as in the provinces, he was never elected Associate of the Royal Academy nor did he join the Office of Works. From 1803 onwards, he acted as surveyor to the estates of the Dean and Chapter of Westminster, a position that he maintained till his death. Byfield differed from Wyatt in so far as he practised in a variety of styles ranging from the Gothic (as in Brockhampton Chapel, near Bromyard, Herefordshire) to a timid but highly competent form of Neo-Greek. The latter is best exemplified in his Sessions House at Canterbury (1806–10) and in the unexecuted designs for Downing College (Figs.8–9 and Pls.III-IV). However, from what little we know about him, it appears that Byfield was not associated with any of the Graecophils in either Cambridge or London, and that his adhesion to the Greek Revival was never accompanied by the noisy statements of some of his contemporaries. How then did he come to be involved with the college?

Amongst the new Fellows of Downing one man, Edward Christian, the Professor of the Laws of England, had directly

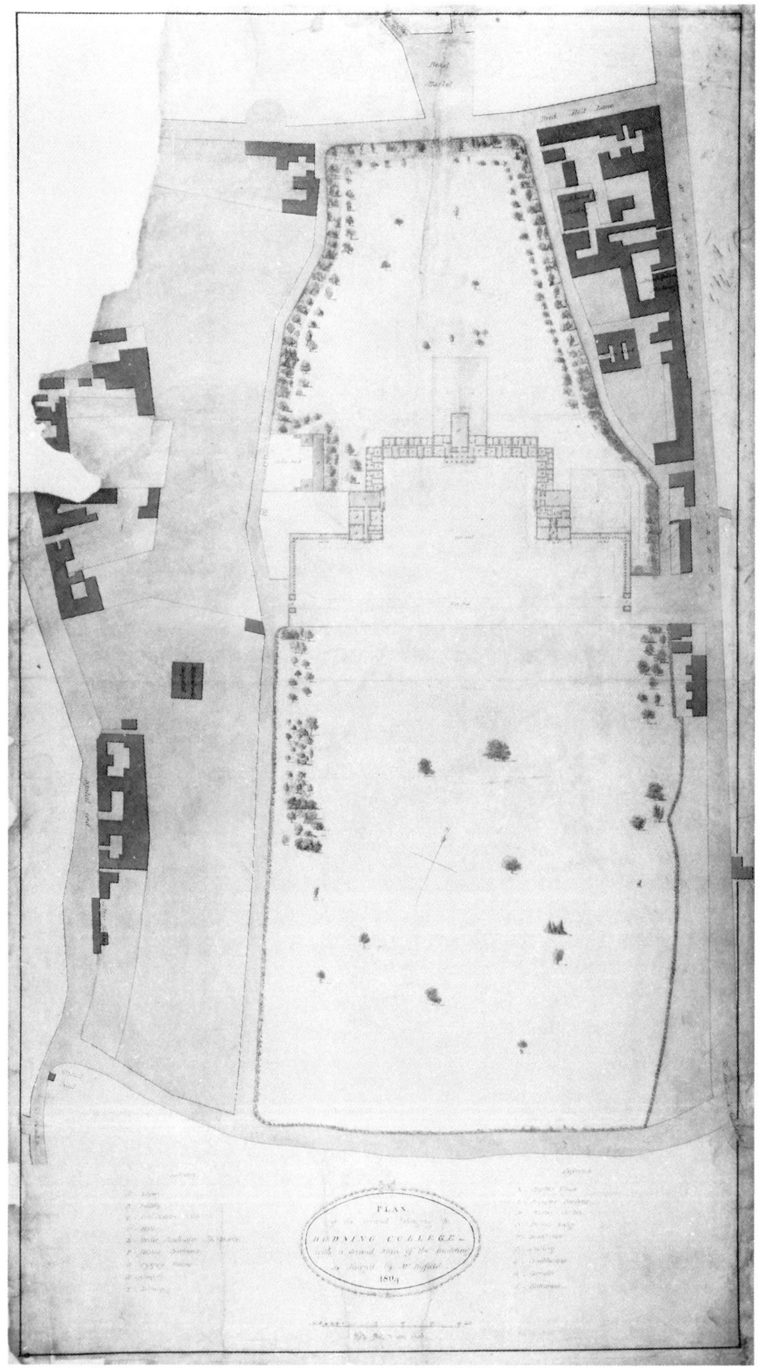

8

8 George Byfield (c.1756–1813), Plan of the site and general plan of the College, 1804

9 George Byfield, Ground Floor Plan, 1804

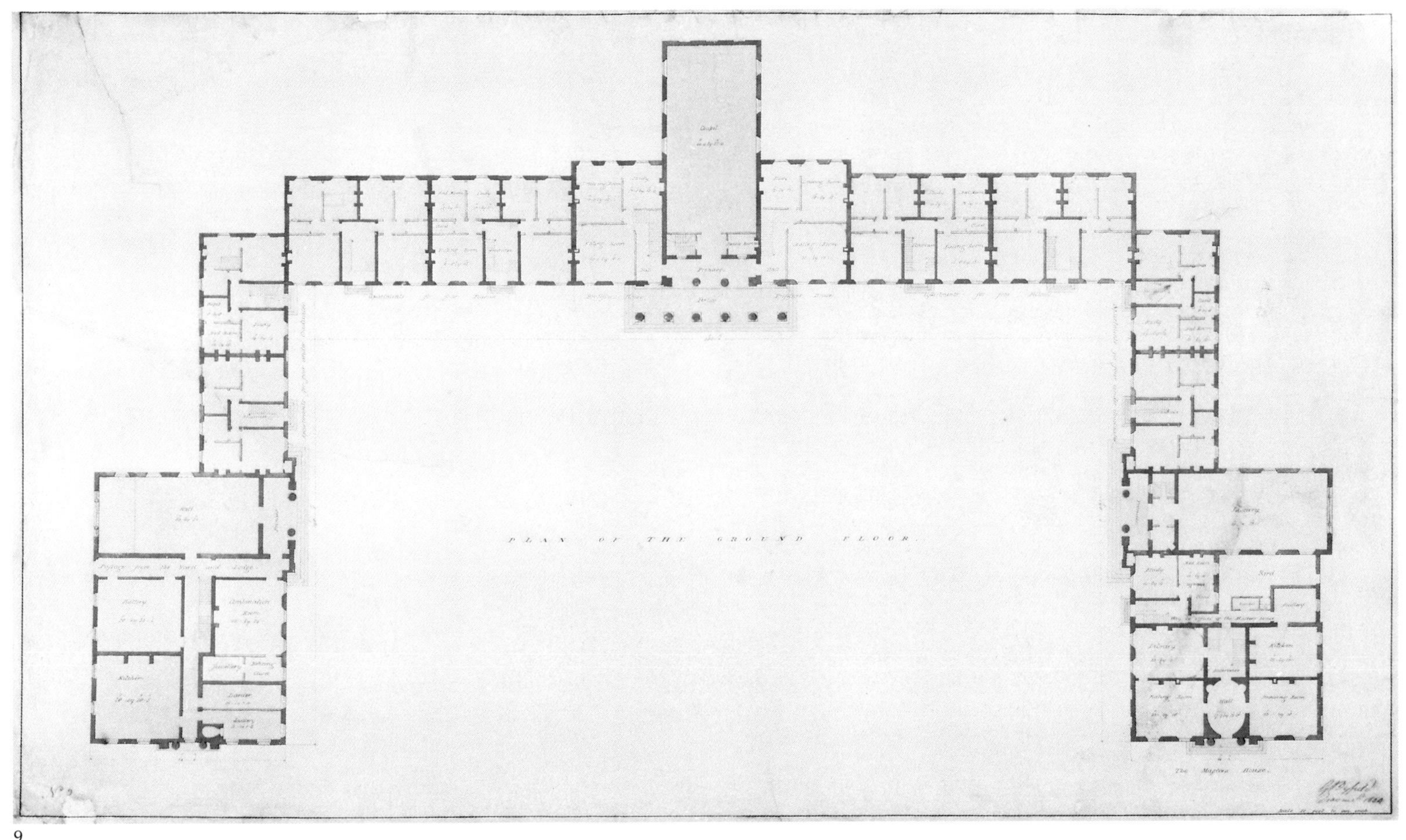

9

benefited from the system of patronage governing the majority of eighteenth century appointments. Indeed he owed almost every step of his career to the continuous protection of the Hardwicke family.[26] The Yorkes, Earls of Hardwicke, had their seat at Wimpole Hall, near Cambridge, and were one of the most powerful families in the county. Starting with Charles, the first Earl and Lord Chancellor, the family had always held the Lord Lieutenantship of the county as well as the High Stewardship of Cambridge University. His son Charles Yorke had been the University Counsel who brought forward the successful Chancery petition of 1764 to establish the trusts of Sir George Downing's will. Furthermore, one of the younger Hardwicke sons had traditionally held the Bishopric of Ely, and the Bishop of Ely also happened to be the Visitor of St. John's College. Indeed it was James Yorke, Bishop of Ely and Visitor of St. John's, who had nominated Christian for the appointment of Chief Justice of the Isle of Ely and who may even have been responsible for his nomination as Professor at Downing. Given Christian's ties with the Hardwicke family, the latter's involvement in the affairs of the university and of St. John's in particular, and the very strong connection between St. John's and Downing, it is reasonable to suppose that Christian brought to the Fellowship's attention an architect patronized by the Hardwickes. In 1790 Byfield had been employed by Jemima, wife of Philip Yorke, the second Lord Hardwicke, to remodel the family's London house at No.4 St. James's Square. In 1791 he appears to have been responsible for the alterations and refacing of Wrest Park, Jemima's family seat.[27] It is not known how Byfield secured the commissions of the Bury St. Edmunds and Cambridge gaols, but it is possible that here too he benefited from the patronage or influence of the Hardwicke family.

After Hope's damning report on Wyatt's designs and the Court of Chancery's request of a second project, the Hardwicke faction, represented by Edward Christian and Dr. Craven, the Master of St. John's (himself a nominee of the Bishop of Ely) found itself in a position to advance its own candidate, George Byfield. Indeed Byfield must have looked ideal: he practised in a tame Greek style, thus answering to the aesthetic requirements laid down by Thomas Hope, and he was already active in Cambridge which meant he knew the local craftsmen and could easily judge tenders and organize appropriate supervision of the works.

During 1804, Byfield must have submitted many drawings, of which only seven survive in the college (see Cat. ns.4–10); these document different phases in the development of his ideas. In his scheme the college was to be sited roughly where the present north range stands and was to be entered from Trumpington Street (Tennis Court Road did not yet exist) as well as from St. Andrew's Street. It was to be U-shaped, with the court open towards the south, and the north range extending for 600 feet. The choice of an open court plan created several problems with regard to the siting of the chapel, hall, library and the residences for the Professors and the Master. Byfield's handling of the ground plan is interesting for its compactness and rationality, but also because it does, in many ways, prefigure the present arrangement. He envisaged the chapel to be placed in the centre of the north range, flanked on either side by the houses of the two Professors (Fig.9). As the surviving ground plan shows, in order not to spoil the symmetry of the whole facade, the entrances to the two residences were cleverly hidden in the vestibule behind the six-columned Ionic portico facing the chapel (Fig.9). The rest of the north range was occupied by apartments for eight Fellows. In the east and west wings there were to be rooms for eight undergraduates, organized around staircases in the traditional Cantabrigian fashion, and followed on each side by a long room housing respectively the library (on the east range) and the Hall (on the west range). These were placed exactly in the centre of the wings and separated the undergraduates' side from the kitchens and offices on the west, and the Master's house on the east. They also marked a change in the shape of the wings, which increased in depth at their southern ends. According to this ground plan, the chapel was to be faced by a projecting portico of six columns, which screened a narrower recessed portico of two, apparently baseless, columns leading into a vestibule. This motif of a recessed portico with vestibule was repeated again in the hall and library, and it reappeared in a simplified form, this time without the vestibule, on the elevation of the Master's House and office blocks (Pl.IV).

According to this ground plan the Master's House was to have a very attractive oval entrance hall leading into two rectangular rooms at the front of the house and into oval rooms at the rear, thus hiding the staircase which was placed immediately behind it. No other architect produced a ground plan for the Master's house as elegant as that of Byfield, who treated it as a fashionable town house for which he borrowed ideas from Claude Nicolas Ledoux's (1735–1806) Parisian houses.[28]

Byfield's only surviving drawing for the elevation of the north range does not match his ground plan in so far as the projecting portico no longer appears to be screening a second recessed portico, nor does the vestibule house the entrances to the Professors' houses (Pl.III). It is not clear why Byfield was prepared to sacrifice the far more archaeological and novel idea of the two types of porticoes combined together. The only possible explanation is that this simplified elevation was dictated by economy, since giant columns such as he had first envisaged were bound to be very expensive. There is no reason, however, to think that the six-columned portico and the rest of the elevation as shown in this drawing differ in any other substantial way from the ideas expressed in the surviving ground plan. The long elevation of twenty-nine bays was extremely simple, the only decoration being provided by the Ionic columns modelled on those of the Erechtheum in Athens, which he knew through Stuart and Revett's *Antiquities of Athens* (1762–1816), and by the Greek fret on the architrave above the doors.

All Byfield's drawings are dated 'Craven Street 1804', but it is possible to be somewhat more precise about the timing of his involvement with the Downing project. The minutes of the Court of Chancery's Decisions[29] show that he swore three affidavits, respectively on 22 June, 11 December, and 18 December, 1804. An inscription on the verso of Byfield's drawing of the south elevation also states that this and other drawings were shown to the Court. The same minutes also reveal that an affidavit was sworn by William Wilkins on 31 December, 1804. This has proved impossible to trace, but must have been an estimate of costs accompanying a set of designs. It is annoying that this first, precise reference to Wilkins is not further qualified and is not supported by the visual evidence of his drawings.

Once again the story can only be hypothetically reconstructed, and it looks as if the presentation of new designs by Wilkins had been a last-minute move prompted by the Graecophils' realization that any further delay would have made it impossible to unsettle Byfield from the very strong position he had gained. Indeed, as late as 10 February, 1805, Joseph Farington could report in his diary that during a visit to the artist Robert Smirke the latter 'had also mentioned that the Commission for building Downing College at Cambridge has been taken from Wyatt & given to Byfield.'[30]

Wilkins and his supporters amongst the Graecophils did not have a quick and easy victory. In fact, between spring 1805 and March 1806 three more architects 'voluntarily'(as the minutes of the Governing Body state) submitted designs for the new college. They were William Porden, Francis Sandys and Lewis Wyatt, James Wyatt's nephew. It is hard to tell what prompted, or who guided their actions since the architect for the college was not intended to be chosen by means of a public competition, but rather through a limited competition between two architects expressly approached by the prospective client. No advertisement had appeared in the press calling for more designs, and in general the national press had not reported widely on the establishment of the new college, certainly not from an architectural point of view. On the other hand, the artistic and architectural circles in London and Cambridge were acutely aware of the importance of the commission, which they discussed not only as a topic of gossip but, more importantly, as a controversial aesthetic issue. Factions had formed immediately inside the Royal Academy over the dispute between Thomas Hope and James Wyatt, which had begun with Hope's pamphlet of February 1804. Robert Smirke, the father of one of the principal exponents of the Greek Revival, condemned Hope bitterly for his pamphlet, which he described as 'an extra-ordinary piece of Egotism' that could be easily answered, and even suggested that 'Porden would do it [the reply] well.'[31] The Academy's council meetings in March and April 1804 had been riddled with arguments as to whether or not Hope should be invited to the Academy's Annual Dinner, a social event from which any recognized member of the artistic establishment could not conceivably be excluded. Wyatt, who aspired to the Presidency of the Academy (and obtained it the following year), commanded the support of the majority of Council members and, despite the resistance put up by George Dance, Benjamin West and John Soane, succeeded in excluding Hope from the dinner. The general commotion did not stop here: a satirical poem entitled *Hope's Garland* was composed by Henry Tresham R.A., and published by Macmillan on the night of the Royal Academy Dinner. The acrimony between the two factions appears to have continued, because in December 1804 Joseph Farington reported West saying that 'Tom Hope is following Wyatt up, having examined many of his works, & is preparing a critical examination of them.'[32] The debate over the schemes for Downing College must have been re-fuelled and gained new momentum, when George Byfield and William Wilkins exhibited their designs in the Royal Academy annual exhibition in April 1805.[33]

By submitting drawings for the college Porden, Sandys and Wyatt were all seeking publicity for themselves, but one suspects that they were also expressing the continuing debate over the aesthetic issues raised by Hope in his pamphlet. Their unprecedented action may also have been dictated by a desire to create obstacles for Hope and his protégé Wilkins, who was just emerging from obscurity and enjoying what might have been perceived as an unfair degree of support. With the exception of the Neo-Palladians, who had found their high priest in Alexander Pope, British architects had never before found themselves backed by 'intellectuals' who could argue their case in print, and articulate their artistic beliefs in a coherent fashion. In the past architects had had to turn themselves into publicists in order to advertise their work – as in the case of Colen Campbell, James Gibbs, Robert Adam, and John Soane to mention but a few – yet none of them had enjoyed the support of men of letters or taste who would champion them in print.

Of the three new architects, Porden was the one who appears to have submitted designs first, possibly spurred by the sight of Byfield's and Wilkins' entries in the April 1805 Royal Academy exhibition. One of his earliest designs, a plan of the site with a block plan of the college, is in fact inscribed 'Sunday April 27' (see Catalogue n.13). Sandys' drawings have not survived and the college records contain no hint as to the date of his submission, while Lewis Wyatt signed his ten drawings, estimates and accompanying general remarks 'December 9th, 1805'. Before we discuss Lewis Wyatt's submission, the events leading to it and those generated by it, something should be said about Sandys and Porden.

Francis Sandys' designs for Downing have not survived although the one for the main elevation had been exhibited at the Royal Academy's April exhibition in 1806.[34] Sandys was a native of Kilrea, Co.Londonderry, who owed much of his education and success as an architect to the patronage of Frederick Hervey, fourth Earl of Bristol and Bishop of Derry. It was probably at Hervey's expense, and certainly with his encouragement, that Sandys, whose brother was domestic chaplain to the Bishop, travelled to Italy in 1791. There he came into contact with the greatest Italian and English neo-classical artists, including the sculptors Antonio Canova and John Flaxman, whose ideas he absorbed. He returned to England in 1796, where he renewed his contacts with Flaxman (who had himself returned from Rome in 1794) and started working for his patron. Joseph Farington records being visited in 1796 by Flaxman accompanied by 'Mr Sandys an Architect; a young man who left Rome at the beginning of April, and is now employed, as he says, in beginning to build a Palace at Ickworth for Lord Bristol.' In fact, Sandys was not entirely responsible for the design of Ickworth, undoubtedly one of the most eccentric neo-classical buildings in this country; he had adapted a design first prepared in Rome for the Earl Bishop by Mario Asprucci the younger.[35] However, Sandys showed at Ickworth great sensitivity and flair for neo-classical architecture as well as an understanding of the interplay between sculpture and architecture, as advocated by the new taste. The death of the Earl Bishop in 1803 interrupted work on the great house and enabled Sandys to carry on with his own modestly successful practice, which had been developing on the side. His activity was chiefly concentrated in Suffolk, with only one recorded foray into Cambridgeshire, namely at Chippenham Park where in 1800 he designed the entrance lodges for John Tharp. In 1804, Sandys had won the commission for the Assembly Rooms, now the Athenaeum, in Bury St.Edmunds, the drawings for which he exhibited together with the design for Downing at the 1806 Royal Academy exhibition. Whether or not Sandys thought he could succeed in getting the commission for Downing, he had nothing to lose by submitting a new scheme, indeed he could only hope to gain some publicity which was always useful as well as needed by one whose patron had suddenly died. Was Sandys acting upon anybody's advice, or did he follow his own initiative? Sadly none of the surviving documents seem capable of answering these questions, but Sandys' frequentation of Academy circles and his friendship with Flaxman, who in 1802 had produced a design for the newly established college's seal, do not exclude the possibility of external pressure and encouragement.

Sandys' own practice in the neo-classical style, and on a building as complex and huge as Ickworth, made him a perfectly plausible architect for Downing. The same could not be said for William Porden (c.1755–1822) whose considerable reputation rested on his Gothic country houses and who, for the purposes of the Downing commission, had the additional misfortune of having been a faithful pupil of James Wyatt. Yet Porden seemed unfettered by these considerations and worked painstakingly on a new scheme for the college which was presented in six beautifully finished drawings, now in the British Architectural Library (Figs.10–15 and Pls.V-VI). These were exhibited in 1806 at the Royal Academy exhibition.[36] It may be noted here that Porden was the man who, according to Robert Smirke, could have successfully replied to Thomas Hope's slanderous attack on James Wyatt in 1804, and that he also enjoyed the favour of George, Prince of Wales who in that same year had commissioned him with the stables, riding-house, tennis-court and other alterations for the Pavilion at Brighton. Porden's work for the prince was in a weird Saracenic/Gothic style, certainly one which would have not endeared him to the Graecophils or even to tamer neo-classicists.

Porden's designs for the college are of great interest, not only because of their departure from the tacitly agreed neo-classical style, but also for his highly unusual conception of the layout (Figs.10 and 11). It would have been reasonable to expect that the choice of Gothic entailed the acceptance of a system of small, intercommunicating courtyards and cloisters. This, after all, was the standard pattern of the other medieval colleges in Oxford and Cambridge and of the monasteries from which they had originated. Porden, instead, proposed a huge quadrangle in which the north and south sides were open and towards the middle of which he placed a cruciform block containing the chapel, hall and library and their related offices. This central block was raised and was approached by means of a rather grand staircase. The buildings on the sides had three floors, with a continuous terrace running round them at the level of the first storey and connecting them with the chapel, hall, library, kitchens and offices at the centre of the quadrangle. The terrace rested on pilasters thus forming on the ground floor a continuous cloister communicating with the gardens and providing, in Porden's words, 'a sheltered communication with every part of the College public and private, and a walk in Winter.'

The Master's House was sited, as by all the other architects, in the south-east corner of the quadrangle, terminating the east range. Its ground plan (Fig.12) was very compact and not dissimilar, in conception, from Byfield's. Here too the visitor entered into a vestibule leading to the public rooms on the front of the house, namely the dining room to the left and the drawing room to the right. Hidden behind the vestibule was a staircase, leading to the bedrooms on the upper floor, and the more private rooms at the back of the house, such as the Master's Room and the library, both of which could thus be easily isolated from the rest of the house. A unit of the same proportions was symmetrically placed at the end of the west range. This, however, was divided into two 'semi-detached' houses for the two Professors. Christian and Harwood can hardly have been pleased with this design which squeezed them into small and not very elegant accommodation (Fig.13). The two houses shared a vestibule which gave access to the entrance of each house. This was, in turn, dominated by the staircase leading to the bedrooms upstairs; the ground floor only contained three rooms: a dining room, a library and a smallish room sandwiched in between the other two.

Compared to the Professors, the Fellows and students were provided for lavishly. Their apartments were traditionally arranged around a staircase, of which there were five on each range, with two sets of rooms for each floor (Fig.14). The standard apartment consisted of an anteroom with press-bed (a foldable bed), a study, a dining room, a bedroom and a water closet.

In his designs, Porden planned to site the college further to the north than any other architect, bringing it much nearer Bird Bolt Lane. The boundary on this side was to be thickly and irregularly planted and access was by means of a large circular drive, the upper half of which was inscribed within the northern ends of the two ranges (Fig.15). The opposite side, on the south, was to be landscaped in a similarly loose and natural fashion: the boundary lines being planted in a thick straight line on the outside but becoming irregular on the inside. Indeed, along the edges the plantations took the shape of flames, with clumps of trees scattered towards the centre of the site. A serpentine river, widening out into an elongated lake with an island, divided the southern end of the site into two almost equal parts. The college could also be approached from the south by means of a winding road running close to the boundary line, and unfolding much more informally than the one to the north.

Such careful planning of the landscaping of the whole grounds was simply unparalleled by any of the many schemes for Downing. The natural, almost pastoral landscape was designed to bring the architecture into full view slowly, hiding it at first from the visitor's view so that it would be revealed all of a sudden in the beauty of its yellow sandstone, as a great surprise. The revelation of a great Gothic pile would have heightened the visitor's sense of surprise, for such a pastoral setting would have suggested classical associations rather than medieval ones. The sight of the overpowering chapel, with the huge Combination Room resembling the choir of some great Gothic cathedral, would have turned the romantic mood generated by the landscape into a sublime one (Pls.V and VI).

Porden's design was as much representative of the aesthetic issues of his times as the neo-classical projects submitted by Byfield and Wilkins. All of them saw the past, be it classical or medieval, as embodying moral, civic and artistic values lost by the moderns. Greek architecture was rational, ordered, finite and serene. In short it was the symbol of man's understanding and could be used as a powerful metaphor of the process of learning and understanding which the new college endeavoured to promote. Gothic architecture, on the other hand, was neither finite nor serene; indeed it sparked off thoughts or intuitions of infinity, of a mysterious connection with higher things, and provoked a perpetual feeling of aspiration. But it was precisely this feeling of aspiration to unwordly ideals which made Gothic equally suitable for a place of learning. Furthermore, Gothic was a style which could be described and was perceived as a native one, embodying the spirit of association and the community of national feelings. Porden's visionary Gothic college was an early and courageous statement of belief in the full expressive power of Gothic as an architectural language. Although generally dismissed as a 'fluke' in previous accounts of the architectural history of the college, Porden's design should be recognized as one of the most carefully thought out projects submitted to the attention of the Fellowship and the most serious challenger, both intellectually and architecturally, of Wilkins' Greek design.

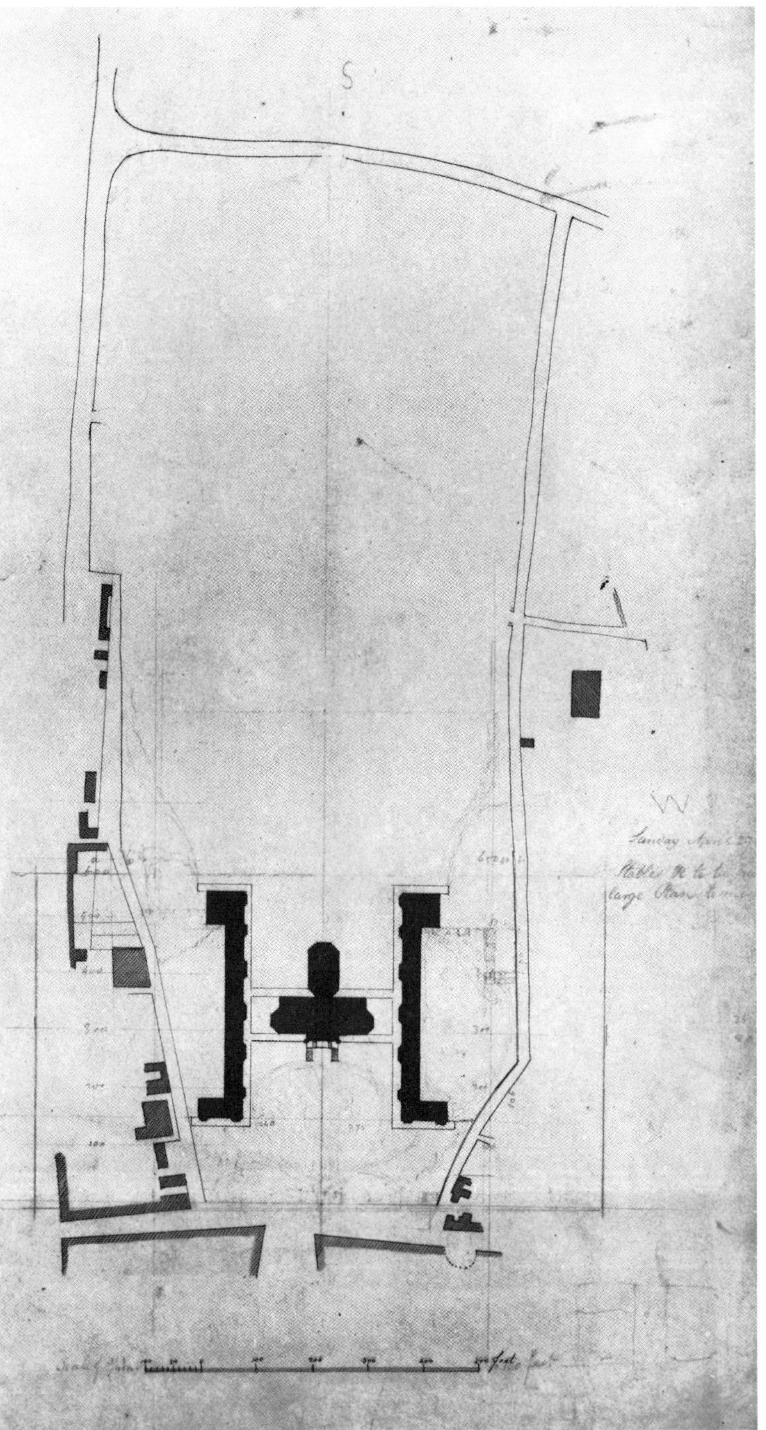

10

10 William Porden (c.1755–1822), Plan of the site with block plan of the college, 1805

11 William Porden, General plan of the college, 1805

11

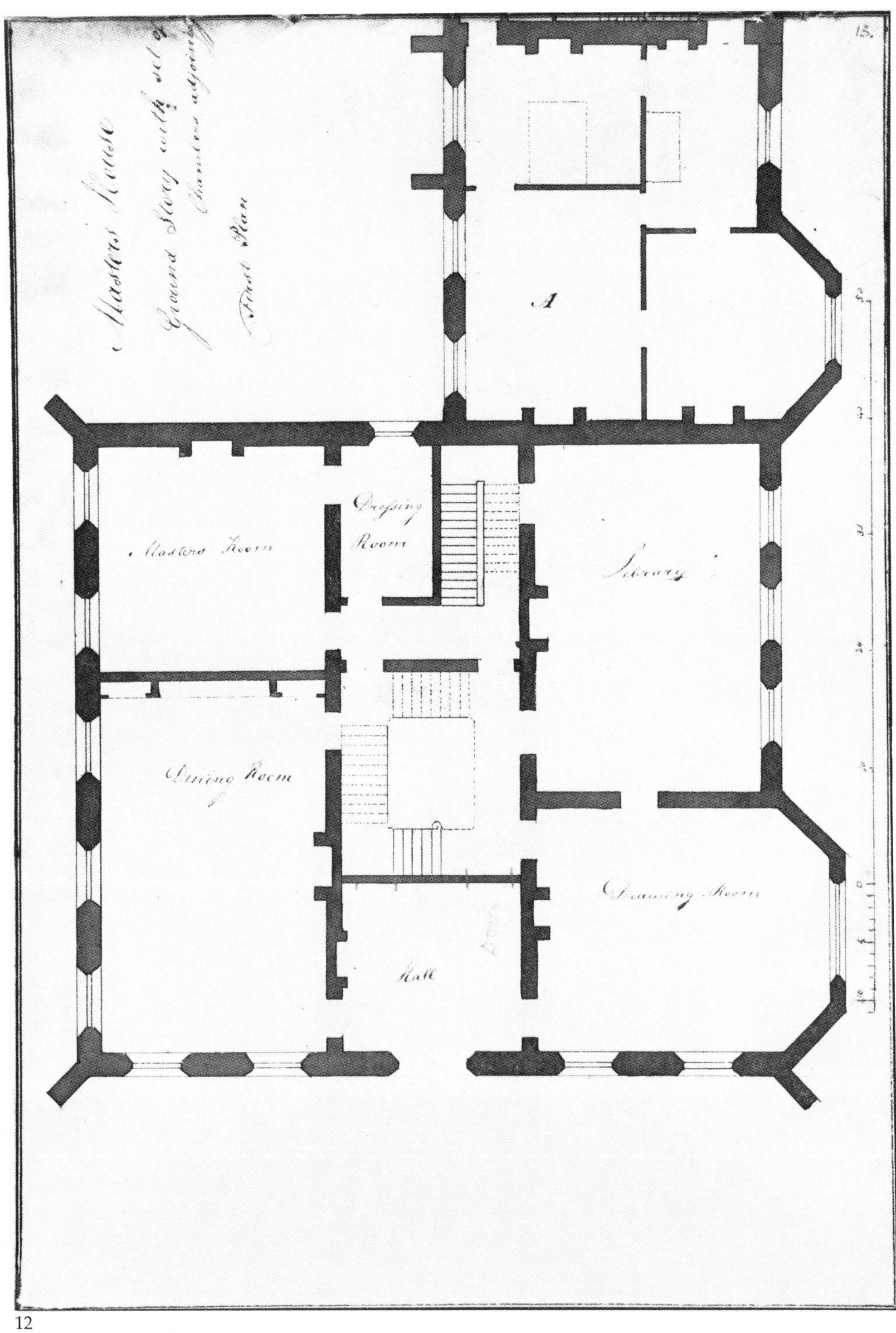

12

12 William Porden, Ground floor plan of the Master's house, 1805

13 William Porden, Ground floor plan of the Professors' houses, 1805

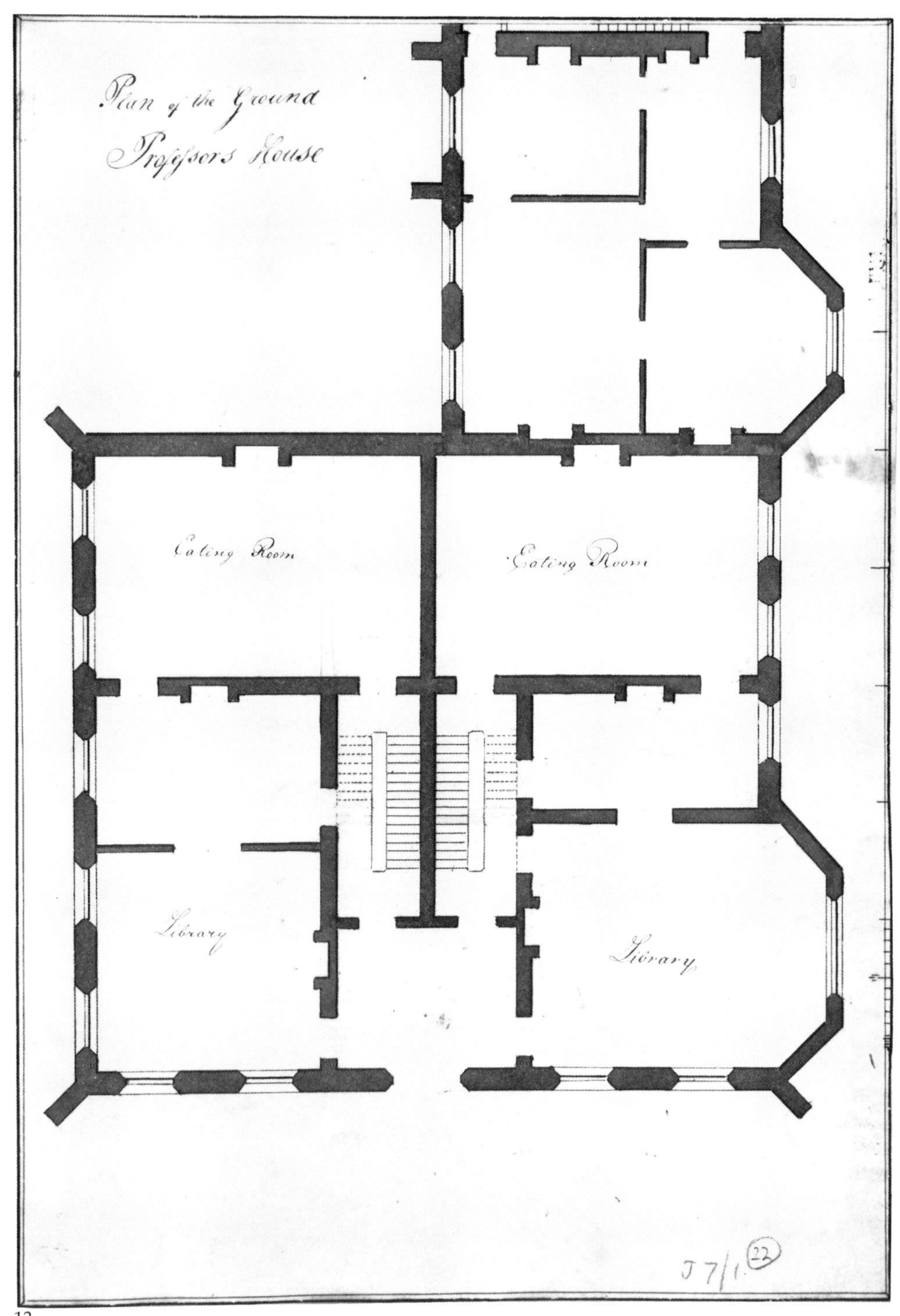

13

14 William Porden, First floor plan of the Fellows' and Students' accommodation, 1805

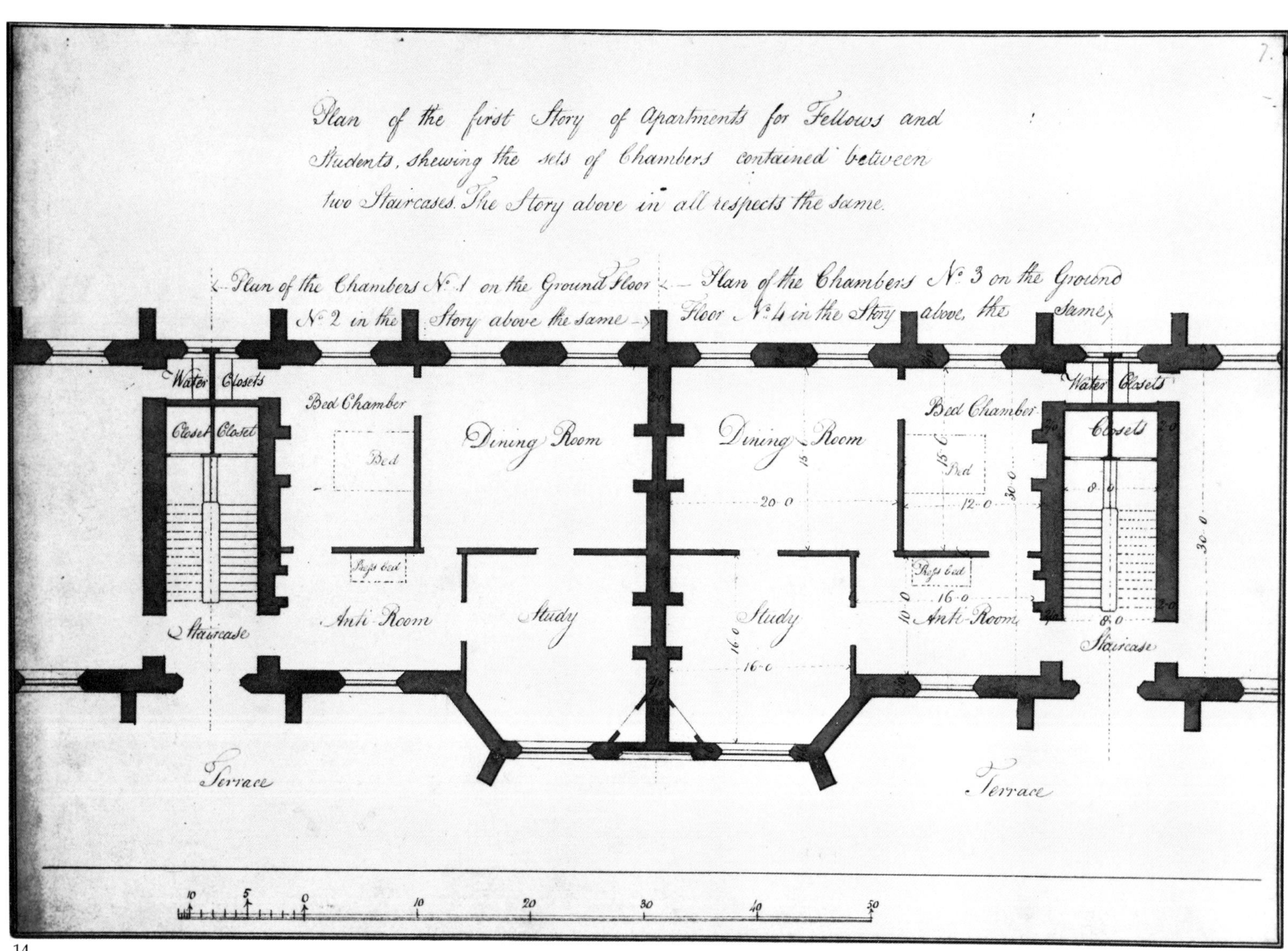

14

15 William Porden, Proposed landscaping of the site, 1805

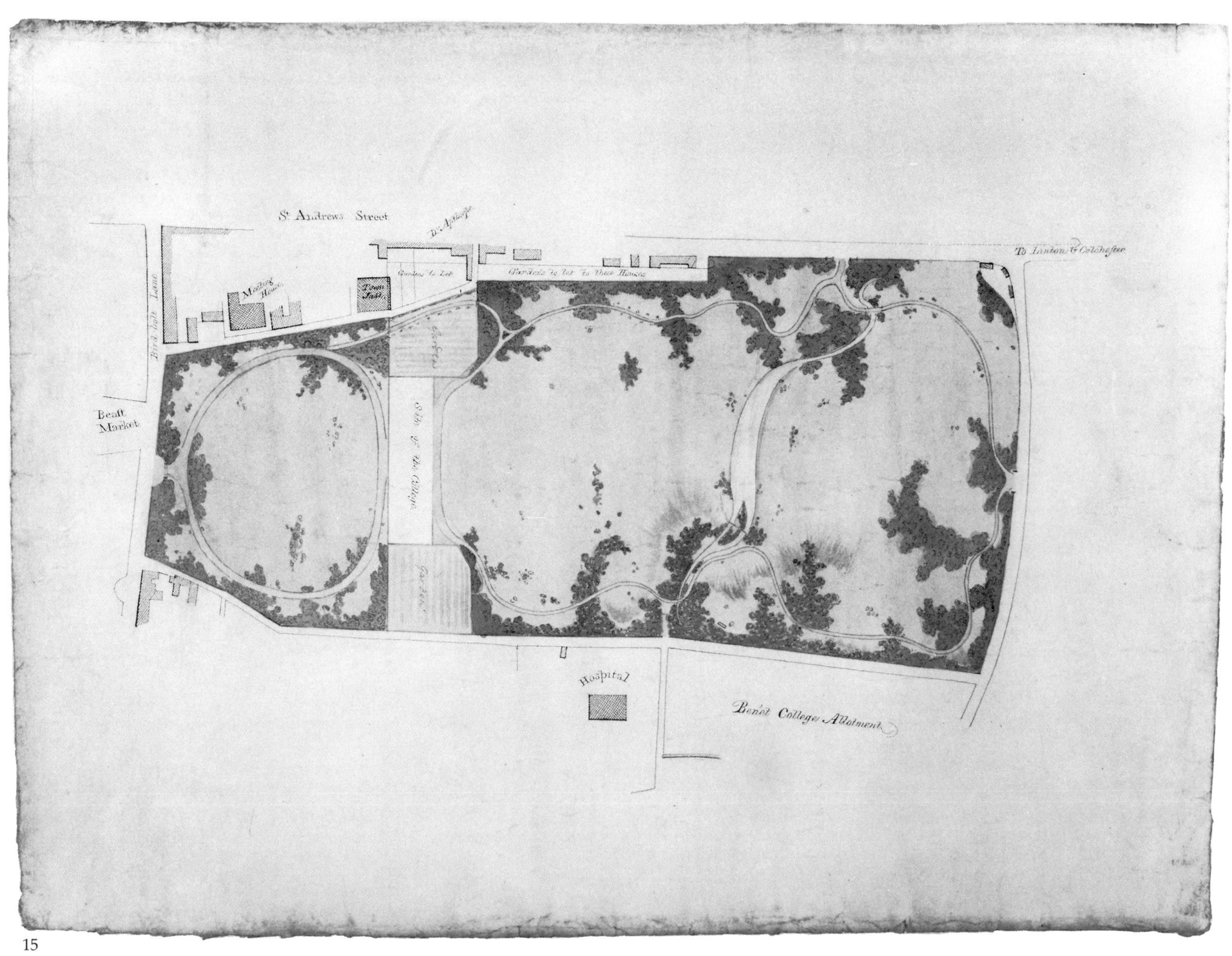

15

III

Wilkins' Imperfect Temple of Learning

On Sunday, 8 December 1805 George Downing Whittington (1781–1807), one of the eldest sons of Captain Jacob Whittington, and a Fellow of St. John's, wrote to his friend Lord George Gordon, fourth Earl of Aberdeen: 'Wilkins is to build the College after his Athenian model, he has been formally advised of this, which is the only satisfaction I have received on the subject since the fatal Decree.'[1] As a member of the defendant family in *Attorney General* v. *Vigor* (1803), the case concerned with the recovery of the Downing properties from Jacob Whittington and George Bowyer, George Whittington could only be upset by the final choice of an architect for the college, since this spelled the inevitability of the court's decisions and, consequently, his family's huge financial losses. On the other hand, the passion for Greek architecture, which he shared with his friends Wilkins and Aberdeen, made him rejoice for the success of their common cause.

Whittington's letter is the only surviving non-legal document referring to the elimination of the various architects who had submitted designs for the college (namely Byfield, Sandys and Porden) and consequently to the choice of Wilkins. Judging from this letter, the decision must have been reached by the Fellowship and communicated to Wilkins, who lived in Cambridge as a Junior Fellow at Caius, in the expectation of no further difficulty or opposition on the part of the court. This, however, was not to be the case for on 9 December 1805, precisely the day after Whittington's letter to Aberdeen, Lewis Wyatt submitted a fresh design for the college.

This was a bad blow for Wilkins, who, that same month, had secured the commission for the East India College at Haileybury, and an unexpected spanner in the careful works of the Graecophils, particularly so because Lewis Wyatt had succeeded in enlisting the backing of some of the heirs-at-law of Sir George Downing.[2] Without this kind of support Lewis Wyatt's designs could have easily been rejected by the Master and Fellows of Downing on the grounds that they had already chosen their architect from a wide enough range of names. Instead, a new candidate was being put forward by the legitimate heirs of Sir George Downing, those same heirs who had fought for the establishment of the foundation and in whose power rested the appointment of the first Master and Fellows. Wilkins' and Lewis Wyatt's plans were first examined by the Master in Chancery on 18 December 1805. No decision was then reached and the architects were in fact asked to introduce some alterations to their designs.[3] Although this smacks of a dilatory move, a reasonable excuse was produced to justify it: the court pointed out the need to provide accommodation for the two Chaplains according to the college's Royal Charter of 1800. Statute XVII of the charter, entitled 'Of Rooms', set out that 'The Chaplains, not being members of the College, shall be entitled to rooms, paying rent for the same.' Lewis Wyatt's reply to the court's order was swift; on 23 December 1805 he produced a document in which he suggested a certain amount of reshuffling of rooms in his original plan, some minor alterations in response to criticism which appears to have been moved against him, and a revised estimate of expenses. Wilkins' response to the new order by the court is unknown but presumably he too limited himself to minor changes.

No decision was made on either of the two projects until the middle of March 1806, when Francis Stratford, the Master of the High Court of Chancery who had been hearing the Downing cause, sought the help of three professional assessors to select the best design. The architects agreed upon by the parties involved were Samuel Pepys Cockerell (1753–1827), George Dance the younger (1741–1825) and James Lewis (c.1751–1820), all three very successful neo-classical architects who would have been sympathetic to both designs. On 19 March 1806, the three assessors, led by Dance, the most senior, wrote to the college's solicitors requesting through them that Master Stratford provide more specific information regarding the nature of their brief. They asked for 'some specific reference . . . to enable us to confine our observations to such particular points as he may wish us to consider, or otherwise that we shou'd report solely upon the general comparative merit of the two designs.' In this same letter the assessors also laid down their own conditions: they would report to the court but they begged leave:

> to state that the entering into any discussion of these designs in presence of their authors wou'd be a task which we cannot undertake.[4]

Master Stratford's resort to the arbitration of professional men on a subject well outside the area of his own competence was normal practice in the courts. However, it was a very unusual way of selecting the architect for a new building. Whether or not he did it consciously, Francis Stratford was setting down some basic rules for the running and assessment of architectural competitions. The client was virtually losing any power of decision and had to accept the judgement of the panel of assessors. This meant that, in the future, renewed importance was to be attached to the drafting of the brief and specifications for the architect, since the only really meaningful contact and exchange of information between the client and the architect occurred at that point in the whole proceedings. The reservations expressed by Dance, Lewis and Cockerell, in their letter of 19 March 1806, about meeting the selected architects and discussing their designs with them, show the profession's slight unease and its reactions to the introduction, however tentative, of new practices. If the architects were gaining power and recognition in so far as they were now being called to decide upon the merits of their colleagues' work, they were also, at the same time, facing the risks of creating deep divisions amongst themselves. This was a particularly serious predicament at a time when the profession still lacked representative bodies and a formally recognized training, outside the system of pupillage under an established architect.

Stratford's reply to the assessors' request of a more precise brief took the shape of three questions, namely:

> 1st. Whether both plans or either of them are proper plans and such as Mr Stratford may safely approve and recommend as fit to be executed. 2ndly. Which plan in your Judgement is upon the whole most proper. 3rdly. To point out the advantages and disadvantages the merits and demerits of each and to state upon what grounds your preference is given.[5]

He was thus asking them to argue their choice on technical as well as on aesthetic grounds and to express clearly the guiding principles underlying the basis of their decision. The document he got back on 26 March 1806 only partially satisfied his requests and showed that eventually, and inevitably, the assessors' decision hinged on aesthetic values. These, of course, were arguable because they were not absolute but rather reflected the general trend at the time and the shift in taste towards the Greek revival.

It is worth quoting extensively from the assessors' report to Master Stratford from which Wilkins' design emerged as the winning one:

> We have carefully examined the aforesaid designs and the written descriptions accompanying each of them and observe as follows.
>
> Each design contains nearly the same number of Buildings for general use and of apartments for the habitation of a Master two Professors and about forty Fellows or Under Graduates or Scholars. The aggregate quantity of Buildings and the gross amount of the estimated Expence are nearly equal in both Designs.
>
> We are of opinion that each Design requires reconsideration and improvement to render it compleatly fit and proper for Execution. The distribution of the several principal parts in each design are somewhat similar but the details of the plan very superior in that of Mr Wilkins whose design in our opinion combines more advantages then that of Mr Lewis Wyatt and is therefore as we are unanimously of Opinion to be preferred 'as upon the whole the most fit and proper'.
>
> The general decorations of Mr Wilkins design adopted from Grecian models possess more grandeur simplicity and classical effect than those of Mr L.Wyatt we think however that the magnificent portico at the Entrance copied from the Propylea in the Acropolys of Athens offers the appearance of affording the means of shelter without the reality on account of the proportionate smallness of its depth.
>
> In examining minutely the design of Mr Wilkins we have to observe that the elevations do not exactly agree with the plan. That there is a considerable dissimilarity between the East and West sides of the Quadrangle as well as of the internal plans of the Masters and professors lodges which with the exposure of the rear of the East Lodge the irregular spaces of the Chimneys of the Kitchen Offices will altogether be Inpurious to the symmetrical appearance of the quadrangle. We are apprehensive that the unpleasant communication between the Kitchen and the Hall or Refectory by a winding subterraneous passage of 140 feet in length from which its termination every thing must be brought up steps exposed to all Weathers thro the floor of the portico of the Refectory will prove very inconvenient and objectionable and in some measure degrade the appearance of the portico itself.
>
> We think it proper to suggest the Consideration whether the Houses of the Masters and professors are not larger than the Endowments may require; and whether it is desirable in all cases to place the undergraduates in the same staircases and immediately under the apartments of the Fellows.
>
> Being unanimously of opinion as we have before stated that the Wilkins's design is preferrable to that of Mr Lewis Wyatt we deam it unnecessary to enter into any discussion of the ultimate particulars of the latter.[6]

Wilkins' style and composition won him the approval of the assessors who, otherwise, were not blind to the flaws of his project. As neither the original six designs submitted to Dance, Lewis and Cockerell, nor Wilkins' written description have survived, it is thus impossible to verify the extent of his weaknesses and the objectivity of the three judges. The assessors' recommendations were substantial since it took Wilkins from the end of March to the middle of June to produce his revised plan. He had conferred with them, heard their views and eventually produced six new drawings which were approved, signed by the three architects, and returned to the court.[7] On 31 July 1806, Master Stratford formally ratified the choice of architect as it had emerged from the limited competition he had organized. Finally, after decades of struggle, the Master and Fellows of the college were allowed to proceed with the building of their institution.

The court's deliberation was a personal victory for Wilkins, for Annesley and his colleagues, and for the Graecophils. Throughout the report it was stated in glowing letters that the architecture was to be Grecian, clearly the most contested issue, and the one on which there should be no doubts in the future. The principal characteristics of Wilkins' design were also minutely described by the report which, in the absence of the original drawings, provides us with the most detailed evidence of what was being agreed upon:

> the general form would be a quadrangle comprehending an area 350 feet long by 214 feet whereof the Southern Division would exhibit the principal front of Grecian architecture of the Ionic Order and would contain a Library 60 feet long by 30 feet wide a Chapel 70 feet long by 20 feet wide. The Northern Division would contain a Grand Entrance from the Town of Grecian Architecture of the Doric Order with Porters Lodges and apartments for 8 Fellows and 10 Undergraduates. The Eastern Division would contain the Public Kitchens & Offices, Lodges for the 2 professors with the necessary Offices & apartments for 4 Fellows and 4 Undergraduates and the Western Division would contain a Lecture Room 24 feet long by 19 feet wide a Lodge for the Master with the necessary Offices and apartments for 4 Fellows 2 Chaplains and 6 Undergraduates comprizing in the whole Accommodation for the Master 2 Professors 16 Fellows 2 Chaplains & 20 Undergraduates as directed by the said Orders. . .[8]

In its July 1806 order, the court in fact ratified a design which differed from the executed buildings in so far as the location of the Master's Lodge and of the Hall were reversed. These were subsequently referred to by the lawyers acting on behalf of the college as 'some few trifling variations not affecting the general design'[9] and they were approved of *a posteriori* by Master Stratford. A subsequent court order was passed on August 6 1806, officially allowing the college to start building and regulating the flow of money to finance the building itself. The money was to be provided by the sale of some of the Bank 3 per cent annuities and it was to be administered by the Accountant General of the Court of Chancery. Before we start looking at the actual building of the college according to Wilkins' designs and under his supervision, it is necessary to pause and consider in some detail Lewis Wyatt's designs, and compare them with Wilkins', in order to understand what was so special about the winning project.

Lewis William Wyatt (1777–1853) was the nephew of James Wyatt, whose designs for Downing College had been so brutally criticized by Thomas Hope in 1804. Lewis was apprenticed first to his uncle Samuel, then to his uncle James; he only began practice on his own in about 1805, the year of his submission of designs for Downing College. He had started exhibiting at the Royal Academy in 1797, initially with drawings of buildings by his father and his uncles. Until December 1805, Lewis had never designed a large scale public building nor, for that matter, supervised the execution of anything he had designed himself; his work had been limited to country houses, the first two of which, respectively in 1803 and 1804, had been executed by his second cousin Benjamin Wyatt of Sutton Coldfield. His last-minute decision to step into the Downing affair, effectively forcing the debate open once again, might have been dictated by a desire to salvage the commission for the Wyatt family as well as to assert his own individuality as an architect. The style adopted by Wyatt in his designs for Downing was the neo-classical manner used by his uncles Samuel and James, but the whole of his composition and use of the orders was more organic, lighter and much more full of interest than in James' earlier design for the college.

Like his uncle James and his rival Wilkins, Lewis Wyatt proposed to arrange the college buildings around a quadrangle placed towards the middle of the site. Access was to be gained from Bird Bolt Lane, with a central avenue directing the view towards the gateway and its flanking arches surmounted by sculpted lions (Figs.16 and 17). The gateway and Porters' Lodges were then linked on the northern side of the quadrangle to square corner blocks for the accommodation of the college servants and four Fellows. On the southern side, facing the entrance gateway, was to be the principal monumental block, containing the chapel, hall and library. The south-west angle building contained the common room, kitchens, bursary and muniment room, whilst the south-east angle building was the Master's Lodge. Wyatt was the only architect to provide the Master's Lodge with a private entrance and drive, to be embellished by a flower garden. Accommodation for the two Professors was provided in the form of two self-contained houses placed in the middle of the east and west ranges (Fig.18). This particular feature was then to be copied by Wilkins in his revised design, since, as will be remembered, Wilkins had originally envisaged the Professors' accommodation to be semi-detached and on the east side of the college. Unlike any of his predecessors and Wilkins himself, Wyatt conceived of a very neat division between Fellows and undergraduates; the latter were to be concentrated on the east side of the college with the Fellows on the opposite side.

The scale of Wyatt's elevations was considerably reduced compared to his uncle's and the stress was not so much on monumentality but rather on elegance of simplicity and proportions. The most architectural of his elevations were those of the gateway (Fig.17) and both the north and south elevations of the south range[10] (Pl.VII). The east and west ranges presented a minimal use of the Doric order – apparently only used to conform to the dictates of Thomas Hope – which only served to mark the corners of the block and the central projecting lodge (Fig.18). However, the Doric order appeared profusely in the south range where it had a structural as well as ornamental purpose. Doric pilasters at the corners, and Doric half-columns framed the sixteen bays of the single-storey southern block the centre of which was marked on the inner side of the quadrangle by a four-columned portico with pediment. The portico with triangular pediment was, in fact, the principal facade of the chapel, placed between the library and the hall. The chapel, which was crowned by a shallow saucer dome, was square in plan with pairs of columns dividing the principal space from the apse at the south (Pl.VIII). This was ingeniously woven into the southern elevation (Pl.VII) so as to look like a fashionable palace

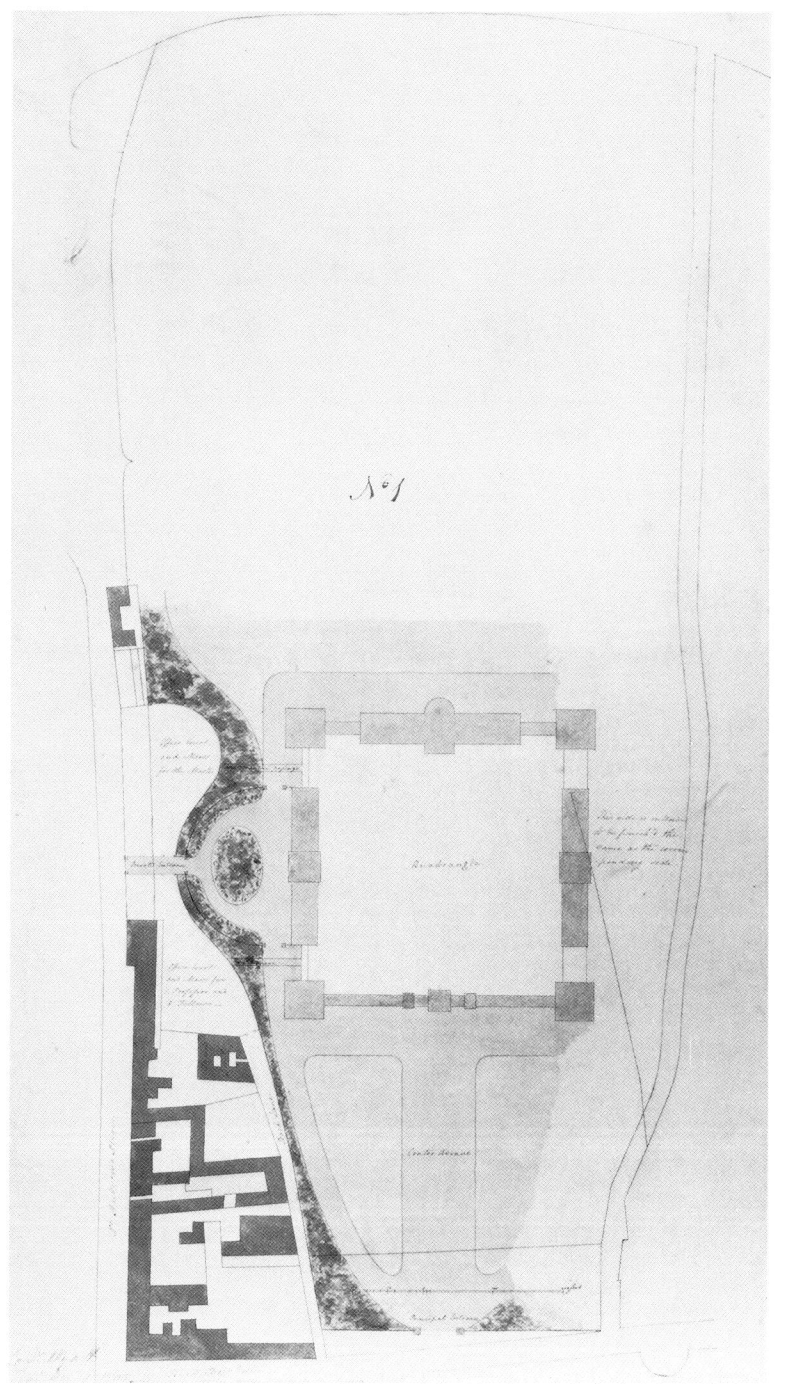

16

16 Lewis William Wyatt (1777–1853), Plan of the site with block plan of the college, December 1805

17 Lewis William Wyatt, Elevation of the south front of the north range, December 1805

18 Lewis William Wyatt, Elevation of the east range with sections of the triumphal arch and chapel, December 1805

17

18

with an apsidal bay, as in Pierre Rousseau's Parisian Hôtel de Salm (early 1780s), rather than the apse of a chapel.[11] Indeed Wyatt's beautiful perspectival view of the southern block could easily be passed for the garden elevation of a London house: there is no loftiness here as in the designs of previous architects, no attempt to use architecture metaphorically. Wyatt seems to have only been concerned with distilling beauty, refinement and elegance in this building. It is annoying that the three assessors asked to express their opinion on the merits and faults of the two rival projects decided not to produce a full-length report on Wyatt's submission, for one suspects that it was precisely this fashionable and sophisticated quality in his design that did not appeal to them.

Wyatt's buildings were meant to be erected in Portland and Country stone for a total cost of £62,800, of which £21,700 were necessary for the southern side of the quadrangle alone. He envisaged the possibility of substantial savings by omitting the columns in the north and south elevations of the library and hall alone, in other words retaining the colonnades linking the whole block to the corner pavilions as well as the columns of the chapel portico and apse. As he realized the impossibility of building the whole college at once, Wyatt suggested that a start be made on the east side of the quadrangle providing temporary accommodation for the Master, two Professors, three Fellows, a chapel, lecture room, hall and offices. This, according to his estimates, would have been habitable in two years and would have cost £9,300.

What were the differences between Wyatt's and Wilkins' design? The lack of Wilkins' very first six drawings, as well as of the revised set dating to June 1806, makes it impossible to go into any detailed analysis, but we can still gauge the basic lines of his plan. One of Wilkins' most crucial departures from his colleague's approach consisted in the rejection of the quadrangle scheme which he replaced with a 'campus' plan. Instead of having a quadrangle entirely surrounded by buildings, Wilkins created a central space around which he distributed twelve pavilions of varying size predominantly linked by means of screen walls (Fig.19). The advantages provided by such an arrangement, inspired by the example of the antique forum, was that it allowed the architect to isolate the various facilities required by the institution within a regular composition. The 'campus' plan entailed other major implications: it concentrated the attention on the facades overlooking the central expanse of lawn, thus freeing the architect from the preoccupation of the ornament and decoration of the outer elevations; moreover, it established a very strong central axis while at the same time preserving the lateral and corner views (Pl.IX). This main axis was naturally destined to house the public core of the college and was the one which received the highest architectural treatment. At Downing the northern end of the axis coincided with the gateway and the southern end with the chapel and library, connected by an entrance hall. This centre building rested on a continuous stylobate which linked it to the pavilions on the side ranges, respectively housing the hall and the Master's Lodge. Both the northern and southern buildings had a strong monumental quality resulting from their scale and the imposing sobriety of their Greek style.

The mood was set by the entrance gateway, consisting of a portico modelled on the Propylaea in Athens, but with the flanking buildings made more regular, and adapted to house a Porters' Lodge and a public lecture room (Fig.20). The Propylaea also served to introduce the eye to the alternating pattern of columns in porticoes which was then taken up and fully developed in the southern range. The outer portico of the Propylaea had six baseless Doric columns supporting the architrave with triglyphs and a rectangular pediment. The portico overlooking the quadrangle, however, was not an identical replica for it had four columns only (Fig.21). The building facing the Propylaea on the south side of the quadrangle, measuring 181 feet, was broken on the north side by a two-columns deep portico of six Ionic columns, modelled on those of the Erechtheum in Athens. These were repeated on the south side but reduced in depth (Figs.22 and 23). Since the portico overlooking the quadrangle on the south side was immediately facing that of the Propylaea it should have been treated as a mirror image of it; instead it reflected the northern portico of the Propylaea. In the original design the four-column portico of the Propylaea reappeared on the sides of the southern block, facing the inner porticoes of the Master's Lodge and of the hall. These two buildings were also given south facing porticoes of four columns each. Wilkins was thus setting out his compositional themes outside the quadrangle on the outer elevations of the Propylaea, but then within the college he broke the rhythm of the pattern by introducing dissymmetry where the viewer, used to Renaissance compositional principles, would have expected symmetry.

19 William Wilkins (1778–1839), Block plan of the college

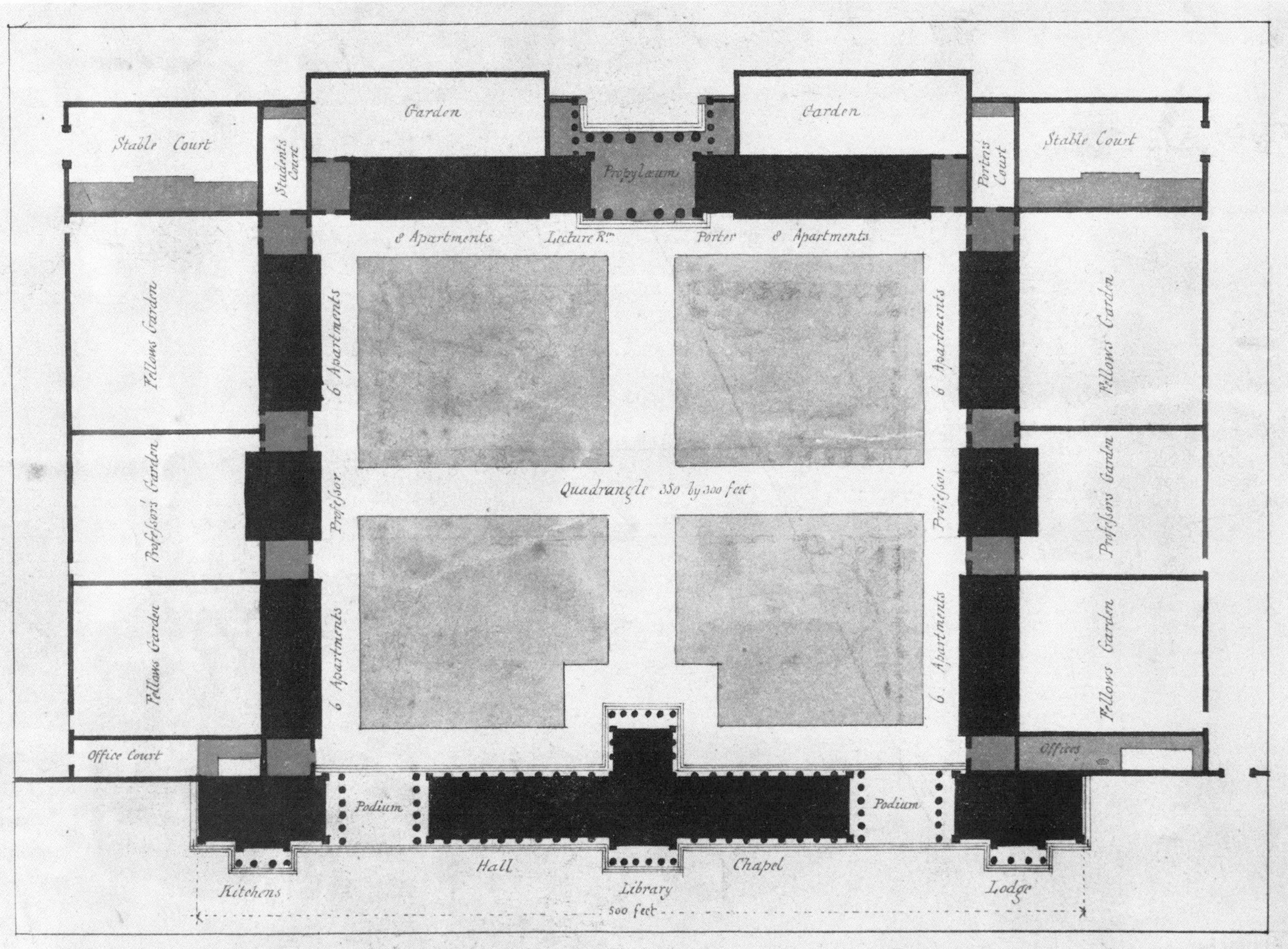

19

20 William Wilkins, North elevation of the Propylaea, 1806

20

21 William Wilkins, Elevation of the south front of the principal portico of the Propylaea, 1806

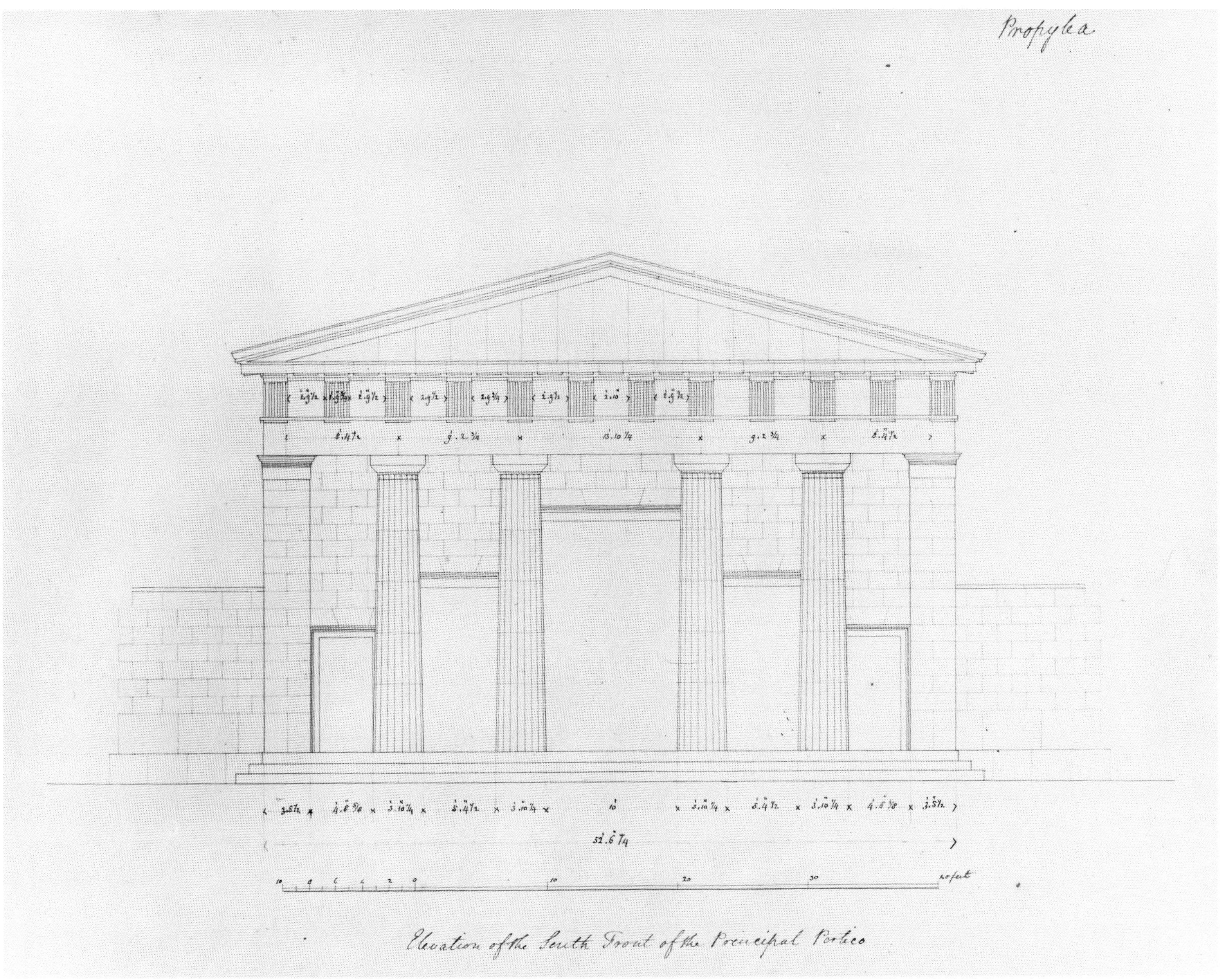

21

22 William Wilkins, Southern half of the general plan of the college, 1806

23 William Wilkins, South elevation of the south range, after 1807

24 William Wilkins, Elevation of the east range, after 1807

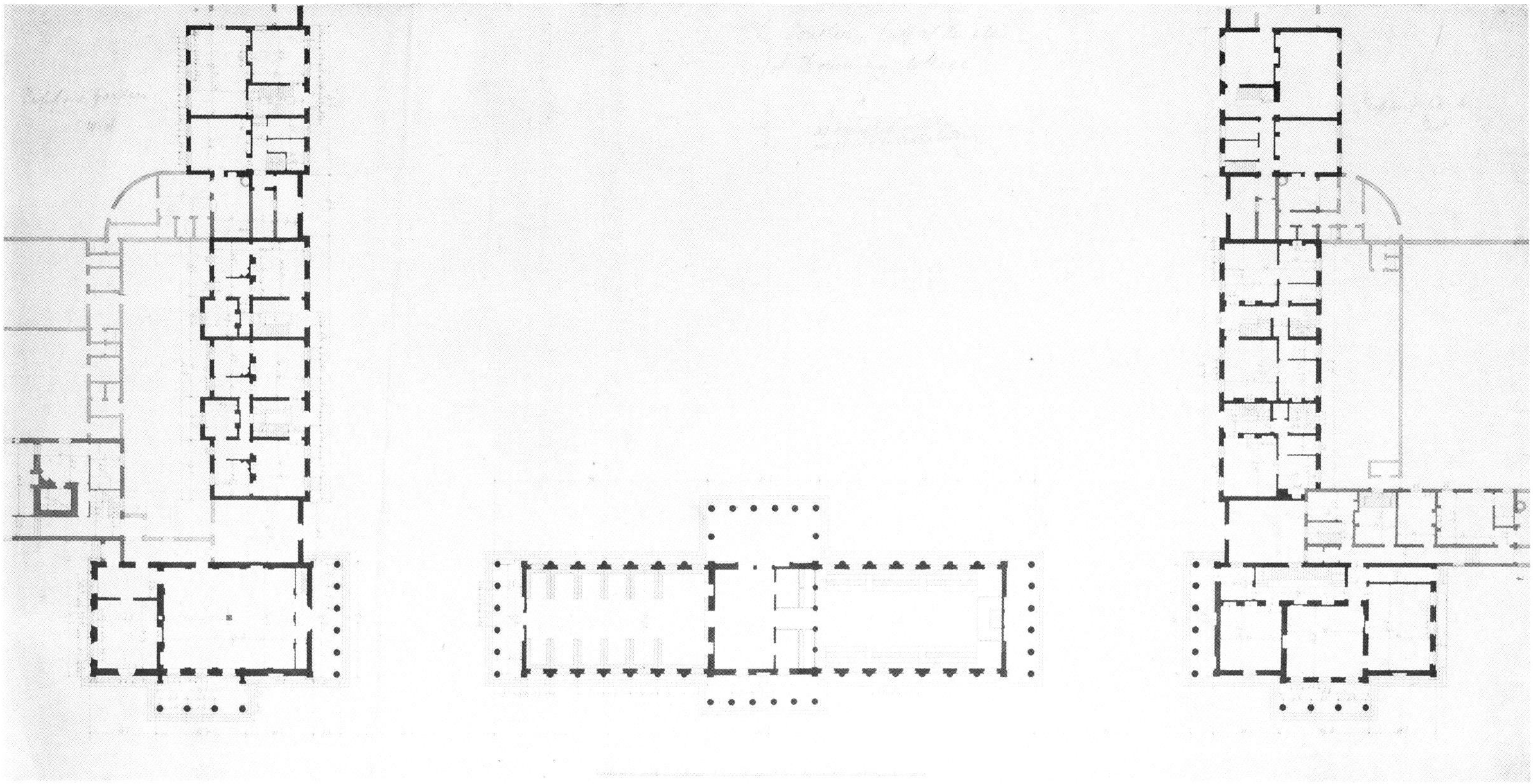

22

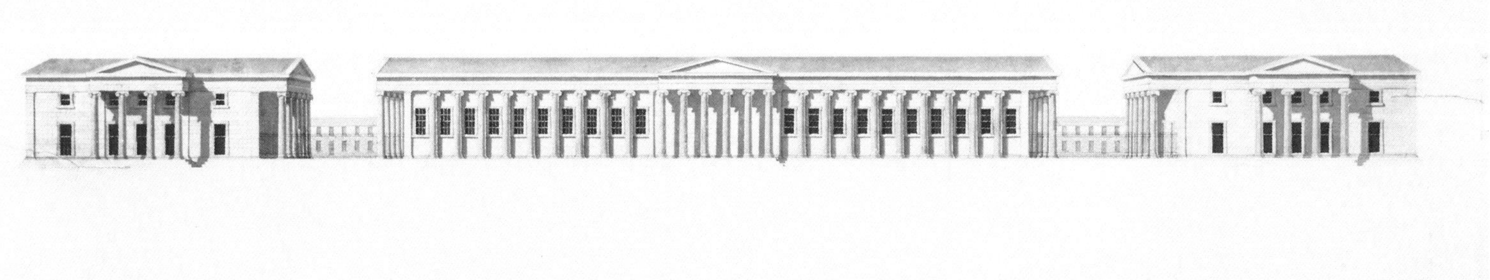

23

The originality of this scheme gained strength from the starkness of the facades of the east and west ranges (Fig.24), which were completely astylar and void of any decorative feature, and also from the contrast between the primitive Doric order of the gateway – as advocated by Hope in his pamphlet – and the elegantly slender engaged and free-standing Ionic columns articulating the whole of the southern block. The Ionic columns, however, were not used as a decorative element but as a structural one for they were meant to represent the pillars supporting the roof as in a primitive wooden hut (Fig.23). Decoration was generally very sparse both externally and internally (Pls.X-XII), being limited to the mouldings and beadings of the relevant order (Figs.25 and 26) and to lions' heads used as gutter headings on the top bed of the cornices, below the roofs of the principal buildings (Figs.27 and 28). The lions' heads appear also inside the hall as purely decorative devices (Fig.29). The chapel and the library were puritanical in their stark simplicity (Fig.30).

Wilkins' architecture for Downing, as for the East India College at Haileybury (Fig.31), was intensely intellectual. It was based on a scholarly study of the classical antiquities of Athens, adapted to the requirements of a modern structure, and it hinged on subtle repetitions and disruptions of rhythms. Very few people had any direct experience of Greek architecture, and, by 1806, few knew of it even through books and publications. These were so rare and expensive that they were restricted to a small élite. Yet, despite its immediately limited appeal, one can imagine the visionary dream that guided both architect and clients: to build up a fragment of Athens in England, and more importantly in Cambridge, where it would embody with magnificent clarity the intellectual and moral values upheld by the academic community.

Unfortunately the modern visitor can hardly appreciate the impact that the original scheme was intended to have because the two crucial buildings, the Propylaea and the southern block, were never executed (Figs. 34 and 35). Furthermore, the general layout of the site bears no relation to what Wilkins had envisaged. He planned thick plantations along the outer edges of the estate and huge, plain expanses of lawn at the centre, with hardly any trees at all; the college would thus have been isolated from the rest of the town, screened off from it. Once inside the belt of trees, however, the visitor would have been faced with the distant view of classical temples, unexpectedly rising from the ground, almost as if he had been transported to some remote plain in Greece, or to the Valley of the Temples in Sicily. The vision would have been imposing and moving, in a way that is entirely lost to us today (Fig.35 and Pls.XVIII–XIX).

24

25 William Wilkins, Frontal view and section of the Ionic capital for use in the Library, Hall and Chapel, 1806

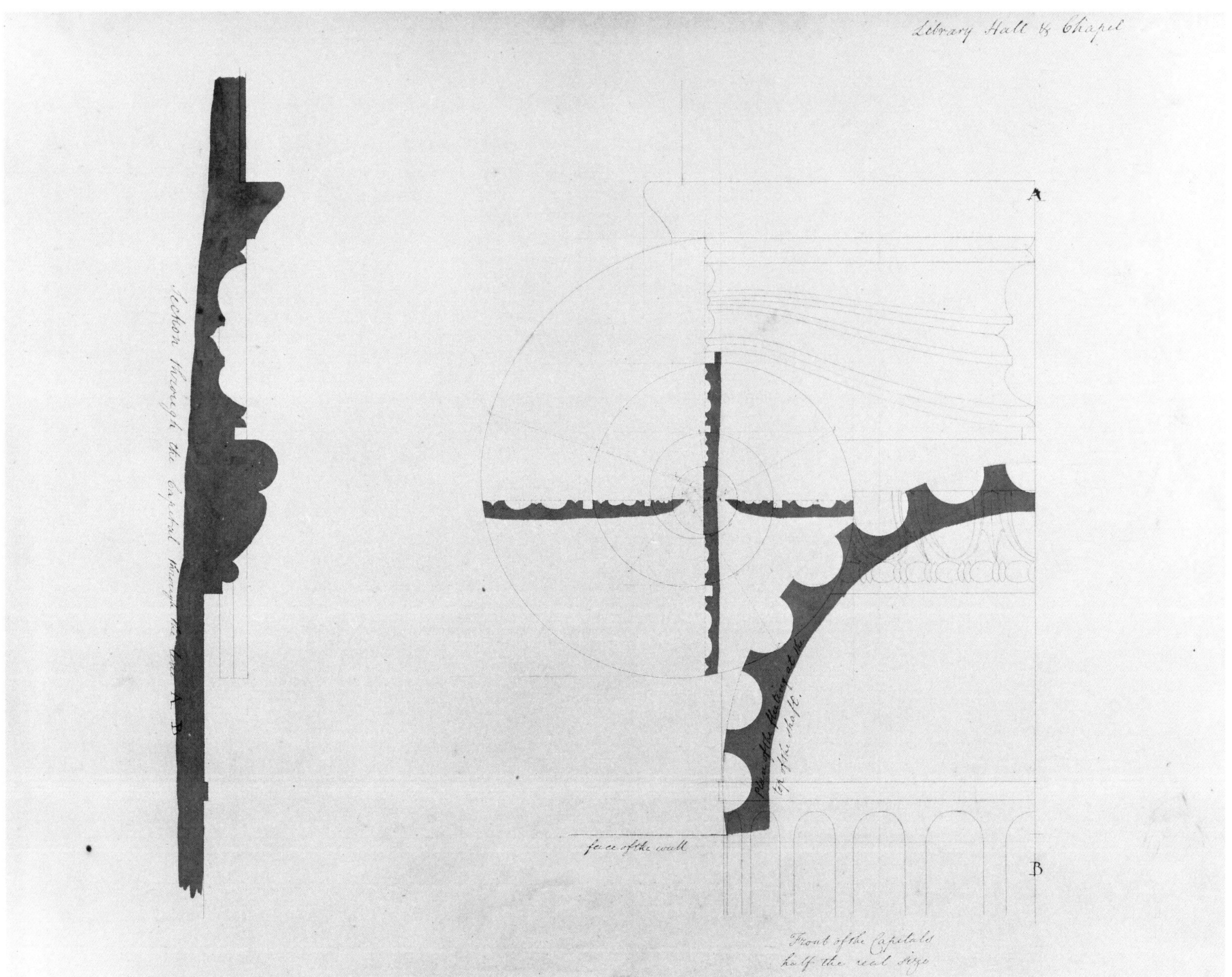

25

26 William Wilkins, Frontal view and section of the Ionic pilaster for use in the Library, Hall and Chapel, 1806

26

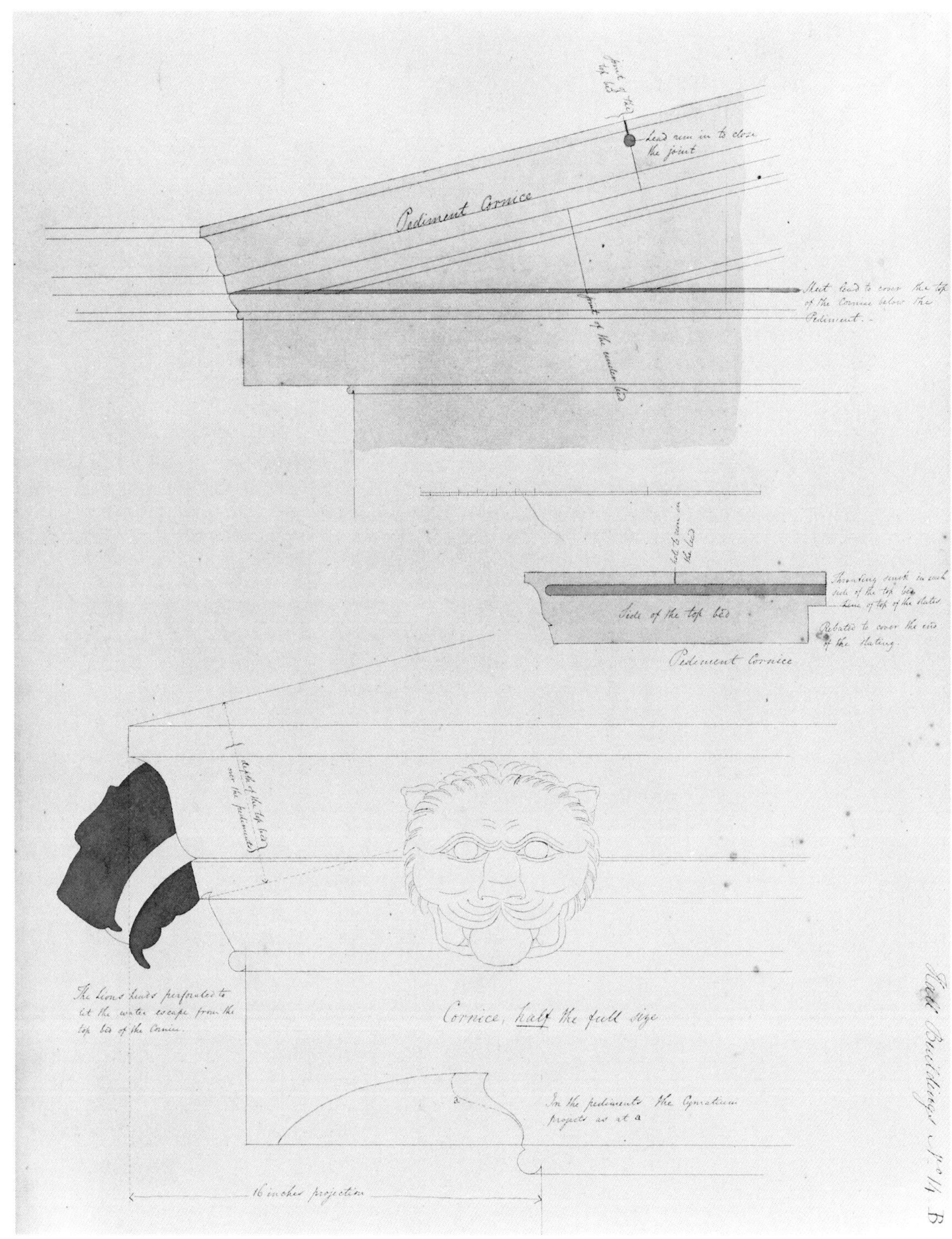
Lead run in to close the joint
Pediment Cornice
Sheet lead to cover the top of the Cornice below the Pediment.
Side of the top bed
Pediment Cornice
The Lions heads perforated to let the water escape from the top bed of the Cornice.
Cornice, half the full size
In the pediments the Cymatium projects as at a
16 inches projection

27

27 William Wilkins, Study of the pediment cornice of the Hall with the perforated lions' heads, 1812

28 Downing College, Detail of the gutter heads as executed

29 Downing College, Detail of the lions' heads inside the Hall

28

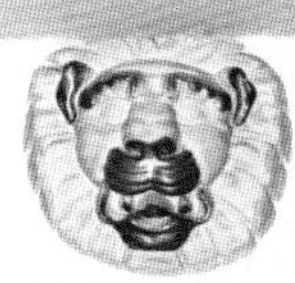
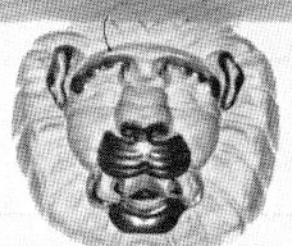
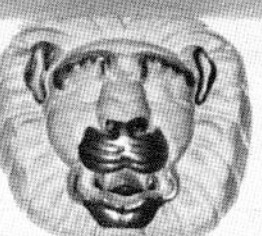
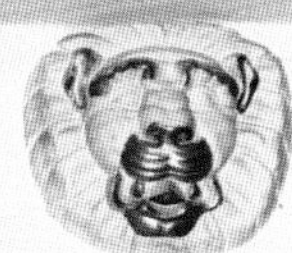
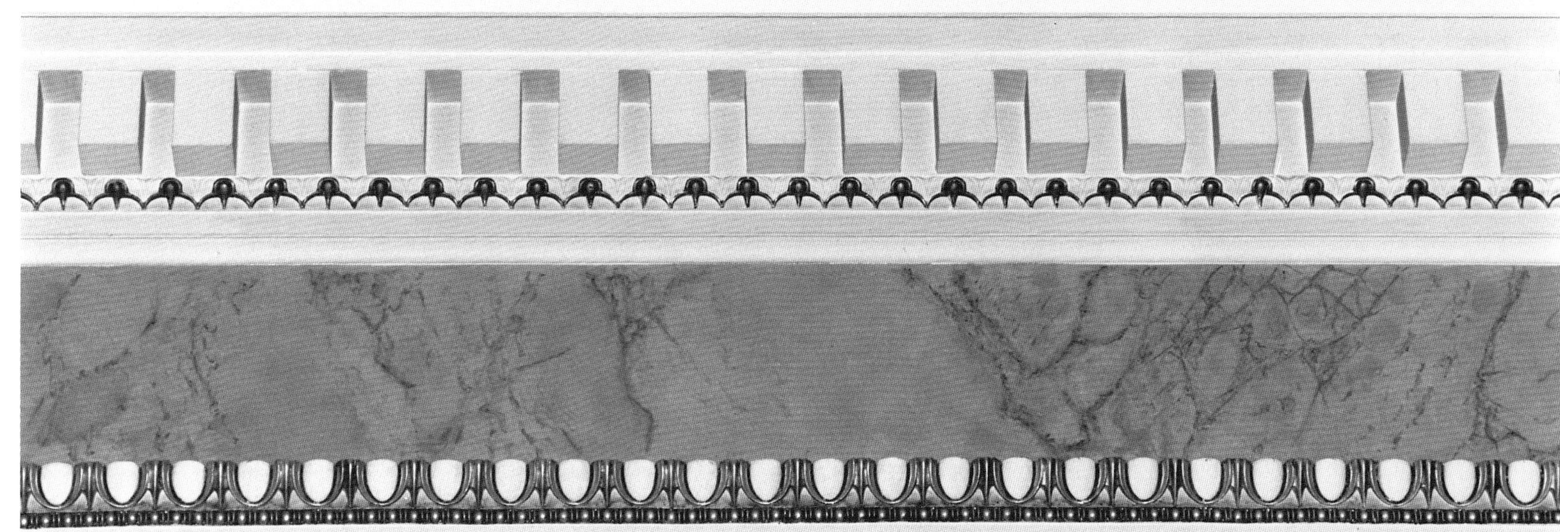

29

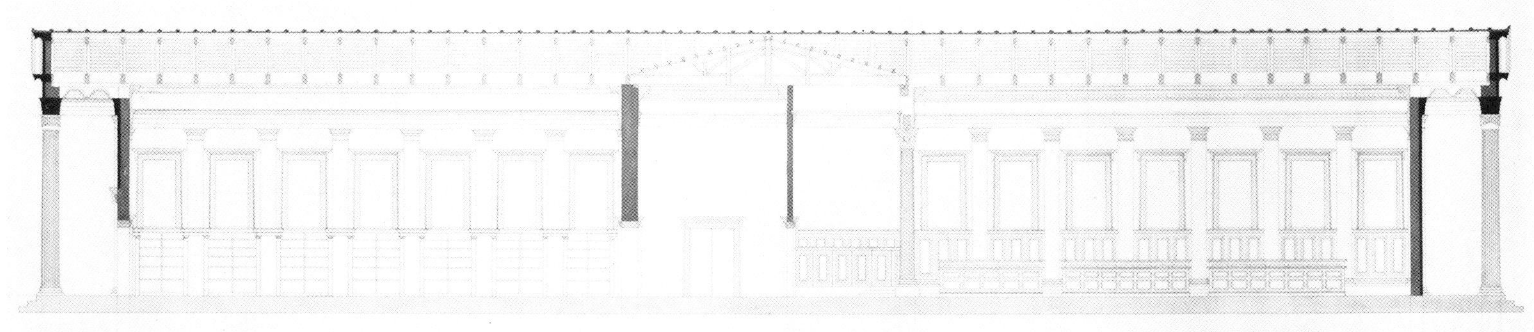

30

31

30 William Wilkins, Section through the southern block showing the interior of the Library and Chapel, c.1806

31 View of the East India College, Haileybury; the chapel was added in 1876 by Sir Arthur Blomfield

32 Downing College, View of the east range

32

33 Downing College, View from south-east of the exterior of the hall

33

34 Downing College, View of the paddock with the Catholic church

34

35 J.Bailey, Perspective from the south-west, 1830

35

Work on Wilkins' 'Temple of Learning' began on 27 November 1806, the summer months having being spent by the architect in producing the detailed working drawings[12] and selecting the contractors. Wilkins chose to employ his brother Henry's firm for all the carpentry work, the stonemasons Edward and Thomas Tomson and the bricklayer Samuel Harris, all local craftsmen on whose skills he could comfortably rely. This was clearly a very important consideration for a novice architect who was embarking on his first commission.[13] During the last months of 1806 and the early ones of 1807, the sewers and drains were built and the foundations dug out; the foundation stone was laid during a public ceremony attended by the Vice-Chancellor of the university and various other dignitaries on 18 May 1807. The following day, 19 May, the Master, Professors and Fellows held a Governing Body meeting in the Lodge of the Provost of King's in the course of which they directed:

> Mr Wilkins to proceed with all convenient expedition to complete the Masters Lodge. The Professors Lodge in the east side of the Court being designed for the residence of Professor Harwood and the six sets of apartments between the two Lodges being for the temporary residence of Professor Christian and Messrs Lens Meeke and Frere.[14]

By the end of July, Wilkins reported to the Court that:

> The Masters Lodge is 13 feet above ground the Offices to the Lodge are 3 feet above ground. The South and West fronts of the Lodge are covered with Stone, the Window and Door architraves to both fronts fixed. The Antae or Pilasters five in number are 12 feet above the floor line or about 2/3 of their intended height. The base molding is fixed the whole extent of the South front. The Window architraves to the West front of the Lodge are also fixed.[15]

Judging from the number of men employed and the frantic pace of the works, the outside of the Master's Lodge must have been more or less completed by the end of 1807 and a serious start made on the rest of the east range.

Although the guiding principles behind the Governing Body's decision of May 1807 are easily understandable, it turned out to be somewhat disastrous because it eventually deprived the project of its most striking and original feature. The decision had a further consequence, that of changing the nature of the relationship between the architect and his client(s). Because building was first started on the Master's Lodge and on that of the Professor of Medicine, rather than on communal buildings such as the hall, the library and the chapel, with which the college as a corporate entity could immediately identify, the architect found himself no longer faced with a 'corporate' patron but with two more traditional individual clients. Both the Master, Francis Annesley, and the Professor of Medicine, Sir Busick Harwood, behaved like any normal private patron who has at heart his personal interest, rather than that of the community, when his own house is being built. They incessantly requested the introduction of alterations to the original design for both functional and aesthetic reasons, and often regardless of the increased expenditure entailed. The Master, for instance, insisted, and obtained that the porticoes of his lodge be given six instead of the original four Ionic columns.[16] Some of the changes requested by Annesley and Harwood, as well as the ones later on introduced by Edward Christian in his lodge on the west range, highlighted Wilkins' pedestrian handling of internal spaces. Even a cursory glance at his plans for the three lodges (Figs.36, 38 and 39) and for the students' and Fellows' quarters (Figs.40 and 41) reveals his lack of inspiration, compared to the interiors proposed by the other architects competing for the Downing commission. It also became obvious that, in designing the three lodges, Wilkins had not taken into consideration the entire range of facilities that the Professors' families would need, particularly those generated by the presence of several young children.

During the course of Annesley's Mastership, Wilkins frequently found himself in open conflict with the Head of the College, who emerges from the documents as a domineering figure who treated the institution as his private possession. The architect was forced to champion the cause of the Fellowship which was witnessing the Master slowly but surely appropriating more and more land for his own garden, as well as erecting all kinds of out-houses and buildings without even seeking the Fellowship's consent. In a letter to Annesley of August 1808, Wilkins had to remind the Master about the aims of the college:

> The chief object in the formation of the plan was the accommodation of every member of the College. This principle must, of course, be violated by anything which tends to abridge the comforts and convenience of those who are so much concerned in the College as the Fellows upon the present Establishment.'[17]

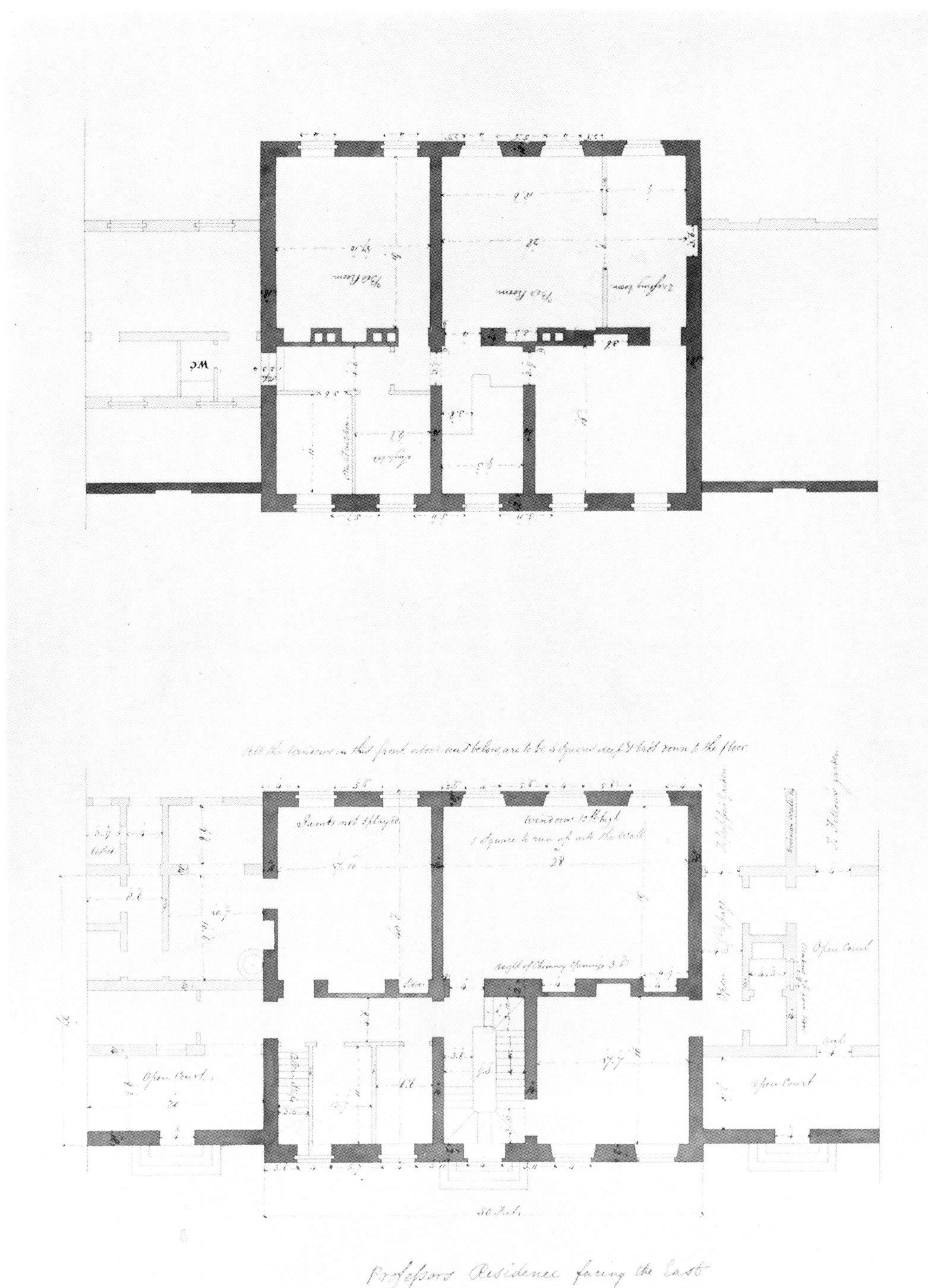

36 William Wilkins, Ground and first floor plans of the West Lodge, 1806

36

37 William Wilkins, Section through the West Lodge, 1806

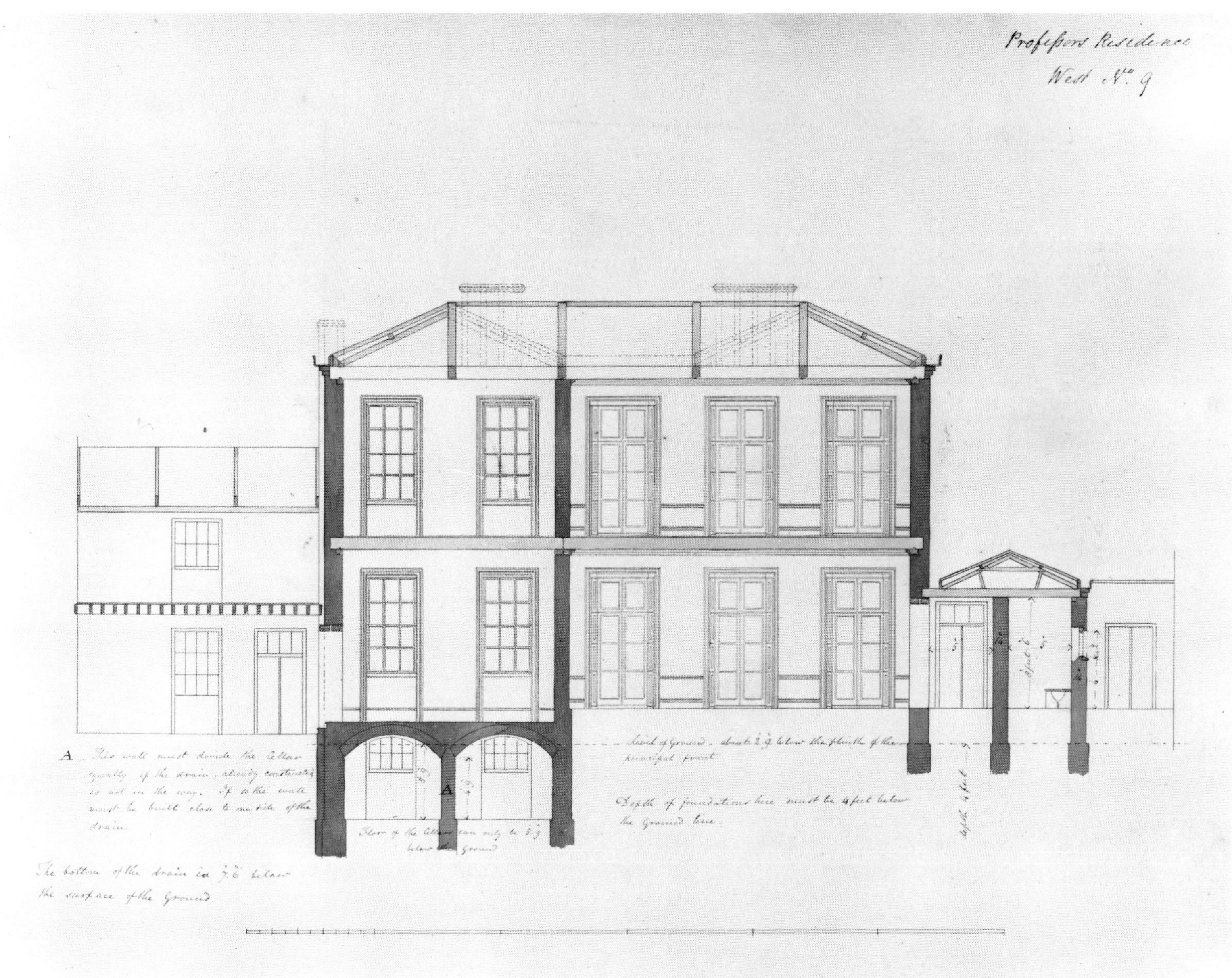

37

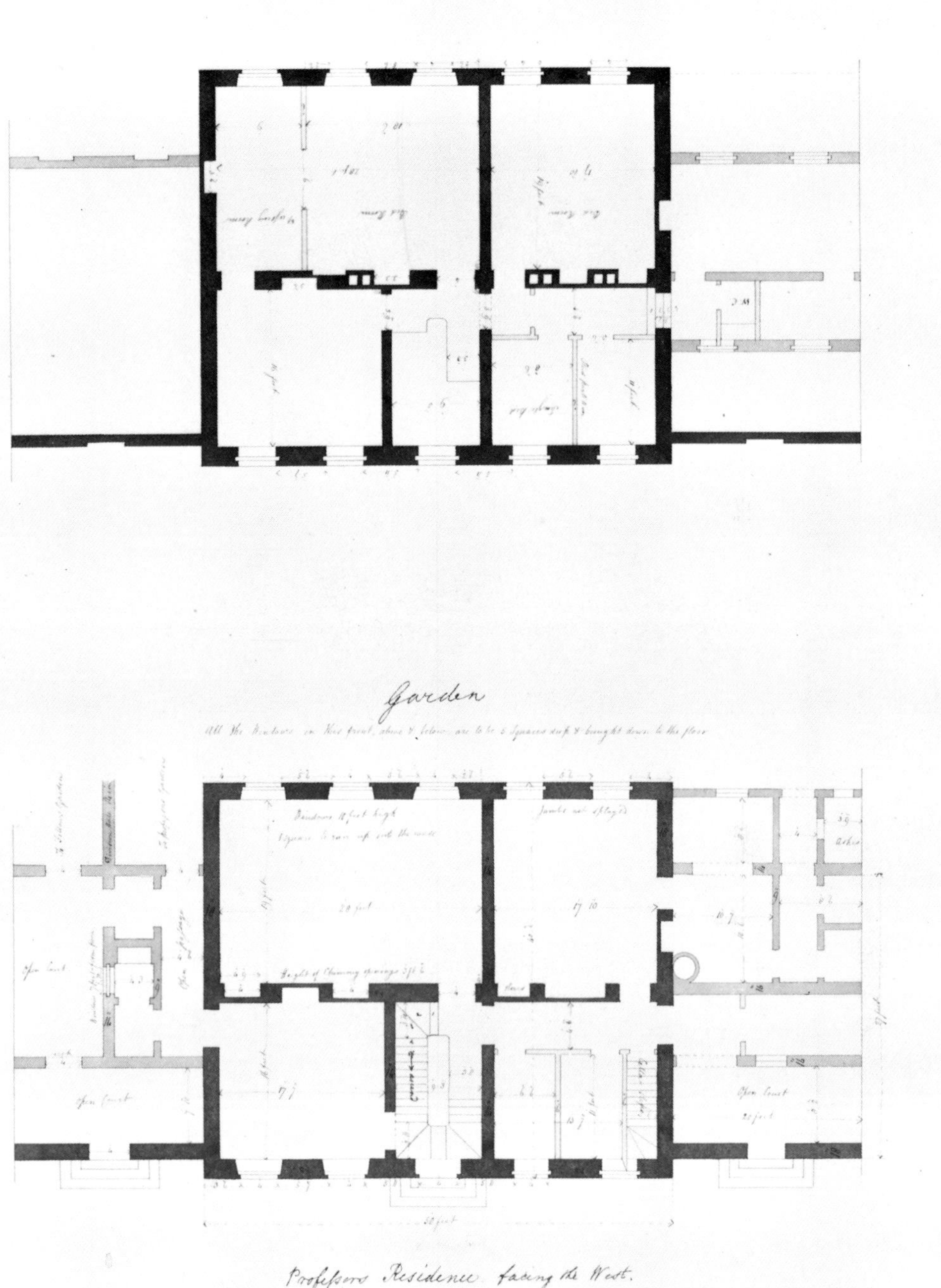

38

38 William Wilkins, Ground and first floor plans of the East Lodge, 1806

39 William Wilkins, Ground plan of the Master's Lodge, 1806

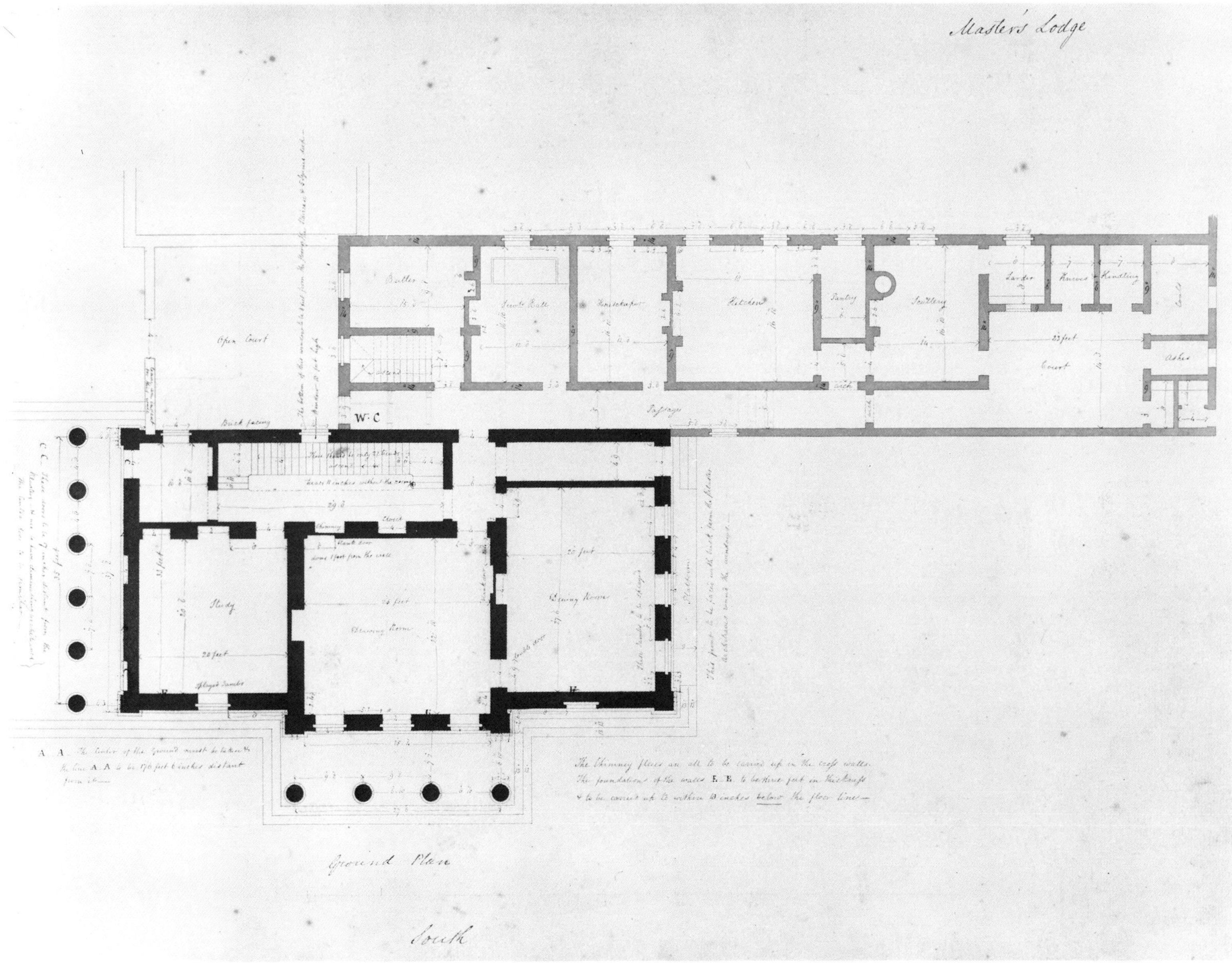

39

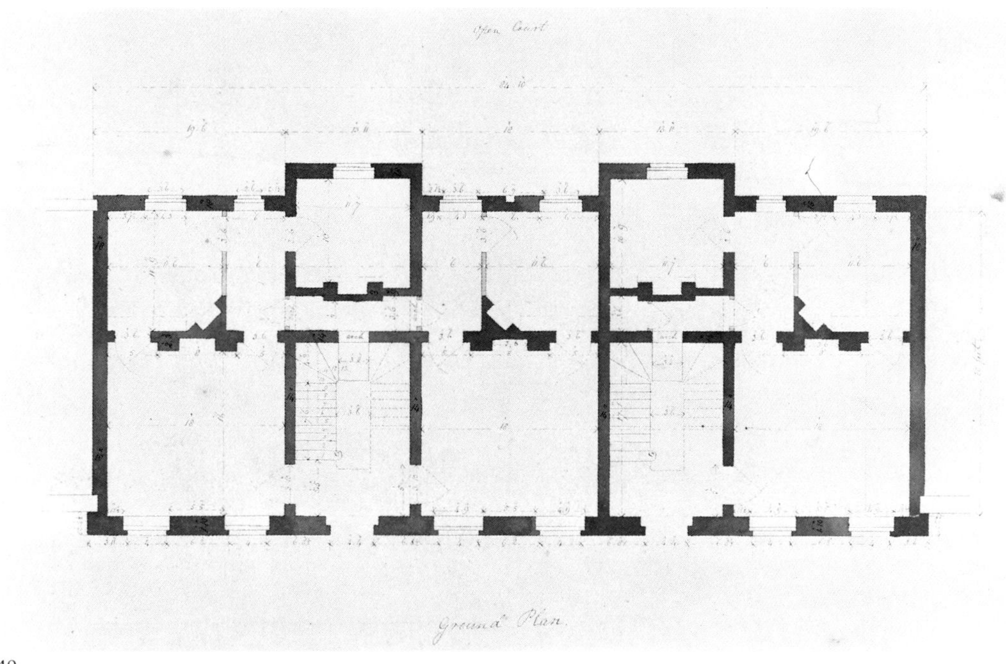

40

40 William Wilkins, Ground plan of students' apartments in the west range, 1806

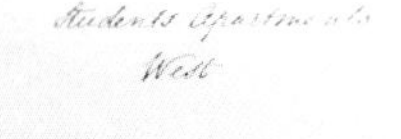

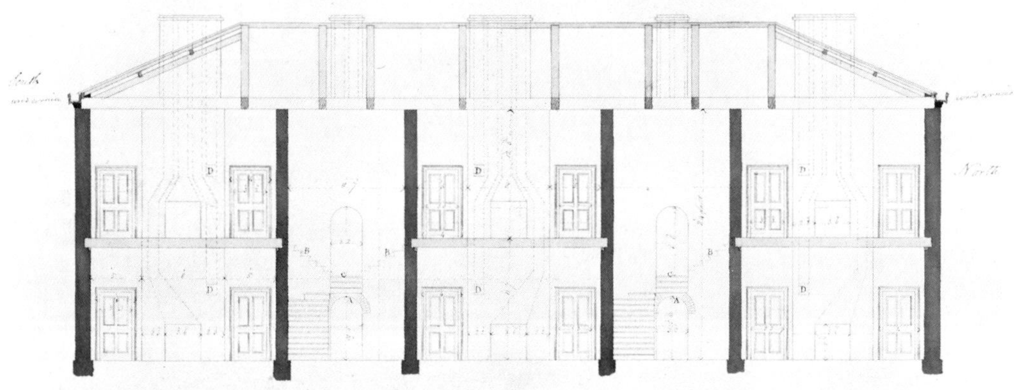

41

41 William Wilkins, Section through the students' apartments in the west range, 1806

Wilkins' problems with the second Master, William Frere (1812–1836), were of a different nature. He was undoubtedly irritated by Frere building a 'cow-house, piggery and seed house' and by the fact that he used the lawn at the centre of the future court as grazing ground for his wife's sheep, but these issues concerned him less than the more serious one about the future of the buildings he had designed. The estimates Wilkins had provided had turned out to be not at all realistic and the building fund, already skimpy, was enormously reduced by the erection of the buildings on the east range; furthermore the construction of six sets of rooms north of the Professor of Medicine's Lodge was not even begun. The college was thus extremely cautious in embarking upon a new building phase and favoured an extensive revision and reduction of the original plans. Wilkins was enormously upset by this stalemate in the construction work and he repeatedly appealed to Frere to carry on according to the original project, pleading with him: 'to let me have the Gateway &c. in since it will be the *only* finished part for the architect to show.' This *cri de coeur* shows the artist speaking, trying to preserve the pivotal part of the design, and the one which would have consecrated his genius. Aware that pleas, although necessary, would not guarantee the desired outcome, Wilkins applied his mind to the problem of increasing the college funds and in 1817 submitted a 'Plan for the Improvement of the Estate belonging to Downing College' (Figs. 42 and 43). In this plan the architect suggested the exploitation of the space available on the Pembroke Leys north and west of the college with a housing development. The Propylaea were moved further to the north, in contrast to the original plan, and flanked by pairs of detached houses; furthermore they were faced by a long avenue lined by sixty terrace-houses, with two terraces of nine houses each terminating the avenue at its southern end. Two more terraces of eight houses each were sited along the western side of the college, along Tennis Court Road (Fig. 43). An alternative layout of the long avenue is shown on a flap attached to the drawing; according to this proposal the terraces were to be pushed further back and screened by a row of lime trees and one of poplars (Fig.42).

Other designs surviving in the college Muniment Room illustrate Wilkins' attempts at reducing the costs of the Propylaea; in one he suppresses the side buildings of the original design, in another he limits himself to reducing the original scale (Figs.44 and 45). Finally, in a general plan, which must have been drawn between 1817 and 1818, he envisages a totally new site for the Propylaea which is moved further north than Bird Bolt Lane and linked by means of quadrant walls to rows of terrace-houses (Fig.46). None of these schemes was implemented and, as far as the Minutes Books reveal, they were probably not even seriously considered.[18]

In the meantime the college decided to petition the Court of Chancery in order to alter the original plan and be allowed to borrow money to finance the continuation of the building programme. William Frere wrote to his brother that he 'proposed to accomplish sufficient part of the building for useful purposes, whithin the probable or possible space of my life, & with the loan of £12,000 only.'[19] This, however, firmly excluded the north range, which Frere did not deem essential for the functioning of the college, although he was not unsympathetic to Wilkins' artistic preoccupations.[20] The petition was successful and Wilkins spent most of the spring and early summer of 1818 preparing a new set of working drawings[21] and then examining the tenders submitted. In choosing the contractors for the west range of Downing, Wilkins took unprecedented care: he employed an unbiased assessor, Mr Benjamin Broadbridge, to check each prospective contractor's estimates against the new set of working drawings and eventually, in November 1818, he selected the Tomson brothers who had already worked on the east range, as well as William and Spicer Crowe.

It was necessary to borrow £27,000, which ensured the completion of the main part of the Domus including the only monumental interior of the college; here, through the serene proportions and colour scheme, the architect successfully recaptured an antique classical interior. The hall was surrounded by *giallo antico* pilasters of scagliola and engaged coupled Ionic columns alternating with Greek tapered openings and panels. The choice of the material, scagliola, was very unusual, the firm of Croggon having begun to produce it only in 1818.[22]

Work on the west range was completed by May 1821 when the first undergraduates were admitted. The college at last existed as an architectural entity of some sort, all its members could be housed and the place could finally produce a communal identity or *esprit de corps*. Wilkins' design, however, had suffered considerably and it must have been clear to him, as well as to his clients, that hopes of completing it were very poor indeed. The east

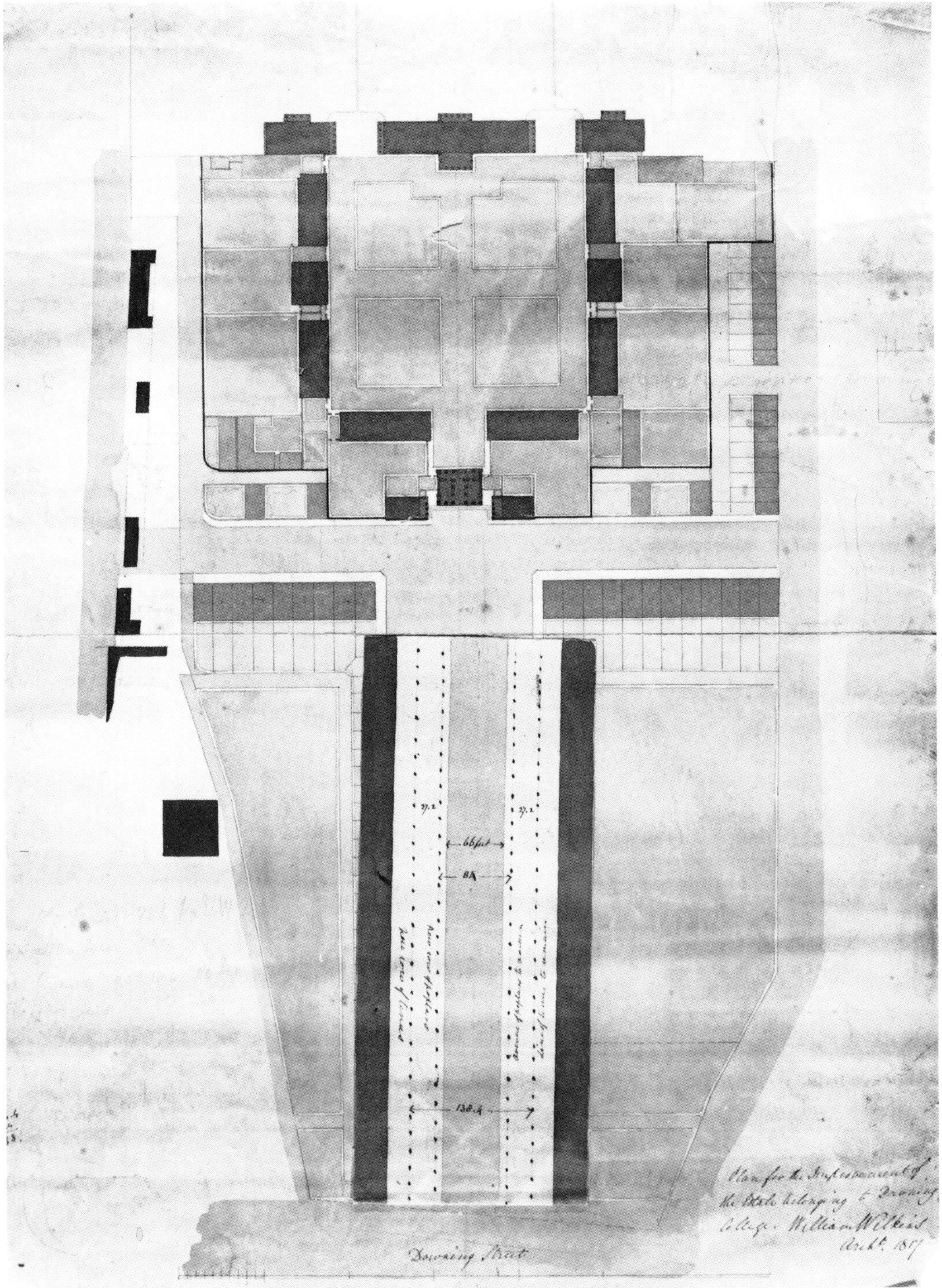

42

42 William Wilkins, Plan for the improvement of the estate belonging to the College, 1817

43 William Wilkins, Plan for the improvement of the estate belonging to the College, alternative proposal, 1817

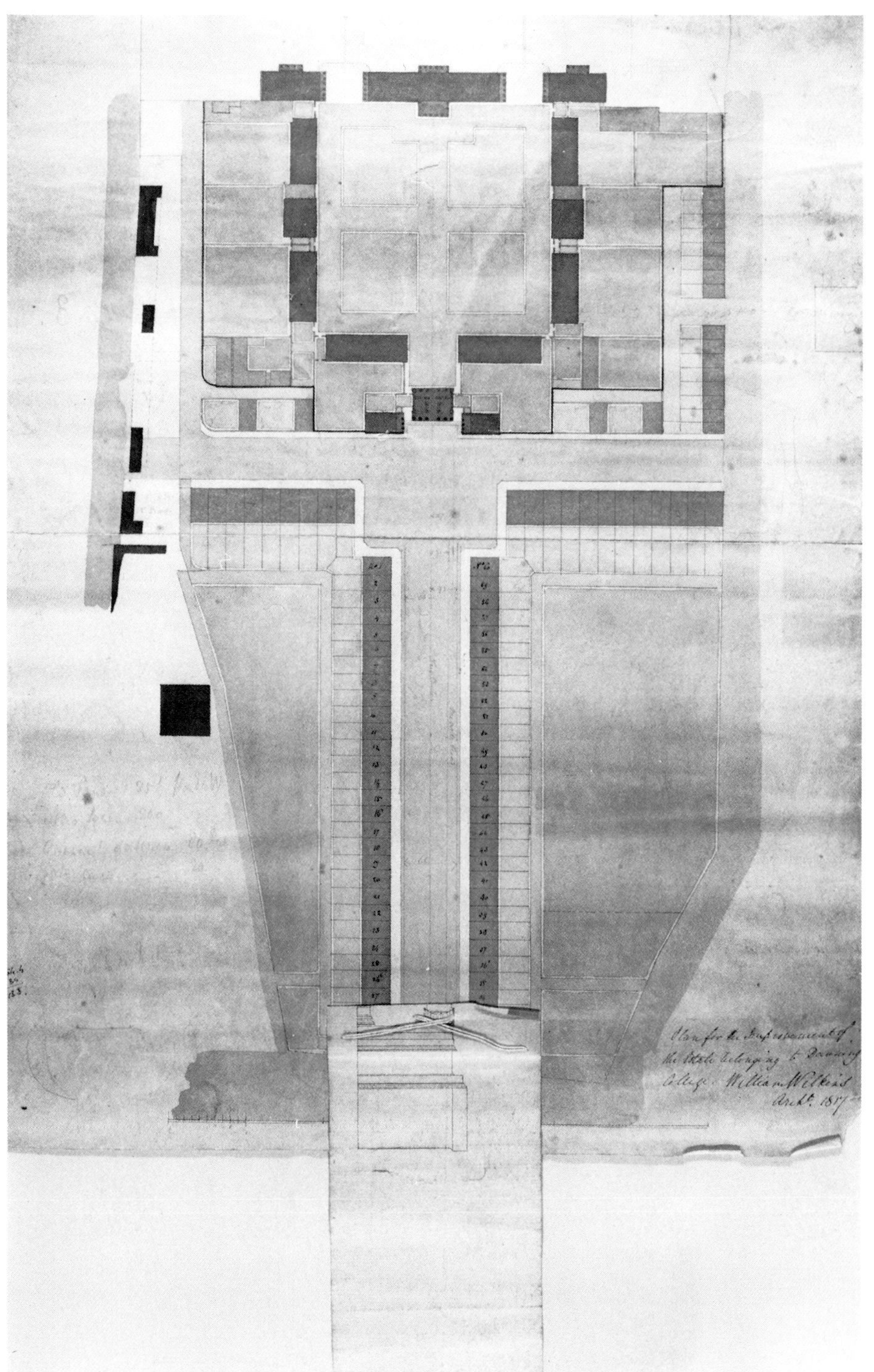

43

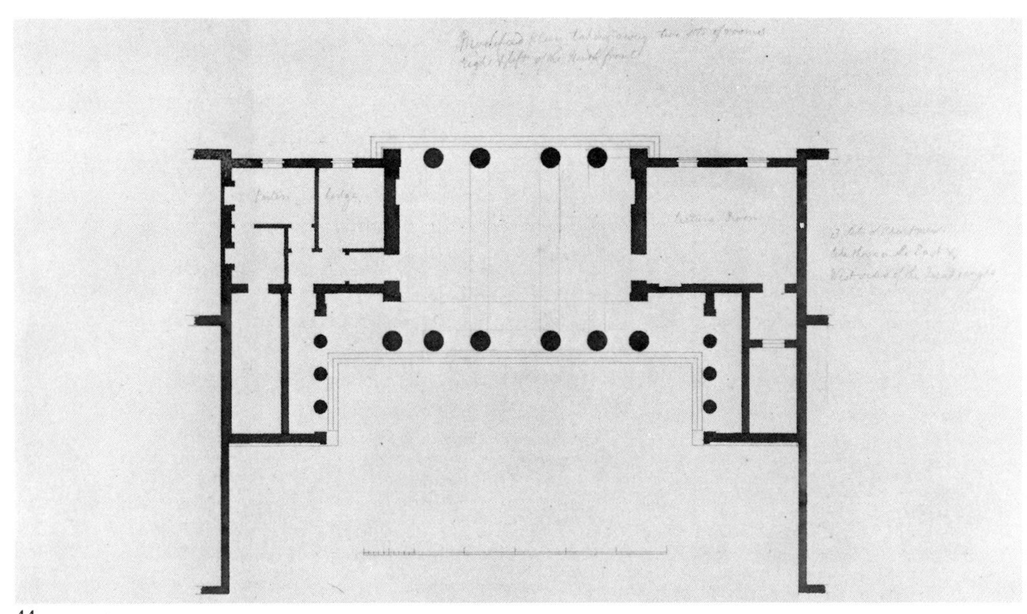

44

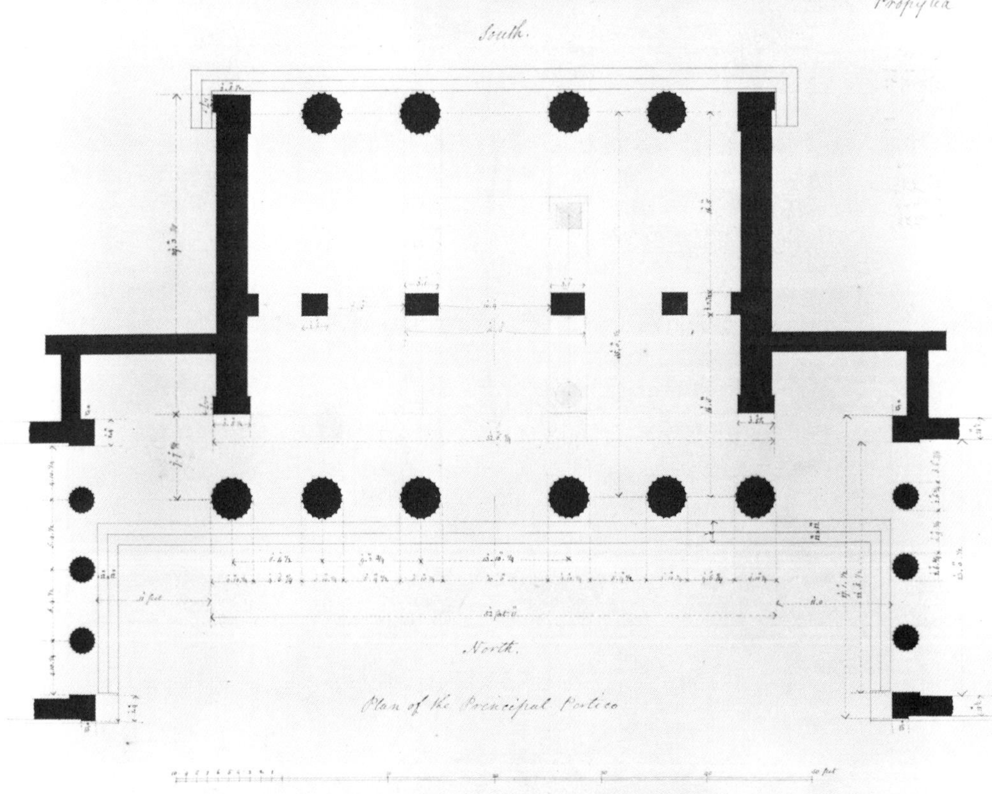

45

44 William Wilkins, Modified plan of the Propylaea, 1817

45 William Wilkins, Plan of the portico of the Propylaea, with reduced proportions, 1817

46 William Wilkins, Revised general plan of the college, 1817–1818

46

47 Downing College, View of the north elevation of the east range

range, as we have already seen, had not been terminated and the west had no proper side elevation since it was meant to connect with the projected north range. Wilkins died on 31 August 1839, at his house in Lensfield Road, unable to see the completion of his very first project. Funds for any major building enterprise had been exhausted and nothing could be done until 1873, with the exception of a small house erected in 1834 in Regent Street to accommodate a college servant and act as a sort of Porters' Lodge.

In February 1873, the architect Edward Middleton Barry (1830–1880) was invited by the college 'to suggest definite plans for the new buildings for the consideration of the College.'[23] Barry's contribution to the aspect of the college can be easily

47

48 Downing College, View of the east elevation of the east range

underestimated, for he chose to adhere strictly to Wilkins' designs for the east range elevation overlooking the court and to treat the northern elevations of both ranges according to Wilkins' principles. The two elevations are conceived of as pseudo porticoes, with paired Ionic pilasters modelled on those by Wilkins at the southern end of the ranges, supporting sloping triangular pediments (Fig.47). Three Greek tapered windows create three bays on each of the two floors. Barry's design was extremely successful in providing an elegant and coherent termination to what otherwise could not be disguised as anything but an unfinished group of buildings. The rest of Barry's work at Downing consisted in alterations to the internal planning, the addition of the Maitland Room and music room which filled in the gap at the north of the west lodge, the creation of a lecture room for the Professor of Medicine, and various alterations to the hall, none of which, however, substantially altered its basic structure.

By 1873 the college appeared to have come to terms with the idea that Wilkins' original project would never be executed in full. This recognition was reflected in Barry's treatment of the outer elevations of his additions to the two ranges: they were faced with stone to be seen from Regent Street which, by this time, had become the main official entrance to the college (Fig.48). Wilkins' dream of a grand gateway in the shape of the Athenian Propylaea was never to materialize.

48

IV
Twentieth Century Architecture at Downing

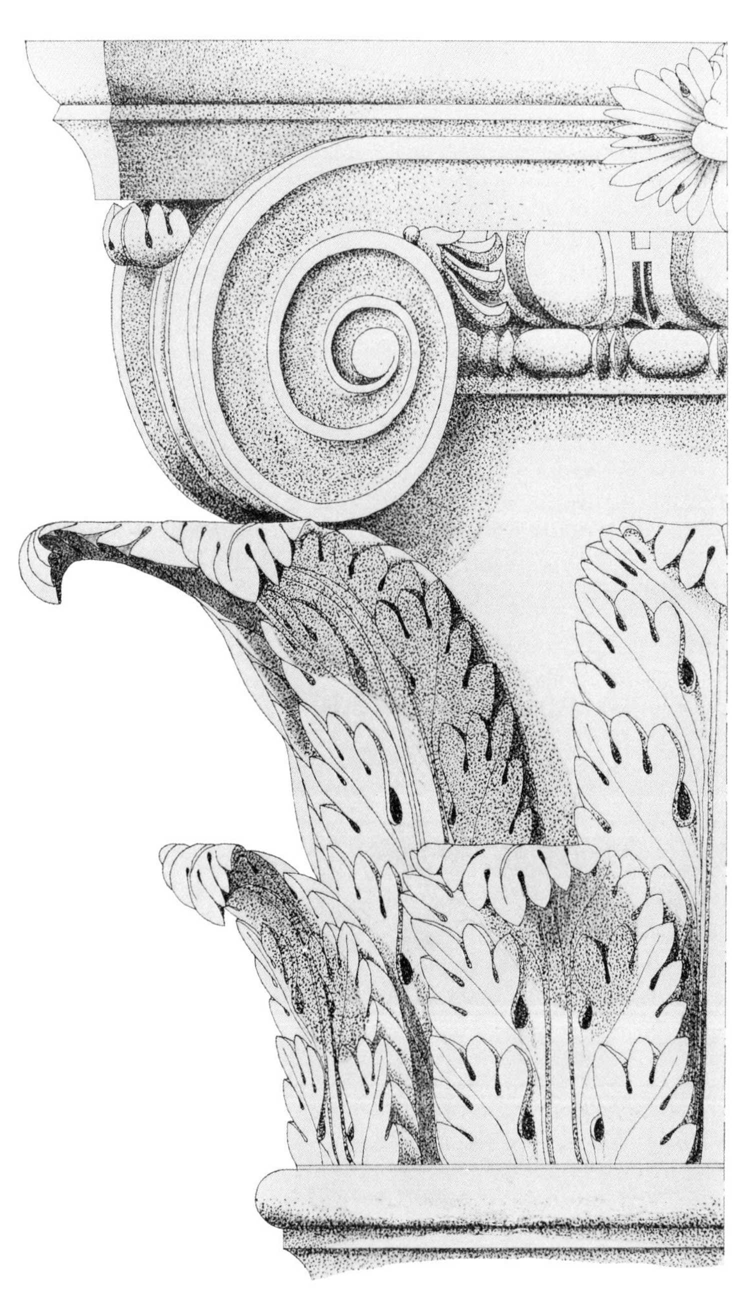

The considerably reduced endowment with which the college started its life not only hampered the architectural schemes of the nineteenth century, but also made its financial security a continuous source of preoccupation. After Barry's additions any further building appeared if not an almost impossible proposition, certainly an extremely remote one. A body of opinion began to grow amongst the members of the Governing Body supporting the idea of selling parts of what appeared to be an unnecessarily large site. This more practical attitude towards a solution of the college's financial troubles developed in the latter two decades of the nineteenth century. At the same time, as a result of the reforms of the 1870s and because of the expansion of the physical sciences, the relationship between the colleges and the university underwent a considerable change. In the course of these years, the university began to take its modern shape: departments were instituted and the need to establish centralized research laboratories became generally felt. The sciences in Cambridge expanded at an unprecedented pace, particularly experimental sciences which required laboratories. This growing trend was first seen in the establishment of the Cavendish Laboratory (1874), perhaps the first physics laboratory in the world, and then in other laboratories for teaching and research. Soon the university was in need of more and more space and the north end of the Downing site, originally the Pembroke Leys, so conveniently placed on the edge of the town centre and yet still very close to some of the colleges, must have been a very appealing possibility. The Downing Fellows, in their turn, must have found it less difficult to part with their land in view of the uses to which it would be put. Their decision to part with some of the college's original site could be interpreted not as a betrayal of their predecessors' actions, but rather as an act imposed by circumstances, yet within the spirit of the college's statutes, which described the aim of the foundation as that of furthering the study of the 'Law, physic and the other useful arts and learning.' In 1895, the Governing Body promoted a Parliamentary bill which would enable it to alienate some of its land; the bill was passed, and two acres along the Downing Street north boundary were immediately sold to the university for £15,000. At the same time the development of the southern edge of the site on Lensfield Road, with substantial red-brick detached houses that the college let on 99-year leases began. In 1897 a further strip on the northern side, forty feet wide and adjoining the one relinquished two years earlier, was sold to the University for £5,000 an acre. Finally, in 1901, the college agreed to sell to the university a further six and a half acres on the northern side; this sale was to take place in three stages at two-yearly intervals, for a price which would yield an annual income of £120 an acre.

During the first decade of the twentieth century the number of undergraduates increased and the need for more students' accommodation soon became evident, if not to the whole of the Governing Body, at least to some of its members. At a meeting on 17 October 1908, Dr Green 'called attention to the desirability of erecting further accommodation for the residence of undergraduates, and expressed the opinion that a building containing 24 sets of rooms might be erected for £7,000.'[1] According to Green's estimates, eight rooms more than the twelve originally planned by Wilkins for the northern range had become necessary. This proposal, however, met with no response or official act on the part of the college. This passiveness irritated the undergraduates. Two years later they submitted a petition which, although principally concerned with the unsatisfactory chapel arrangements, pointed to the generally cramped conditions of life in Downing. The petition was presented to the Governing Body at its meeting of 5 March 1910, and was accompanied by the sum of £70.10s., the subscription offered by seventy-seven of the signatories. They complained about the current location of the chapel which was placed above the hall, and 'suggested the erection of an Iron Chapel; or (alternatively) the conversion of the present Libary on staircase K and other premises adjoining the North side of the house of the Professor of Medicine, into a Chapel.'[2]

The reply of the Governing Body was a dilatory one: alterations to the library on staircase K, could not be contemplated because they would be too inconvenient and expensive, and the proposal of erecting an iron church required consideration at a subsequent meeting when the Governing Body would be 'in possession of fuller information as to the details and the prospects of this proposal.' An iron church must have sounded an odd suggestion to anybody who was not acquainted with this type of building. In England the use of iron had been confined to strictly functional buildings, such as railways, exhibition pavilions and shopping arcades, but it had not been extended to houses or churches; in France, on the contrary, it was relatively well developed by the architects Victor Baltard, Louis-Auguste Boileau and Anatole De

Baudot in the churches they built in Paris between 1854 and 1904.[3] The mere suggestion of using iron for the chapel must have generated horror amongst the Fellows who must have had visions of their grounds spoilt by a functionalist, modern building. Inevitably no subsequent meeting of the Governing Body discussed the proposal, and the subject seems to have been successfully put to rest until March 1913, when the undergraduates produced a new salvo of complaints. Once again these took the form of a petition, principally concerned with the unsatisfactory arrangements for religious worship, but this time also vehemently clamouring for the provision of at least twenty new sets of rooms. This time the Master, Howard Marsh, 'pointed out the desirability of erecting a permanent Chapel' (as opposed to the undergraduates' renewed suggestion of a temporary structure built with funds collected amongst themselves), and the Governing Body found itself engaged in a discussion, in the course of which a sum of £10,000 was identified as necessary for building a chapel and twenty sets of rooms. The meeting also appointed a committee of enquiry charged with producing a report on the necessary buildings and their likely cost.[4]

This new committee reported to the Governing Body on 4 June 1913; the members believed that 'for about £11,000 a chapel and 24 sets of rooms might be erected near the North West corner of the Domus' and they asked permission to consult an architect in order to obtain rough plans for the scheme, but without involving the college in any expense for his work. Permission was readily given and the committee proceeded to the choice of an architect, who later turned out to be C.G.Hare (1875–1932). No papers survive documenting the work of the Marsh Committee, thus we do not know how the architect was selected nor how many drawings he was asked to submit. On 22 November 1913, the Governing Body was informed about the plans produced by the still unnamed architect which, however, the Committee 'considered to be open to various criticisms.' Presumably the architect was asked to revise his designs and nothing more was heard on this subject until May 1914. At the meeting of the Governing Body of 16 May the question of extending the College buildings was revived and 'the plans (as revised by Mr Hare, the architect) were produced by the Committee. Besides the Chapel and the centre-block (which would contain twenty sets of rooms), they included a library, with four sets of rooms, but *not* for immediate erection.'[5]

C.G.Hare was not a particularly fashionable or distinguished architect; in 1911–1912 he had worked at Queens', first restoring the President's Gallery and then on the Dokett Building in Friars' Court. Except for Downing, he had no other connection with Cambridge until 1928 when he was employed at Christ's for substantial alterations to the Combination Room. Hare practised in a style which is commonly described as Edwardian Classicism; its characteristics are large scale public buildings in which the Baroque classicism of Wren and Vanbrugh is revived. Only one drawing by Hare appears to have survived in the college (Fig.49) and this has never been published or discussed before. It shows the influence of Vanbrugh's and Hawksmoor's architecture on Hare's composition and decoration. The building that Hare proposed was to be H-shaped, consisting of two public blocks, the library on the west and the chapel on the east, linked by a central block of seven bays containing the twenty sets of rooms. From the drawing it is difficult to gauge the exact siting of the building, but the Marsh Committee had originally proposed the north west corner of the Domus for new developments. This decision was probably dictated by a desire to keep whatever remained of the north end free, but a building such as the one designed by Hare could not be tucked away in a corner; indeed its extension and general monumental quality suggest that it might have been meant to provide a northern termination to the court. The Governing Body reacted favourably to the design but a study of the estimates of costs provided by the architect revealed that 'the scheme could only be carried out if a large sum were raised by voluntary subscriptions.' This called for the drafting of a circular calling for such donations which was to be submitted to the approval of the Governing Body at its next meeting of 19 May 1914. The drafts were approved, reprinted and officially distributed after 24 May 1914. Thus began Downing's first public appeal for fresh building funds.

This appeal turned out to be a failure because of the outbreak of World War I in August 1914. Building schemes were abandoned, only to be resumed in July 1920 – and then with a revised scope. The then Master, Professor Albert Seward, laid before the Governing Body on 20 July 1920 'the draft of a circular as to the revival of the Building Fund, with a view to the erection of new rooms for undergraduates, as a War Memorial.' The circular was printed, sent to the members of the Fellowship for their suggestions and eventually approved on 30 July 1920. It appears

49 C.G.Hare (1875–1932), Perspective of proposed new building, 1914

49

that there was no energy or will (or even experience at fund-raising) to pursue the matter, since the Governing Body minutes give no signs of anything happening until the late 1920s. Following an earlier modification of the original Charter, the college had been released from the obligation to provide a stipend and accommodation for the Downing Professors of Law and Medicine. This new measure had not been implemented yet, but in 1924 the Governing Body eventually agreed to the severing of the two Professorships from the college, thus relieving – albeit very slightly – the continuing problem of insufficient space. This had the immediate effect of freeing the two lodges and thus providing some of the much needed accommodation.

In March 1929, the Master and Bursar were authorized by the Governing Body to consult Sir Herbert Baker (1862–1946), one of the most prominent architects of the time, as to the fee that he would be likely to ask for producing some designs for new additions to the college. In particular the Governing Body wished Baker to explore the possibility of building 'between Regent Street and the College Court.'[6] This detail is important because it shows a considerable shift from 1914, when the possible site for building was identified with the north-west corner of the Domus (the area now occupied by Kenny Court). In 1929, the suggested area for expansion has moved to the north-east and, presumably could stretch further down along the east side of the college. One possible reason for this drastic change may have been the clearer recognition of the need for a proper entrance to the college.

Once again the college records do not throw any light on the process by which the name of Herbert Baker was reached; but it is clear that, consciously or not, the college abhorred the idea of choosing its architects through competitions, by now a commonly used means of selection. Sir Herbert Baker was without doubt one of the architectural stars of the period, but he was far from being the only one: his contemporaries included Sir Edwin Lutyens and Sir Giles Gilbert Scott, for instance. Of these two only Scott had worked in Cambridge before Baker's appointment at Downing.[7] Why did the choice fall on Baker? Possibly because his architecture, particularly in buildings such as the Union Buildings at Pretoria (1909) and the Secretariats at New Delhi (1912), had a simplicity and strength unparalleled by his contemporaries, and strangely akin to Greek revival architecture. This latter quality should not surprise us, considering that Baker had enjoyed in South Africa the patronage of Cecil Rhodes who had wanted him to 'visit the old countries of the Mediterranean to get inspiration for any thoughts he [Rhodes] might undertake.'[8] In particular, Rhodes wished Baker to see Rome, Paestum, Agrigentum, Thebes and Athens, and many years later Baker could say that he 'had the opportunity of putting to proof at Pretoria some of the knowledge gained on my tour.'[9] It was perhaps the impression that Baker could provide a starker form of classicism, which would match and complement Wilkins' incomplete buildings, that led the college to appoint him.

In his first letter to Baker, the Bursar asked him to advise 'upon extensions to the College and upon the lay-out of the site as a whole.' The key points of the brief were expressed in one sentence: 'More accommodation is needed for Students and fellows, and also a new Chapel, Library and Entrance Gate.' The Bursar went on to stress that:

> we are a poor Society unfortunately, but we have a substantial legacy in prospect and there is always a possibility if really fine plans are prepared that benefactors may come forward. At all events such pressure is being put upon the Colleges to admit more students and we are one of the few Colleges that has scope for extension that we feel we ought to be getting out plans. In addition to the prospects of obtaining benefactions by so doing we are anxious that nothing should be done in the shape of additions or alterations to the existing buildings till a well thought out scheme for the whole of the site has been prepared. The site is such a splendid one and its possibilities are so great, and a College is such an important institution that we feel we ought to have the very highest opinion obtainable, and therefore are venturing to appeal to you in the hope you may be able to help us.[10]

No enquiry was made regarding the size of Baker's fees for producing a scheme of this kind as had been requested by the Governing Body. Indeed the Bursar's letter had not the tone of an enquiry but rather that of a formal invitation to Baker to become the college's new architect.

Baker's positive reply came on 25 March 1929 and it was followed by the almost immediate establishment of personal contacts with the college. These took the shape of visits on the part of the Bursar to Baker's country seat at Cobham in Kent, and then of Baker coming to stay at the Master's Lodge during the first week of April 1929. As early as 16 April 1929, Baker could write to the Bursar announcing that he was working on the plans for the college and requesting photographs of the site, levels of the ground and other similar material which could be used before undertaking a full-scale survey of the site. Letters were exchanged with increasing frequency, sometimes at the rate of one a day. Right from the moment of Baker's appointment the college and the architect appear to have enjoyed a uniquely happy relationship, which continued unchanged throughout the years and, after Baker's death, also with his partner Alex Scott.

The first designs were sent to the Bursar on 17 May 1929, accompanied by a long covering letter explaining the nature of the scheme in great detail.[11] Since none of the five sketch plans submitted by Baker at this time survive, his letter to the Bursar is a crucial document if we are to understand the principles guiding his design as well as the problems he was faced with. He believed that the chapel, library, assembly room and common room ought to be combined all in one block of great architectural interest. Such a block should command a central position between the two existing buildings (the west and east ranges), and more precisely at the north end of the site. This, he argued, would be a similar position, although on the opposite side, to the one originally envisaged by Wilkins. Baker did not feel that building at the south end of the site was preferable to building on the area indicated by the college. Indeed he perceived great architectural scope in the development of an east-west axis which would run from an imposing gateway on Regent Street through the court, ending at a more modest but still monumental gateway on Tennis Court Road. The new central block on the north side would be graced by a six-columned portico similar to the wider porticoes of the Master's Lodge and hall and would be continued by slighlty receding blocks of rooms. Meeting the central unit at right angles there would be two separate blocks of rooms which would thus face the old buildings and be divided from them by means of the new pathway running from Regent Street to Tennis Court Road. These blocks of rooms had a highly architectural treatment: they terminated with four-columned porticoes echoing the smaller south-facing porticoes of Wilkins' buildings.

The importance attributed by Baker to the east-west axis can be more fully appreciated when we consider that, in order to increase its architectural effect, he planned to add twin porticoes on to the pilasters of Barry's northern terminations to the original buildings. This way the vista from underneath the projected Regent Street gate would have been like that of an ideal *Via Sacra*, with a sequence of porticoes alternating with cypress trees and terminated by a modern version of a triumphal arch. H.G. Pilkington's watercolour of 1929 (Fig.50) vividly conveys the spirit of Baker's ideas for this vista, together with the force of his classical vision.[12]

Despite his careful study of the layout of rooms in other colleges, at this stage Baker still had some problems in finding the best solutions for the distribution of bedrooms and study-rooms. Furthermore he wrestled with the purely architectural problem of relating the larger scale of the chapel to the smaller one of the blocks of rooms. His letter reveals his deep concern to secure the comfort and privacy of undergraduates and Fellows, and at the same time, the lack of direction he had received from the college on this very subject. This type of practical problem was eventually resolved in the course of a Governing Body meeting on 5 June 1929, which the architect was invited to attend. The plans then met with general approval and only a few unimportant suggestions were made for alterations. By 13 June Baker submitted the revised plans for the rooms, and these greatly pleased the Governing Body who inspected them on 17 June. At that meeting it was decided to ask the architect for perspective drawings and plans in a form suitable to be included in an appeal brochure that the College intended to produce during the forthcoming months.

The apparent rush of the Dons to get the appeal under way was, however, broken by the summer vacation – which did not match the intensity of Baker's enthusiasm: towards the end of September 1929 Baker wrote to the Bursar asking in a humorous yet nervous fashion 'When do you all come to life again?'[13] Baker clearly took an active interest in the production of the brochure, for which he not only provided drawings and plans but also a lengthy description of his scheme. The prospect of the drawings' publication meant that all the essential features of the design, and particularly of the elevations, had to be fixed with absolute precision and it is from these drawings, published in early 1930, that we can appraise the importance of Baker's contribution to Downing (Figs.51–53).

Baker's north block of thirty-five bays, with its six-columned portico behind which rose a stepped saucer dome, its niches filled in with sculpture and the beautiful mullioned arched windows on either side of the main portico, was not a Greek Revival building, nor did it attempt to be such. Yet it provided

50

50 H.G.Pilkington, View of the new east-west axis from the Porters' Lodge, 1929

51 H.Baker (1862–1946), General plan of the college, 1929–1930

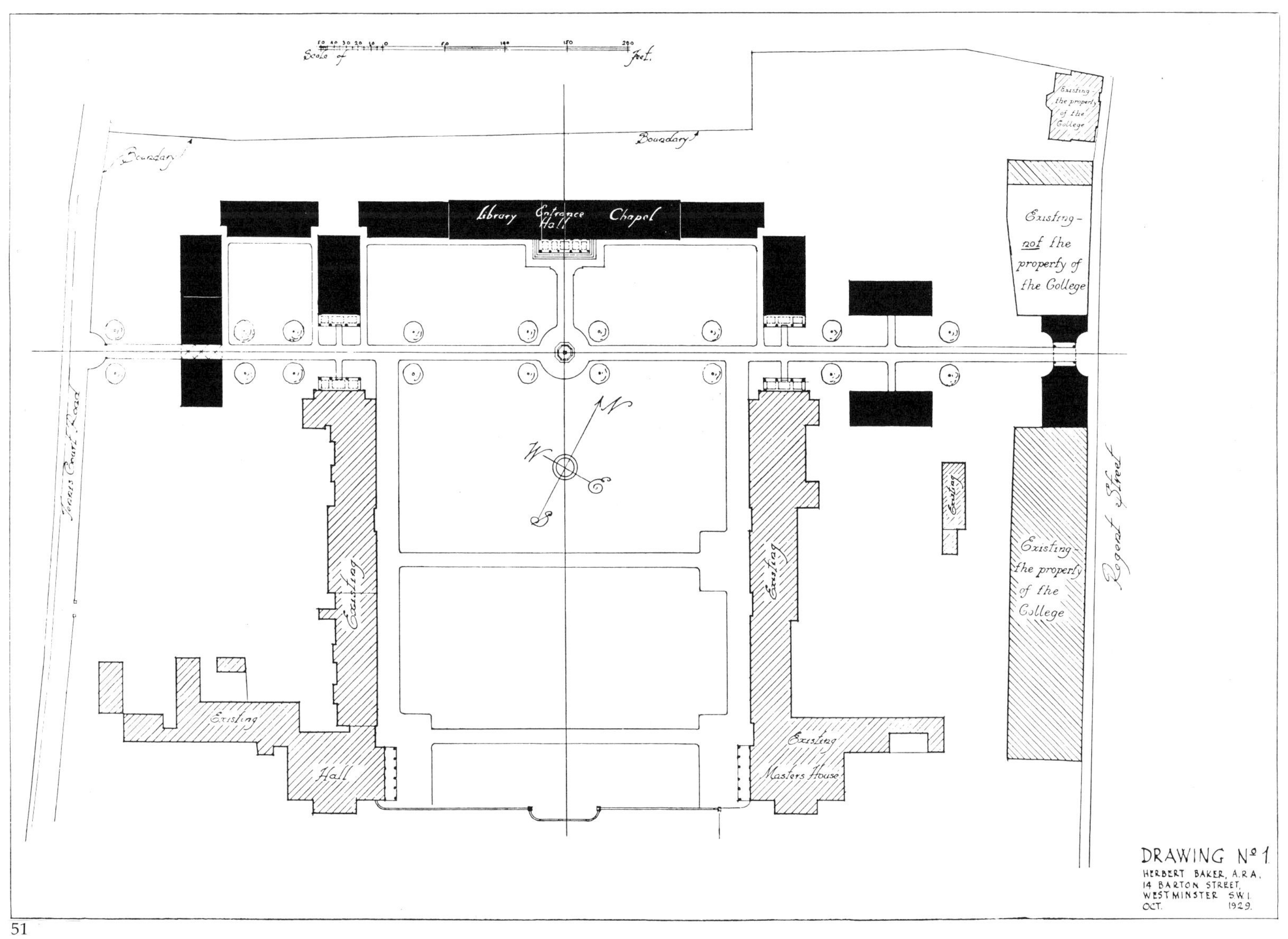

51

52 H.Baker, Elevation and plan of the central block, 1929–1930

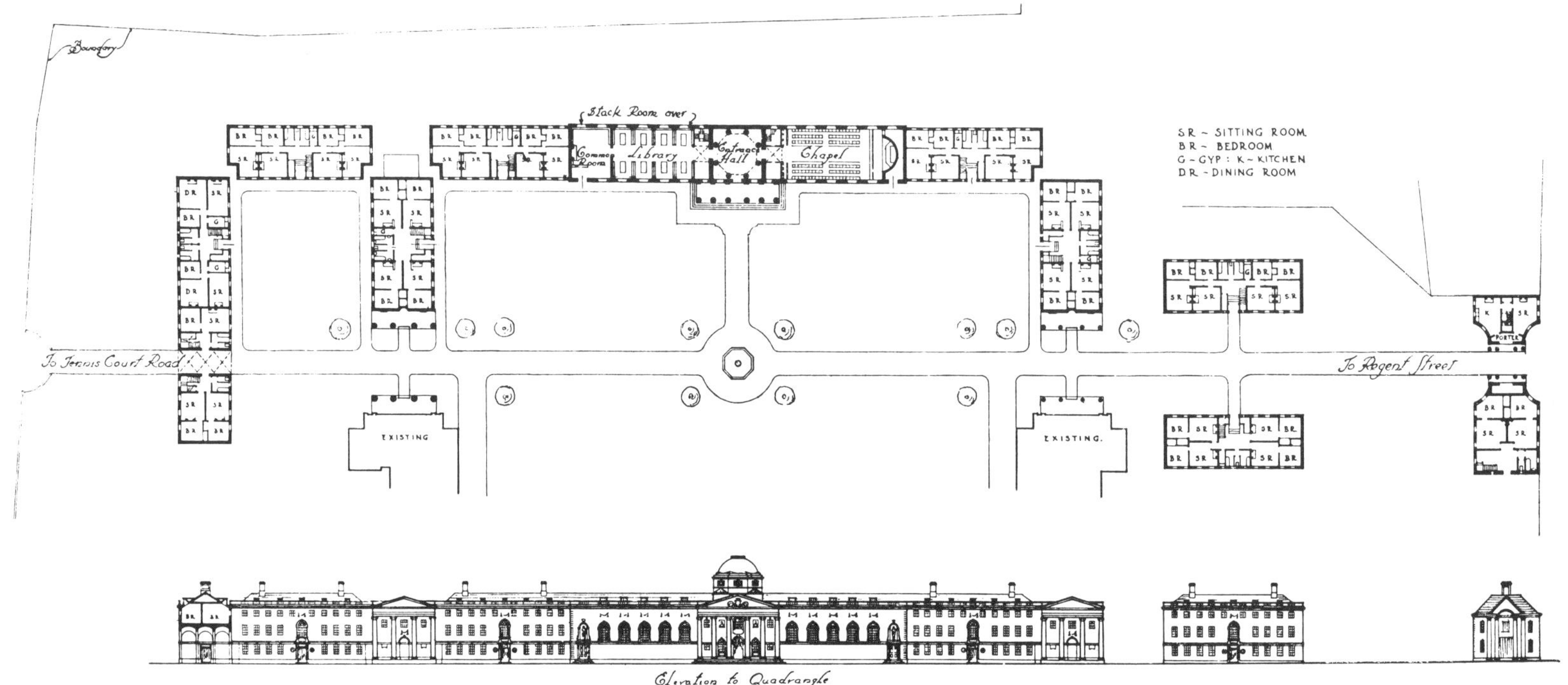

52

53 H.Baker, Elevation of entrance gate and Porters' Lodge, 1929–1930

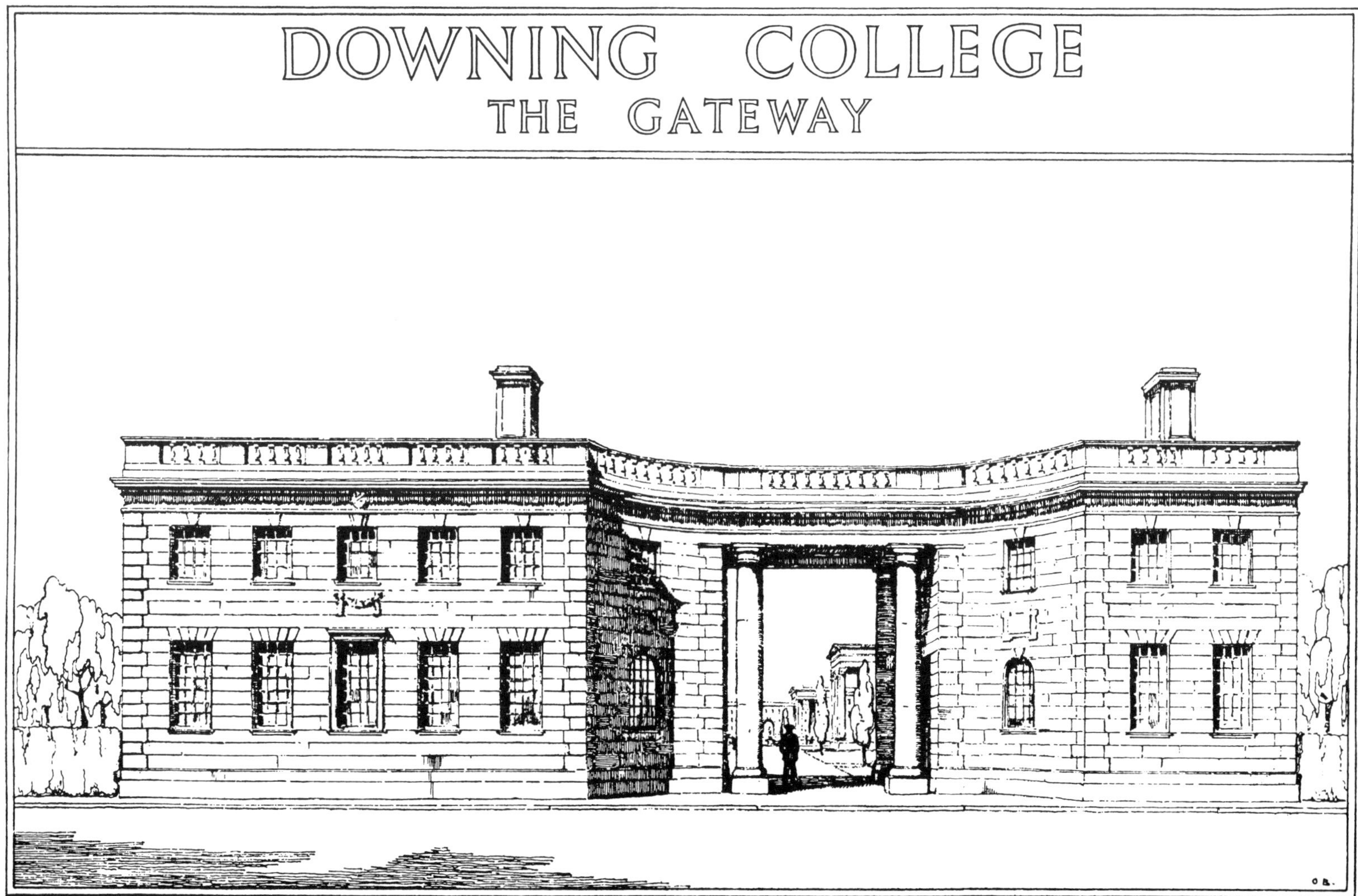

53

a powerful match to Wilkins' original plan. Baker's buildings shared the grand vision which was reflected in those designed by Wilkins, and like them, displayed a deep empathy with the classical world. Unfortunately, like Wilkins', Baker's scheme was not entirely executed, for in December 1929 the Governing Body decided to proceed with only four blocks of rooms, delaying the erection of the central block (the one on which the whole design hinged) until the end of the appeal.

Work on the new buildings began in the summer of 1930 and was almost completed by 1932. The architect's task stretched to designing all the internal fittings and taking care of the most minute details (Figs. 54 and 55). By the time the buildings were occupied not enough money had been raised to proceed with the second phase of the scheme, and all further projects were temporarily abandoned. Baker, however, remained hopeful and in constant touch with the college to which, in 1932, he had been elected Honorary Fellow. In 1932 he designed the Kenny Gates to Tennis Court Road, the generous gift of the daughters of the former Professor, C.S. Kenny, and in November 1936 he provided the college with a revised design for an entrance gate on Regent Street.

The 1936 idea of a new Regent Street gate was part of a scheme devised by the college to produce much needed revenue. In the nineteenth century, Wilkins had been concerned with similar projects and, as will be recalled, had thought of a housing development on the northern side of the site to provide for the rapidly growing population of Cambridge. In the twentieth century college officials were planning to exploit the commercial potential of Regent Street which, by this time, was no longer a road leading into the countryside but the main route to the busy railway station (built in 1845). Baker's new design for the main gate differed from the one illustrated in the appeal brochure of 1930, since it now extended to include two floors for students' accommodation above a ground floor entirely occupied by shops that the college intended to let on long leases (Fig.56). The increased height of the building also determined some changes in the use of the columns which in the 1929 design framed the vista into the college. The giant Doric columns were now replaced by four Ionic columns resting on the cornice above the shop level and framing an archway surmounted by the college arms.[14]

This scheme, however, was not brought to fruition, possibly owing to the death of the Master, followed also by a change of

54 Downing College, View of the portico in H.Baker's west wing

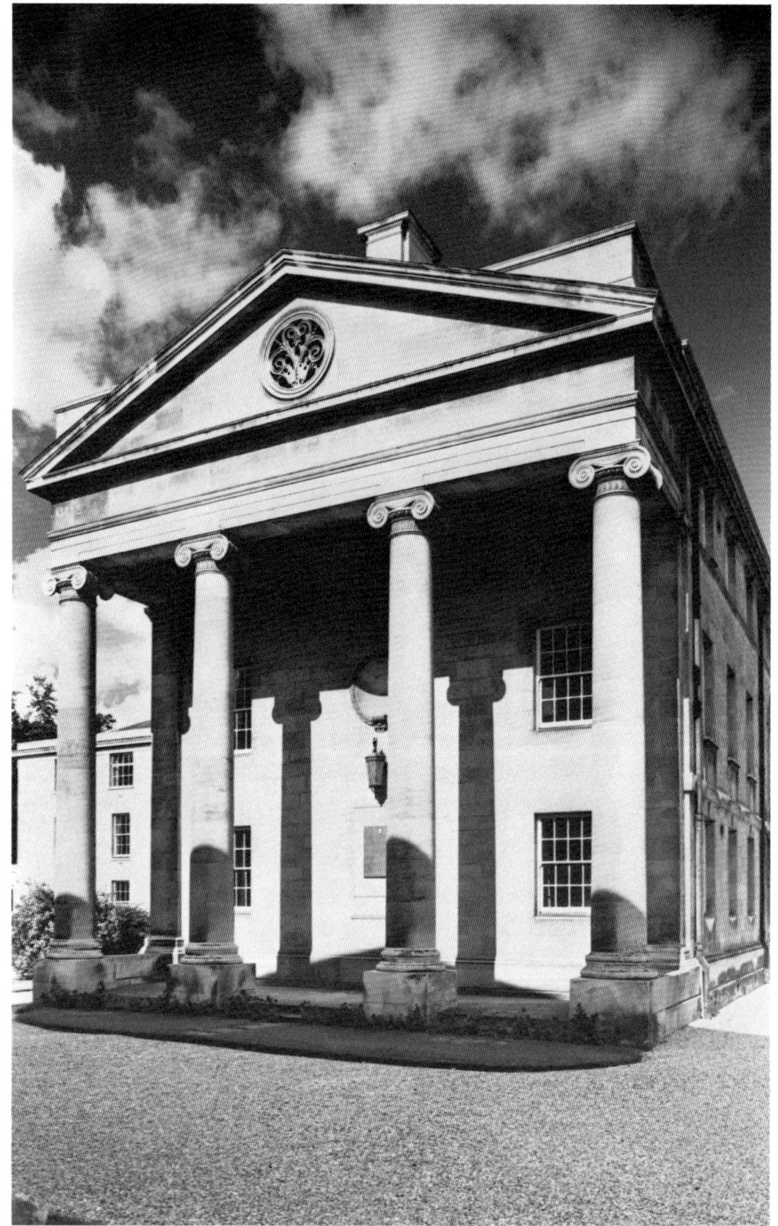
54

55 Downing College, View of the west wing staircase

55

56 H.Baker, Revised design for the Regent Street Gate, 1936

56

Bursars. A general reassessment of the college's finances took place, and on 30 May 1939 the new Master, Admiral Sir Herbert Richmond, wrote to Baker asking for a meeting to discuss:

> how our prospects now stand of undertaking the centre block and the gateway portion; the remaining part of the suggested scheme, – the Kenny Gate buildings and two other blocks which were originally suggested, will I fear never come into being, for unless some wholly unexpected windfall were to come our way, our present and prospective resources will be entirely absorbed by the centre and gateway building.'[15]

Even these considerably reduced plans could not be pursued. The outbreak of World War II in September 1939 completely upset the normal life of the country and of the college, which was continuously occupied by the Royal Air Force. The ordeal of six years of war did not, however, diminish the desire to complete the northern end of the college. Demobilisation, and the increased need for student accommodation, combined with the determination to build a better future and a return to normal life, stimulated swift activity. The initiative was taken by Sir Herbert Richmond, a remarkably strong and determined Master. As early as 24 September 1946, he circulated a memorandum amongst the members of the Governing Body asking them to 'consider now, and to decide during the coming months, whether we desire to carry out the scheme of building the Chapel and Library as approved in the existing Baker designs, or whether a modification of these designs be desirable.' He went on to list what in his view were the objections that could be raised against the Baker design; these were principally of a financial and utilitarian nature. In particular he pointed out how 'The Entrance Hall and Combination Room, handsome and dignified though they be, serve no practical purpose, and may even be considered to some degree as pretentious. The Dome, in my eyes, is a costly excrescence besides being out of harmony with the restrained simplicity of the original buildings. Neither Entrance Hall, Combination Room or Dome are revenue producing.' The Master's memorandum was circulated amongst the Fellowship together with a sketch illustrating his proposal (Fig.57). He favoured the building of the chapel in the central block, but its position was to be considerably changed. According to Richmond the chapel should be placed transversely, using the two spaces on either side to provide an additional twenty-four sets of rooms. In his opinion, financial reasons advised against a six-columned portico facing the chapel, although considerations of decorum would make it desirable. The dome he proposed to remove but 'in order to give an added definition and dignity to this part of the building, to put in its place a graceful lantern: Emmanuel, Pembroke and Clare, for example, have such lanterns. They are not out of keeping – as I feel the Dome is – with the general classical design of the College buildings.'[16] On this count he was blatantly wrong, as a lantern would have offended Wilkins' restrained simplicity as much as, if not more than, Baker's Roman dome. Furthermore he proposed to move the Master's House to the west lodge which would have been smaller and more manageable. Wilkins' Master's Lodge could then be used to house the library for which the space had become totally insufficient.

Richmond's memorandum was followed by the Fellows' written replies, all very long and detailed, which kept streaming in until the end of Michaelmas Term 1946. The majority of the Fellows expressed support for the Master whilst reiterating their commitment to both the Wilkins and Baker plans. Everybody recognized that the general lay-out of the college suggested by Baker should be adhered to, for it identified with great precision the lines for future expansion. With two exceptions, namely the Senior Tutor and Mr. Clive Parry (then a young University Lecturer) all the Fellows were prepared to accept compromises in order to streamline and reduce the costs of Baker's central block. The Senior Tutor was loath to depart from Baker's scheme; he wrote:

> An architect of great reputation was employed, his plans received fairly general, and, I think, enthusiastic approval and it was for the carrying out of these plans that an appeal was made for funds to old members of the College. To this appeal a very generous response, (in the light of the then prevailing economic conditions and of the small number of old Downing men, most of whom did not come from the more prosperous classes), was forthcoming. In my view a College should endeavour to expand its buildings systematically, as funds become available, according to an approved plan in the hope that the final result, which will stand for centuries, will be satisfactory. Any piecemeal development, snatching perhaps at temporary advantages, is misguided and runs the risk (I consider a most serious risk) of marring the final result. Sir Herbert Baker gave us an objective, which provided for a dignified chapel and library and adequate sets of rooms, and towards this

57 H.Richmond, Revised ground plan and elevation of the north block, 1946

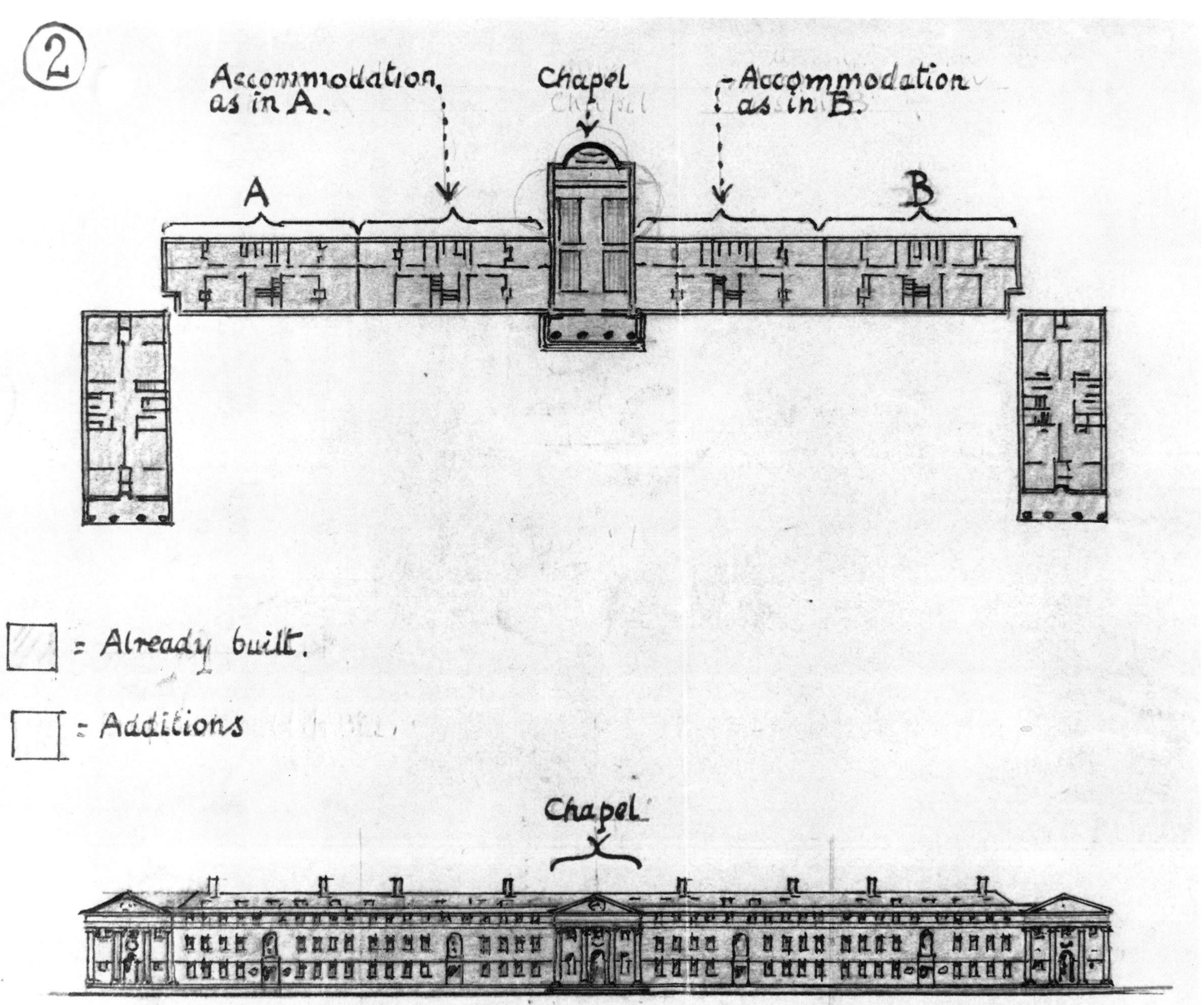

57

objective I consider that we should move progressively as funds permit. Such ordered development will in my view be most likely to receive substantial financial support from members of the College and can moreover be placed, perhaps, before the University Grants Committee or any other public bodies in years to come.[17]

Clive Parry's reply was equally interesting and uncompromising, showing the lingering power of Wilkins' design a century and a half after its conception:

I personally should like to see the Chapel and Library erected to the design of Wilkins and in the place he intended – between the Lodge and the Hall. But I believe I am in a minority of one in this regard. Were, however, the majority to be converted to my view, the gap between the new (Baker) buildings could be filled in with residential blocks – designed so as to avoid monotony in some fashion which I am incompetent to indicate. If, however, the court is always to remain open and the Chapel is to be built where Baker intended, then I do not think that any convincing reason has been adduced to justify a departure from Baker's plan. I feel that the different modifications of Baker's plan which have been suggested by various members of the College, including yourself, all tend to detract from that quality of spaciousness of conception which characterised the work of both Wilkins and Baker. I do not doubt that building costs have much increased and that it would be very difficult to obtain just now the permissions requisite for building anything as 'useless' as a dome. But I cannot help feeling that the College will live a very long time and will in all probability survive contemporary restrictions. I am, therefore, averse to endowing it with a 'utility' chapel. And I feel that posterity might respect us more if we were now to refuse to modify Baker's scheme and to proceed with the blocks designed to stand outside the court rather than with the Chapel.[18]

At a Governing Body meeting held on 13 December 1946 it was decided that: 1) a chapel was to be built according to the Baker plan or some modification of it, 2) that a building licence should be requested for the erection of sets of rooms, a library and a chapel, but without specifying a date on which the building operations would commence, 3) that the Master's Lodge should be retained as such, and 4) that Alex Scott, Baker's partner and now principal member of the firm, should be consulted on the desirability of modifying the original Baker design.[19]

Alex Scott was immediately approached in writing by the Master who, however, died early in 1947. He was replaced by Sir Lionel Whitby who, with the help of James Grantham, the Bursar, kept the project alive. Throughout 1947, 1948 and 1949 Scott was busy designing a new elevation and plans for the northern block which would fill the gap between the Baker wings (Fig.58 and Pl.XXI), as well as helping with the re-structuring of the east lodge in order to accommodate the library. Scott's chapel and the adjoining rooms provided a compromise solution between Baker's original plan and Richmond's proposal. Baker's six-columned Ionic portico (Pl.XXII) was retained but the dome was removed and not replaced with anything else. The chapel was given a pannelled antechapel and a well proportioned apsed end for the altar, pierced by narrow arched windows (Figs.59–60 and Pls.XXIII–XXIV). The apse, however, ended up more reminiscent of a Romanesque church than of a Greek temple adapted to modern Christian worship (as the portico implies). Undergraduates' rooms on either side of the chapel replaced the original Baker layout. This change was accordingly reflected in the elevation which was no longer vaguely inspired by the river elevation of Wren's Library at Trinity, but merely repeated the structure of the Baker wings with three storeys and severe mullioned windows. Building could only be started in 1950, and in 1953 the Chapel was officially consecrated. This, however, did not mark the definitive end of the Baker-Scott era since in 1960–1961 Scott and his partner Vernon Helbing, were again employed to modify Baker's original designs for two blocks of rooms between Tennis Court Road and the Baker wings (Fig.61). The two blocks were the gift of Agnes Kenny, the surviving daugther of Professor C.S.Kenny, and form what is now known as Kenny Court.

In the Introduction to the Cambridgeshire volume of *The Buildings of England* series, commenting on twentieth century architecture in Cambridge, Sir Nikolaus Pevsner wrote:

What has gone up in the years between the two world wars? No one can say that the authorities did not go to architects of renown. Lutyens built for Magdalene, Sir Herbert Baker for Downing, Sir Edwin Cooper for the University, Sir Giles Gilbert Scott for Clare and the University. The question remains how these and other architects tackled the special problems involved, *genius loci*, contemporaneity of spirit, planning and materials, and the unique blend of domesticity and display on which colleges can insist for their new ranges of sets. . . . Sir Herbert Baker was Sir Herbert Baker, i.e. far too convinced of himself. Downing called for nothing

> but a faithful completion of as much as possible of Wilkins's plan – at least externally. Baker's attempt at remaining superficially similar to Wilkins and yet replacing the Wilkins idiom by a Baker idiom is decidedly unsuccessful.[20]

Pevsner's judgement of Baker's work at Downing seems excessively harsh and his opinions concerning what was architecturally correct for Downing are open to serious question. Indeed this very opinion, according to which Downing calls for 'a faithful completion of as much as possible of Wilkins's plan', constitutes the core of the college's architectural dilemma in the latter part of the twentieth century. Should a replica of an early nineteenth century building be erected in the twentieth century? Or should the college maintain faith in Wilkins' vision, but find a contemporary classicist expression of that vision?

Wilkins' plan for Downing reflected a daring and powerful ideal. This ideal became the heritage of subsequent generations of students and scholars of the college. The incomplete state of the buildings did not undermine the power of that original architectural vision. The two completed blocks, terminated by the Master's Lodge and by the Hall, with their elegant but severe porticoes, could in fact be beheld as beautiful architectural objects in their own right, but they could also be perceived as romantic 'ruins' suggesting visions of the much more perfect beauty that the completed scheme might once have afforded. They stood, in their present form, as the fragments of a temporarily lost monument, one which called out for reconstitution. They kept reminding generations of Fellows that the home they inhabited was but a ghost of what it had been intended to be, and filled them with the desire to make that dream become reality. Wilkins' drawings, together with those of some of the architects who had competed against him, were jealously kept within the college and they too acted as a continuous, powerful reminder of what the Domus might have been like. All of this certainly helped in shaping the architectural taste of generations of Fellows, and made them acutely aware of the need to complete the college if not following the letter of the original designs, at least in their broad lines.

Thus there have been two possibilities open to the Governing Body throughout the present century: either to go to an architect specialising in restoration work, simply asking him to copy Wilkins and complete the latter's plan to the last detail, or to turn to a first rate architect practising in a classicist style, who could design something entirely original yet sympathetic to the existing buildings. The latter has consistently been the course chosen by the senior members of the college, so that they turned to Sir Herbert Baker in 1929, to Howell, Killick, Partridge and Amis in 1964 for the new Senior Combination Room and Parlour, and lately, in 1983, to Quinlan Terry for the Howard Building.

No architect, no creative artist, can be asked to be a copyist. It is precisely on these grounds that Pevsner's criticism of Sir Herbert Baker can be proved to be wrong, misconceived and blindly insensitive. Baker could not be asked to deny his own personality in order to immerse himself in the mentality and style of a different man who had lived a century before. What he could do, and what he did, was precisely what had been asked of him: to express in his own language and according to his own artistic feeling the classical spirit of his own age. Bill Howell and Quinlan Terry have responded to the same demands and have provided the 1960s Modern Movement and the 1980s Post-Modern Movement answers to this problem.

In 1964, the college decided to restore the hall according to Wilkins' original design and to build a new Senior Combination Room and kitchens block. Howell, Killick, Partridge and Amis were selected from a wide and varied range of names which included the following architectural partnerships: Brett and Pollen; Casson, Condor and Partners; D.Clarke Hall; Cubitt and Partners; A.B.Davies; Raymond Erith; Robert Matthew and Johnson-Marshall; Denis Lasdun; James Stirling, and finally the Oxford Architects Partnership. The staunchest representatives of the Modern Movement, namely Lasdun and Stirling, were not included in the short-list, a sign that the majority of the Fellows found the Brutalism of Lasdun's concrete architecture and the functionalism of Stirling irreconcilable with the existing architecture of the college. Eventually they chose to interview Erith, Howell, Casson and Johnson-Marshall; of these four Erith was in those days the least fashionable. He obstinately persisted in practising in a form of new classicism ostracized by all the architectural schools. Classicism was an obsolete language; it had been swept away from the schools where the Bauhaus ideology [21] was now being taught by the émigré German architects and designers on their way to the United States.

The chosen design could be defined, in one way, as the college's concession to the Modern Movement, and in another as

58 Downing College, View of the north block with the chapel seen from south-west

58

59

59 Downing College, View of the chapel from the vestibule

60 Downing College, Interior of the chapel

60

61 Downing College, View of Kenny Court

61

62 Downing College, View of the senior combination room from the south-east

the architects' illustration of the common, rationalist roots of both Modern and Classicist forms of architecture. Howell's Senior Combination Room (Figs.62–64 and Pl.XXV) is one of the cleverest modern buildings in Cambridge; the twentieth century three-dimensional illustration of the archetype of architecture, the primitive hut described by Vitruvius in antiquity, by the Abbé Laugier in the eighteenth century, and by Sir John Soane in the nineteenth century.[22] The Senior Combination Room repeats, in a simplified and modern way, the principles of the classical temple, which had been the sources of Wilkins' pavilions. It stands on a stepped base which continues the stylobate of the hall; the concrete pilasters supporting the concrete beams on which the roof rests are modern versions of Wilkins' columns, and the four broken, triangular terminations of the roof reflect the pediments of the Hall and Master's Lodge. Similarly the long, blank wall connecting the hall to the Senior Combination Room pavilion, interrupted only by a thin, tall strip housing a window and door, is deeply indebted to the classical tradition. It reflects Wilkins' idea of blank screen walls connecting separate pavilions, but also manages to capture the primitive strength of Greek archaic architecture, as in the Lions' Gate at Mycenae for instance.

62

63 Downing College, West elevation of the senior combination room

63

64 Downing College, View of the interior of the senior combination room

64

In more recent years, the college has had once again to face the hard choice of modern versus classical. The great generosity of the Howard Trust has suddenly made it possible to build a lecture theatre and a series of public rooms for the undergraduates who, in the 1980s, still sorely miss such facilities. The site chosen for this new development was one originally designated for building by the Baker plan, almost facing the Kenny Court and north-west of Wilkins' west wing. The architectural climate of the 1980s is of course very different from that of the 1960s. Modernism has changed considerably and Post-Modern Classicism, that is a return to a witty form of Classicism, has become one of the strongest trends in the United States as well as on the Continent. Thus, the architectural choices open to the college in 1983 were considerably more varied than in 1964, although perhaps more subtle and open to criticism. The 1980s offer lively and fanciful architectural possibilities, but they also face any prospective architectural patron with unprecedented obstacles created by the conservationist lobbies on the one hand, and, on the other, the RIBA rules for competitions, which tend to favour modernist architects.

When it became clear that the Howard Trust donation to the college was a concrete reality, public opinion was still shocked by the disastrous outcome of the international competition for the new National Gallery Extension in London (coincidentally adding to a Wilkins building). The RIBA appointed panel responsible for the selection of the winning design had taken no consideration at all of the trustees' wishes and had chosen a design which failed to satisfy the Gallery's requirements and clashed with the adjoining buildings in Trafalgar Square. The college was worried by this episode because it highlighted the weak position of the patron under the present system of open competitions – the standard way of choosing architects for major public buildings. The patron simply loses all power of decision and control and is, indeed, almost forced to implement a scheme whether it likes it or not. A further worry was generated by the consideration of the stylistic preferences of any RIBA appointed panel of assessors: they would inevitably have been supporters of the Modern Movement, and, as the National Gallery experience had taught, would show little concern for stylistic harmony with the pre-existing buildings. It was easy to envisage a situation in which a modernist, high-tech design was selected against the better judgement of the college; it would then be referred to the Royal Fine Arts Commission for approval who would reject it on the grounds that it was not suitable for the site. The design would then go back to the drawing board and, possibly, after a series of inconclusive sessions with the Royal Fine Arts Commission, the whole procedure of the competition would have to be started again. In the worst possible case the college might simply have been forced to build some 'monstrous carbuncle' on such a prime, historical site.

All these visions advised against the promotion of a competition and a much more traditional approach was preferred: senior members of the college were asked to propose names of architects for consideration by the benefactor and the New Buildings Committee. In 1964, on the occasion of the choice of an architect for the Senior Combination Room, the Fellows' response had produced a mixed bag of names; in 1983, however, no architect of real calibre was proposed. The dissatisfaction of the benefactor and of some of the members of the committee led to a more thorough examination of recent architectural trends, in the conviction that the site called for an architect of international standing, capable of re-interpreting the language of classical architecture. The college also believed that it had a duty to promote the highest architectural standards. It was at this stage that some really exciting architects began to be considered; they included Philip Johnson, Leon Krier, Terry Farrell, Arata Isozaki, Arthur Erickson, and Quinlan Terry. Some of these architects were unknown to the members of the committee who had no close acquaintance with the revolutions taking place on the international architectural scene, so that it became necessary to familiarize members of the committee with current architectural literature. Where possible, visits were made to buildings which had been executed by the architects under consideration.

Although there was a fundamental stylistic coherence linking most of the architects on whom attention had now concentrated, they were sufficiently different to enable some relatively easy exclusions, and an immediate and remarkably general agreement was reached by the committee and the benefactor over the name of Quinlan Terry. Their recommendation of Terry's name to the Fellowship as a whole met with equal, unanimous consensus and Mr. Terry was consequently issued with a formal invitation to meet the committee with a view to preparing designs for a new lecture theatre and Junior Combination Room block, as well as for a residential building in the West Lodge garden. That encounter took place on 26 May 1983 and eventually led to the architect's appointment.

Why was Quinlan Terry chosen for the new Howard Building? His architecture has been described by Charles Jenks[23] as 'Super-realist Classicism' – in other words his buildings are so classical that they look as if designed by a seventeenth or eighteenth century architect. However, his originality lies in his profound understanding of the classical language of architecture, which enables him to expand and re-interpret it, sometimes in a whimsical fashion, while maintaining an absolute faithfulness to its principles and materials. Unlike other Post-Modern architects, whose classicism is mostly pastiche and often of a very ephemeral nature, Terry's buildings have the grace and long-lasting virtues of the monuments of past centuries.

Terry's first design for the new Howard Building perpetuated the restrained classicism of Downing. Like its neighbouring elevation by Edward Barry, and the Baker portico, the main facade was subdivided by a giant order of pilasters and half columns resting on a plinth. The order, however, departs from the traditional use of the Ionic because of the different function of the new building; its theatrical nature calls for a richer, more elaborate order, namely the Corinthian. The final design (Fig.65, 68 and Pl.XXVI), which was exhibited in the 1986 Royal Academy Summer Exhibition, develops these themes further and introduces a delightful play between more complex stone textures in the rustication of the end bays. These are an elaboration of a theme previously explored by Terry at the Heseltine Summerhouse, Thenford, in 1982. The central bay has also been given a new richness by the introduction of half columns of the Composite order and of an elaborate door (Fig.69) surmounted by a broken pediment. In its final version the Howard Building is an architectural *tour de force*; in it Terry has set himself the challenge of employing in one building all the four classical orders: the Doric (Fig.70) is used on the south front colonnade, Ionic pilasters grace the interior of the lecture theatre, while both Corinthian and Composite orders are displayed on the principal, north elevation (Figs.65 and 72). Here the combination of Corinthian and Composite, as well as that of columns and pilasters, is directly based on the precedent of Bramante's cloister of Santa Maria della Pace, Rome (1500–1504), a building much admired by Terry and closely studied by him in the course of his 1967 Rome scholarship. Terry's final design departs from the stark classicism of Wilkins and introduces new elements of variety and curiosity which are more akin to Baker's brand of classicism. This should not be considered a fault; on the contrary it should be remembered that the Howard Building is engaged in a direct dialogue with the buildings designed by Sir Herbert, rather than with the Wilkins' end of the college.

In choosing Quinlan Terry as its architect for the 1980s the college has shown once again its lasting commitment to classicism. Although for the Fellows it may have been an extremely easy choice to make, almost an instinctive one, it was a daring decision since no other Post-Modern classical building has been attempted at either Oxford or Cambridge. The large majority of the public, sometimes insensitive to architectural issues and stultified by three decades of ugly modern architecture, can easily think of a building like this as a folly or as the expression of a backward looking society. For Downing it has been the concrete expression of the college's belief in the liveliness of its cultural heritage and the continuation of a tradition, embodying a classical version of avant-garde taste in architecture.

Downing College as it stands today reflects two centuries of different but consistent visions of morality and beauty. The buildings of the two major projects were never completed in the way that their architects had envisioned, yet there is no real clash or contradiction in what we see. If other colleges in Oxford and Cambridge testify to continuous wealth and development, Downing is a monument to the power exerted by the architectural environment on the human imagination, the power to generate visions and the desire to transmit them to future generations. The desire to build, to expand the community and the facilities of the college remains as strong today as ever. Recent history has shown that the college can continue to build efficient, cost-effective, architecturally innovative and striking buildings, and yet remain faithful to its founders' dreams and those of generations of benefactors.

65 Quinlan Terry (1937–), Principal elevation of the Howard Building, 1986

65

66 Quinlan Terry, General plan of the proposed new West Lodge quadrangle, 1983

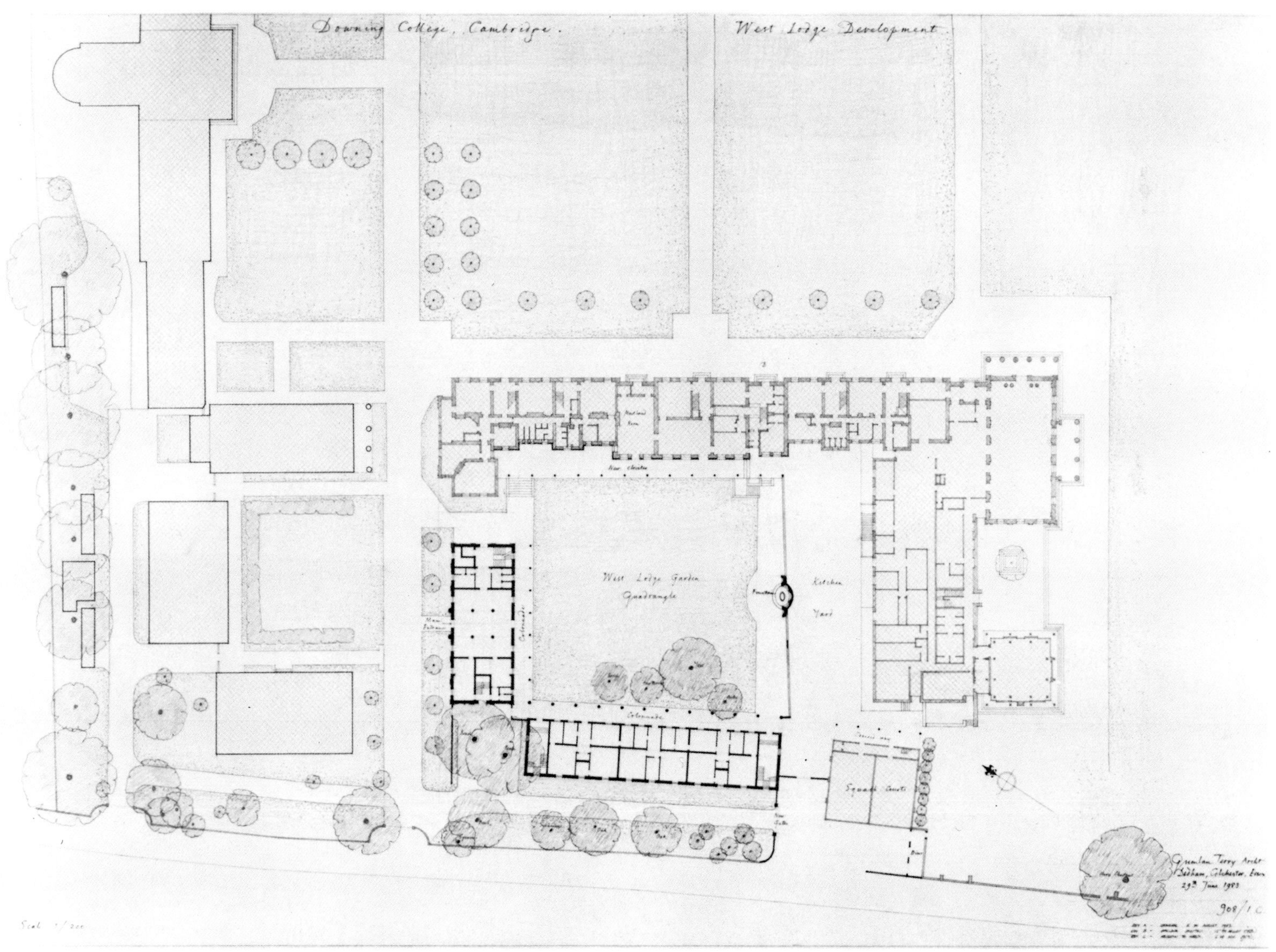

66

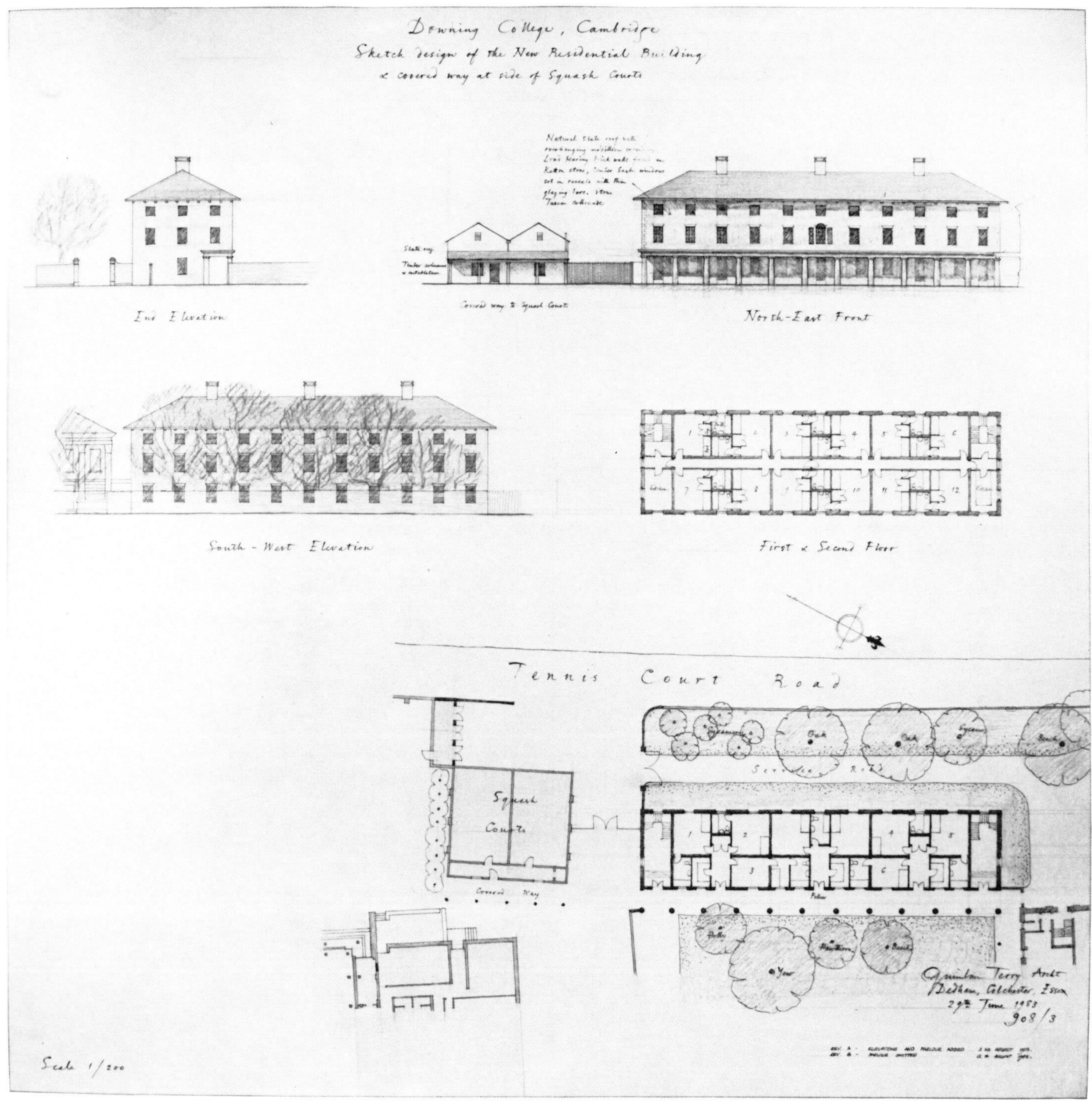
Downing College, Cambridge
Sketch design of the New Residential Building
& covered way at side of Squash Courts
End Elevation
Covered way to Squash Courts
North-East Front
South-West Elevation
First & Second Floor
Tennis Court Road
Service Road
Oak
Squash
Courts
Covered Way
Quinlan Terry Archt
Dedham, Colchester, Essex
29th June 1983
908/3
Scale 1/200

67

67 Quinlan Terry, Elevation, profiles and plans of the proposed residential accommodation in the West Lodge garden, 1983

68 Quinlan Terry, Plans of the ground, first and mezzanine floors of the Howard Building, 1986

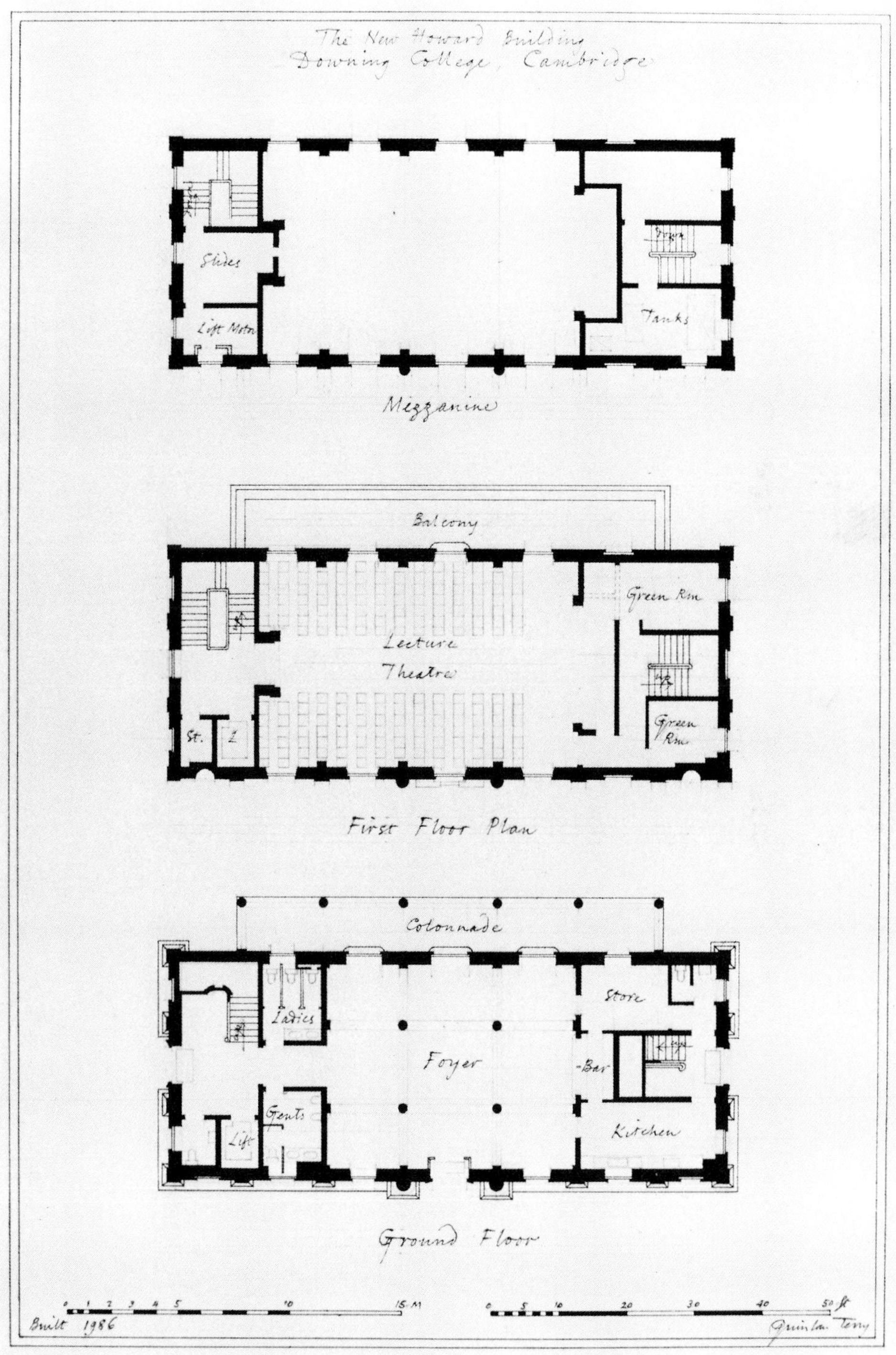

68

69

69 Quinlan Terry, Elevation of the north door of the Howard Building, 1986

70 Quinlan Terry, Profile of the Doric colonnade and balcony, 1986

70

71

71 Quinlan Terry, Elevation of the east door of the Howard Building, 1986

72 Quinlan Terry, The Corinthian capital used in the Howard Building, 1986

72

Colour Plates

I
Thomas Gainsborough (1727–1788)
Lady Margaret Downing

II

II James Wyatt (1746–1813), Perspective of the courtyard looking south, 1804

III George Byfield (c.1756–1813), Elevation of the south front with sections of the east and west wings, 1804

III

IV George Byfield, Elevation of the Master's Lodge and termination of the west wing, 1804

IV

V

V William Porden (c.1755–1822), Elevation of the south front, 1805

VI William Porden, Elevation of the east front, 1805

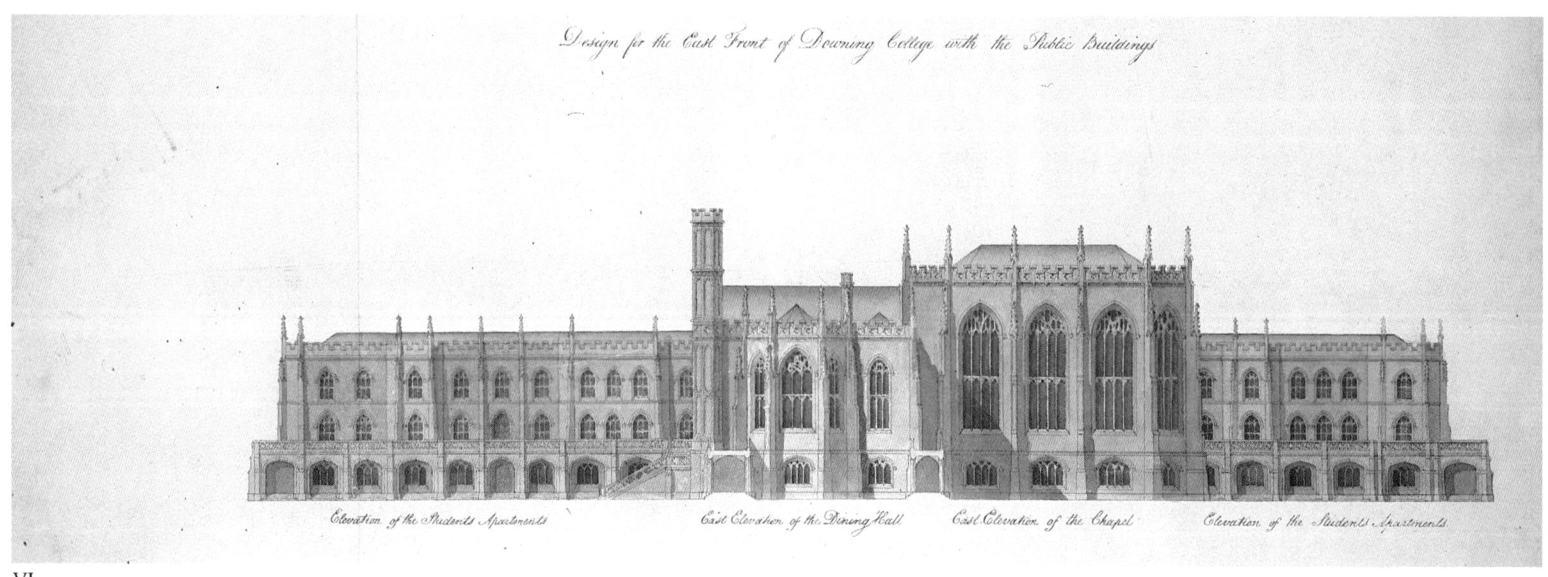

VI

VII

VII Lewis William Wyatt (1777–1853), Elevation of the south range, 1805

VIII Lewis William Wyatt, Section through the Chapel, 1805

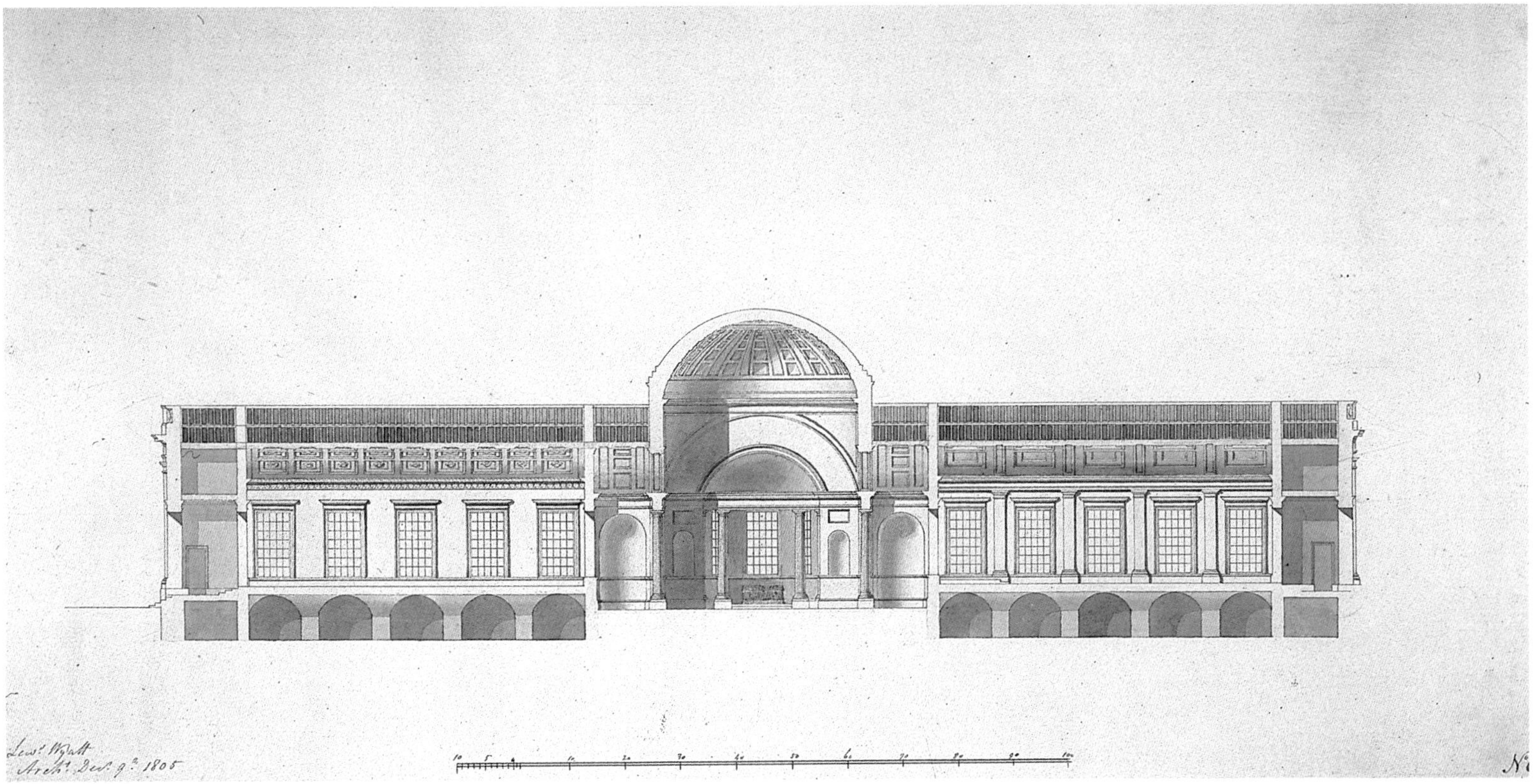

VIII

IX

IX William Wilkins (1778–1839), Elevation of the south block, after 1812

X

X Downing College, View of the exterior of the Hall from south-west

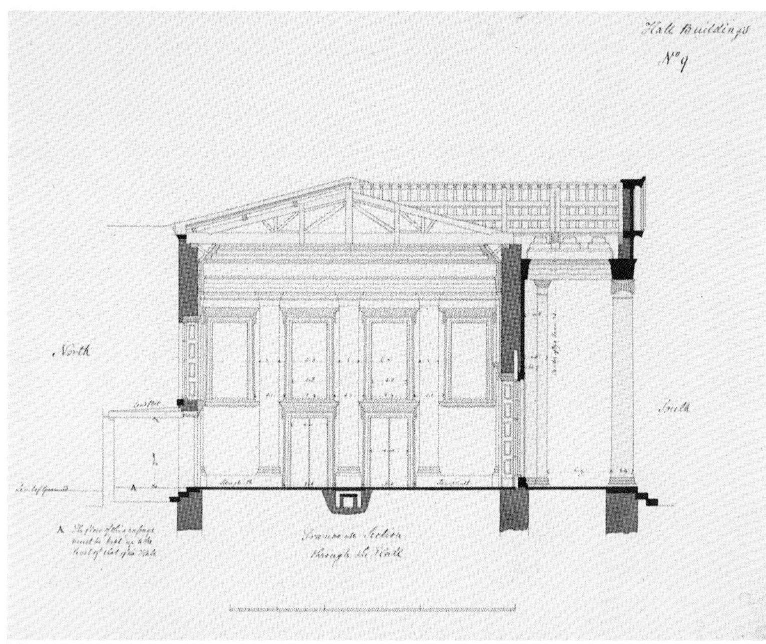

XI

XI William Wilkins, Transverse section through the Hall, 1806

XII William Wilkins, Elevation of the north side of the Hall, 1806

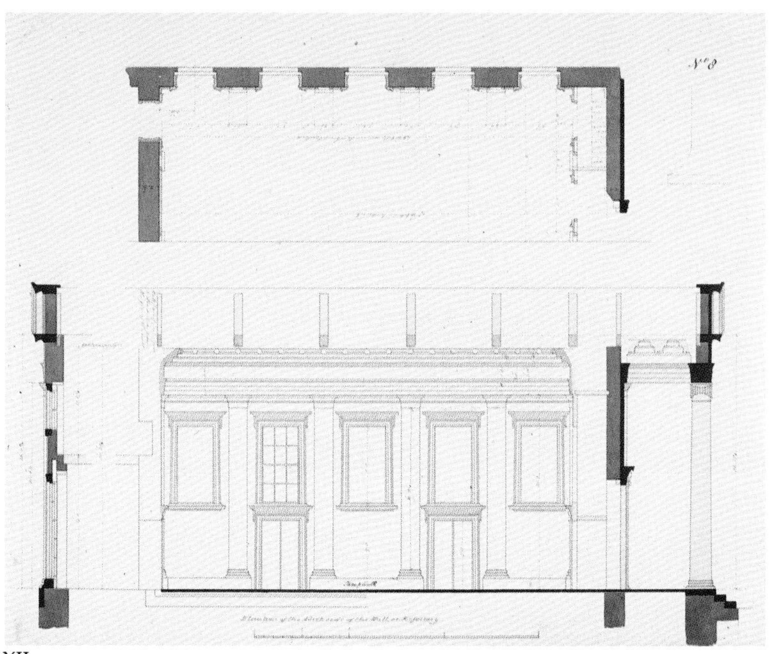

XII

XIII

XIII William Wilkins, Details of the principal roof of the Hall, 1806

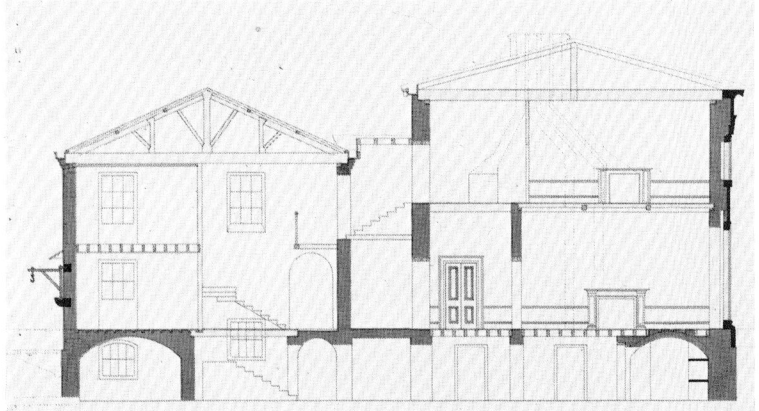

XIV

XIV William Wilkins, Transverse section through the West Lodge, 1806

XV Downing College, View of the west range as executed

XV

XVI Downing College, View of the Master's Lodge from south-east

XVII Downing College, View of the Master's Lodge from south-west

XVI

XVII

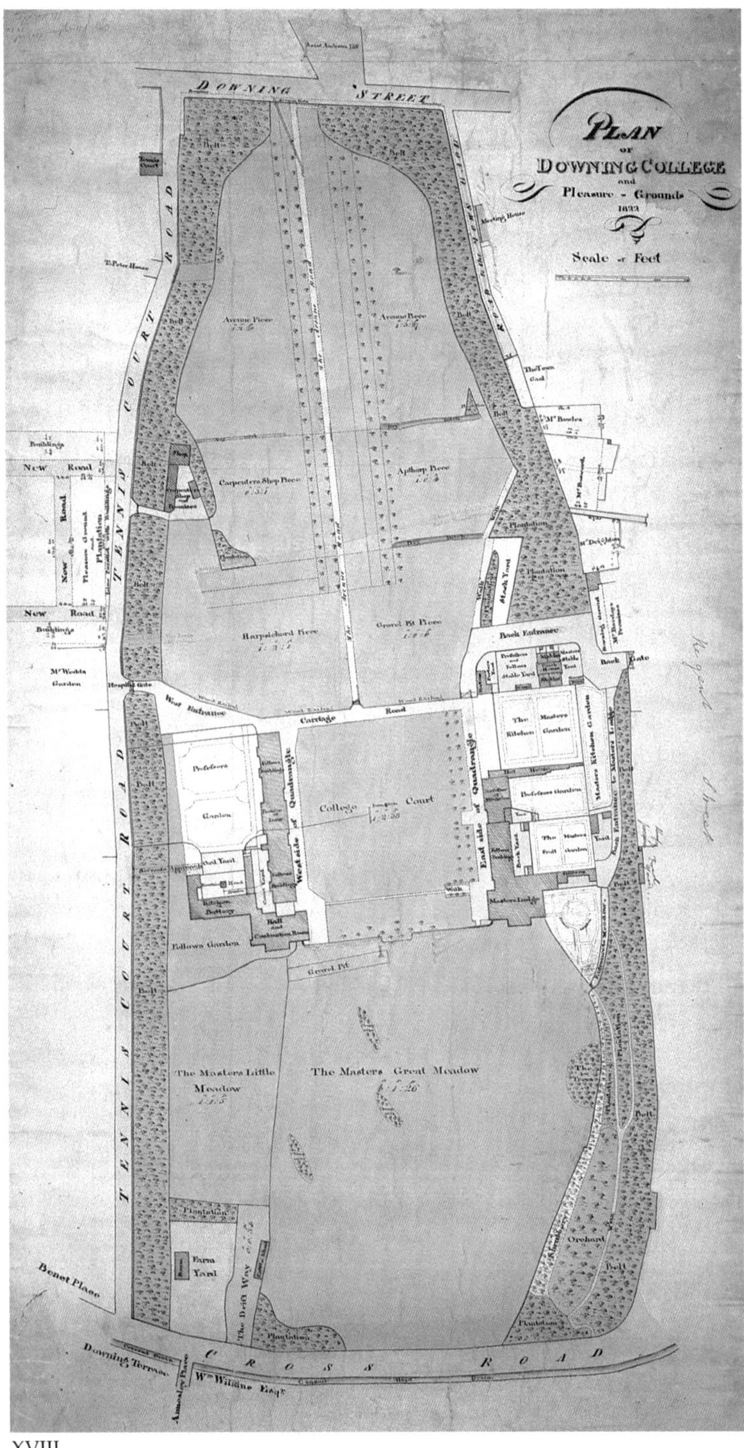

XVIII

XVIII William Wilkins, Plan of Downing College and Pleasure Grounds, 1822

XIX Downing College, General view from the air looking west

XIX

XX

XXII

XX Downing College, Western elevation of H.Baker's east wing

XXI Arthur Betts del., Principal elevation of the north range including the Chapel and Students' rooms, 1950

XXII Downing College, View of the north range with the Chapel designed by A.Scott

XXI

XXIII
Arthur Betts del.
Perspectival view of the Chapel's interior looking north, 1950

XXIV
Arthur Betts del.
View towards the south end of the Chapel, 1950

XXIII

XXIV

XXV Downing College, West elevation of the senior combination room

XXV

XXVI Quinlan Terry (1937–), Principal elevation of the Howard Building, 1986

XXVI

Notes

CHAPTER I

1 The authors wish to acknowledge their considerable debt to *The History of Downing College* by Stanley French (Cambridge, Downing College Association, 1978), upon which they have relied extensively throughout.

2 'Any property which the wife had owned as a single woman became the husband's on marriage', J.H.Baker, *An Introduction to English Legal History*, (2nd ed.1979) p.396.

3 For an explanation of the workings of a strict settlement, see A.W.B.Simpson, *An Introduction to the History of the Land Law*, (Oxford, 1961) pp.218–224.

4 An entail or estate tail is an interest in land which descends lineally. The land can be enjoyed only by the person to whom it descends (the tenant in tail) for his or her lifetime, and then passes to the person next entitled – the tenant in tail's son or daughter. If the line dies out, the land reverts to the grantor, or whoever he has specified should receive it next. An entail may be general, so that in default of male issue, the land will pass through the female line, or it can be limited to pass only to either male issue (a tail male) or female issue (a tail female). Methods were developed in the later Middle Ages by which an entail could be 'barred', that is to say, turned into a full fee simple (a freehold). The owner of a fee simple enjoyed powers of alienation over the land which a tenant in tail lacked.

5 Barnardiston was a barrister and law reporter. He published two volumes of cases in the King's Bench (covering the period 1726–1734) of rather indifferent quality, and a rather better set of reports of Chancery cases for the year 1740–1741. He became a serjeant-at-law in 1736.

6 The will contained a name and arms clause requiring the person who received the estates under the will to take the name of Downing if he did not already have it.

7 There are several reports of the case. The judgment of Sir John Wilmot in the first part of the case is the only one that is fully reported: Wilmot 1. There is a short report in Dickens 414 which has a brief summary of all aspects of the case. Ambler – who was later briefed in the Downing cause – reported the argument at Ambler 550 and a summary of the second part of the case at 571. There are demonstrable errors in Ambler's report. A good summary of the proceedings is also to be found in *Attorney-General* v. *Bowyer* (1798) 3 Ves. Jun. 714, 715–7.

8 For a summary of the development of the law of mortmain, see A.H.Oosterhoff, 'The Law of Mortmain: An Historical and Comparative Review', *University of Toronto Law Journal*, XXVII (1977), p.257.

9 In feudal times such grants deprived lords of their most valuable feudal privileges. They also operated to disinherit the grantor's family and often took the form of a gift to an ecclesiatical foundation made as a dying act of piety. Such grants could lead to land being tied up indefinitely. There were repeated statutory attempts to regulate grants in mortmain from Magna Carta onwards and a royal licence came to be required before land could be conveyed to a corporation.

10 The Preamble to the Statute contained a list of objects – of a secular character – which in Elizabethan times were regarded as charitable. The modern law of charity has developed from this Preamble by a process of analogy. Curiously, the Preamble is based on a passage in Langland's *Piers the Ploughman*, which probably dates from the 1370s.

11 A statute of 1736 which extended the mortmain laws to charitable gifts of land was held to be inapplicable to Sir George Downing's will because it was made 19 years before the statute.

12 If property is given for a charitable purpose which fails, a court may in certain circumstances apply the property instead for some analogous charitable purpose. On this aspect of the case, see Gareth Jones (the present Downing Professor of the Laws of England), *History of the Law of Charity 1532 – 1827*, (Cambridge 1969), p.138ff.

13 At the time they were Catherine Cornwall, Elizabeth Neale, Frances Barrell, Mary Annesley, Sarah Goate, and Elizabeth Ewer.

14 Letter dated London 20th June 1768; DC Muniments, 10/d.

15 Yorke died in January 1770, three days after having been appointed Lord Chancellor; in 1768, the year of his election as MP for the University, the Senate of the University voted their thanks to him for 'having proved an effective advocate for us in the great cause whereby an estate worth £4000 a year is secured to the University for building and endowing a new college'.

16 DC Muniments, 2/66, 66A and 67.

17 *Whittington* v. *Attorney-General* (1783), Dickens 616. The case was heard by Lord Loughborough, Ashurst J. and Hotham B. The case was set for a long hearing. Lord Loughborough dismissed the bill of review after just three days on the basis that as each of the parties intended to appeal to the House of Lords, it was a waste of time and money for the Commissioners to hear it. He therefore dismissed the bill 'without the least scintilla of opinion'. The authors have been unable

to trace any appeal to the House of Lords, and from the reports of later proceedings, it appears that none was made.

18 *Attorney-General* v. *Bowyer* (1798) 3 Ves.Jun. 714. In that case Lord Loughborough, the Lord Chancellor, and a friend to the Downing cause, rejected the contention that the decree of 1769 could no longer be implemented because of lapse of time. He declared that the trustees were at liberty to lay a plan before the Master in Chancery for founding and establishing the College. The Master was required to report on it.

19 *Attorney-General* v. *Bowyer* (1800) 5 Ves. Jun. 300, Lord Loughborough. The last reported case on the Downing cause was concerned with details of the recovery of the properties from Whittington and Bowyer: *Attorney-General* v. *Vigor* (1803) 8 Ves.Jun. 256; Lord Eldon, Lord Chancellor.

20 The fourth adviser, Dr Tocklington, Master of Clare Hall, had refused to assist the Downing cause since as long ago as 1781.

21 See footnote 18.

CHAPTER II

1 BM, Add. MSS.6772, ff.173–174 v.

2 Quoted in Robert Willis and John Willis Clark, *The Architectural History of the University of Cambridge and of the Colleges of Cambridge and Eton* 3 vols., (Cambridge 1886), vol.ii, pp.756–57.

3 Minute Books (49) 1800–1807, f.1; the first Governing Body meeting was held 'soon after the date of the Charter' and on this occasion Wyatt's appointment was formally recorded.

4 PRO C33/534, f.731v, Court Decisions, 20 May, 1805.

5 DC Muniments, 80/9.

6 Respectively WyJas [4] 1, 2 and 3.

7 D.Watkin, *The Triumph of the Classical. Cambridge Architecture 1804–1834*, (Cambridge 1977), p.17.

8 DC Muniments, 80/16.

9 PRO C33/524, f.130v–131v.

10 Cf. D.Watkin, *Thomas Hope 1769–1831 and the Neo-Classical idea*, (1968).

11 For a list of Hope's writings see D.Watkin, *Thomas Hope* cit., pp.261–2.

12 In 1799 Hope acquired a house in Duchess Street, Portland Place, where he planned to accommodate his collection. He gradually enlarged and remodelled the building which he decorated and furnished in a sophisticated neo-classical style. In 1804 Hope started issuing invitations to visit the house to the members of the Royal Academy.

13 Cf. D.Watkin, *Thomas Hope* cit., p.62.

14 Wilkins was presented as 'a gentleman conversant in the History of the Antiquities of Great Britain and especially in the ancient architecture of this Kingdom'.

15 For a more extensive treatment of this subject, see M.L.Clarke, *Greek Studies in England 1700–1830*, (Cambridge 1945).

16 Three of the six founding members of Downing came from St. John's: the master, Francis Annesley, was the son of the Rev. Martin Annesley, D.D. of St. John's, and he himself had matriculated at St. John's at Easter 1800; Edward Christian, Professor of the Laws of England, was a Fellow of St. John's; John Lens had been Fourth Wrangler at St. John's. Of the other three, Busick Harwood was originally at Christ's and then became a Fellow Commoner at Emmanuel, John Frere had been at Trinity and was about to sit for a Trinity Fellowship when he was offered one at Downing; finally William Meeke was a Fellow Commoner at Emmanuel.

17 Cf. W.Otter, *Life of Clarke*, (1824), pp.505–506.

18 The literature on Neo-Classicism has been steadily growing and gaining in depth of analysis. The following are some of the key studies on the period: H.Honour, *Neo-Classicism*, (Harmondsworth 1968); Arts Council of Great Britain, *The Age of Neo-Classicism*, (London and Harlow 1972); R.Rosenblum, *Transformations in late Eighteenth Century Art*, (Princeton 1974).

19 On this subject see W.Herrmann, *Laugier and Eighteenth Century French Theory*, (1962); E.Kaufmann, 'Piranesi, Algarotti and Lodoli. A controversy in XVIIIth century Venice', *Essays in Honour of Hans Tietze*, (Paris 1958), pp.309–16; D.Wiebenson, *Sources of Greek Revival Architecture*, (1969) and J.Mordaunt Crook, *The Greek Revival. Neo-Classical Attitudes in British Architecture 1760–1870*, (1972).

20 On the Society of Dilettanti, see L.Cust, *History of the Society of Dilettanti* ed.S.Colvin, (1898).

21 The only other likely arbiters of taste that Annesley might have consulted were Sir William Gell and the Earl of Aberdeen. In 1804, Gell was travelling in the Peloponnese, and Aberdeen was also travelling in the Mediterranean – on 15 February, 1804 he arrived in Venice from Corfu and Pola.

22 Thomas Hope, *Observations on the Plans and Elevations designed by James Wyatt Architect, for Downing College, Cambridge; in a Letter to Francis Annesley, Esq. M.P.*, (1804), p.14.

23 DC Muniments, 49.

24 *The Gentleman's Magazine*, 1813 (ii), p.299.

25 They were only three, in Bury St.Edmunds (1803), Cambridge (1802–1807) and Canterbury (1806–1810).

26 See Christian's correspondence with the third Lord Hardwicke in the British Museum, Add. MSS.35, 393, ff. 133; Add. MSS.35, 687, ff.200, 259, 263, 272.
27 Cf. H.Colvin, *A Biographical Dictionary of British Architects 1660–1840*, (1978), sub vocem BYFIELD, G., pp.176–77; and J.F.J.Collett-White, *The Old House at Wrest*, (Bedford 1983).
28 On Ledoux see A.Braham, *The Architecture of the French Enlightenment*, (1980), in particular the Hôtel de Thelusson.
29 PRO, C33/534, ff.731v–732.
30 Kathryn Cave ed., *The Diary of Joseph Farington, vol.VII January 1805–June 1806*, (New Haven and London 1982), p.2514.
31 Quoted in D. Watkin, *Thomas Hope* cit., p.10.
32 Kenneth Garlick and Angus Macintyre eds., *The Diary of Joseph Farington, vol.VI April 1803–December 1804*, (New Haven and London 1979), p.2478, entry dated Sunday 23 December 1804.
33 Cf. A.Graves, *The Royal Academy of Arts. A Complete dictionary of contributors and their work from its foundation in 1769 to 1904*, 8 vols., (1905), vol.i p.368 and vol.viii p.276.
34 Cf.A.Graves, *The Royal Academy* cit., vol. vii, p.17, n.841 in the original catalogue.
35 On the history of Ickworth see Pamela Tudor-Craig, 'The Evolution of Ickworth', *Country Life*, 17 May 1973, pp.1362–65.
36 Cf. A.Graves, *The Royal Academy* cit., vol.vi, p.183, n.791 in the original catalogue.

CHAPTER III

1 BL, Aberdeen Correspondence, Add. MSS.43229, f.117v.
2 The report of the final order of the Court of Chancery on the choice of architect for Downing, dated 6 August 1806, states that '. . .a plan of ye buildings for ye said College according to a design by Mr Wilkins of Caius College in ye University of Cambridge Architect has been proposed before him [Master Stratford] by or on behalf of ye Petitioners & another plan of ye said Buildings according to a design by Lewes Wyatt of Queen Anne St. East in ye Co. of Middlesex Architect has been proposed before him by or on behalf of ye defendants ye heirs at law of ye said testor Sir George Downing. . .'; PRO C33/542, f.792.
3 PRO C33/542, f.792: '. . .by a subsequent order dated ye 18th day of December 1805 it was ordered yt in considering ye plan of ye buildings for ye said College ye said Master should have regard to ye circumstances yt Rooms might be wanted according to ye Statutes for Chaplains paying rent for ye same.'
4 Letter to Messrs Forster, Cooke and Frere; DC Muniments, 80/24.
5 Assessors' statement, dated London March 26, 1806; DC Muniments, 80/15.
6 DC Muniments, 80/15.
7 The assessors produced a 'Certificate' approving the new drawings on 14 June 1806, in which they were at pains to stress that they had been concerned exclusively with the 'merit of the design. . .independent of any consideration of the expence of executing it'; DC Muniments, 80/6. Their fees came to 15 Guineas each; DC Muniments, 80/24.
8 DC Muniments, 80/29.
9 DC Muniments, 80/29.
10 Wyatt explained his guiding principles in his *General Remarks* of 9 December 1805, 'I have consider'd the Buildings as capable of being arrang'd under two distinct classes. The Habitable and the ornamental, confining each as much as possible to its peculiar situation. In the former I have endeavour'd to combine convenience with simplicity & aeconomy, and to compress the whole into as small a size, as the Number, & dimensions of the Rooms requir'd, would admit of. . .The Hall, the Chapel, and the Library being necessarily Rooms of large dimensions, are more applicable to the purpose of producing a good effect, when concentrated into one Building, this advantage I have avail'd myself of, and have plac'd them as a centre Building on the South side of the Quadrangle, bestowing upon it every enrichment of which I conceived it capable.'; DC Muniments, 80/16.
11 Rousseau's Hôtel de Salm clearly acted as a model, but ultimately one can see some of the seeds of Wyatt's southern elevation for Downing in his uncle James' garden front of Heaton Hall, Lancashire, 1772.
12 These are still preserved in the college, see Catalogue Section nos.51–153.
13 The detailed account of the workmen employed at Downing and the payments they received is contained in four documents, DC Muniments, 80/1, 2, 3 and 4.
14 Minutes Books 1800–1807; DC Muniments, 49.
15 William Wilkins' affidavit of 29 July 1806; DC Muniments, Trunk 4/4.
16 Cf. William Wilkins' affidavit of 23 March 1809, and James Lewis' report to the Court upon the state of the buildings dated 24 September 1812; DC Muniments, 80/50.
17 Letter dated London, 9 August 1808; DC Muniments, 63/21.
18 The only reference to these plans occurs in the minutes of a Governing Body meeting of 24 January 1818, in which it was

'resolved that the alterations proposed by Mr Wilkins in the Northern side require further consideration but that in as much as there is no immediate prospect of proceeding with these parts of the Building which will be affected thereby it will be convenient that the consideration of the same be postponed to a future time'; DC Muniments, 49/3A.

19 Letter dated Downing Lodge 15 December 1817; DC Muniments, 80/18.

20 Cf. letter mentioned above, footnote 19.

21 Preserved in the college and of larger size than those produced in 1806, cf. Catalogue p. 138.

22 Cf. Croggon Order Book, July 1819, 'Downing College Cambridge for Mr Wilkins 14 flat pilasters 16ft 10 ¼ ins. projection, same imitation of giallo antique as Covent Garden £402. 0s. 0d.', quoted in Alison Kelly, 'Coade Stone in Georgian Architecture', *Architectural History*, XXVIII (1985), pp.71–102. Scagliola is a type of Italian plasterwork imitating marble or stone.

23 Governing Body minutes, 8 February 1873; DC Muniments.

CHAPTER IV

1 Governing Body minutes (1860–1915) p.473; DC Muniments, 51.

2 Governing Body minutes (1860–1915) p.487; DC Muniments, 51.

3 The churches were St.Eugene (1854–55), St.Augustin (1860–71), Notre-Dame-du-Travail (1899–1901), St.Jean de Montmatre (1894–1904).

4 Governing Body minutes (1860–1915) pp.542v–543; DC Muniments, 51.

5 Governing Body minutes (1860–1915) p.567; DC Muniments, 51.

6 Governing Body minutes (1915–1930) pp.439–40; DC Muniments, 52.

7 Scott had built the new building at Clare between 1923 and 1934.

8 Cf. Herbert Baker, *Architecture and Personalities* (1944), p.35.

9 Cf.Herbert Baker, *Architecture* cit., p.36. On Baker's career see Dougal O.Malcom, *Dictionary of National Biography 1941–1950*, (Oxford 1959) *sub vocem* BAKER, Sir Herbert pp.41–3 and Doreen E.Greig, *Sir Herbert Baker in South Africa*, (Cape Town 1970).

10 Letter dated 20 March 1920; DC Muniments, Ref. 3/1/16.

11 The letter is reproduced in full in Appendix II; the whole correspondence with Sir Herbert is preserved in DC Muniments, Ref. 3/1/16–20.

12 Pilkington produced the watercolour during October 1929; this was the second drawing of the vista that Baker had made, as the first one had not satisfied him. In a letter to the Bursar, dated 4 October 1929 (DC Muniments, Ref.3/1/16), referring to the unsatisfactory small drawing of the view from the entrance Baker said 'I think it wants a wash drawing in order to show the perspective and atmosphere.'

13 Letter dated 24 September 1929; DC Muniments, Ref.3/1/16.

14 The correspondence between the Bursar, J.Grantham, and Baker on the subject of the new gateway and shops is in DC Muniments, Ref. 3/1/17.

15 DC Muniments, Ref. 3/1/14.

16 Cf. DC Muniments, Ref. 3/2/1.

17 H.C.Whalley-Tooker to the Master, dated 28 October 1946; DC Muniments, Ref. 3/2/1.

18 Clive Parry to the Master, dated 8 December 1946; DC Muniments, Ref. 3/2/1.

19 Baker had died in 1946.

20 Nikolaus Pevsner, *The Buildings of England. Cambridgeshire*, (Harmondsworth 1970), pp.38–9.

21 Founded in Weimar in 1919, the Bauhaus school united the Academy of Art and the School of Arts and Crafts; it immediately attracted the best and most innovative designers of the day. On the Bauhaus see: H.Wingler, *The Bauhaus: Weimar, Dessau, Berlin, and Chicago*, (Cambridge, Mass. 1969), M.Franciscono, *Walter Gropius and the Creation of the Bauhaus in Weimar*, (Chicago and London 1971), and K.Frampton, *Modern Architecture. A Critical History*, (1980).

22 Cf. W.Herrmann, *Laugier* cit., (1962) and J.Soane, *Lectures on Architecture: Delivered to the Students of the Royal Academy from 1809 to 1836 in Two Courses of Six Lectures Each.* Edited by A.T.Bolton, (1929).

23 Charles Jencks, 'Introduction', *Architectural Design Profile. Post-Modern Classicism the New Synthesis*, 5/6 (1980), p.10.

Appendices

APPENDIX I

MASTERS OF DOWNING COLLEGE

1800–1812	Francis Annesley
1812–1836	William Frere
1836–1885	Thomas Worsley
1885–1888	W. L. Birkbeck
1888–1907	Alex Hill
1907–1915	Howard Marsh
1915–1936	Albert Seward
1936–1947	Herbert Richmond
1947–1957	Lionel Whitby
1957–1972	W. K. C. Guthrie
1972–1978	Morien Morgan
1978–1987	John Butterfield

APPENDIX II

SIR HERBERT BAKER'S REPORT OF MAY 1929

On 17 May 1929, Sir Herbert Baker sent to the Bursar a first set of five sketch plans for the new buildings. None of these drawings survive in Downing but the covering letter accompanying them has been preserved.

Dear Mr Smith, I now have the pleasure of submitting to you sketch plans for the new buildings at your College:
(1) & (2) Small scale block plans.
(3) 1/16″ scale plan showing sections and elevations.
(4) & (5) Alternative schemes for the sets of rooms to 1/8″ scale.

General Plan. I think there can be no doubt that the central group of major buildings, consisting of the chapel, library, assembly room and common room should be on the north side of the site in the centre between the two blocks; in fact they would be in a similar position but on the opposite side to the original conception of the architect who designed your present buildings, the change of position being necessitated by the selling of your land beyond.

An important point, I think, is to link up the new buildings with the old by blocks of rooms leaving between them an open vista as seen from the new entrance gate. To give good architectural effect to this I suggest as an ultimate ideal, building twin porticoes on to the inner pilasters of the present northern facades and corresponding porticos on to the new blocks opposite. The vista may be terminated by an archway through a further block leading to a back entrance along Tennis Court Road. My first scheme shown on the main drawing, No. 3, and block plan, No. 1, is to build blocks of rooms continuous with the new central block at the end of the chapel and library respectively. There are certain architectural difficulties in fitting the scale of the block with its small rooms, to the bigger scale of the chapel and library necessitated by the higher rooms and to the central portico. This change of scale is however a common feature, due to the same cause, in most college buildings at Oxford and Cambridge. A further possible objection to this scheme is that one half of the rooms with the blocks running east and west would have a northern aspect; and this is a point which requires your consideration.

I am therefore suggesting an alternative plan on block plan No. 2, showing the blocks of rooms running only north and south with east and west aspects, thus leaving a gap between the rooms and the central block which might be planted with an avenue of trees to give some architectural continuity. Central Block. I have suggested that the chapel, the library and the assembly room should be entered from a common hall approached from a portico similar to the wider portico with six columns of the present building. I have placed the common room at the end, approached by a separate entrance from the outside, but communicating with the library. Over both library and common room I am suggesting a stack-room for the storage of the less used books, by which means the library itself could be made into a pleasanter reading room not overloaded with bookcases. If there had not been a vacant space above, the stack room might have been put in what is perhaps the more usual position, a basement below, but this would be more costly as your sub-soil being, I believe, good, there is no need for deep foundations.

As regards architectural treatment, I think it is important to carry on the treatment of the porticos and to have a uniform cornice line so as to give architectural unity to the whole of the ultimate college buildings. Working to the same cornice line and keeping the ground floor line a little lower would enable us to get three sets of reasonably high rooms where you have now two sets of rooms of reasonable height. So I think there is no doubt that this should be done in spite of the change of scale due to the smaller rooms and fenestration.

The Sets of Rooms. I have studied other colleges and given a good deal of thought to the planning of the sets of rooms and submit two alternative schemes, but I am well aware that there are other methods of planning possible. Very much depends on the requirements and a change of methods may radically alter the scheme. A plan can only be decided upon when it is definitely settled whether the men will have bathrooms, whether they will wash in their rooms or in lavatories, and the number of gyp rooms, &c. required; also the methods of heating. In these plans I have assumed that they will have separate bathrooms; about two baths, one closet and one gyp's room to each floor of four rooms; but I am not quite certain whether there should be basins with water laid on in each bedroom.

I am aware that it would be a convenience, as is done in many colleges, that there should be a separate entrance to the bedroom for the bedmaker, but this necessitates either a corridor between the bedrooms, thus widening the block by about four feet, or else having two instead of four sets on each floor served by one staircase. In other words that system would imply double the number of staircases with attendant conveniences.

I think my plan, however, would largely overcome this difficulty by providing projecting bookcases acting as a screen to the fire-places so that a man should not be disturbed by anyone going to the bedroom. There could if desired be double doors to the room.

In scheme 'A' I have placed a more compact staircase opposite to the entrance, which gives a little more accommodation but involves drainage on two sides; one is anxious to concentrate the plumbing both for initial and maintenance economy as well as possibly for external appearance, i.e. if the pipes must be outside.

Drawing 5, plan 'B' shows the staircase at the side of the entrance and schemed over it. By this means all the drainage is on one side, but the staircase is perhaps rather extravagantly large on the upper floors.

In scheme 'B' the height can only be obtained by raising the ground floor three or four steps above the entrance and this involves pushing up the floors and making each room a little higher, but the windows of the top floor become rather small under the present cornice height, and to these upper rooms, as shown on the sections, a dormer window would, I think, have to be added. Architecturally, however, I think I prefer this scheme 'B' as being perhaps a little quieter and bigger in scale than scheme 'A'. Scheme 'B' would of course cost a little more on account of the extra height and of the dormer windows. Both schemes may indeed have to be modified when we decide on the general principles and probably other plans tried.

My plan shows a possible 9 blocks containing 108 rooms or fewer by as many don's rooms we provide, which practically means throwing two sets of rooms into one.

Gateway. My suggestion for the gateway, but I admit it wants rather more consideration, is to repeat the idea of the columns of the porticos shortened in the base but with the same cornice level, and recessed from the street so that from the street you would look through an avenue of columns with long intervals with connecting trees. The columns may necessitate rather a higher building than perhaps necessary and we shall have to consider what to make of this on the wider side, supposing the porter is housed on the narrower.

Catalogue of Drawings

The following is a catalogue of the drawings for Downing preserved in public collections, that is to say in the college's Muniment Room and in the British Architectural Library. The bulk of the collection now at Downing is represented by Wilkins' drawings. At the beginning of this century these drawings were bound into two albums of different sizes. The smaller album (here referred to as SWP – small working plans) contained one hundred and three small size drawings produced by Wilkins between 1806 and 1817. The larger album gathered together sixty-eight working drawings, all large (46.4×67.9 cm.) versions of the drawings for the west range in the small album. These large working drawings, made in 1818, were shown to the Court of Chancery and used by the builders as the documents against which their work was assessed and measured. Because they are basically repetitive of what is already to be found in the small album they have not been individually catalogued here.

The college's Muniment Room and the British Architectural Library have very small holdings of twentieth century drawings, particularly by Sir Herbert Baker. The British Architectural Library has recently acquired a hundred drawings for Downing from the Baker and Scott partnership (RIBA XI/e). They are all working drawings dating from Scott's time as head of the partnership and they are for the chapel. The majority of these drawings are on tracing paper and many are also reprographic copies; generally they are of poor quality and are in very poor condition.

The following catalogue is arranged by artist and chronologically. Measurements are given in centimetres, with height preceding width. All inscriptions are transcribed starting from the top right of the sheet and then moving clockwise, although some of the illustrations in the catalogue have been rotated to facilitate viewing. Unless otherwise stated, all inscriptions are in the handwriting of the author of the drawing.

1. James **WYATT** (1746–1813)
Perspective from south-west. (see Fig.6, p.27)
Pen and washes within ruled border; 24.7×72.7 cm. Signed: 'James Wyatt Arch.t' on lower left corner. *Exhibited*: 'The Age of Neo-Classicism', London, 1972; 'The Triumph of the Classical. Cambridge Architecture 1804–1834', Cambridge 1977. *Reproduced*: G.Walkley, 1938, 1014; A.Dale, 1956, pl.41; J.M.Crook, 1964, p.10; D.Linstrum, 1973, fig.29; P.Bicknell, 1982, fig.4. *Location*: British Architectural Library, WyJas[4],1, purchased 1937.

This view shows the south front of the south range and the elevation of the west range in Wyatt's design for a quadrangle 250 feet square. The portico and the tower excited Thomas Hope's sharp criticism; he described the tower as 'an entire distinct building, piled upon another' with 'four huge flower pots that terminate its angles' (p.28).

2. James **WYATT**
Perspective from north-west. (see Fig.5, p.27)
Pen and washes within double ruled border; 25.6×72.3 cm. Signed: 'James Wyatt Arch.t' on lower left corner. *Exhibited*: 'The Age of Neo-Classicism', London, 1972; 'The Triumph of the Classical. Cambridge Architecture 1804–1834', Cambridge 1977. *Reproduced*: G.Walkley, 1938, 1015; D.Linstrum, 1973, fig.30. *Location*: British Architectural Library, WyJas [4],2, purchased 1937.

The drawing shows the elevation of the north range with the entrance gateway in the shape of a triumphal arch.

3. James **WYATT**
Perspective of the courtyard looking south. (see Pl.II)
Pen and washes within ruled border; 32.0×78.5 cm. *Exhibited*: 'The Age of Neo-Classicism', London, 1972; 'The Triumph of the Classical. Cambridge Architecture 1804–1834', Cambridge 1977. *Reproduced*: J.M.Crook, 1968, pl.14; D.Linstrum, 1973, fig.31. *Location*: British Architectural Library, WyJas [4],3, purchased 1966.

This is the most striking of the three surviving drawings by James Wyatt for the College. The use of the Roman Doric colonnade was criticized by Hope.

4. George **BYFIELD** (c.1756–1813)
Plan of the site with block plan of the College. Pen and washes within double ruled border; 76×38.5 cm. Signed and dated: 'G. Byfield/ Craven St. 1804'. Inscribed: 'PLAN/ of part of the Town of/ CAMBRIDGE/ showing the Site of/ DOWNING COLLEGE/ agreably to the Place/ Designed by Mr. Byfield'. *Location*: Downing College, Cambridge.

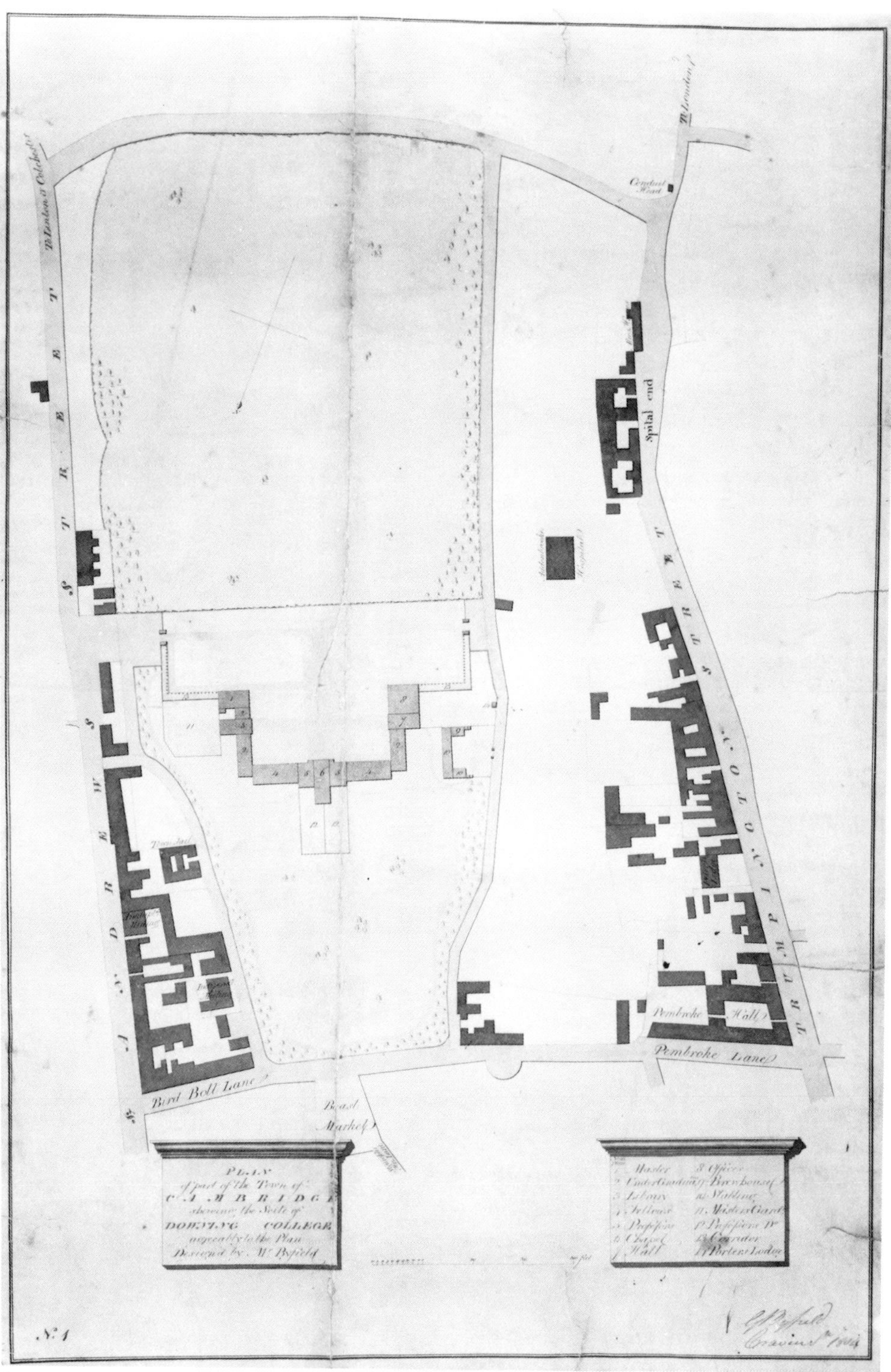

4

5. George **BYFIELD**
Plan of the site and general ground plan of the college. (see Fig.8, p.37)
Pen and washes within ruled border; 85.5×40.5 cm. Inscribed: 'PLAN/ of the general settlement of/ DOWNING COLLEGE/ and a Ground plan of the Buildings/ as designed by Mr. Byfield/ 1804'. *Location*: Downing College, Cambridge.

6. George **BYFIELD**
Plan of the basement storey.
Pen and ink with pink, brown, blue and grey washes within ruled border. Signed and dated 'G.Byfield/ Craven St. 1804' in lower right corner. Inscribed: 'PLAN of the BASEMENT STORY' in the centre; 'N.o 1' in lower left corner; 'Scale 6 feet to an inch' in lower right corner. *Location*: Downing College, Cambridge.

7. George **BYFIELD**
Plan of the ground storey. (see Fig.9, p.35)
Pen and ink with brown, black and grey washes within ruled border; 55.5×162 cm. Signed and dated: 'G.Byfield/ Craven St. 1804'. Inscribed with measurements, 'PLAN OF THE GROUND FLOOR' in the centre. The lower left corner is missing. *Location*: Downing College, Cambridge.

8. George **BYFIELD**
Plan of the first floor.
Pen and ink with brown and black washes within ruled border; 55.5×162 cm. Inscribed with measurements, 'PLAN OF THE FIRST FLOOR' in the centre; 'N.o 3' in lower left corner. The lower right corner is missing. *Location*: Downing College, Cambridge.

9. George **BYFIELD**
Elevation of the south front with sections of the east and west wings. (see Pl.III)
Pen and washes within ruled border; 55.5×162 cm. Signed and dated: 'G.Byfield/ Craven St. 1804' on lower right corner. Inscribed: 'N.o 4' (in lower left corner) and 'Section of Under Graduates Apartments ELEVATION OF THE SOUTH FRONT Section of the Under Graduates Apartments' (along the lower margin). VERSO: Inscribed: 'E This plan was shewn to Henry Hale Seward, John Phillips, Charles Beazley, George Tappen and

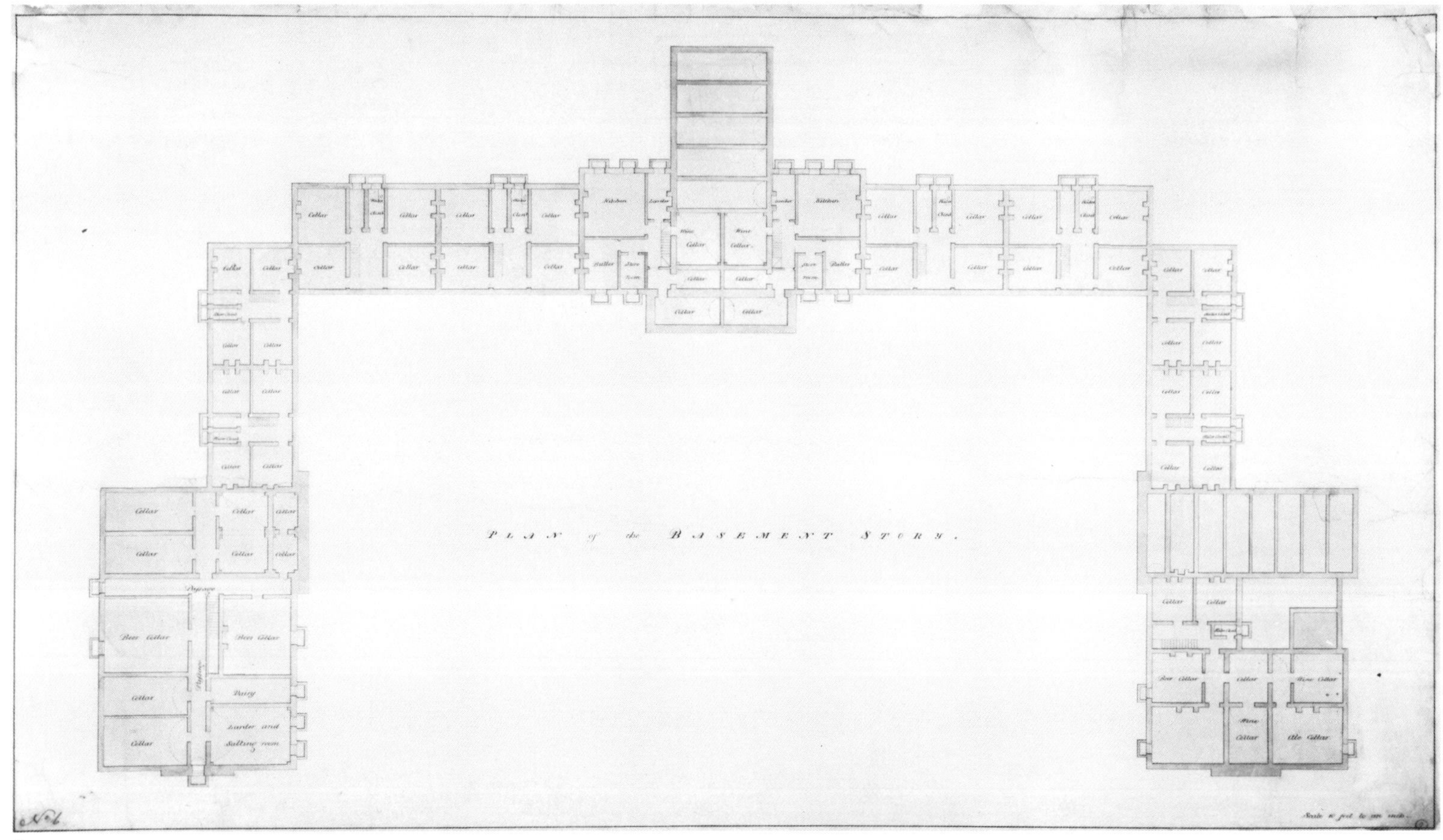

6

George Frere at the times of their exam[inati]ons in Chancery on the part of George Byfield in a Cause wherein his Majesty's Att[orne]y Gen[era]l is inform[an]t against Timothy Stonehouse Vigor & o[ther]s Def[endan]ts/ I.A.Berrey/ D[utifull]y Exam[ine]d'. *Location*: Downing College, Cambridge.

Byfield envisaged a quadrangle open to the south with the Chapel placed in the centre and flanked by the Master's and Professors'Lodges.

10. George **BYFIELD**
Elevation of the Master's Lodge and termination of the west wing. (see PI.IV)
Pen and washes within ruled border; 39.5×56.5 cm. Signed and dated: 'G.Byfield/ Craven St. 1804'. Inscribed: 'ELEVATION of the MASTER'S HOUSE and END of the WEST WING' along the lower margin; 'N.o 6' in the lower left corner; 'Scale six feet to an inch' in the lower right corner. *Location*: Downing College, Cambridge.

This drawing, like the ones listed above, has never been published or exhibited before. It reveals Byfield's unknown and somewhat unexpected degree of committment to Greek revival architecture as early as 1804.

11. William **PORDEN** (c.1755–1822)
Site plan. (see Fig.15, p.45)
Pen and watercolour; 70.5×55.9 cm. Various inscriptions. *Location*: Downing College, Cambridge.

12. William **PORDEN**
Plan of the site.
Pen and watercolour; 42.2×28 cm. Inscribed: 'Land for Downing College, Cambridge'; 'Establishment/ Master/ 6 Fellows maybe 12 or 14/ 40 Students/ Viz. 10 or 12 Fellow Comm.rs/ 20 Pensioners/ 8 or 10 Scholars/ East 2 Professors'; 'whole length about 1860 Feet'. Scale: ¾ in. to 100 ft. *Literature*: J.Lever, 1976, p. 90. *Location*: British Architectural Library, J7 [1], presented by H. Garling 1855.

Both site plans show Porden's ideas for the landscaping of the college grounds; the drive on the north end of the site is conceived much more as the approach to a country house than to an educational institution.

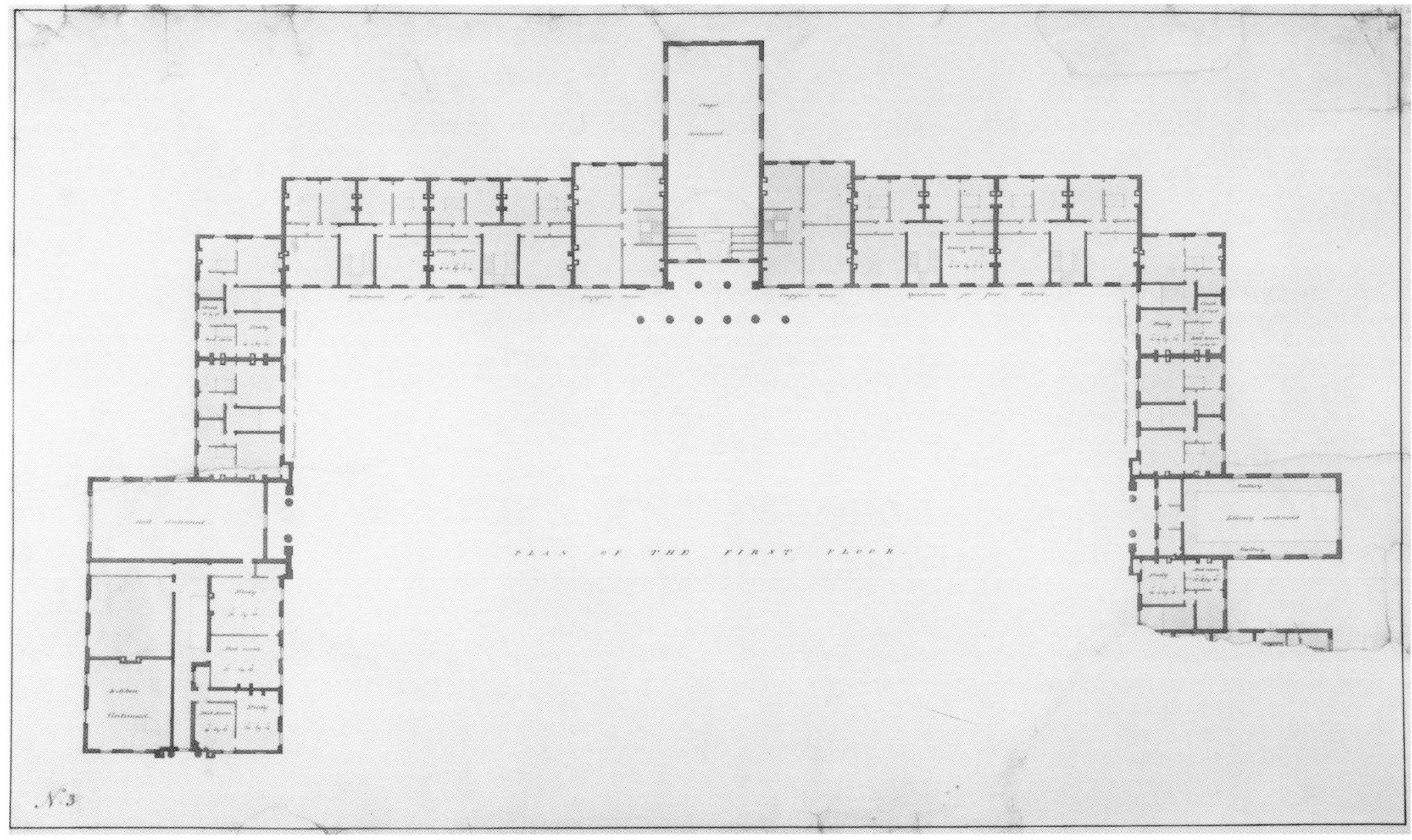

8

13. William **PORDEN**
Plan of the site with block plan of the college. (see Fig.10, p.40)
Pen and ink with black wash; 50.8×35 cm. Inscribed in pencil: 'Sunday April 27/ Stables &c to be. . .to/ large Plan to. . .'. Scale: ¾ in. to 100 ft. *Literature*: J.Lever, 1976, p. 90. *Location*: British Architectural Library J7 [1], 2, presented by H. Garling 1855.

Porden is here pushing the buildings further north than any other architect before or after him.

14. William **PORDEN**
Preliminary design for the central block containing an octagonal chapel.
Pen and ink; 34×50 cm. Scale: ½ in. to 10 ft. *Literature*: J.Lever, 1976, p. 90. *Location*: British Architectural Library, J7 [1], 3, presented by H. Garling 1855.

15. William **PORDEN**
Elevations and two sections of the central block.
Pencil; 52×33.5 cm. Scale: ½ in. to 10 ft. *Literature*: J.Lever, 1976, p. 90. *Location*: British Architectural Library, J7 [1], 4, presented by H. Garling 1855.

16. William **PORDEN**
Plan and rough part-elevation of the central block seen from the south end.
Pencil; 49.5×33.5 cm. Scale: ½ in. to 10 ft. Inscribed: 'Chapel', 'Library', 'Dining Room'. *Literature*: J.Lever, 1976, p. 90. *Location*: British Architectural Library, J7 [1], 5, presented by H. Garling 1855.

17. William **PORDEN**
North elevation of the chapel and central block.
Pencil; 33.5×49.5 cm. Scale: ½ in. to 10 ft. *Literature*: J.Lever, 1976, p. 90. *Location*: British Architectural Library, J7 [1], 6, presented by H. Garling 1855.

18. William **PORDEN**
Ground plan of the central block.
Pencil; 34×52 cm. *Literature*: J.Lever, 1976, p. 90. *Location*: British Architectural Library, J7 [1], 7, presented by H. Garling 1855.

19. William **PORDEN**
Elevation of the Fellows' Building showing an alternative treatment of the windows.
Pen and ink over pencil underdrawing; 26.5×34.5 cm. *Literature*: J.Lever, 1976, p. 90. *Location*: British Architectural Library, J7 [1], 8, presented by H. Garling 1855.

20. William **PORDEN**
Preliminary drawing for the elevation of the Fellows' Building.
Pen and ink over pencil underdrawing; 26.5×34.5 cm. *Literature*: J.Lever, 1976, p. 90. *Location*: British Architectural Library, J7 [1], 9, presented by H. Garling 1855.

21. William **PORDEN**
Alternative elevation of the Fellows' Building, with square-headed windows in the upper storeys.
Pen and ink over pencil underdrawing; 26.5×34.5 cm. *Literature*: J.Lever, 1976, p. 90. *Location*: British Architectural Library, J7 [1], 10, presented by H. Garling 1855.

22. William **PORDEN**
Preliminary elevation of the east and west ranges.
Pen and ink over pencil underdrawing; 26.5×34.5 cm. *Literature*: J.Lever, 1976, p. 90. *Location*: British Architectural Library, J7 [1], 11, presented by H. Garling 1855.

23. William **PORDEN**
Main elevation of the east and west ranges.
Pen and ink over pencil underdrawing; 26.5×34.5 cm. *Literature*: J.Lever, 1976, p. 90. *Location*: British Architectural Library, J7 [1], 12, presented by H. Garling 1855.

24. William **PORDEN**
Elevation and part-plan showing a classical colonnade instead of a Gothic one.
Pencil; 25×33.5 cm. *Literature*: J.Lever, 1976, p. 90. *Location*: British Architectural Library, J7 [1], 13, presented by H. Garling 1855.

25. William **PORDEN**
Elevation and part-section showing a classical colonnade.
Pencil; 35×33 cm. *Literature*: J.Lever, 1976, p. 90. *Location*: British Architectural Library, J7 [1], 14, presented by H. Garling 1855.

26. William **PORDEN**
Section through the east and west ranges.
Pencil; 35×33 cm. *Literature*: J.Lever, 1976, p. 90. *Location*: British Architectural Library, J7 [1], 15, presented by H. Garling 1855

27. William **PORDEN**
General plan of the college. (see Fig.11, p.41)
Pen and wash within ruled border; 52.5×65 cm.; over the central block is a flier (35.5×25 cm.) showing an alternative plan. Inscribed: 'Plan for a College to be built at Cambridge/ pursuant to the will of the late Sir Jacob [sic] Downing/ consisting of a House for the Master, Houses for two Professors, and Chambers for Forty Fellows and Students/ a Chapel, a Library, a Dining Hall and suitable Offices to each'; 'Under the Terrace a Cloister is proposed forming a sheltered Communication with every part of the College, in Wintry Weather'; 'Residence for the Master of the College/ Four Stories'; 'Two Houses for/ the two Professors'; 'Plan of the First story of Apartments for fellows and Students'. *Exhibited*: 'The Triumph of the Classical. Cambridge Architecture 1804–1834', Cambridge 1977. *Literature*: J.Lever, 1976, p. 90; D. Watkin, 1977, p.18. *Location*: British Architectural Library, J7 [1], 16, presented by H. Garling 1855.

28. William **PORDEN**
Elevation of the north front.
Pen and watercolour within double ruled border; 34×67.5 cm. Signed: 'W.Porden Architect' in lower left corner. Inscribed: 'North front of the Design for Downing College'; 'North Front of the Apartments for the Fellows and Students', 'Elevation of the Library/ Principal Entrance to the Chapel Library and Dining Room Elevation of the Dining Room', 'North Front of the Apartments for the Fellows and Students'. *Exhibited*: 'The Triumph of the Classical. Cambridge Architecture 1804–1834', Cambridge 1977. *Literature*: J.Lever, 1976, p.91; D. Watkin, 1977, p.19. *Location*: British Architectural Library J7 [1] 17, presented by H. Garling 1855.

29. William **PORDEN**
Elevation of the south front. (see Pl.V)
Pen and watercolour within double ruled border; 34×53 cm. Signed: 'W.Porden Architect' in lower left corner. Inscribed: 'South Front of Downing College', 'Elevation of the Professors' Houses', 'Elevation of the Combination Room', 'South End of the Chapel', 'Elevation of the Reading and Muniment Rooms', 'Elevation of the Master's House'. *Exhibited*: 'The Triumph of the

Classical. Cambridge Architecture 1804–1834', Cambridge 1977. *Literature*: J.Lever, 1976, p.91; D.Watkin, 1977, p.19, pl.3. *Location*: British Architectural Library J7 [1] 18, presented by H. Garling 1855.

30. William **PORDEN**
Elevation of the east front. (see Pl.VI)
Pen and watercolour within double ruled border; 34×67.5 cm. Signed: 'W.Porden Architect' in lower left corner. Inscribed: 'Design for the East Front of Downing College with the Public Buildings', 'Elevation of the Students Apartments', 'East Elevation of the Dining Hall', 'East Elevation of the Chapel', 'Elevation of the Students Apartments'. *Exhibited*: 'The Triumph of the Classical. Cambridge Architecture 1804–1834', Cambridge 1977. *Literature*: J.Lever, 1976, p.91; D.Watkin, 1977, p.20. *Location*: British Architectural Library J7 [1] 19, presented by H. Garling 1855.

31. William **PORDEN**
Plan of the basement storey of the fellows' and students' residential block.
Pen and ink with grey wash; 25×35.5 cm. Scale: ⅛ in. to 1 ft. Inscribed: 'Plan of the Basement Story of the Apartments for/ Fellows and Students, between each two Staircases', 'Cloister on the level of the Courts and Gardens forming a sheltered communication/ with every part of the College public and private, and a walk in Winter'. *Literature*: J.Lever, 1976, p.91. *Location*: British Architectural Library J7 [1] 20, presented by H. Garling 1855.

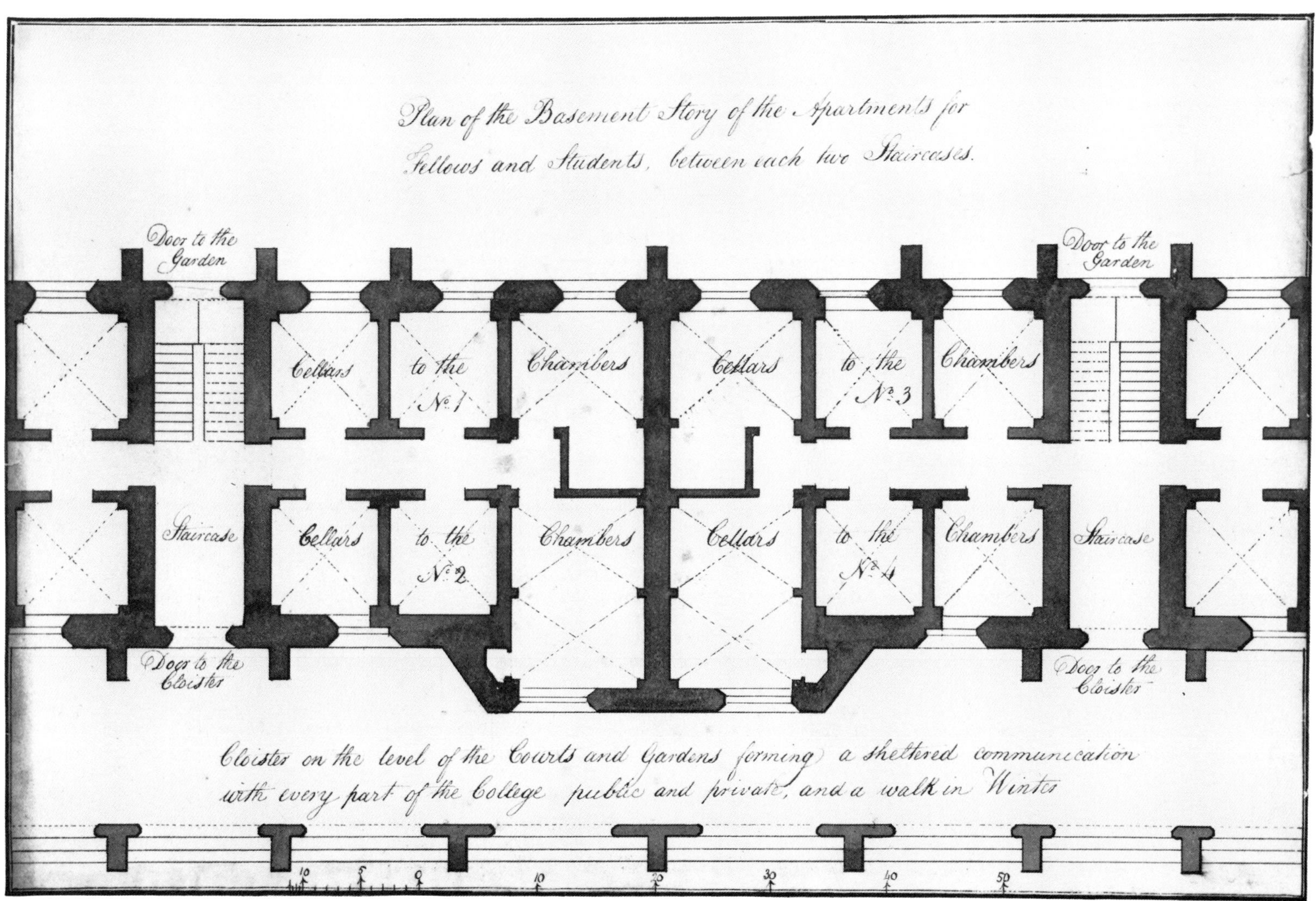

31

32. William **PORDEN**
Plan of the first floor of the fellows'and students'residential block. (see Fig.14, p.44)
Pen and ink with grey wash; 26.5×35.5 cm. Scale: ⅛ in. to 1 ft. Inscribed: 'Plan of the first Story of Apartments for Fellows and/ Students shewing the sets of Chambers contained between/ two Staircases. The Story above in all respects the same'. *Literature*: J.Lever, 1976, p.91. *Location*: British Architectural Library J7 [1] 21, presented by H. Garling 1855.

33. William **PORDEN**
Plan of the ground floor of the Professors' houses. (see Fig.13, p.43)
Pen and ink with grey washes; 35×24.5 cm. Scale: ⅛ in. to 1 ft. Inscribed: 'Plan of the Ground/ Professors House'. *Literature*: J.Lever, 1976, p.91. *Location*: British Architectural Library J7 [1] 22, presented by H. Garling 1855.

34. William **PORDEN**
Plan of the first floor of the Professors' houses.
Pen and ink with grey wash; 35.5×24.5 cm. Inscribed: 'Plan for the Bed Chamber/ Story for the/ Professors Houses'. *Literature*: J.Lever, 1976, p.91. *Location*: British Architectural Library J7 [1] 23, presented by H.Garling 1855.

35. William **PORDEN**
Alternative ground plan for the Professors' houses.
Pen and ink with grey wash; 26×34.5 cm. Inscribed: 'Professors Houses/ Ground Story'. *Literature*: J.Lever, 1976, p.91. *Location*: British Architectural Library J7 [1] 24, presented by H.Garling 1855.

36. William **PORDEN**
Alternative plan for the first floor of the Professors' houses.
Pen and ink with grey wash; 26×34.5 cm. *Literature*: J.Lever, 1976, p.91. *Location*: British Architectural Library J7 [1] 25, presented by H.Garling 1855.

37. William **PORDEN**
Plan of the ground floor of the Master's house. (see Fig.12, p.42)
Pen and ink with grey wash; 25×35.5 cm. Scale: ⅛ in. to 1 ft. Inscribed: 'Masters House/ Ground Story with Set of/ Chambers adjoining/ First Plan'. *Literature*: J.Lever, 1976, p.91. *Location*: British Architectural Library J7 [1] 26, presented by H.Garling 1855.

38. William **PORDEN**
Plan of the first floor of the Master's house.
Pen and ink; 26×35 cm. Scale: ⅛ in. to 1 ft. Inscribed: 'Chamber/ Plan of Masters House'. *Literature*: J.Lever, 1976, p.91. *Location*: British Architectural Library J7 [1] 27, presented by H.Garling 1855.

39. William **PORDEN**
Alternative ground plan of the Master's house.
Pen and ink over some pencil underdrawing; 25×35.5 cm. Scale: ⅛ in. to 1 ft. Inscribed: 'Masters House/ Ground Story'. *Literature*: J.Lever, 1976, p.91. *Location*: British Architectural Library J7 [1] 28, presented by H.Garling 1855.

40. William **PORDEN**
Alternative plan for the first floor of the Master's house.
Pen and ink over some pencil underdrawing; 26×34.5 cm. Scale: ⅛ in. to 1 ft. Inscribed: 'Masters House/ Bed Chamber Story', 'Porch'. *Literature*: J.Lever, 1976, p.91. *Location*: British Architectural Library J7 [1] 29, presented by H.Garling 1855.

41. William **PORDEN**
Rough plan of the stables and coach-houses.
Pencil; 33×53 cm. Scale: ⅛ in. to 1 ft. Inscribed: 'Downing College/ Plan of the Stables & Coachhouses'. *Literature*: J.Lever, 1976, p.91. *Location*: British Architectural Library J7 [1] 30, presented by H.Garling 1855.

42. Lewis William **WYATT** (1777–1853)
Plan of the site with block plan of the College. (see Fig.16, p.50)
Pen and washes within ruled border; 35.5 × 60 cm. Signed and dated: 'Lew.s Wyatt/ Arch.t Dec.r 9th 1805'. Inscribed: 'N.o 1' top centre; *Location*: Downing College, Cambridge.

43. Lewis William **WYATT**
Plan of the basement storey.
Pen and ink with grey and black washes within ruled border; 35.5 × 55 cm. Signed and dated: 'Lew.s Wyatt/ Arch.t Dec.r 9th 1805'. Inscribed: 'Basement Story Downing College/ N.o 2' in the centre. *Location*: Downing College, Cambridge.

44. Lewis William **WYATT**
Plan of the first floor.
Pen and ink with grey wash within ruled border; 35.5 × 55 cm. Signed and dated: 'Lew.s Wyatt/Arch.t Dec.r 9th 1805'. Inscribed: 'Chamber Story Downing College/ N.o 4' in the centre. *Location*: Downing College, Cambridge.

45. Lewis William **WYATT**
Plan of the attic storey.
Pen and ink with grey washes within ruled border; 35.5 × 60 cm. Signed and dated: 'Lew.s Wyatt/ Arch.t Dec.r 9th 1805'. Inscribed: 'Attic Story Downing College/ N.o 5' in the centre. *Location*: Downing College, Cambridge.

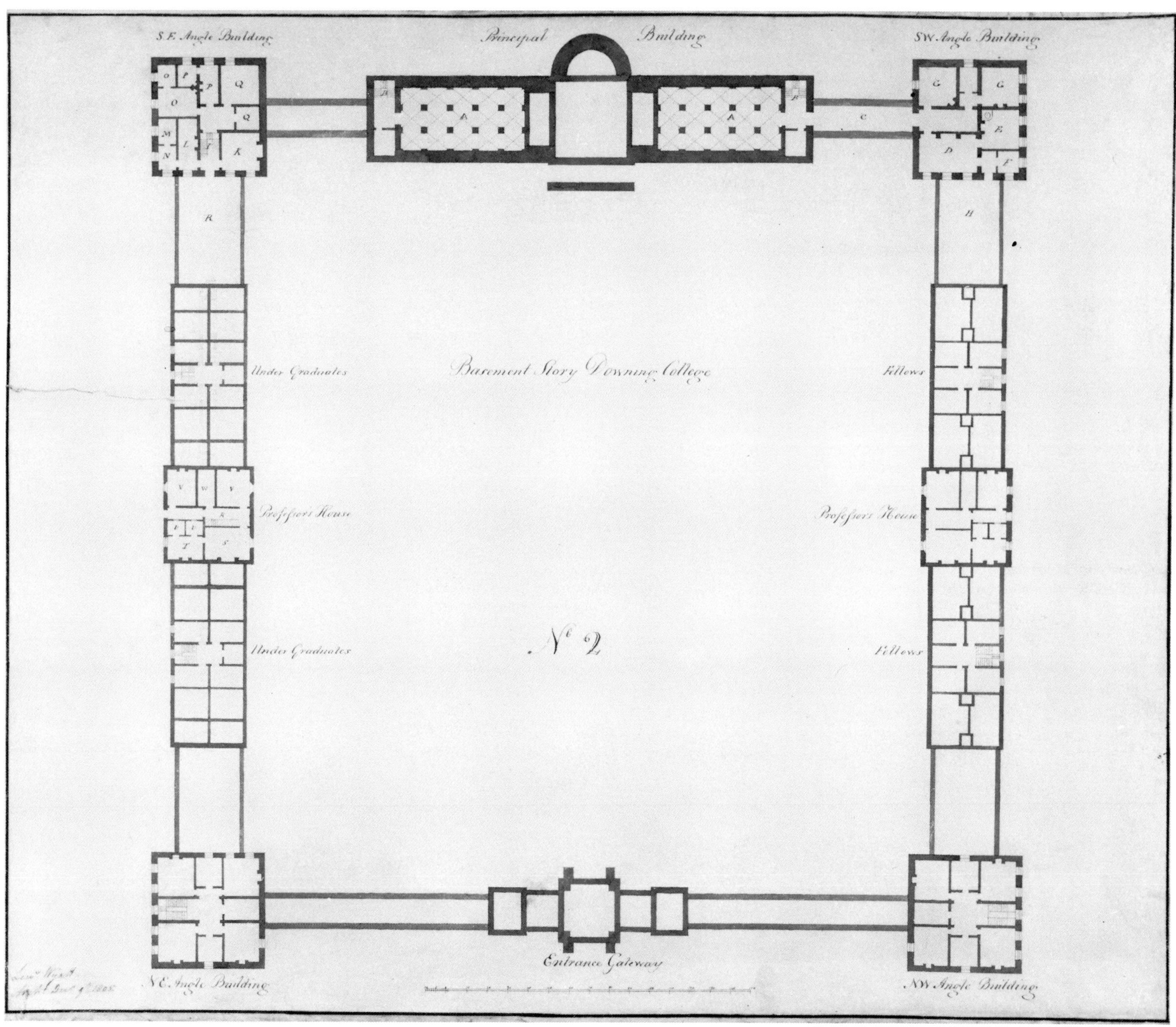
S.E. Angle Building
Principal Building
SW Angle Building
Basement Story Downing College
Under Graduates
Fellows
Professors House
Professors House
Under Graduates
Fellows
No 2
Entrance Gateway
N.E. Angle Building
NW Angle Building

43

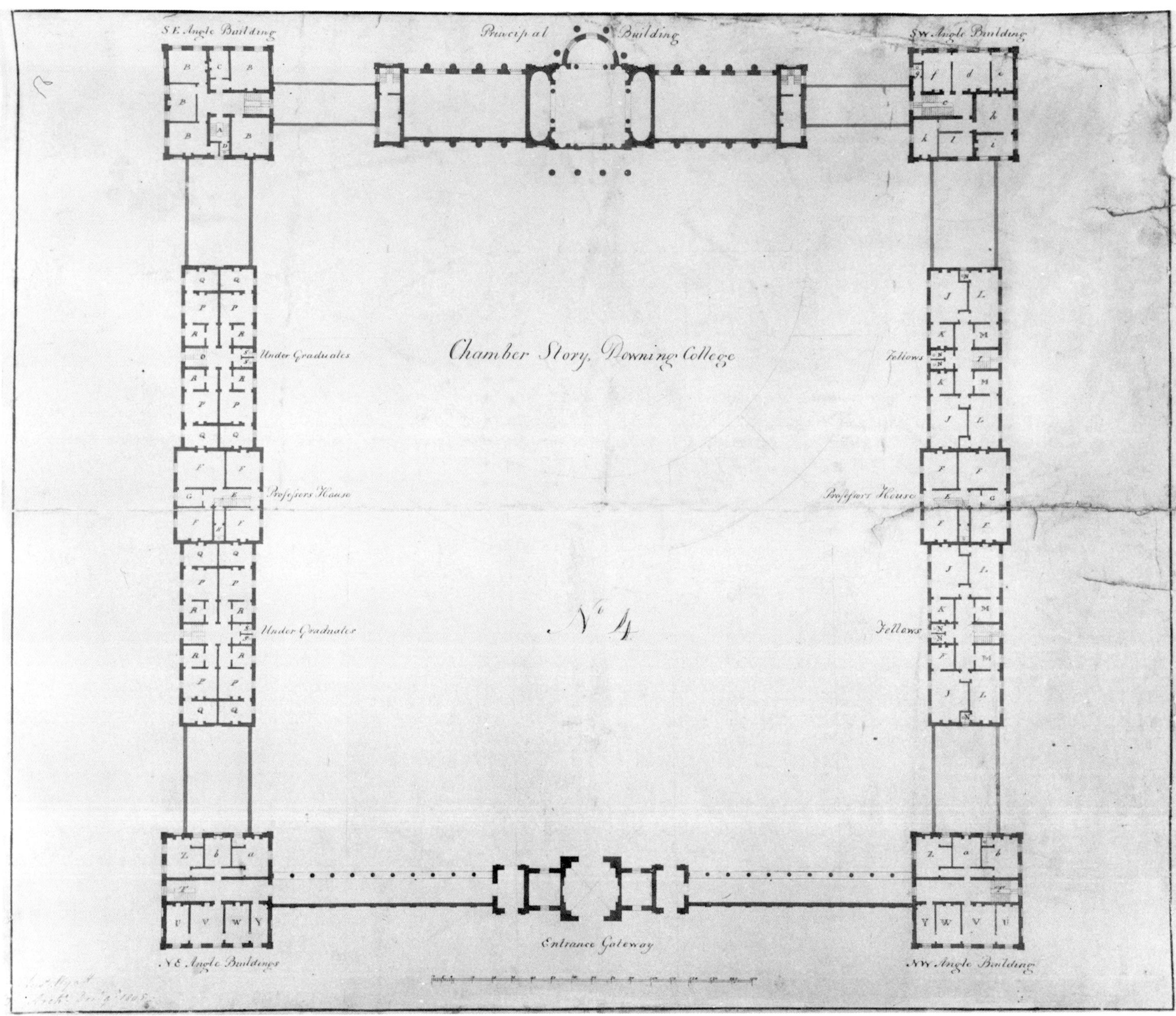
S E Angle Building
Principal Building
SW Angle Building
Under Graduates
Chamber Story, Downing College
Fellows
Professors House
Professors House
Under Graduates
No 4
Fellows
Entrance Gateway
N E Angle Buildings
NW Angle Building

44

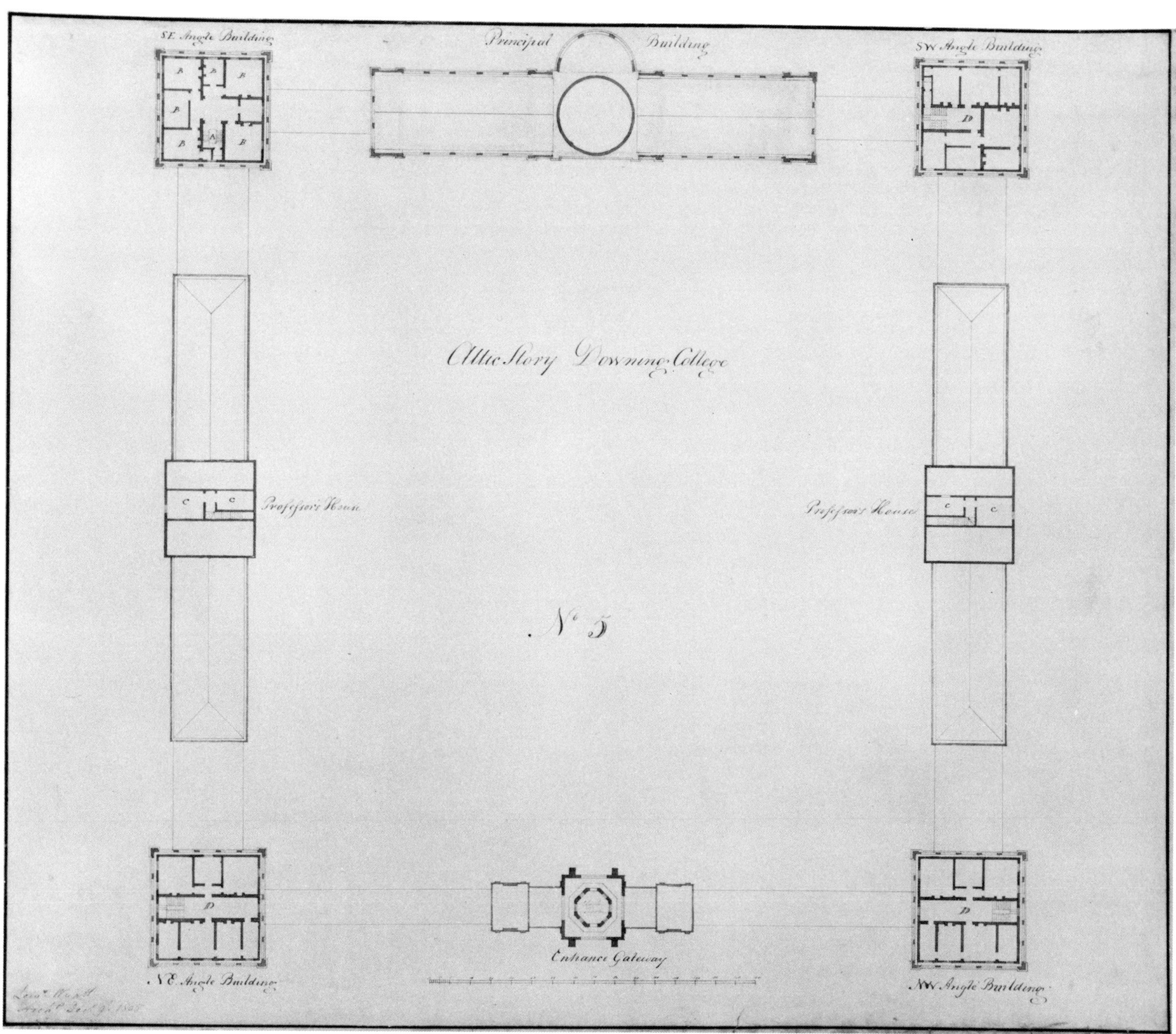
S.E. Angle Building
Principal Building
S.W. Angle Building
Attic Story Downing College
Professor's House
Professor's House
No. 5
N.E. Angle Building
Entrance Gateway
N.W. Angle Building

45

46. Lewis William **WYATT**
Elevation of the south front of the south range. (see Pl.VII)
Pen and washes within ruled border; 35.7×115.5 cm. Scale: 1:100. Signed and dated: 'Lew.s Wyatt/ Arch.t Dec.r 9th 1805' in lower left corner. Inscribed: 'N.o 1' in lower right corner. *Exhibited*: 'The Age of Neo-Classicism', London, 1972; 'The Triumph of the Classical. Cambridge Architecture 1804–1834', Cambridge 1977. *Reproduced*: B.Little, 1971, pp. 190–201; D.Watkin, 1977, pl.2. *Location*: Downing College, Cambridge.

Lewis Wyatt's design for the College pivotted round this highly refined elevation. He proposed a quadrangle closed on the south by the building illustrated here which contained the Chapel, a library and the Hall.

47. Lewis William **WYATT**
Elevation of the south front of the north range. (see Fig.17, p.51)
Pen, ink and grey wash; 35.5×115.5 cm. Scale: 1:100. Signed and dated: 'Lew.s Wyatt/ Arch.t Dec.r 9th 1805' in lower left corner. Inscribed 'N.o 7' in lower right corner. *Exhibited*: 'The Triumph of the Classical. Cambridge Architecture 1804–1834', Cambridge 1977. *Location*: Downing College, Cambridge.

Access into the quadrangle was through a reduced triumphal arch surmounted by a clock-turret placed in the middle of the north range. A Doric colonnade linked the Porter's Lodge to corner pavilions on the east and west sides.

48. Lewis William **WYATT**
Elevation of the east range with section of the triumphal arch and chapel. (see Fig.18, p.51)
Pen and washes; 34.2×114.5 cm. Scale: 1:100. Signed and dated: 'Lew.s Wyatt/ Arch.t Dec.r 9th 1805' in lower left corner. Inscribed 'N.o 8' in lower right corner. *Location*: Downing College, Cambridge.

The east and west ranges were plain, the only decoration being provided by pilasters marking the projecting three-bayed centre of the building.

49. Lewis William **WYATT**
Section through the Chapel. (see Pl.VIII)
Pen and washes; 34.5×70.5 cm. Signed and dated: 'Lew.s Wyatt/ Arch.t Dec.r 9th 1805' in lower left corner. Inscribed: 'N.o 9' in lower right corner. *Location*: Downing College, Cambridge.

The interior of the chapel was to be decorated with rich plaster work.

50. William **WILKINS** (1778–1839)
Perspective of the south front of the south range. (see pl.IX)
Pen and washes within triple ruled border, on three sheets of paper joined together; 49.6×178.5 cm. *Exhibited*: 'The Age of Neo-Classicism', London, 1972; 'The Triumph of the Classical. Cambridge Architecture 1804–1834', Cambridge 1977. *Reproduced*: B.Little, 1971, pp. 190–201; D.Watkin, 1977, pl.2. *Location*: Downing College, Cambridge.

51. William **WILKINS**
Sectional view of the chapel and library. (see Fig.30, p.62)
Pen and ink with yellow, grey, red and black washes; 46×91.6 cm. Scale unnumbered. Inscribed in pencil: 'Library', 'Chapel'. *Reproduced*: R.W.Liscombe, 1980, pl.15. *Location*: Downing College, Cambridge SWP1.

52. William **WILKINS**
Elevation of the south front of the south block.
Pen and ink with grey wash; 46×118 cm., four sheets of paper pasted together. Scale unnumbered. Inscribed: 'Elevation of the/ South Front', 'Library', 'Chapel', and measurements. *Reproduced*: R.W.Liscombe, 1980, pl.14. *Location*: Downing College, Cambridge SWP2.

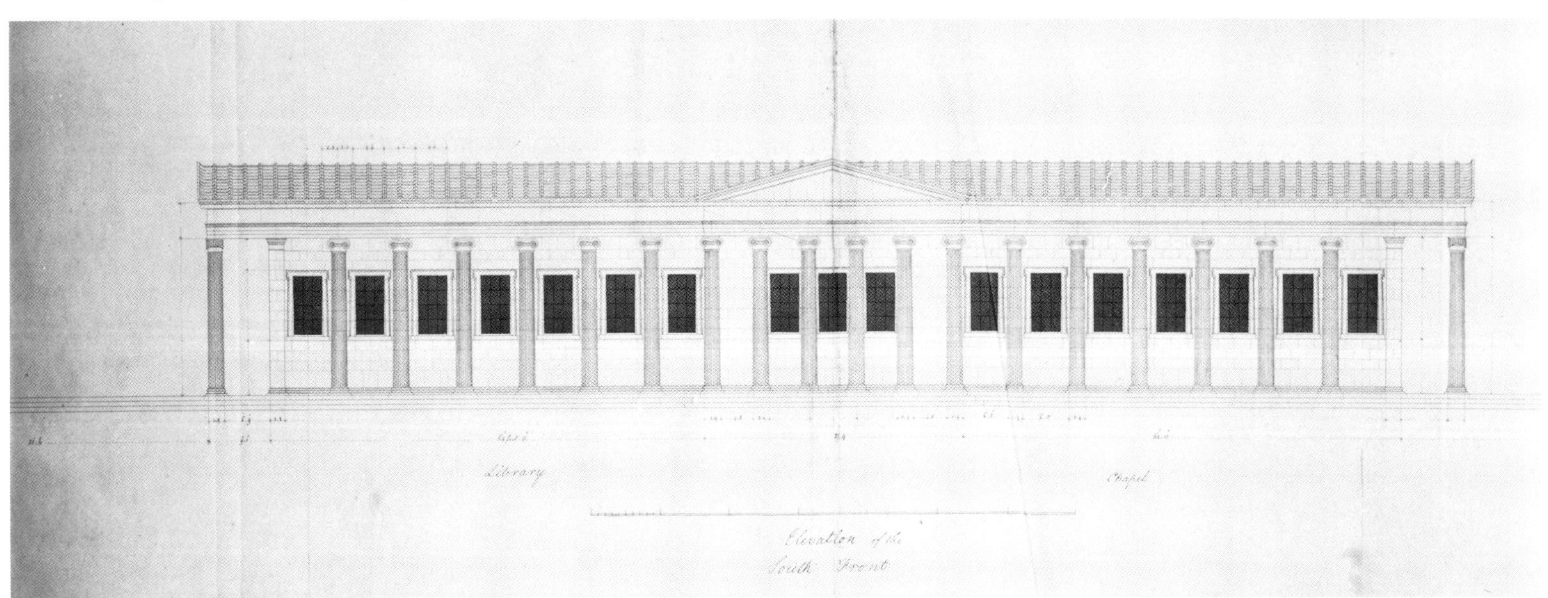

52

53. William **WILKINS**
Section through the chapel.
Pen and ink with yellow, red, black and grey washes; 45.7×58.7 cm. Scale unnumbered.
Inscribed in pencil: 'West End of the Chapel'.
Location: Downing College, Cambridge SWP3.

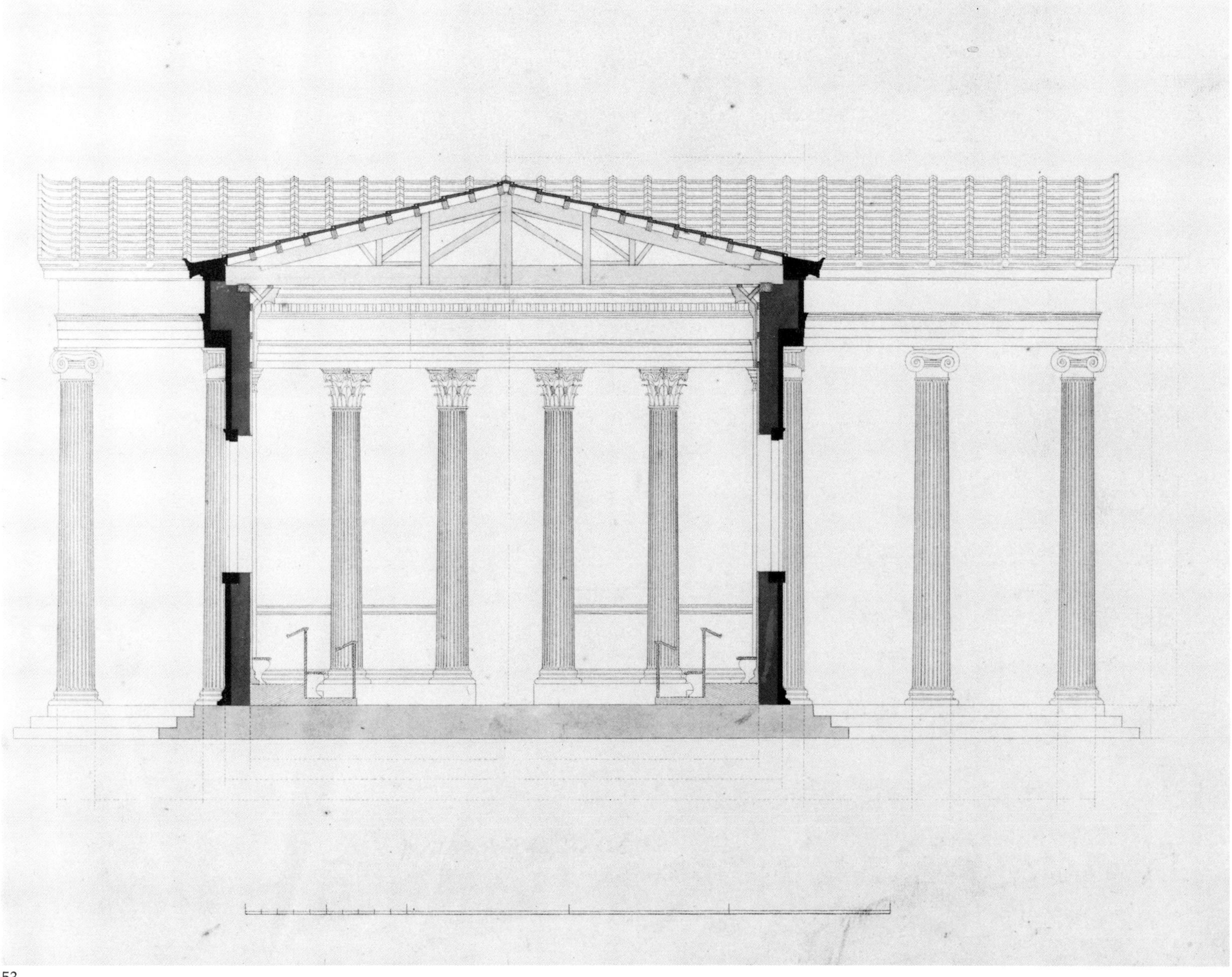

53

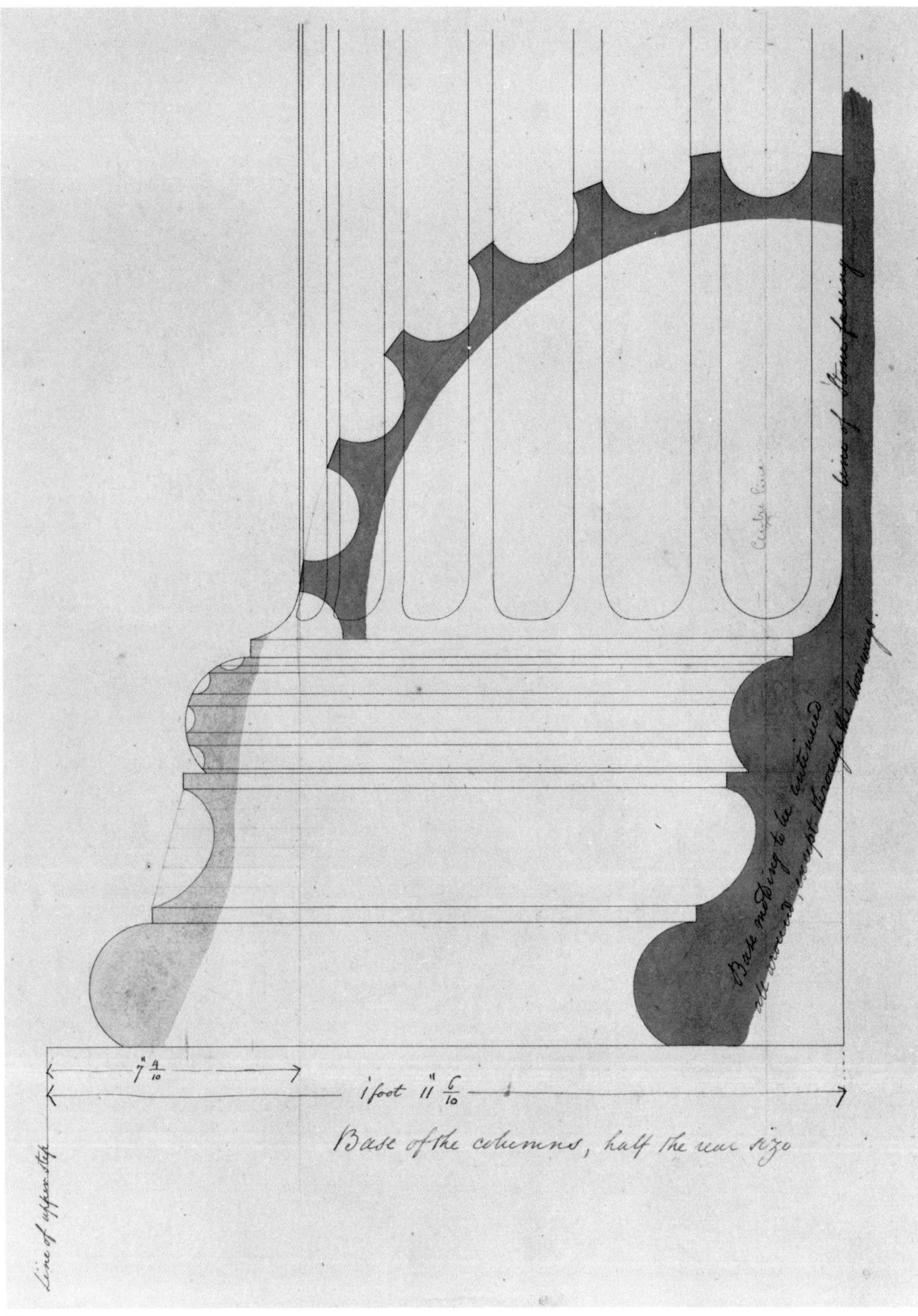

54

54. William **WILKINS**
Details of the base of the Ionic order to be used in the chapel, hall and library.
Pen and ink with pink and grey washes; 46.2×59.5 cm. Inscribed with measurements and 'Chapel, Hall and Library' (along the right upper margin); 'Base moulding to be continued/ all around, except through the door ways'; 'Line of Stone facing'; 'Base of the Columns, half the new size'; 'Line of upper step'; 'Centre line'. *Location*: Downing College, Cambridge SWP4.

55. William **WILKINS** (1778–1839)
Details of the Ionic capitals to be used in the library, hall and chapel. (see Fig.25, p.58)
Pen and ink with grey wash; 46.1×59.5 cm. Inscribed with measurements: 'Library Hall & Chapel' (along the right upper margin); 'Plan of the fluting at the/ top of the shaft'; 'face of the wall'; 'Front of the Capitals/ half the real size'; 'Section through the Capital through the line AB'. VERSO: some measurements inscribed in pencil. *Location*: Downing College, Cambridge SWP5.

56. William **WILKINS**
Profile and section of the volute of the Ionic capital to be used in the chapel, hall and library.
Pen and ink with grey wash; 46.1×59.5 cm. Inscribed with measurements: 'Chapel, Hall & Library' (along the upper right margin); 'Section of the Capital through the line CD'; 'Flank of the Capital, half the real size/ The engaged columns are more than semi-columns/ they project before the face of the wall 13½ inches at/ the necking of the capital and exceed semi-columns by/ half a fluting and a fillet. The excess above semi-columns/ is represented at E'; 'Section of the volute through the line AB'; 'face of the wall'. *Location*: Downing College, Cambridge SWP6.

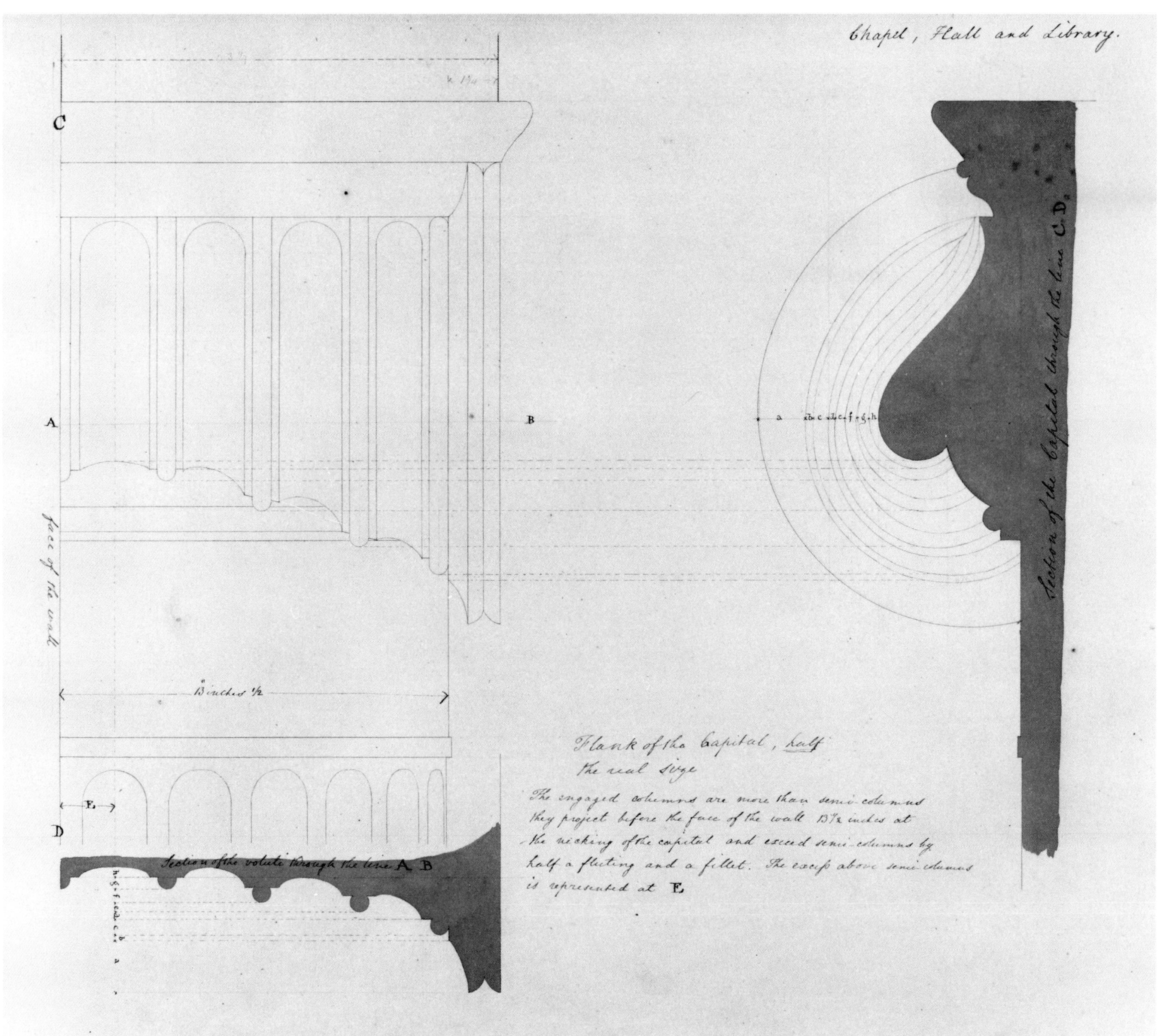
Chapel, Hall and Library.
C
A
B
D
E
face of the wall
13 inches ½
Section of the volute through the line A B
Section of the capital through the line C D
Flank of the Capital, half
The real size
The engaged columns are more than semi-columns they project before the face of the wall 13½ inches at the necking of the capital and exceed semi-columns by half a fluting and a fillet. The excess above semi-columns is represented at E

56

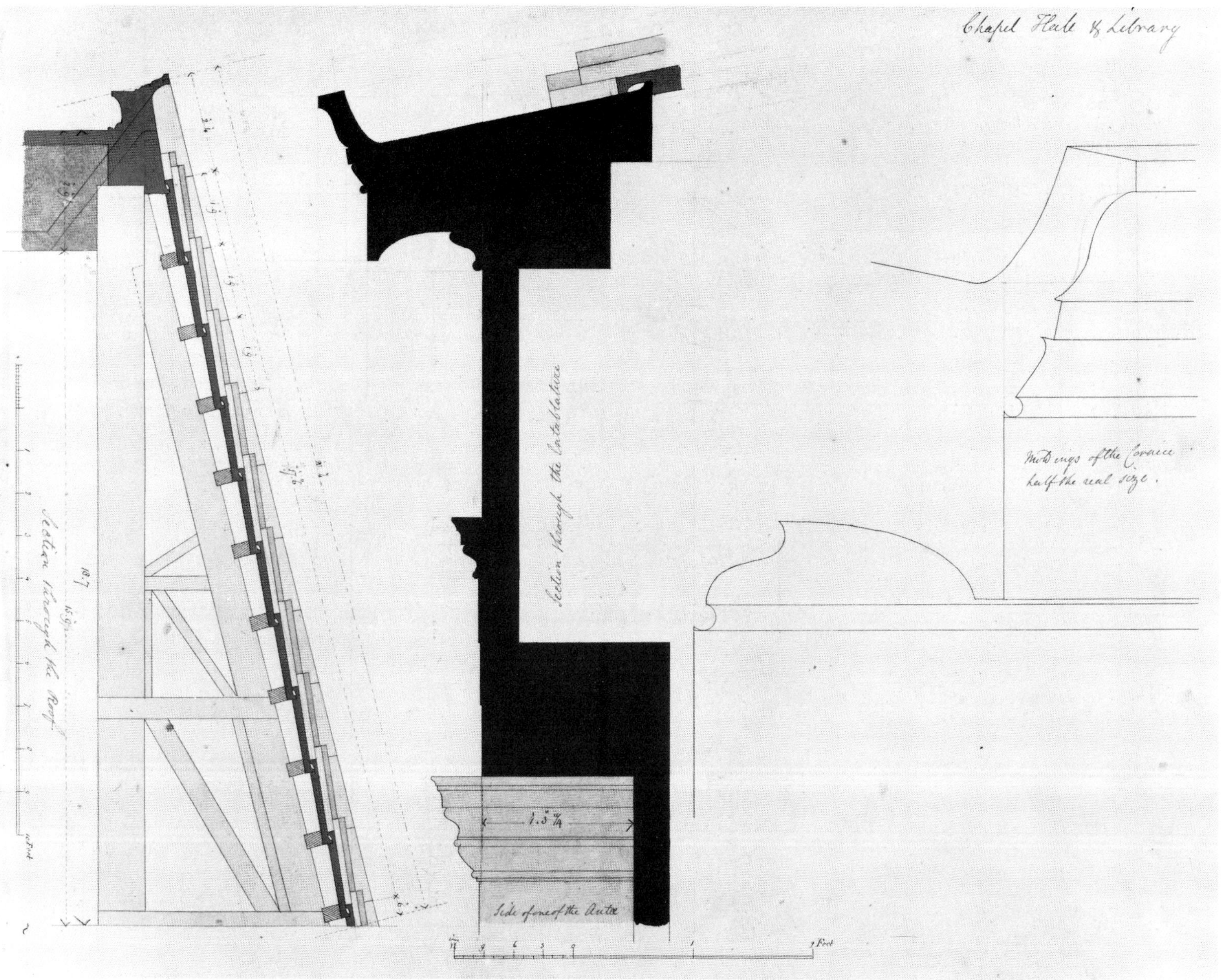
Chapel Hall & Library
Section through the Entablature
Mouldings of the Cornice
Half the real size.
Side of one of the Antae
Section through the Roof

58

57. William **WILKINS**
Profile and detail of the decoration of the Ionic pilaster to be used in the chapel, hall and library. (see Fig.26, p.59)
Pen and ink with grey wash over some pencil underdrawing; 46.5×59.5 cm.
Inscribed: 'Buildings of the South front' 'Chapel Hall & Library' (both along the upper right margin); 'External antae, or pilasters, half the/ Full Size'; 'Section'. *Location*: Downing College, Cambridge SWP7.

58. William **WILKINS**
Sectional views of the entablature, roof, and profile of the cornice to be used in the chapel, library and hall.
Pen and ink with yellow, red, brown, black and grey washes over some pencil underdrawing; 46.1×59.8 cm. Inscribed: 'Chapel Hall & Library' (along the upper right margin); 'Section through the Roof'; 'Section through the Entablature'; 'Side of one of the Antae'; 'Moldings of the Cornice/ half the real size'. *Location*: Downing College, Cambridge SWP8.

59. William **WILKINS**
Plan of the portico of the Propylea.
Pen and ink with grey washes over some pencil underdrawing; 46.5×59.7 cm. Scale: 1/16 in. to 1 ft. Inscribed with measurements: 'Propylea' (upper right corner); 'North/ Plan of the Principal Portico' (along the lower margin). *Location*: Downing College, Cambridge SWP9.

60. William **WILKINS**
Plan of the main portico of the Propylea at roof level.
Pen and ink with yellow, red, grey and black washes; 46.4×59.7 cm. Scale unnumbered. The left side of the drawing shows the portico's ceiling with its square coffers, the right hand side shows the beams supporting the plastered ceiling and the actual roof tiles. *Location*: Downing College, Cambridge SWP10.

61. William **WILKINS**
Elevation of the north front showing the Propylea flanked by the Porters' Lodge and the lecture room. (see Fig.20, p.54)
Pen and ink; 46.2×92.2 cm. Scale unnumbered. Inscribed in pencil: 'North Front'; 'Porters' Lodge &c.'; 'Propylea or Entrance facing the Botanic Garden'; 'Lecture Room'. *Reproduced*: R.W.Liscombe, 1980, pl.17. *Location*: Downing College, Cambridge SWP11.

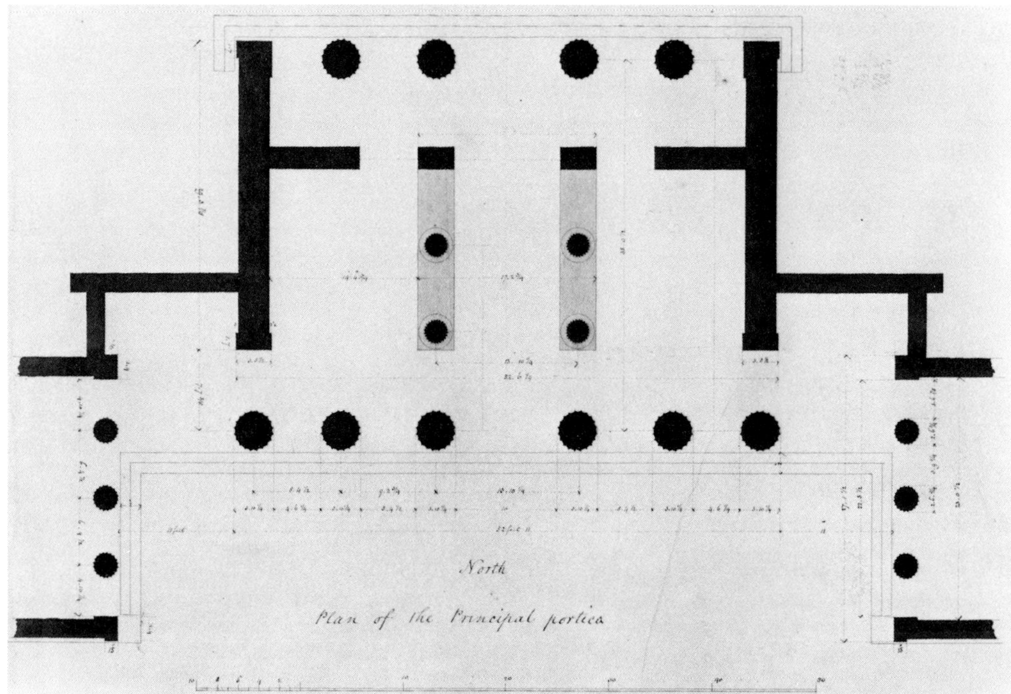

59

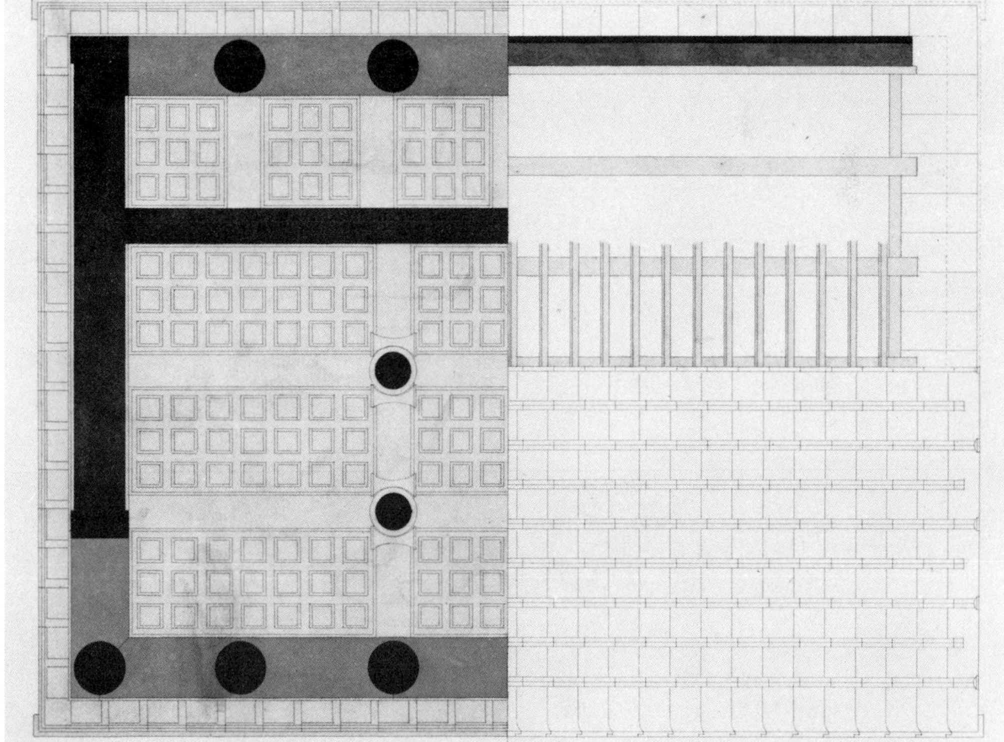
60

62. William **WILKINS**
Elevation of the principal portico of the Propylea with sectional views of the porticoes of the Porters' Lodge and lecture room.
Pen and ink with red and black washes over some pencil underdrawing; 46.2×92.2 cm. Scale ⅒ in. to 1 ft. Inscribed with measurements: 'Propylea' (in the upper right margin); 'The Epystilia must be single stones in length/ they may be two stones in width./ The tympanum of the pediment to have no/ horizontal joints' (on the left); 'Porters' Lodge'; 'Elevation of the Principal Portico/ facing the North'; 'Lecture Room'. *Reproduced*: D.Watkin, 1968, pl.17. *Exhibited*: 'The Triumph of the Classical. Cambridge Architecture 1804–1834', Cambridge 1977. *Literature*: D.Watkin, 1977, p.23. *Location*: Downing College, Cambridge SWP12.

63. William **WILKINS**
Sectional view of the Propylea with a view of the principal elevation of the Lecture Room.
Pen and ink with yellow, red, brown and black washes; 46.6×59.7 cm. Scale unnumbered. Inscribed in pencil: 'front of the lecture Room/ facing the East'; 'Section through the Propylea'. *Location*: Downing College, Cambridge SWP13.

64. William **WILKINS**
West elevation of the Propylea with a view of the principal elevation of the Porters' Lodge.
Pen and ink over some pencil underdrawing; 46×60.1 cm. Scale ⅒ in. to 1 ft. Inscribed with measurements: 'Propylea' (along the upper right margin); 'North'; 'South'; 'Flank of the Principal Portico/ facing West./ The Portico in the distance is the front of the Porters' Lodge'. VERSO: some measurements inscribed in pencil. *Location*: Downing College, Cambridge SWP14.

65. William **WILKINS**
Elevation of the south front of the principal portico of the Propylea. (see Fig.21, p.55)
Pen and ink over some pencil underdrawing; 46×58.6 cm. Inscribed with measurements: 'Propylea' (on the upper right margin); 'Elevation of the South Front of the Principal Portico' (along the lower margin). *Location*: Downing College, Cambridge SWP15.

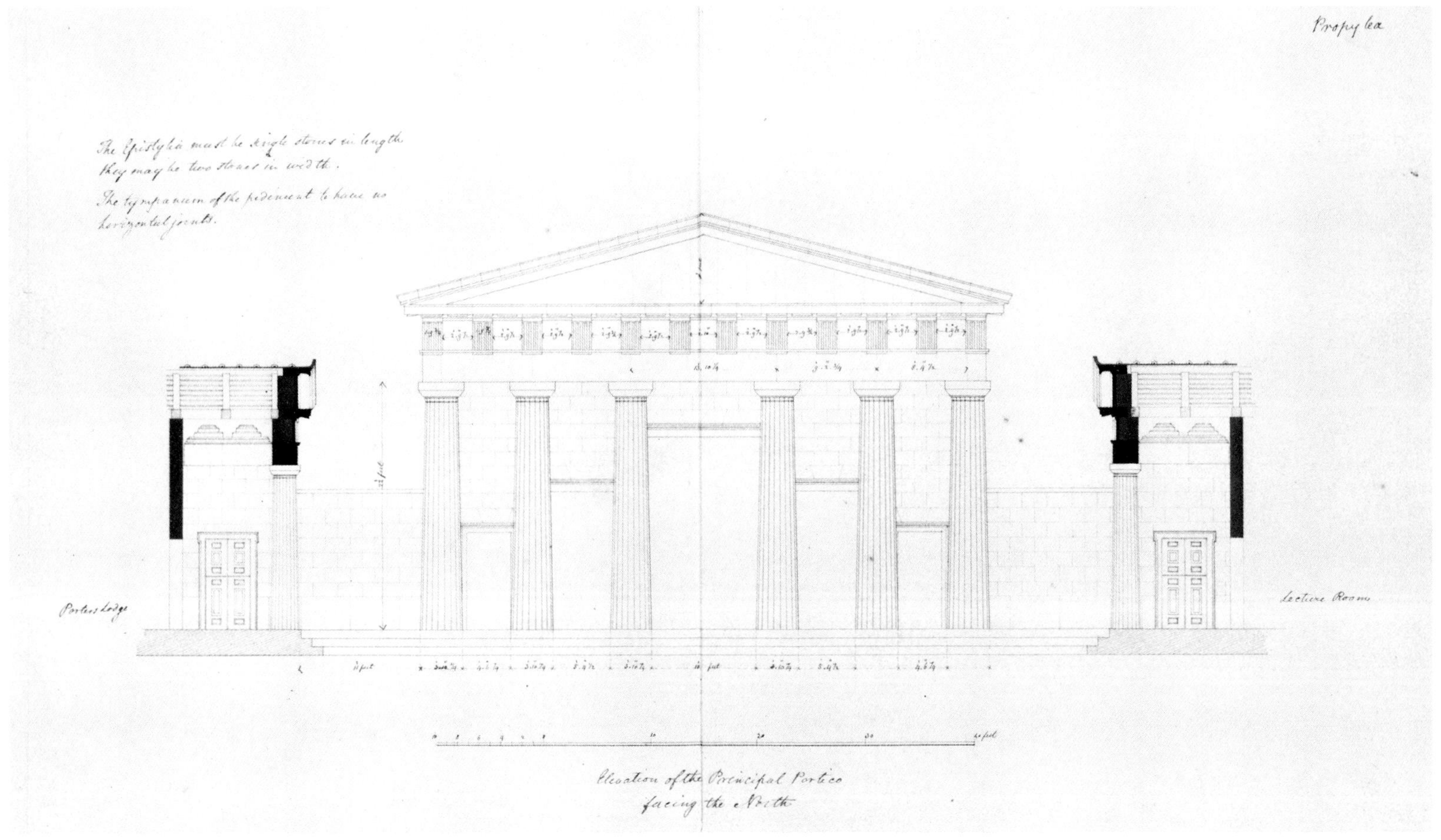

62

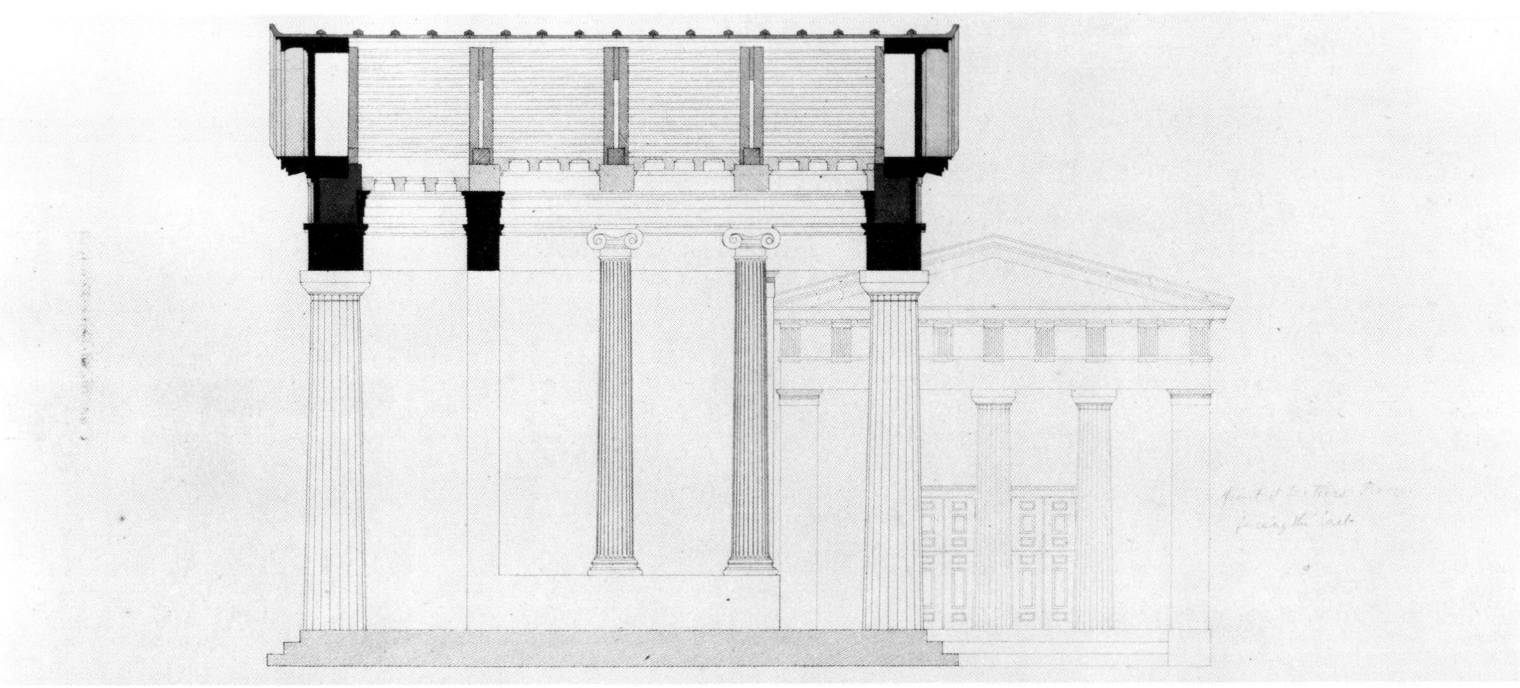

63

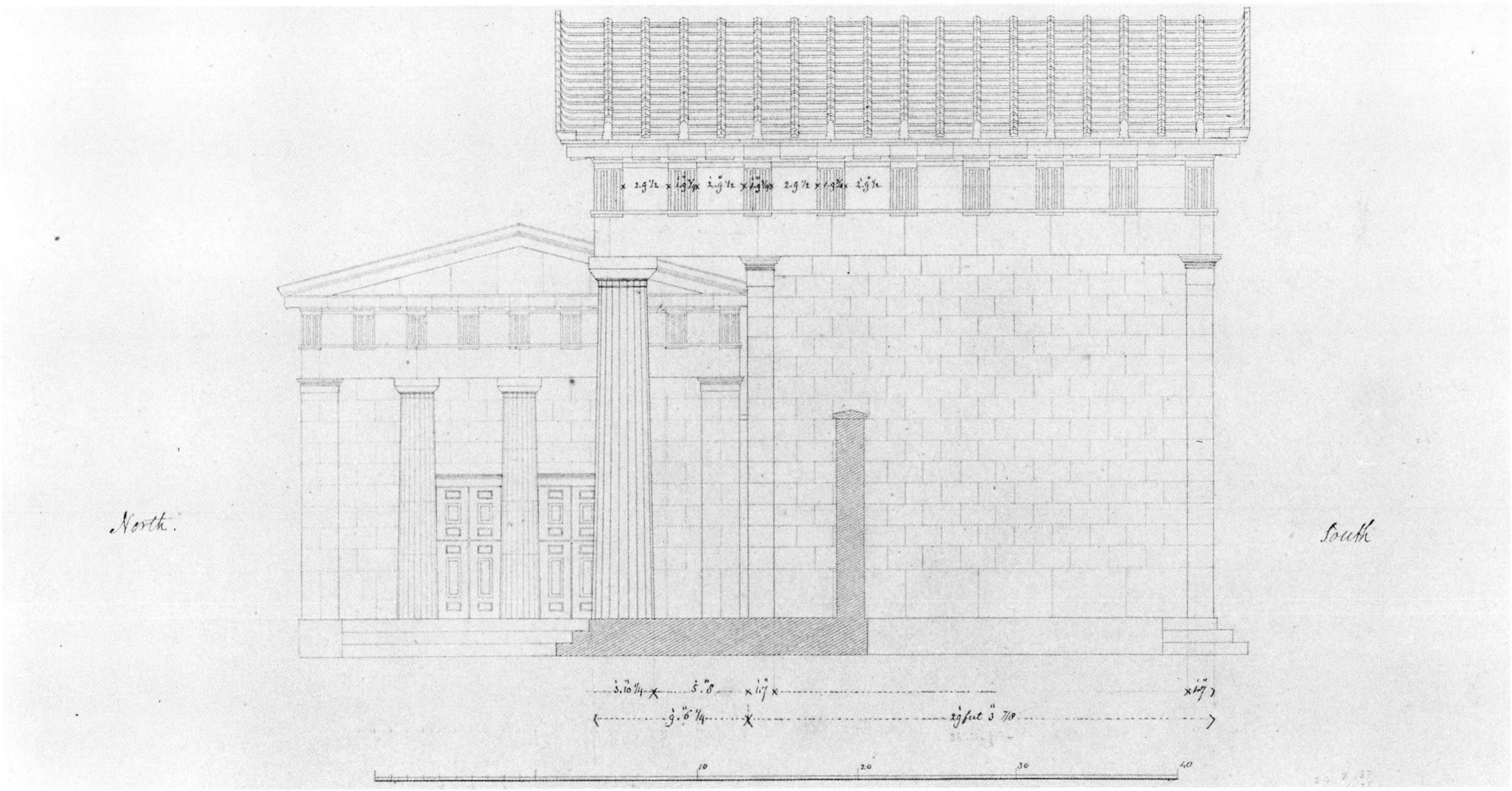

64

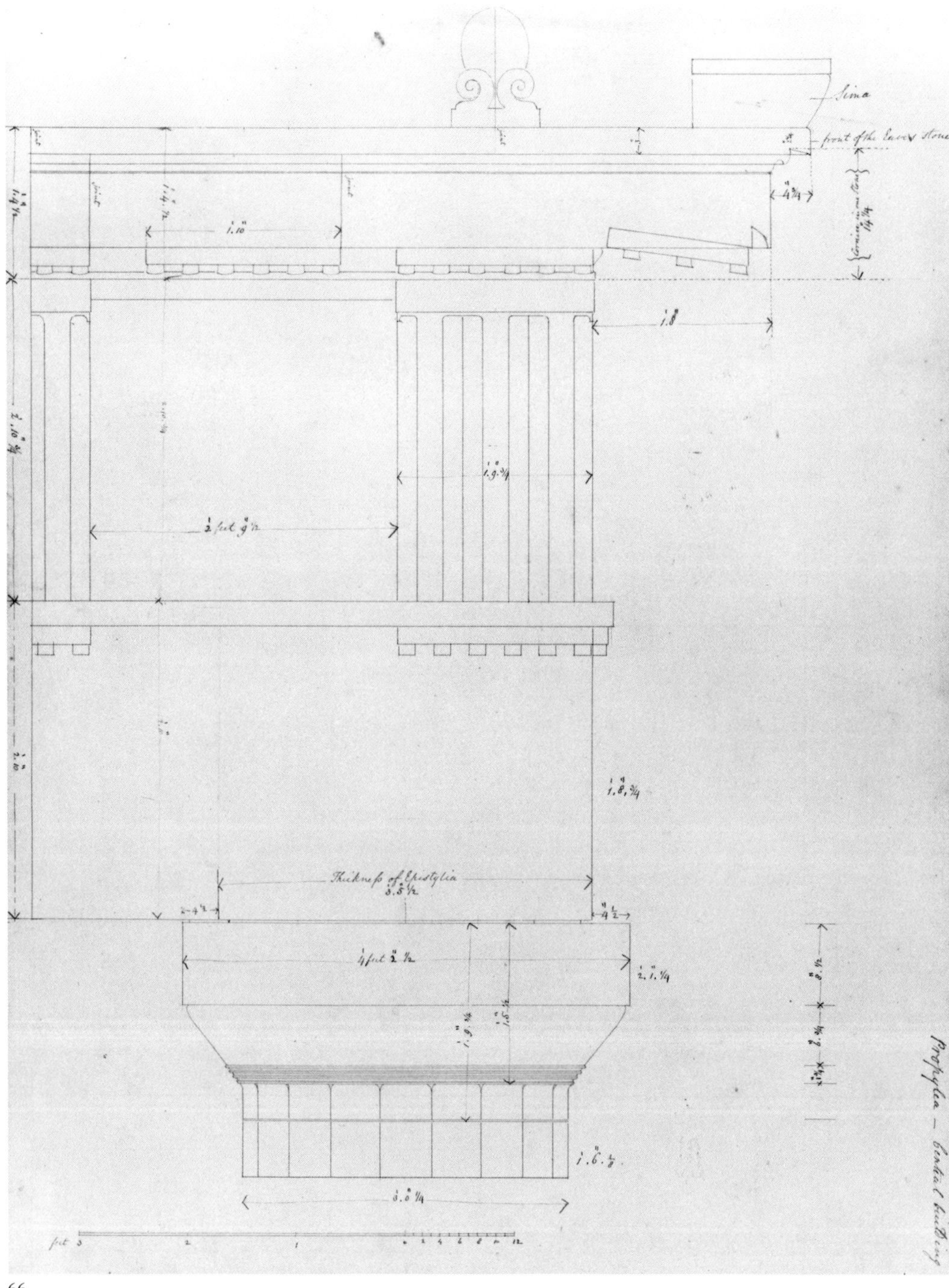

66

66. William **WILKINS**
Profile of the Doric entablature in the main building of the Propylea.
Pen and ink over some pencil underdrawing; 60.2×46.3 cm. Scale ½ in. to 1 ft. Inscribed with measurements: 'Propylea – Central building' (along upper right margin); 'Sima'; 'front of the Eaves stone'; 'Cornice in one stone'; 'Thickness of the Epistylia'. VERSO: some measurements inscribed in pencil. *Location*: Downing College, Cambridge SWP16.

67. William **WILKINS**
Frontal view and profile of the Doric capital for the central building of the Propylea.
Pen and ink with grey wash over some pencil underdrawing; 46.6×60 cm. Inscribed: 'A small rise in the centre of the Abacus to prevent the Epistylia from bearing upon its edges'; 'Propylea. Central Building'; 'Capital of the Antaea real Size'; 'Annulets & contour of the Ovolo of the Capital Real size'; 'Half the Capital of the columns/ Half the real size'; 'In one stone'. *Location*: Downing College, Cambridge SWP17.

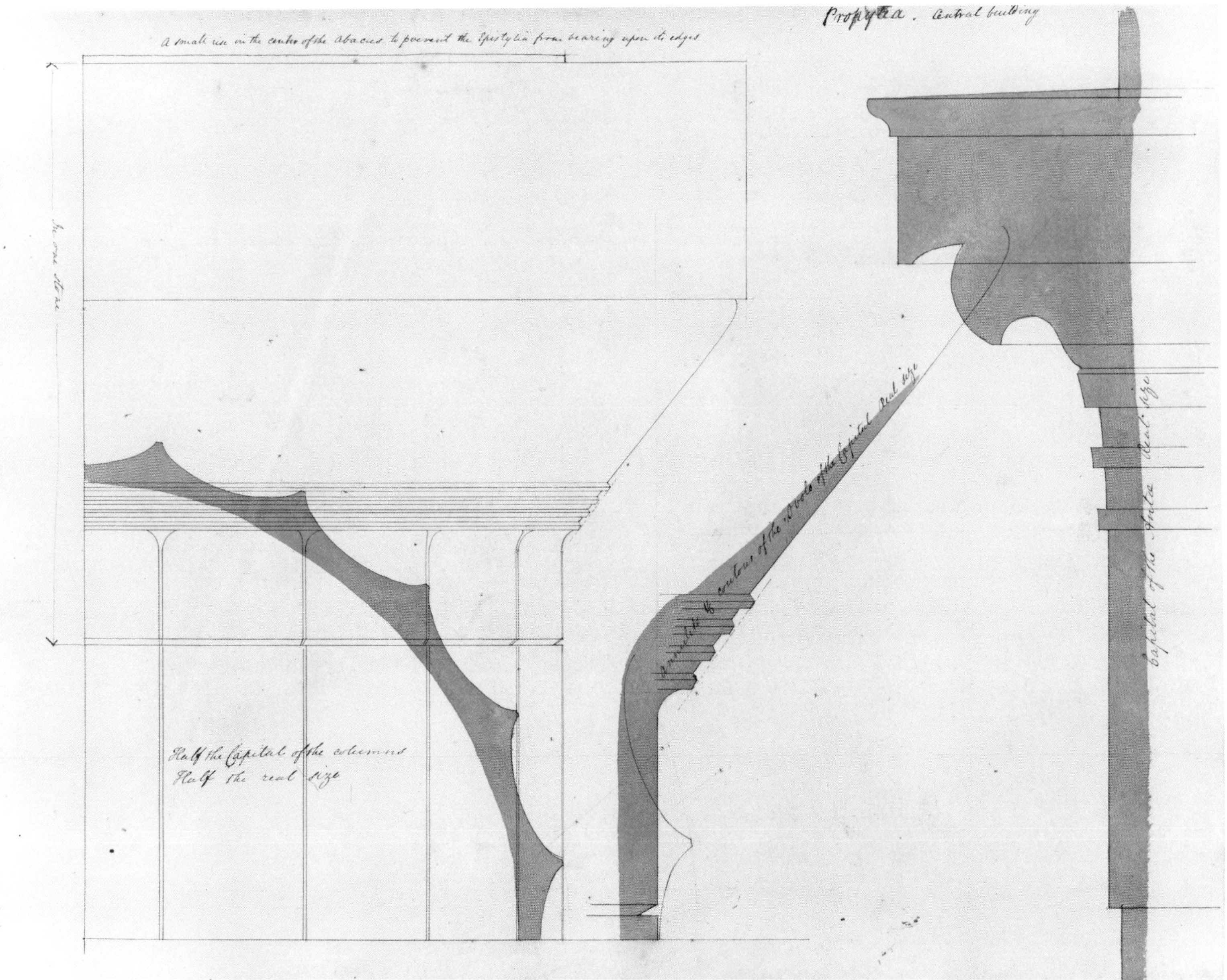

67

68. William **WILKINS**
Section through the roof of the main portico of the Propylea.
Pen and ink with yellow, brown and grey washes over some pencil underdrawing; 46.3×59.7 cm. Scale unnumbered. *Location*: Downing College, Cambridge SWP18.

68

69. William **WILKINS**

Plan and elevation of part of the roof of the central building of the Propylea, with details of the upper- and under-faces of the tiles.

Pen and ink with grey and brown washes over some pencil underdrawing; 46.4×60 cm. Scale 1/12 in. to 1 ft. Inscribed: 'End of the stones forming the Sima upon the pediment'; 'The tiles and capping tiles to be of/ artificial Stone'; 'Propylea Central part/ the raking stones forming the eaves, in the/ flanks of the Central building, must be worked/ out of blocks 4′7¼″ long, 2′3″ wide & 10¼″ in depth. In the centre of each block a check/ is worked out (A.A) to stop the capping tiles./ The ends are saddled as shewn at B.B. The/ joints here will be covered by the capping tiles/ which extend to the edge of the Eaves & are/ terminated by a flowered ornament'; 'Eaves raking stones'; 'Upper face of the tiles'; 'Under face of the Tiles'; 'Plan of part of the Roof'. *Location*: Downing College, Cambridge SWP19.

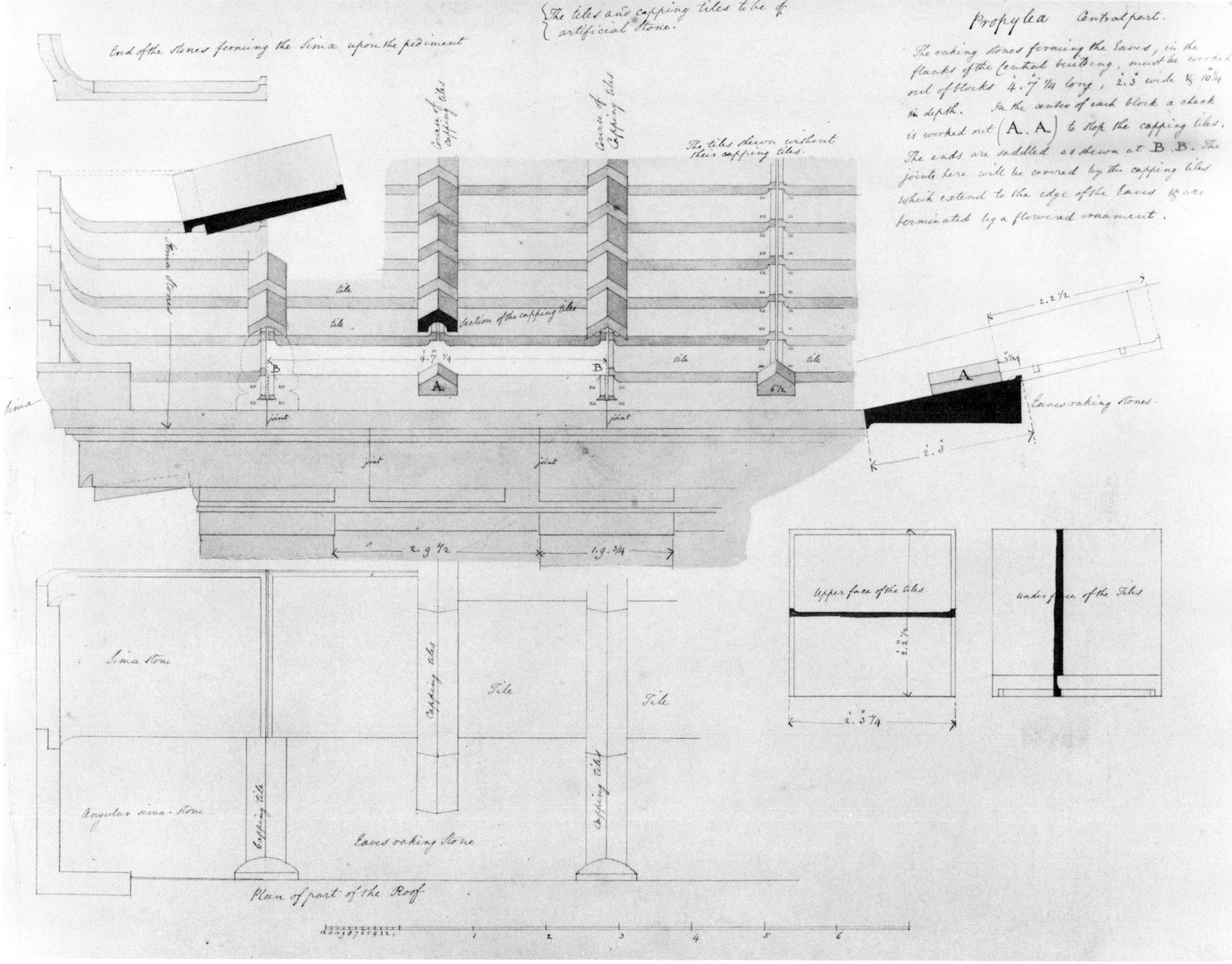

69

70. William **WILKINS**
North elevation of the wings of the Propylea. Pen and ink over some pencil underdrawing; 46.2×59.8 cm. Scale 1/10 in. to 1 ft. Inscribed with measurements: 'All the cornice stone excepting the two at the angles and that in the centre to be precisely the same width viz. 19⅛‴' (on the left); 'The stone forming the cornice over the centre Triglyph to be only the width of the mutule'; 'Propylea-Wings' (upper right corner); 'North side of one of the Wings/ for the Porters' Lodge' (along the lower margin).
Location: Downing College, Cambridge|SWP20.

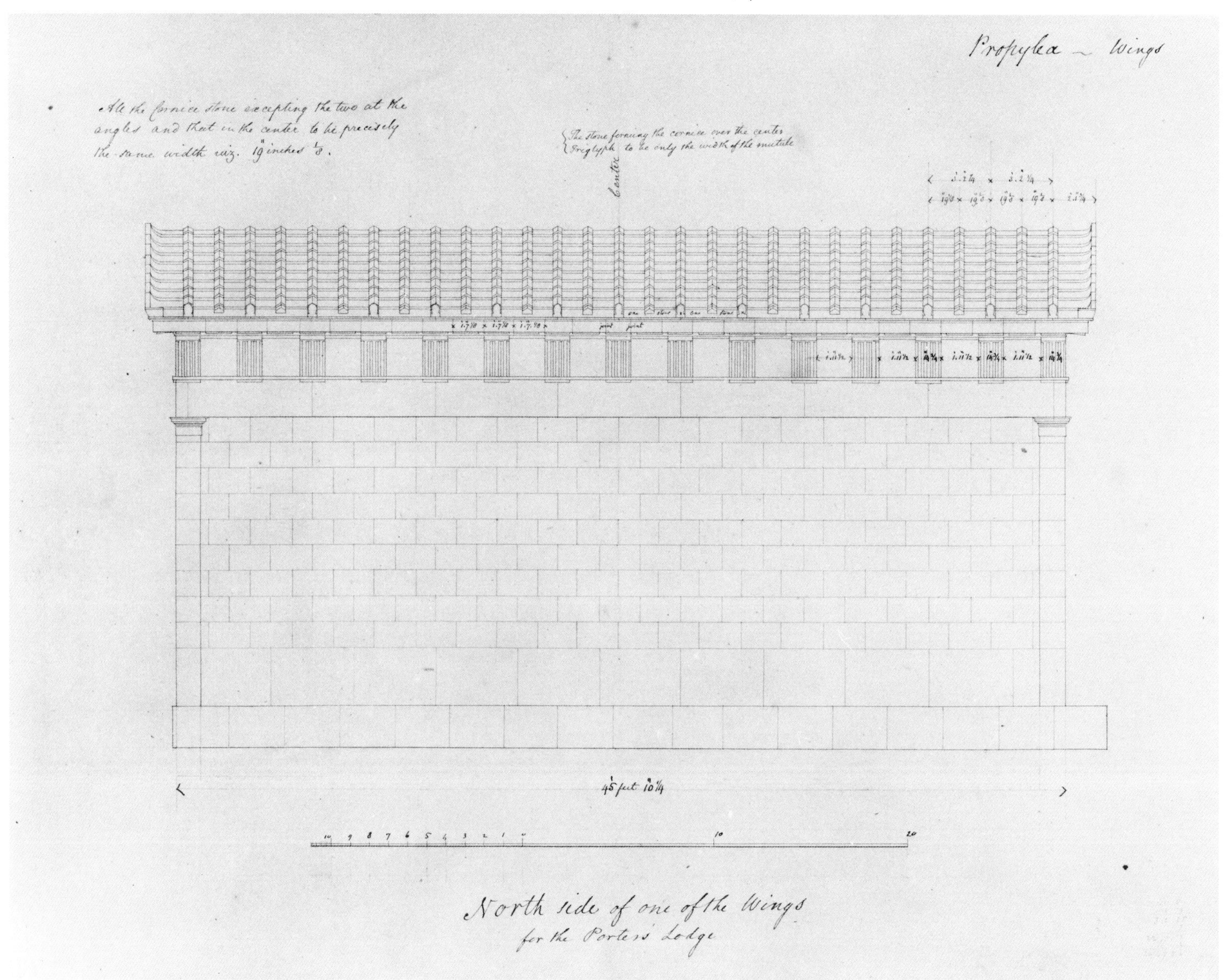

70

71. William **WILLKINS**

Principal elevation of the Porters' Lodge.
Pen and ink over some pencil underdrawing; 46×59.8 cm. Scale 1/10 in. to 1 ft. Inscribed with measurements: 'Propylea – Wings' (upper right corner); 'Front of one of the smaller porticoes/ facing the West' (along the lower margin).

Location: Downing College, Cambridge
SWP21.

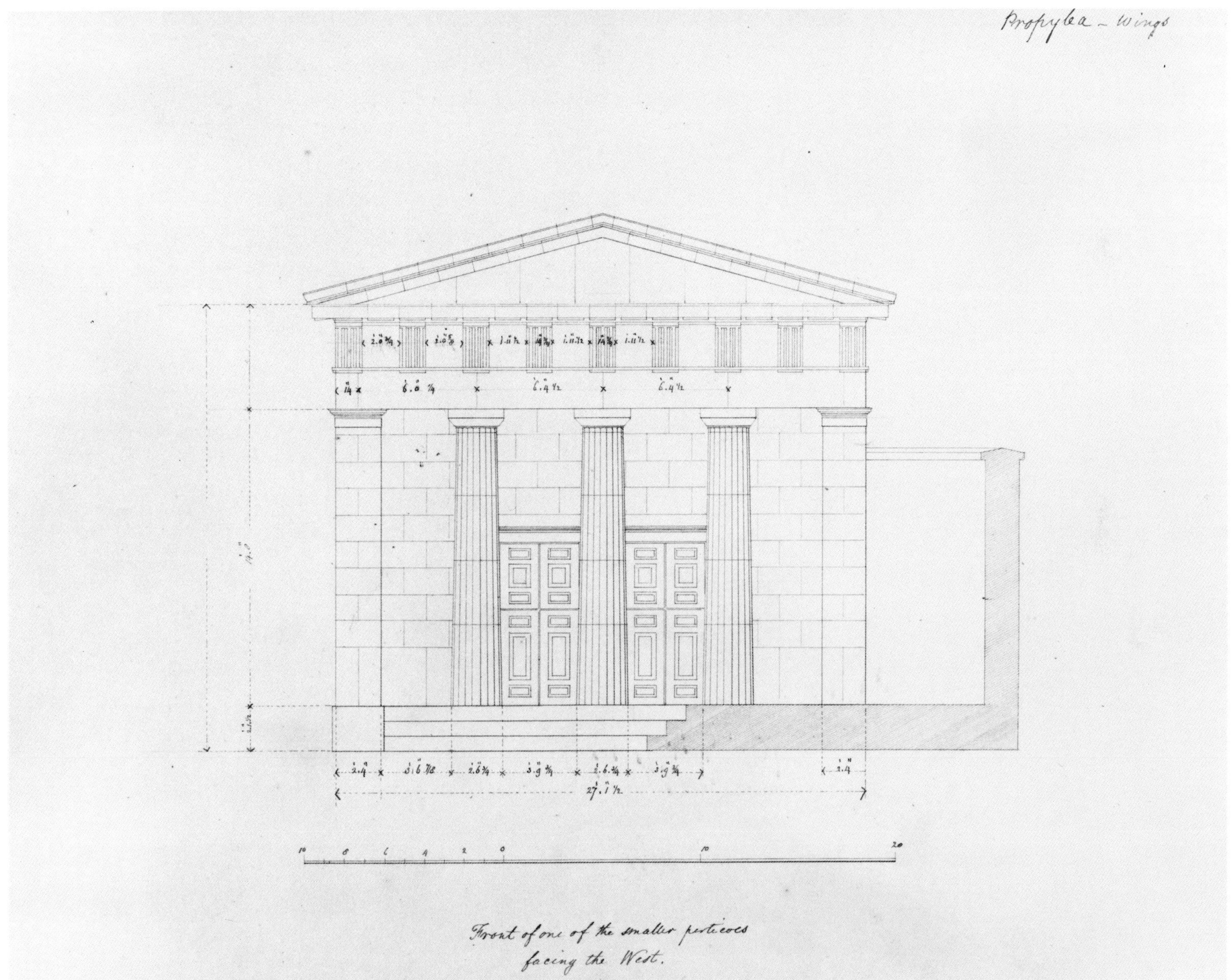

71

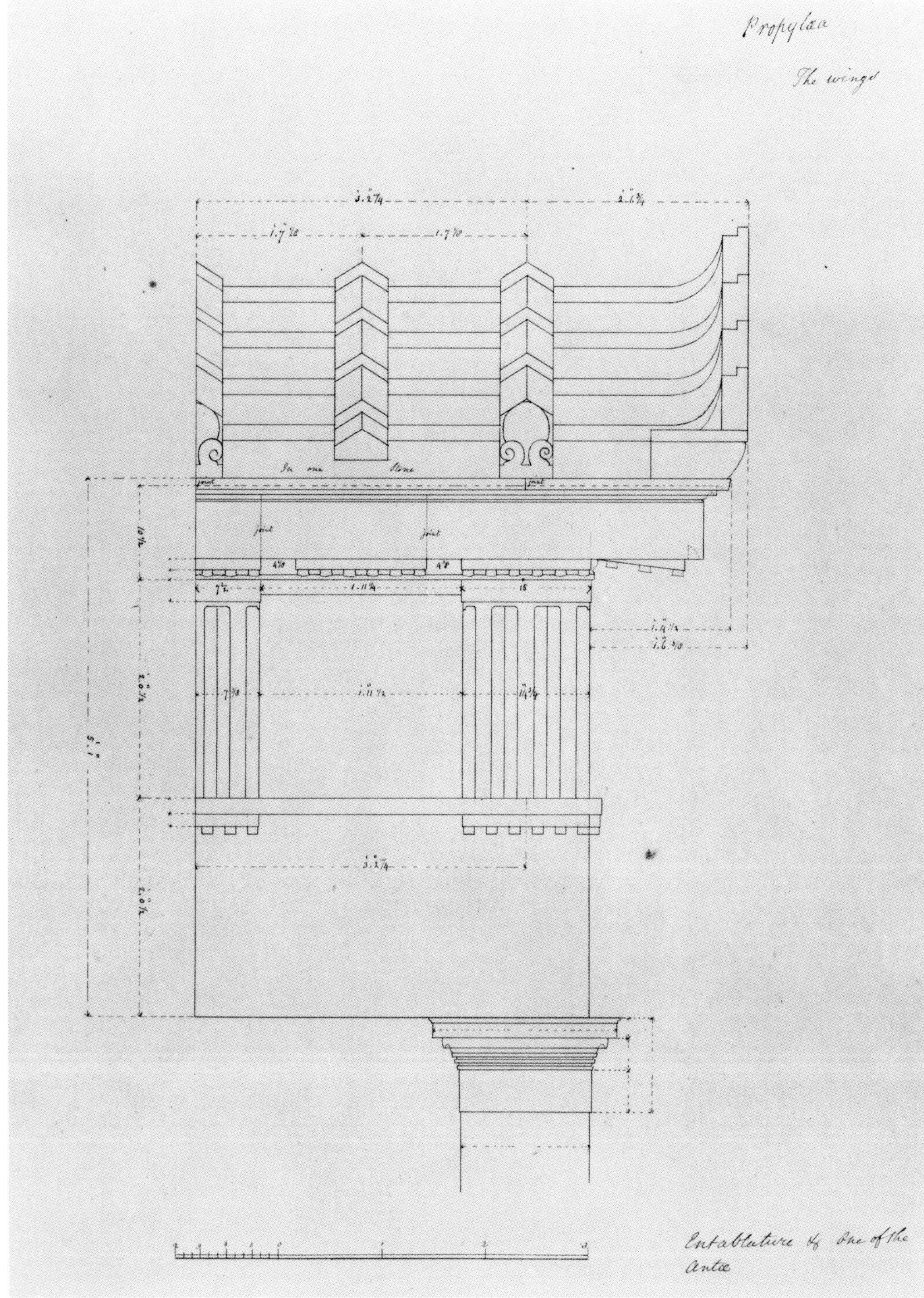

72

72. William **WILKINS**
Profile of the entablature and of one of the antae in the wings of the Propylea.
Pen and ink; 59.9×46.1 cm. Scale 1⁄12 in. to 1 ft.
Inscribed with measurements: 'Propylaea/ The Wings' (upper right corner); 'Entablature & one of the/ Antae' (lower right corner).
Location: Downing College, Cambridge
SWP22.

73. William **WILKINS**
Section through the roof of one of the wings of the Propylea.
Pen and ink with brown, yellow, black, grey and red washes over some pencil underdrawing; 59.9×46.4 cm. Scale 1/12 in. to 1 ft. Inscribed with measurements: 'Propylea/ The Wings' (upper right corner); 'Section through the Roof of one of the Porticoes' (lower right corner). *Location*: Downing College, Cambridge SWP23.

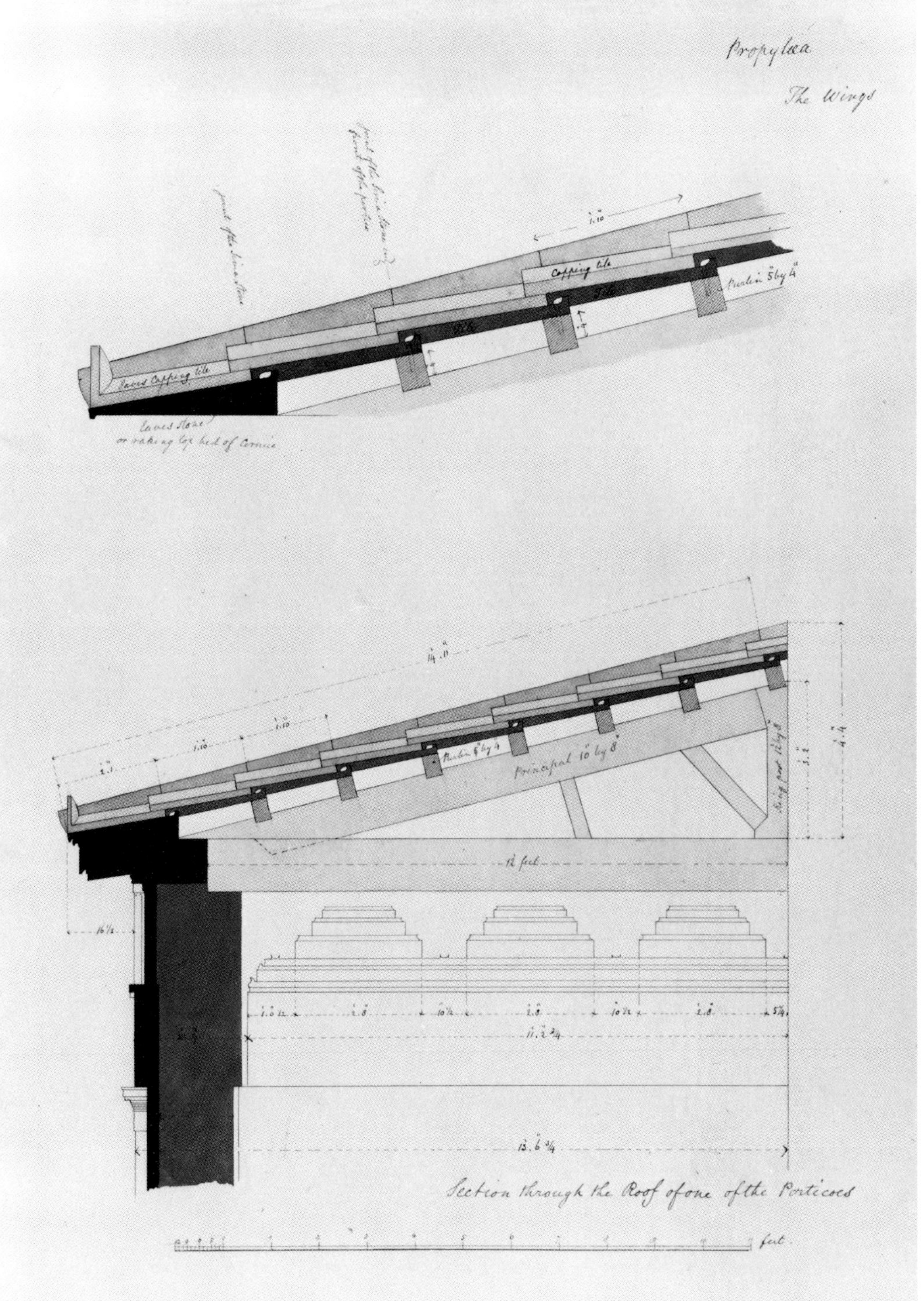

73

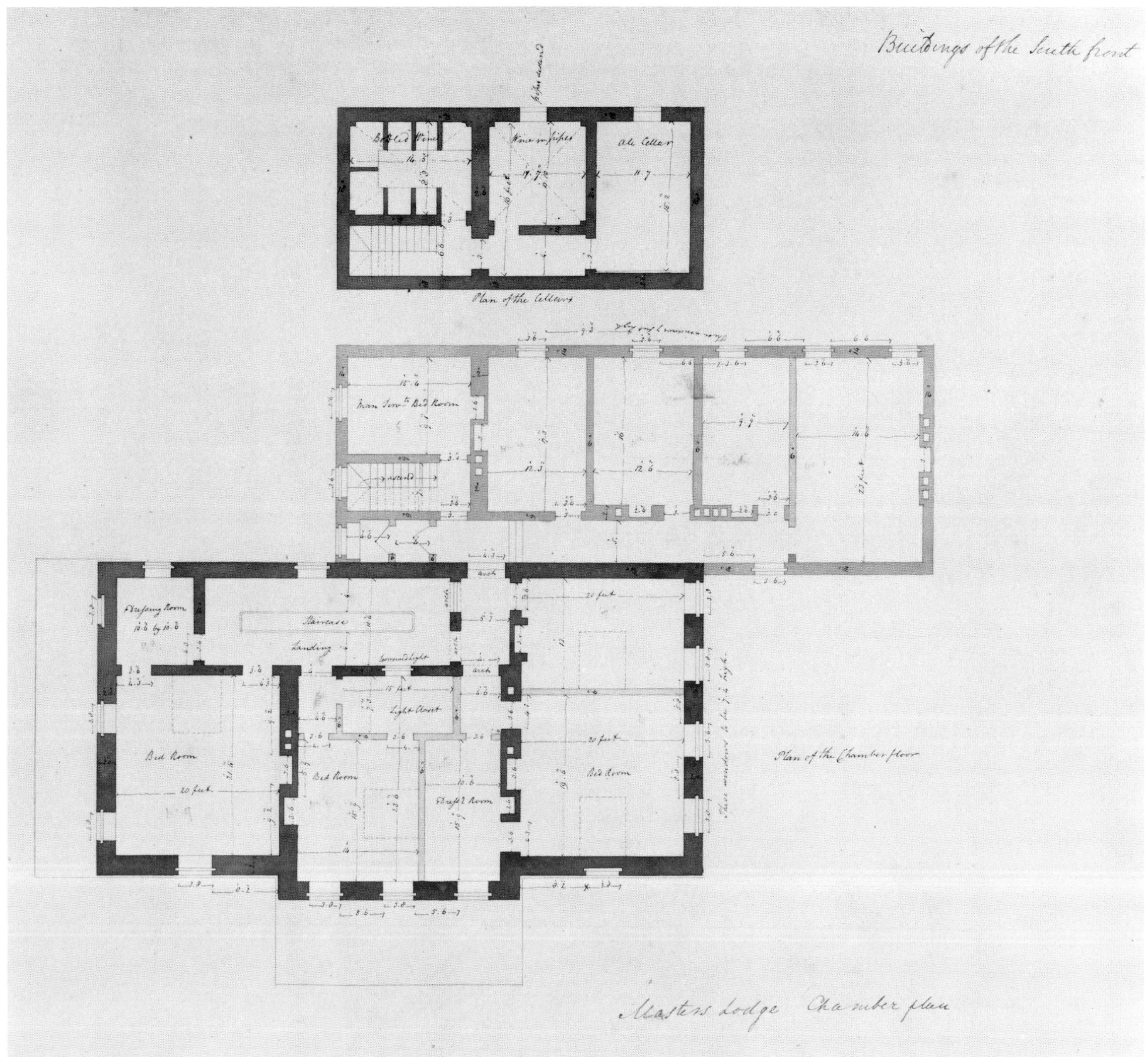
Buildings of the South front
Bottled Wine
Wine in pipes
Ale Cellar
Plan of the Cellars
Man Servts Bed Room
Dressing Room
Staircase
Landing
Light Closet
Bed Room
Bed Room
Bed Room
Plan of the Chamber floor
Masters Lodge Chamber plan

76

74. William **WILKINS**
Elevation of part of the East range including the Master's Lodge. (see Fig.24, p.27)
Pen and ink with some traces of pencil on two sheets of paper joined together; 46.2×112.8 cm. Scale unnumbered. *Location*: Downing College, Cambridge SWP24.

75. William **WILKINS**
Plan of the ground floor of the Master's Lodge. (see Fig.39, p.71)
Pen and ink with grey and black washes over some traces of pencil; 45.9×59 cm. Inscribed with measurements: 'Master's Lodge' (upper right corner); 'Ground Plan/ South' (lower left margin); 'AA The centre of the ground must be taken & the line AA to be 176 feet 6 inches distant from it'; 'The Chimney flues are all to be carried up in the cross walls. The foundations of the walls EE to be three feet in thickness & to be carried up to within 10 inches below the floor line'; 'This front to be faced with brick from the pilaster/ Architrave round the windows'; 'The bottom of this window to be 11 feet from the floor of the Staircase & 5 Squares deep'; 'Window 10 feet high'. *Location*: Downing College, Cambridge SWP25.

76. William **WILKINS**
Plans of the cellars and of the first floor of the Master's Lodge.
Pen and ink with yellow and grey washes over some traces of pencil; 46.3×59.6 cm. Inscribed with measurements: 'Buildings of the South front' (upper right corner); 'Plan of the Chamber floor' (in a different handwriting); 'Masters Lodge Chamber plan' (along the lower right margin); 'Plan of the Cellars' (in a different handwriting, along the bottom). *Location*: Downing College, Cambridge SWP26.

77. William **WILKINS**
Sections through the roof of the kitchens and of the Master's Lodge.
Pen and ink with yellow, red and black washes, over some pencil underdrawing; 59.7×46.4 cm. Scale 1/10 in. to 1 ft. Inscribed with measurements: 'Buildings of the South front' (along the lower right corner); 'Section through the Roof over/the Masters Lodge & the College Kitchens' (along the bottom). *Location*: Downing College, Cambridge SWP27.

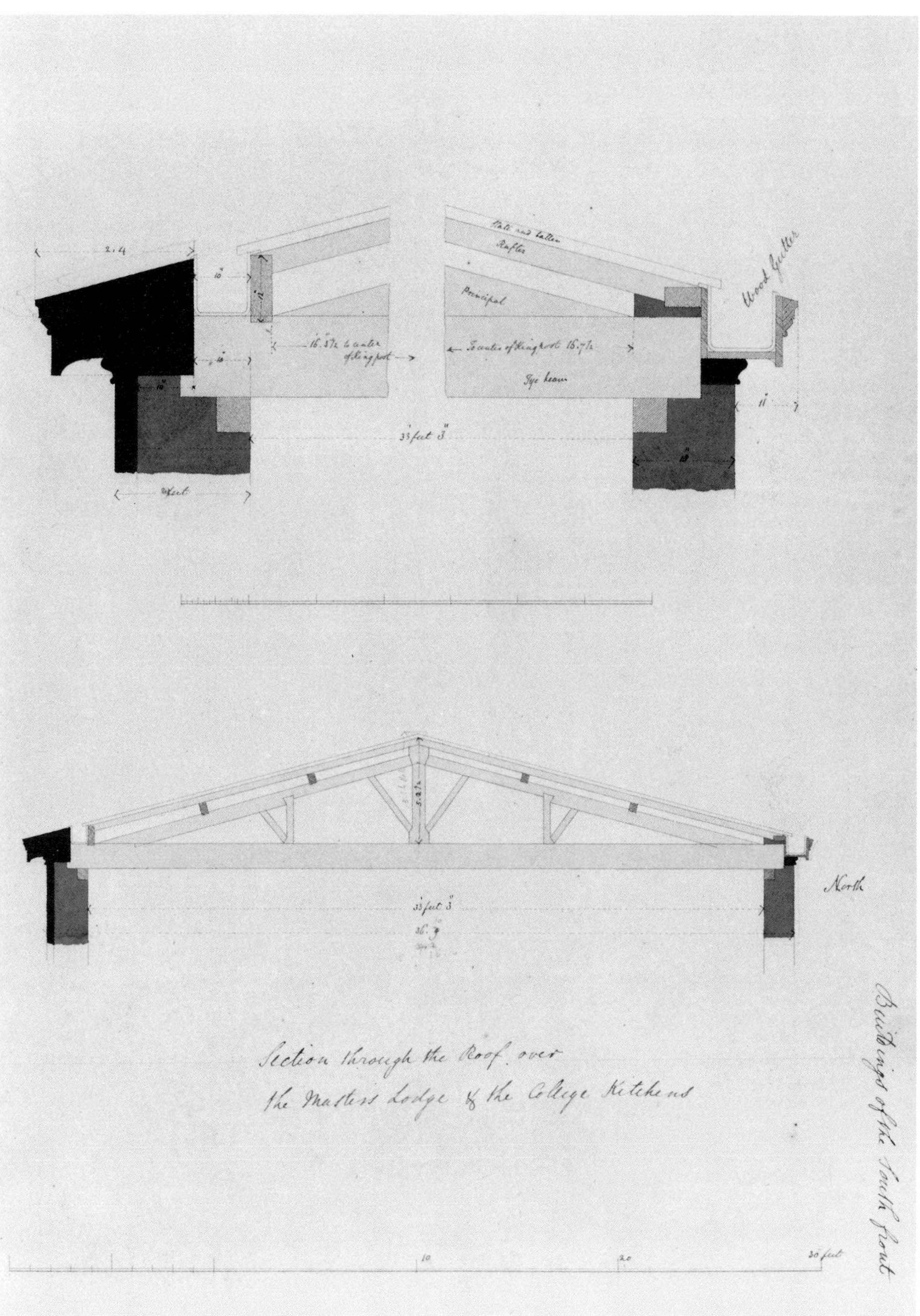

78. William **WILKINS**

Elevation of the windows on the south front of the Master's Lodge and profiles of their architrave mouldings.
Pen and ink with grey washes over some pencil underdrawing; 46.3×59 cm. Inscribed with measurements: 'Buildings of the South front/ Masters Lodge' (upper right corner); 'This width diminishes to ½ an inch at the top of the Window Opening'; 'The same width the Upper Windows'; 'Architrave moldings round the Windows & Doors in the South & West Fronts <u>at Large</u>'; 'Line of the upper fillet of the Base molding'; 'Elevation of the Windows of the South Front'; 'The Three Doors in the West Front are to be 8 feet by 4 feet in the clear of the openings. The Architrave moldings to be the same and inclosed in the same manner, as those round the Windows./ The three Attic Windows in the West Front under the Portico, are to be precisely the same as those in the South front'. *Location*: Downing College, Cambridge SWP28.

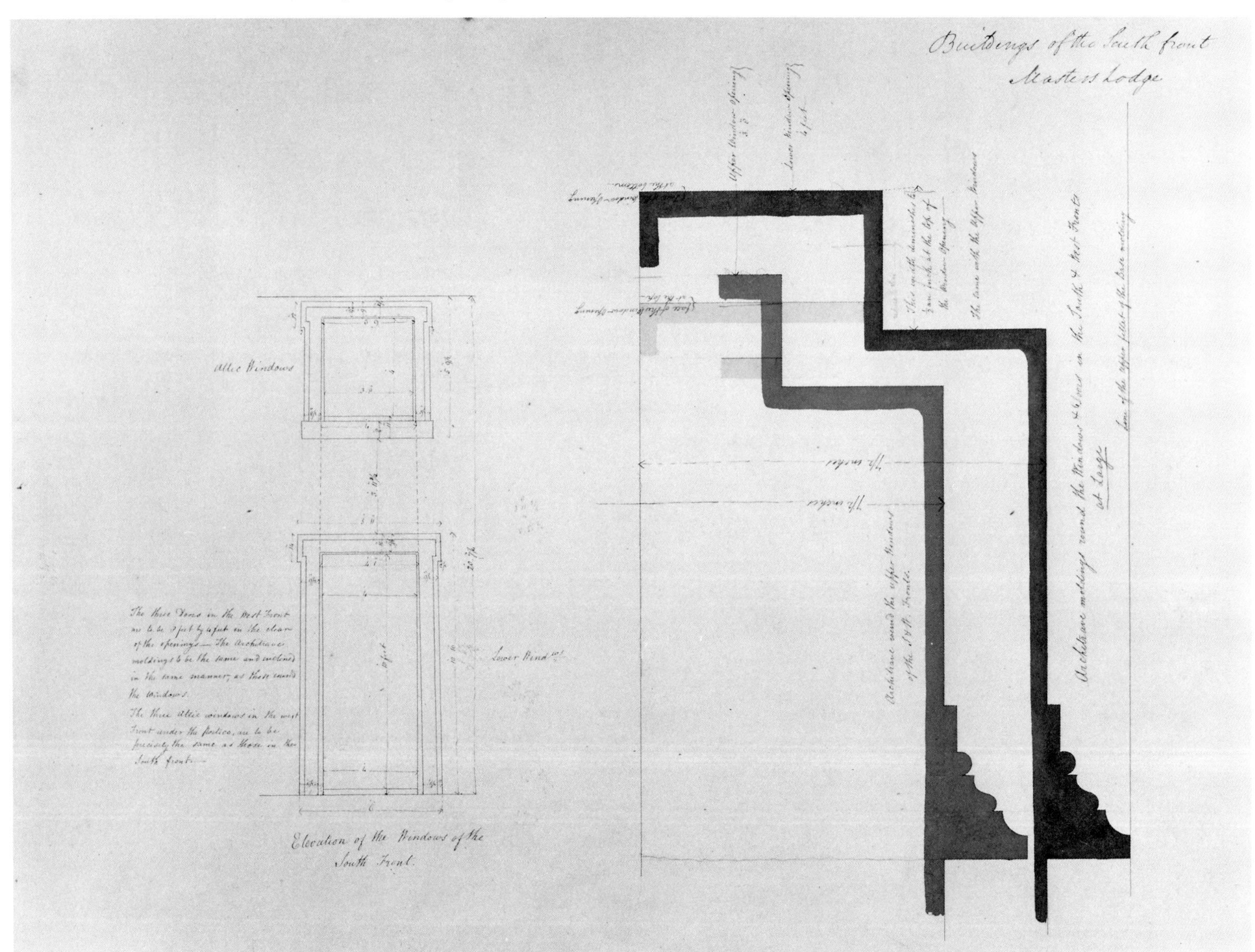

78

79. William **WILKINS**
Plan of the ground floor of the students' apartments and plans of the cellars underneath. Pen and ink with yellow and grey washes over some traces of pencil; 46.2×59.3 cm. Inscribed with measurements: 'Cellar floor 9 feet below the floor of the Students apartments'; 'Indents 6 inches square left of the wall for rain-water pipes'; 'Corner of the Lodge offices'; 'D. Be careful to make this pier as it is here drawn two feet by 14 inches & also in the Cellar below'; 'Plan of the Ground floor'; 'N.B. All the flues to be 14 inches by one foot excepting where the sections shew the contrary. They may go up this width in every case, as far at least as the Chamber floor'. *Location*: Downing College, Cambridge SWP29.

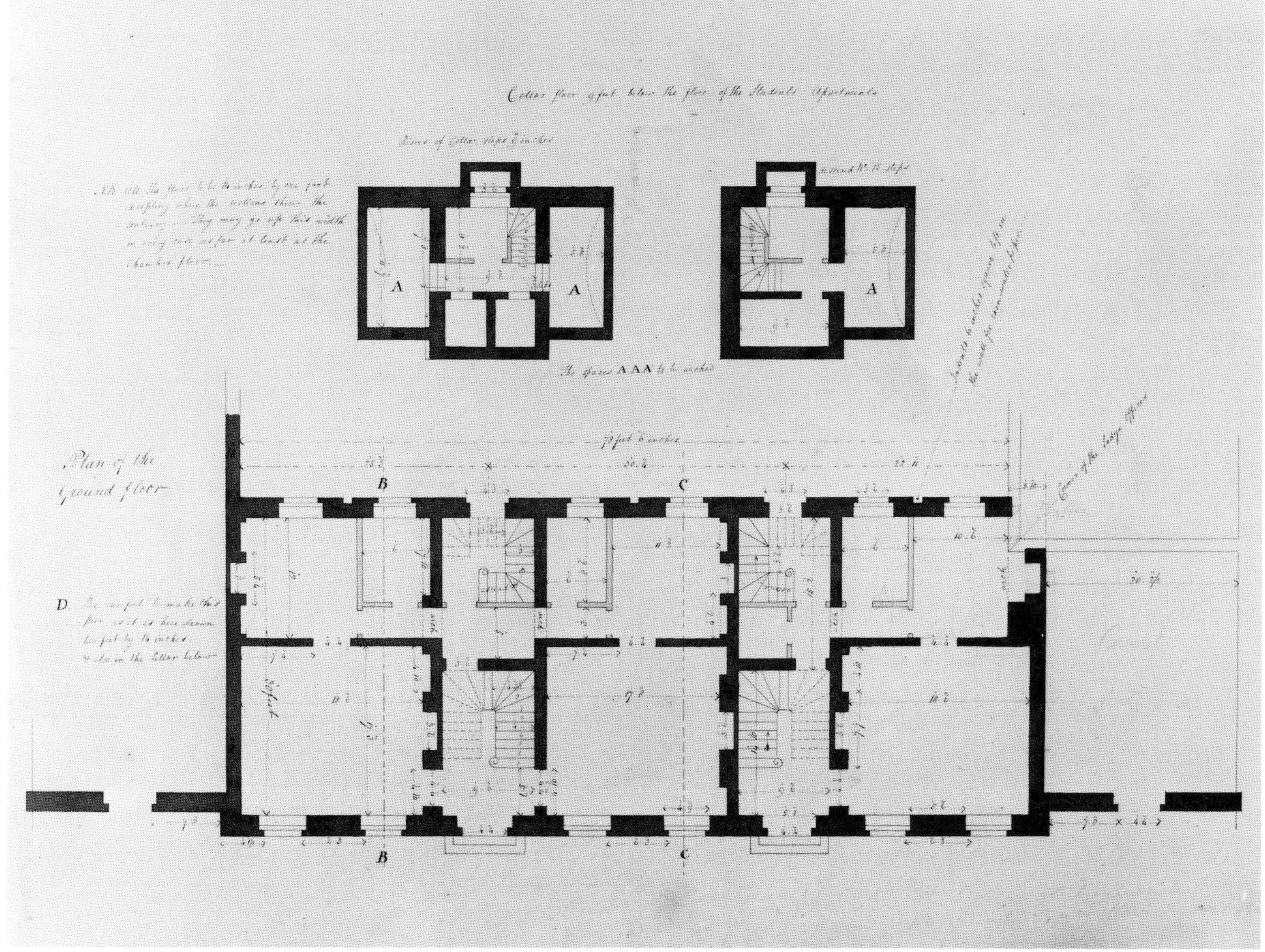

79

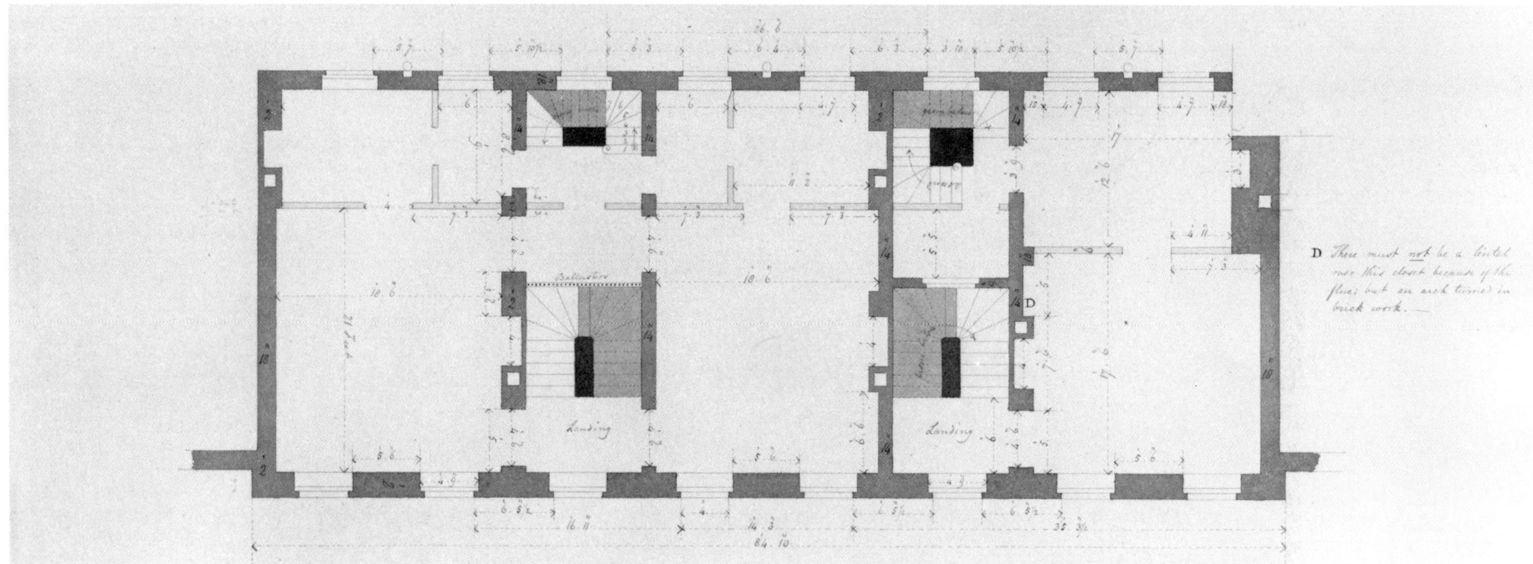

Ballusters
Landing
Landing
D There must not be a lintel over this closet because of the flues but an arch turned in brick work.

80

Gutter
Upright stud work covered with slates
Section thro' one of the Windows
Gutter
Risers of these steps 6½
Lead flat
Queen post
Landing
Queen post
No 3

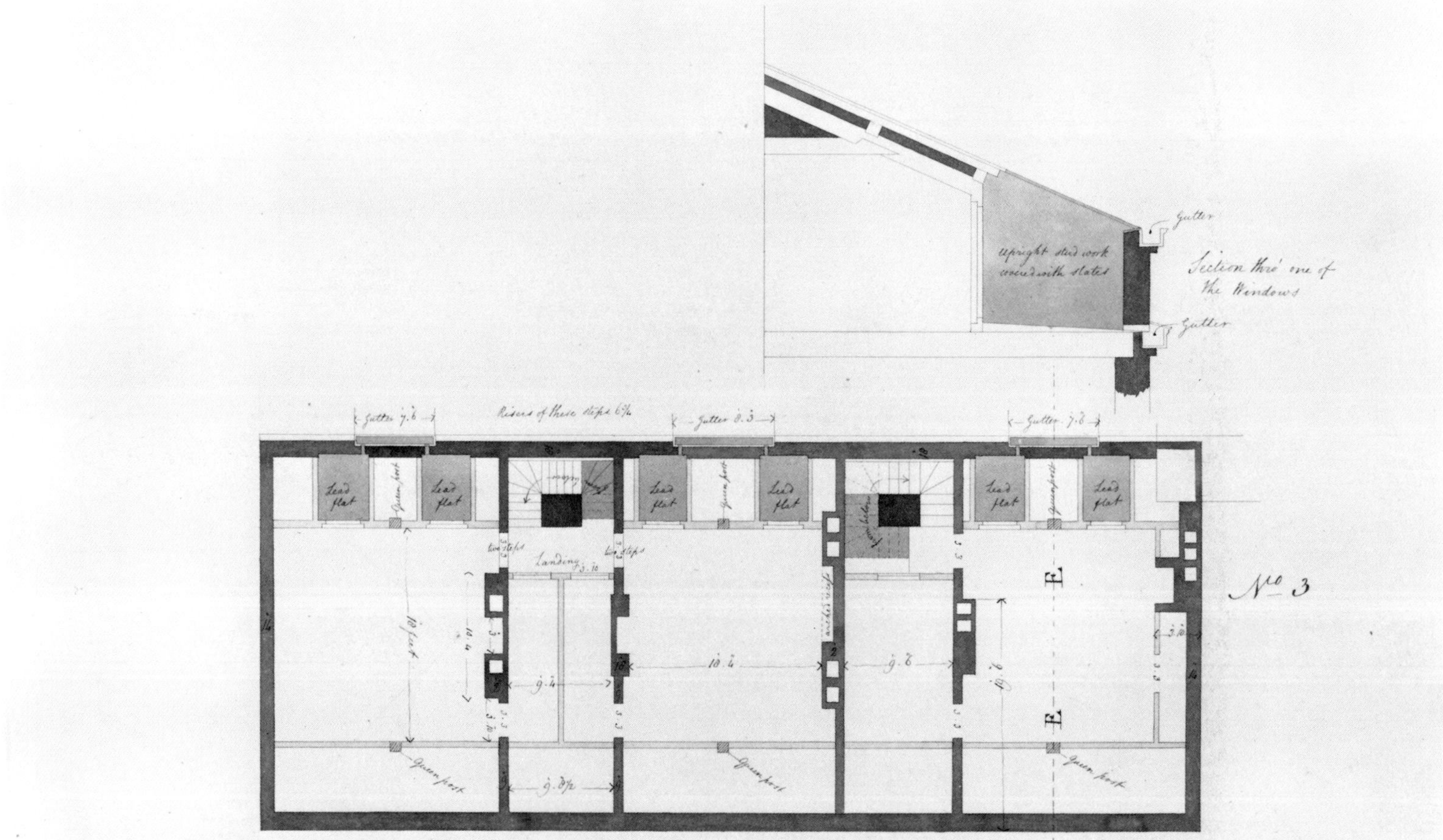

81

80. William **WILKINS**
Plan of the first floor of the students' apartments in the east range adjoining the Master's Lodge.
Pen and ink with yellow, black and grey washes over some pencil underdrawing; 46.2×59.9 cm. Scale 1/10 in. to 1 ft. Inscribed with measurements: 'D. There must <u>not</u> be a lintel over this closet because of the flue; but an arch turned in brick work'. *Location*: Downing College, Cambridge SWP30.

81. William **WILKINS**
Plan of the attic floor of the students' apartments in the east range with the section of a window.
Pen and ink with yellow and grey washes over some traces of pencil; 45.9×59.1 cm. Inscribed with measurements: 'Upright stud work covered with slates'; 'Section thro' one of the Windows'; 'N.3'; 'Chamber plan'; 'Risers of these steps'. *Location*: Downing College, Cambridge SWP31.

82. William **WILKINS**
Rear elevation of the students' apartments in the east range with detail of the window sash.
Pen and ink over some pencil underdrawing; 46.3×59.8 cm. Scale 1/10 in. to 1 ft. Inscribed with measurements: 'The upper sash only hung upon which is a frame work of Iron boxing up into the wall'; 'Windows of the Students' Rooms next the Garden'. *Location*: Downing College, Cambridge SWP32.

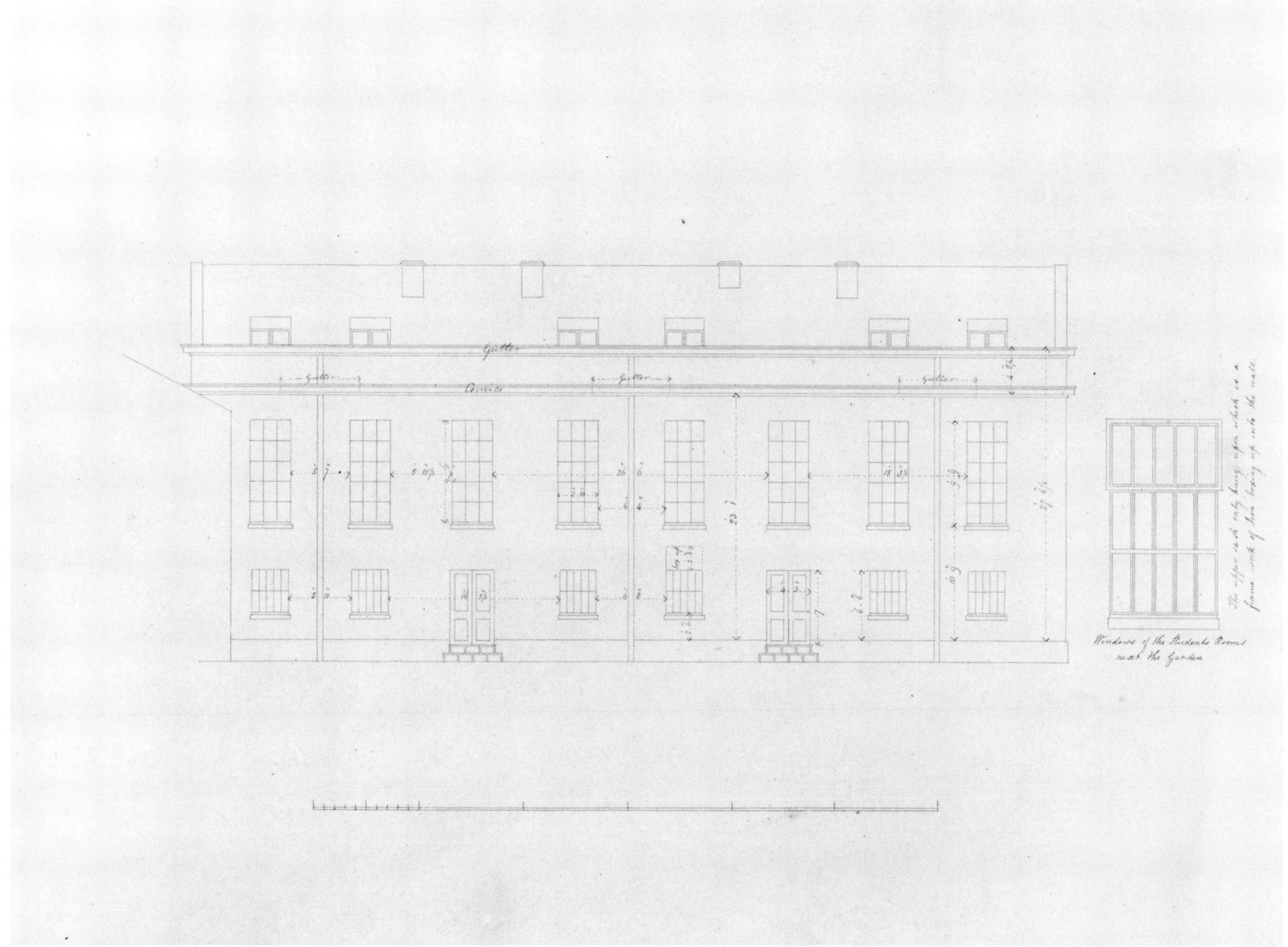

82

83. William **WILKINS**
Sections through the students' apartments in the east range.
Pen and ink with yellow, black and grey washes over some pencil underdrawing; 45.9×59.4 cm. Inscribed with measurements: 'Slanting of the Roof'; 'N.5'; 'Section through the line CC of the ground plan'; 'A. line of the top of plinth'; 'Section through the line BB in the Ground plan'; 'wherever this Gutter occurs an indent of half a brick to be left for it – one foot deep'; 'These flues a foot square'. *Location*: Downing College, Cambridge SWP33.

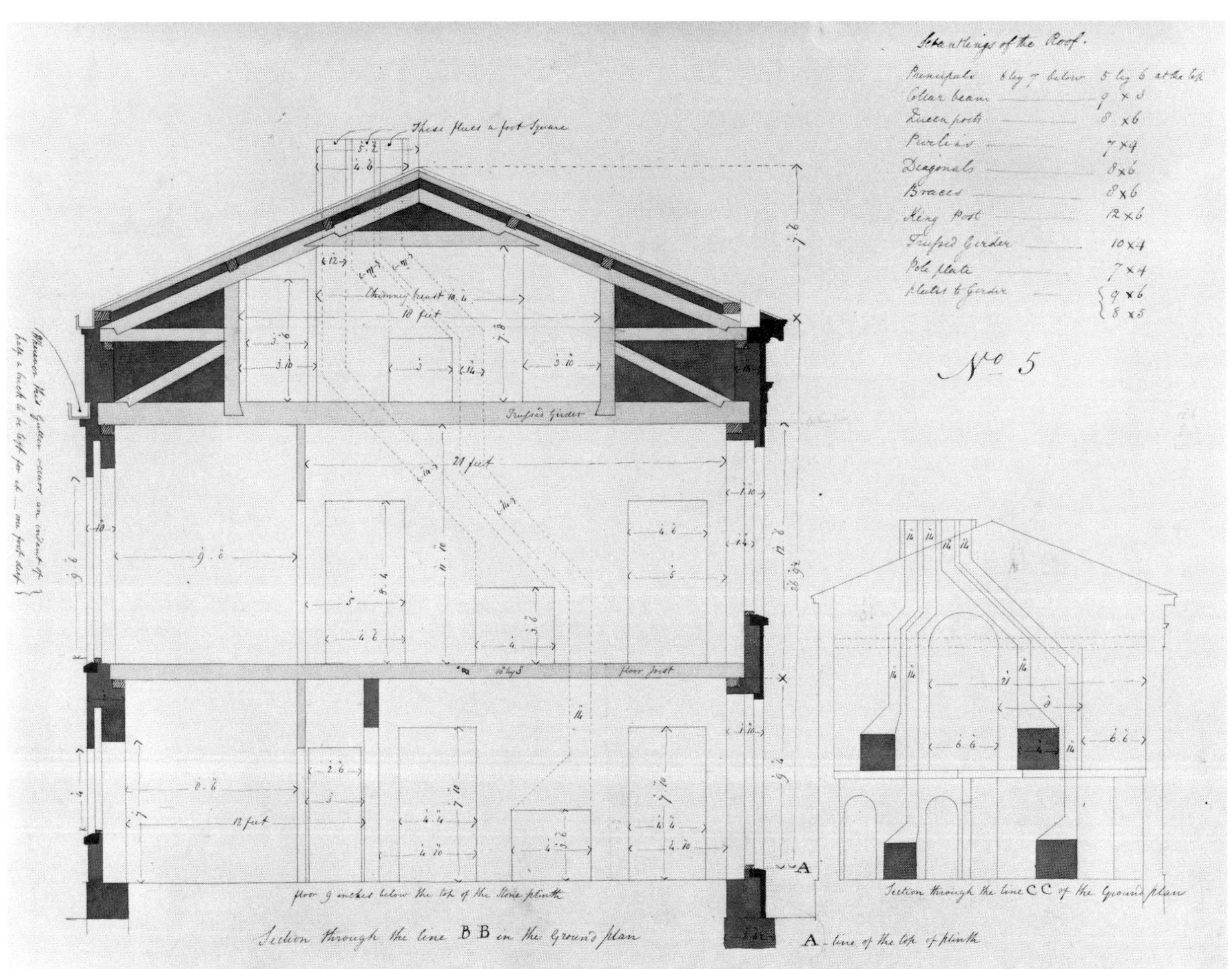

83

84. William **WILKINS**
Section through the attic floor of the students' apartments in the east range.
Pen and ink with grey wash over some pencil underdrawing; 46×59 cm. Inscribed with measurements: 'N.6'; 'Purlins 7' by 4"'; 'Section through the Chamber floor in the line EE. See N.3'; 'Brick work cover'd with slates'. *Location*: Downing College, Cambridge SWP34.

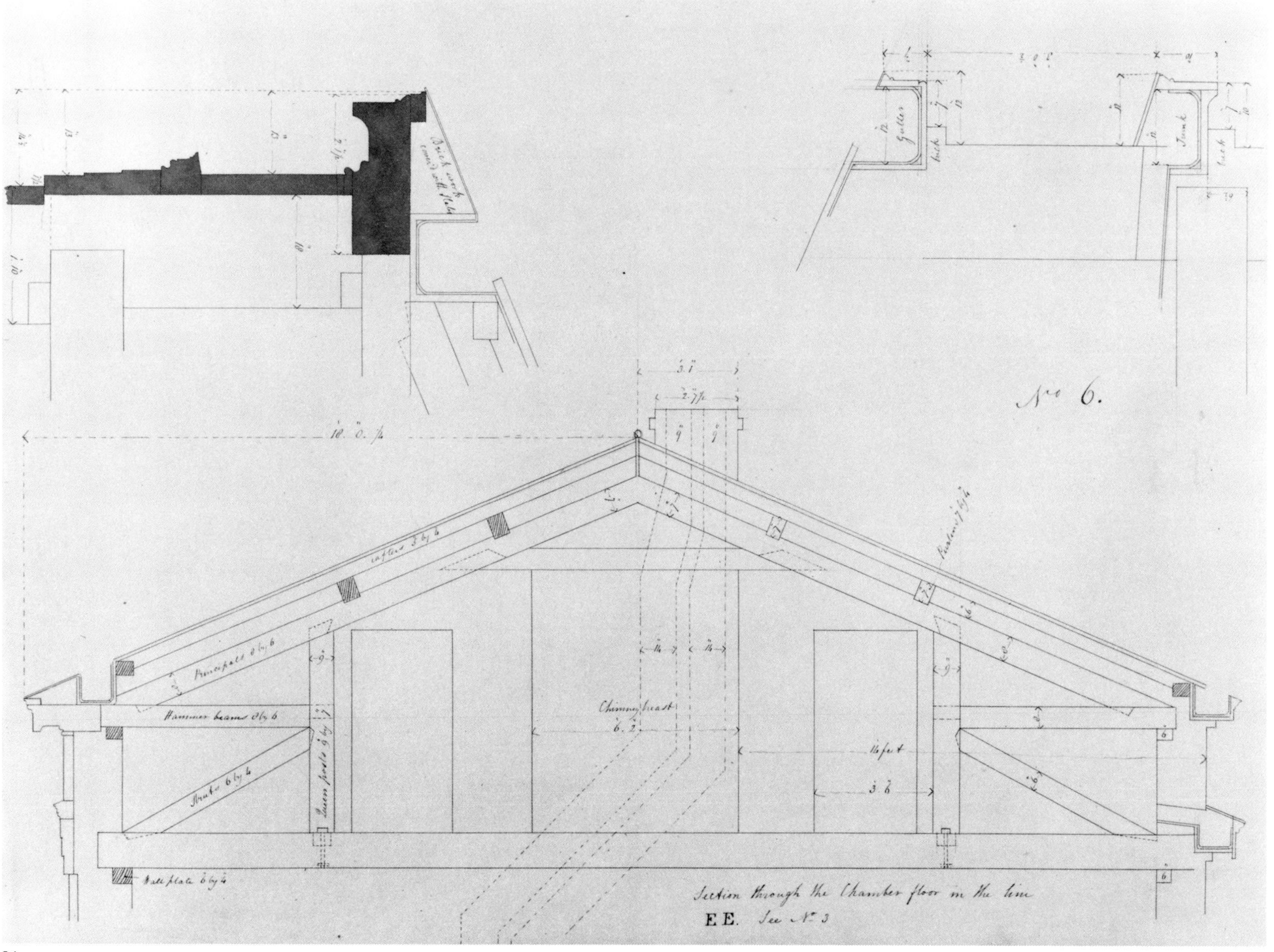

84

85. William **WILKINS**
Elevation of the Professor's Lodge in the east range, with section through one of the front rooms.
Pen and ink over some pencil underdrawing; 45.7×59.5. Scale 1/10 in. to 1 ft. Some measurements inscribed in pencil. *Location*: Downing College, Cambridge SWP35.

86. William **WILKINS**
Plans of the ground and first floors of the Professor's Lodge in the east range.
(see Fig.38, p.70)
Pen and ink with grey washes over some pencil underdrawing; 58×46.2 cm. Inscribed with measurements; 'Garden/ All the windows in this front, above & below, are to be 5 Squares deep & brought down to the floor'; 'Windows 10 feet high 1 square to run up into the wall'; 'height of Chimney openings 3 ft.6'; 'Professors Residence facing the West'. *Location*: Downing College, Cambridge SWP36.

85

87. William **WILKINS**
Ground plan of the coach-house.
Pen and ink with grey washes over some pencil underdrawing; 46.1×59.7 cm. Inscribed with measurements; 'Stable Court'; 'pier for Gate 2 feet Square'; 'Plan of the Stables for Downing College'; 'This Area to be sunk 4 feet for 6 long'. *Location*: Downing College, Cambridge SWP37.

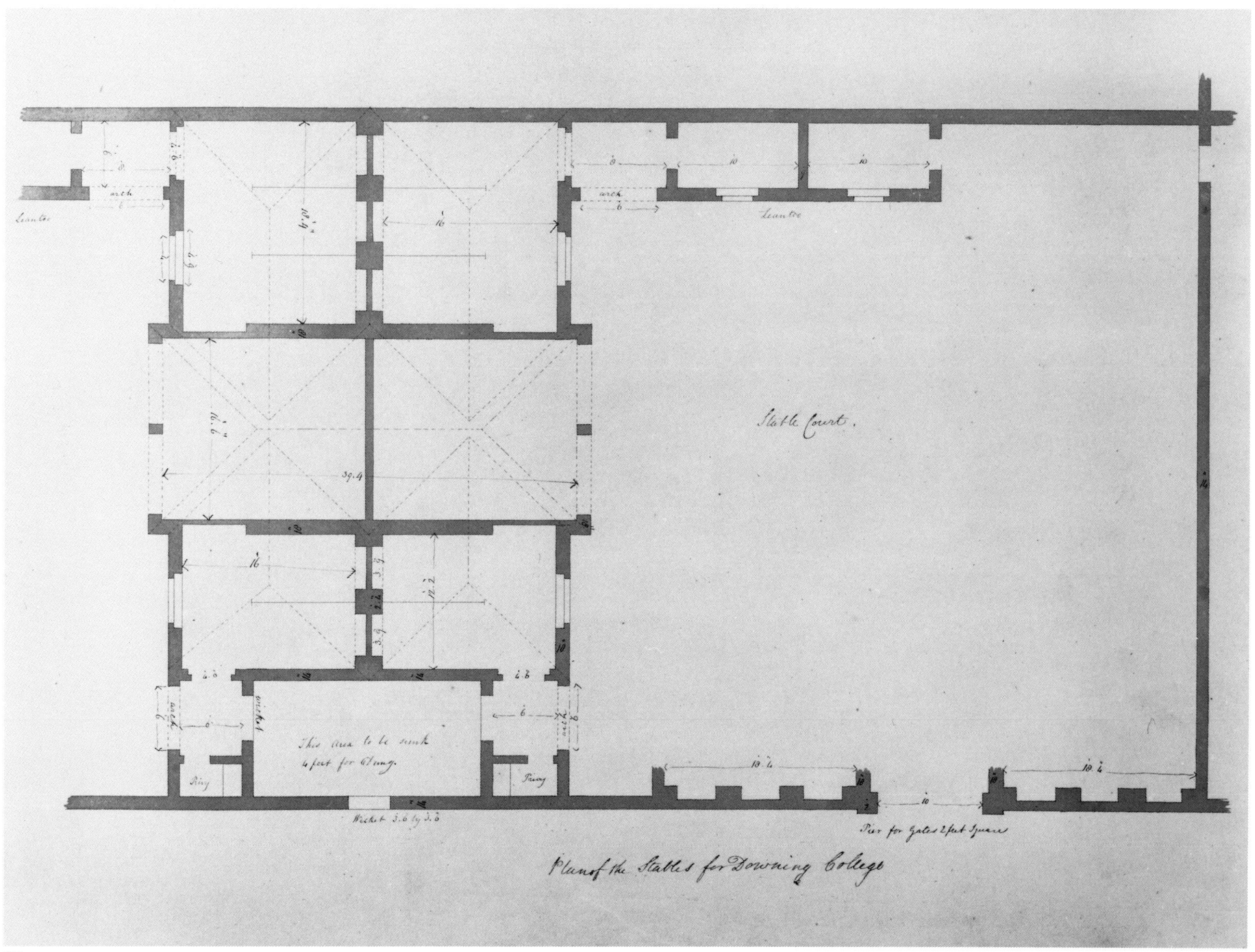

87

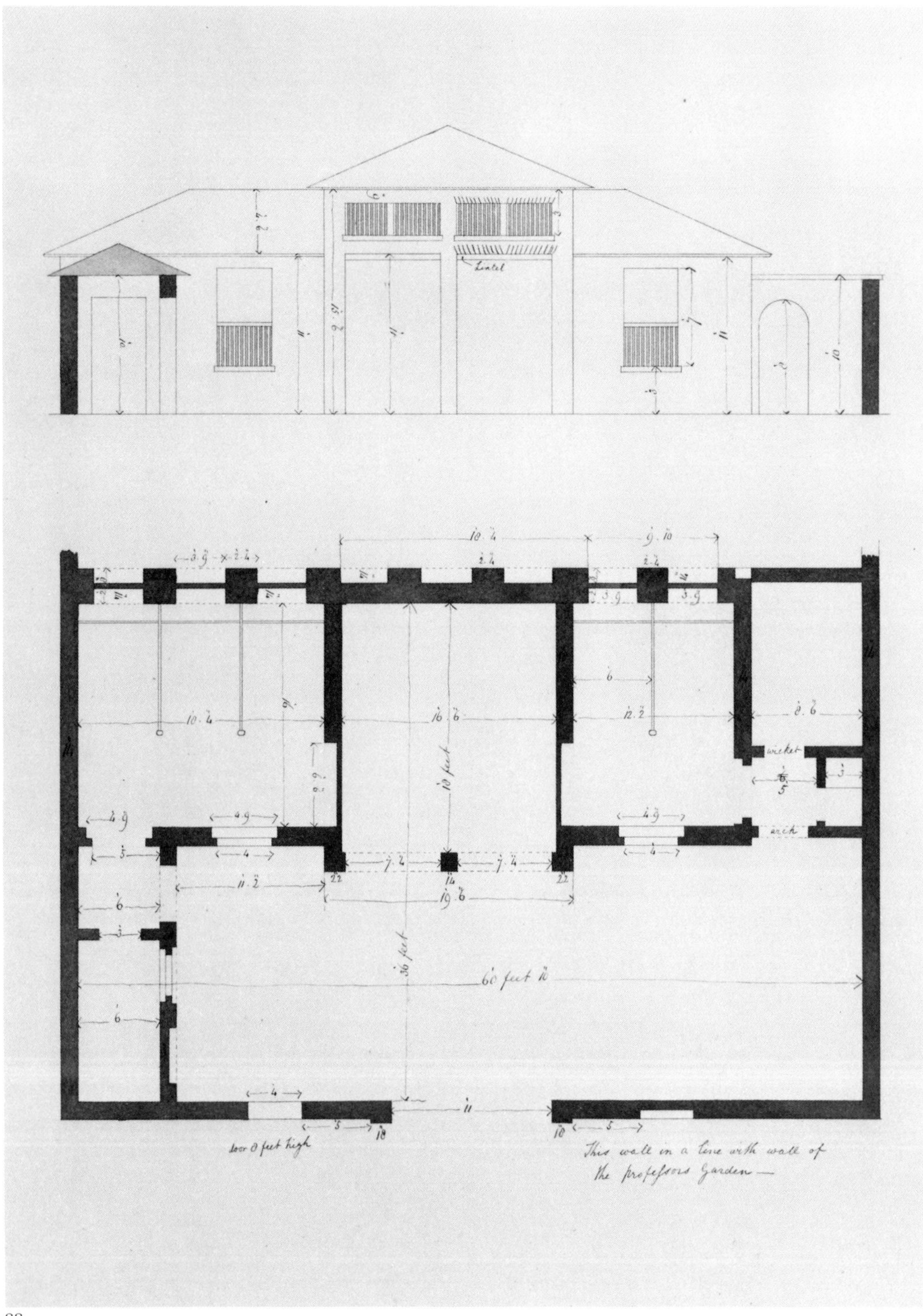

88

88. William **WILKINS**
Ground plan and elevation of the stables.
Pen and ink with grey washes over some pencil underdrawing; 59.7×45.8 cm. Inscribed with measurements; 'This wall in a line with wall of the professors Garden'; 'door 8 feet high'. *Location*: Downing College, Cambridge SWP38.

89. William **WILKINS**
Section and elevation of the stables.
Pen and ink with grey and black washes over some pencil underdrawing; 46.1×59.6 cm. Inscribed with measurements; 'Provide Timber for 18 Square of flooring and for 26 Square of Roofing'; 'Principals 6/2 by 5 at bottom 5/2 by 5 at the top'; 'Dripping Eaves all around & likewise to the Coach houses. The Centre Gutter between the Stable roofs to discharge the water at each end'; 'For all the particulars of the partitions, Racks, Mangers &c. &c. see the Fellows Stables at Caius Coll:'; 'Rafters 4 by 2½"'; 'Purbins 5 by 4 notched an Inch into the principals'. *Location*: Downing College, Cambridge SWP39.

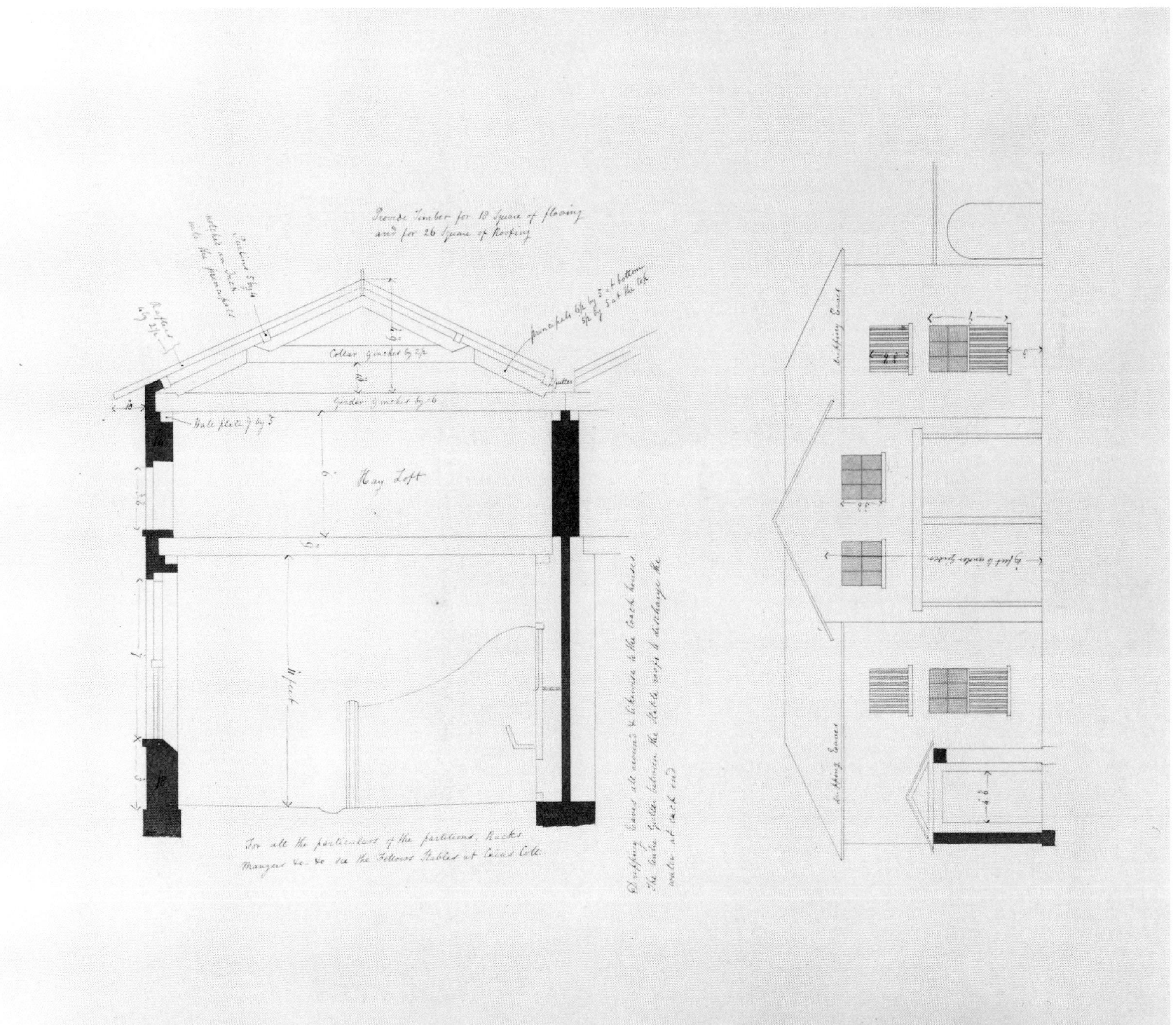
Provide Timber for 18 Square of flooring
and for 26 Square of Roofing
Collar 9 inches by 2½
Girder 9 inches by 6
Wall plate 7 by 3
Hay Loft
11 feet
For all the particulars of the partitions, Racks
Mangers &c. &c. see the Fellows Stables at Caius Coll:
Dripping Eaves
Dripping Eaves

89

90. William **WILKINS**
Plan of the drainage system for the west range.
Pen and ink with grey and pale blue washes over some pencil underdrawing; 46.2×59.9 cm. Scale 1/10 in. to 1 ft. Inscribed in pencil along the upper margin 'First one Wanted begin here'.
Location: Downing College, Cambridge
SWP40.

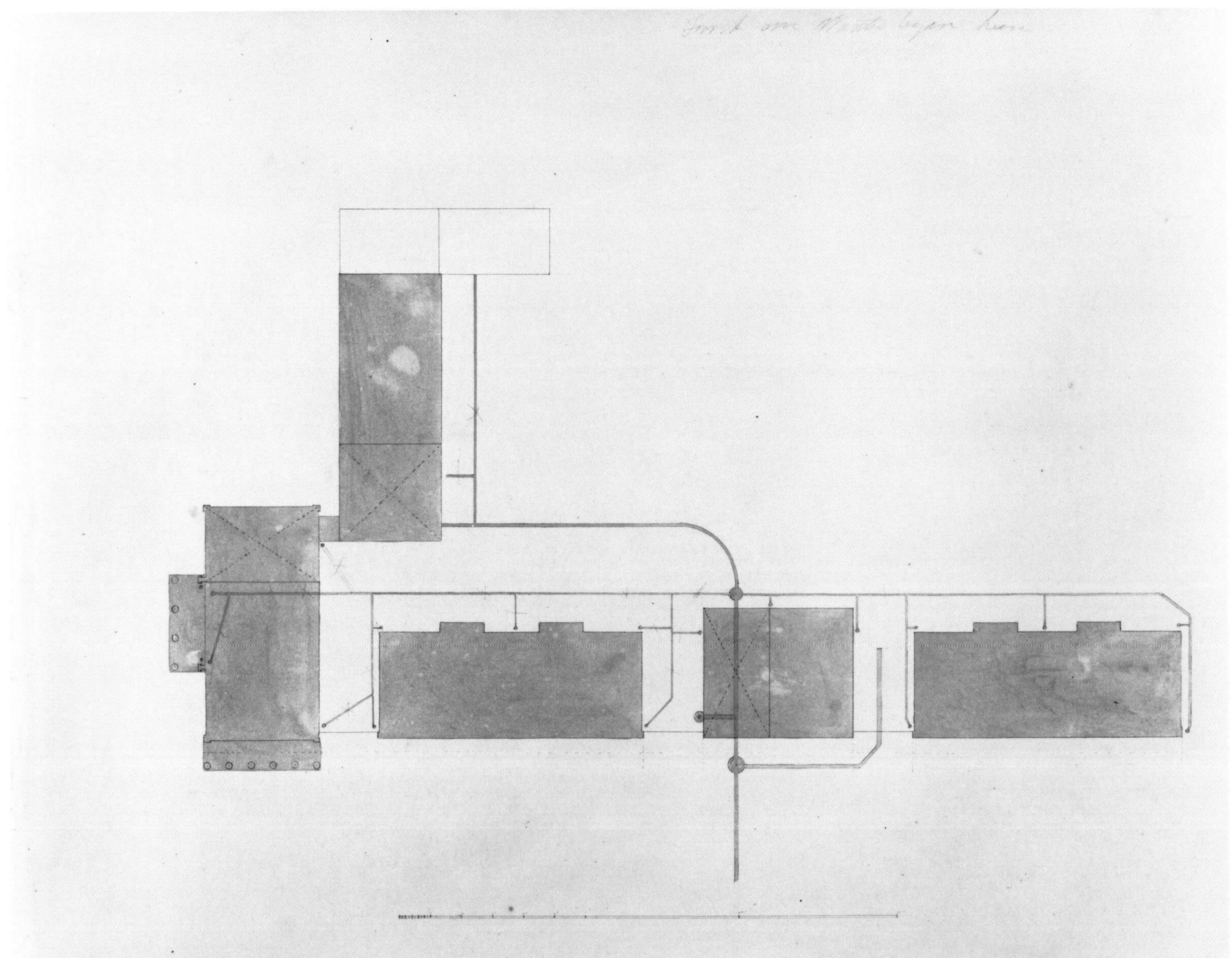

90

91. William **WILKINS**
Plan of the basement storey of the hall and kitchens.
Pen and ink with grey and yellow washes; 46.1×92.1 cm., the flap measures 8×9.4 cm. Scale 1/10 in. to 1 ft. Inscribed with measurements; 'Hall Buildings N.o 2'; 'A The drawing shews the projection of the face of the pilaster, before the wall, too little, it ought to have been 3 feet 4'; 'East'; 'South'; West'; 'descend 3 steps to the level of the Kitchen &c.'; 'Kitchen Court. North'. *Location*: Downing College, Cambridge SWP41.

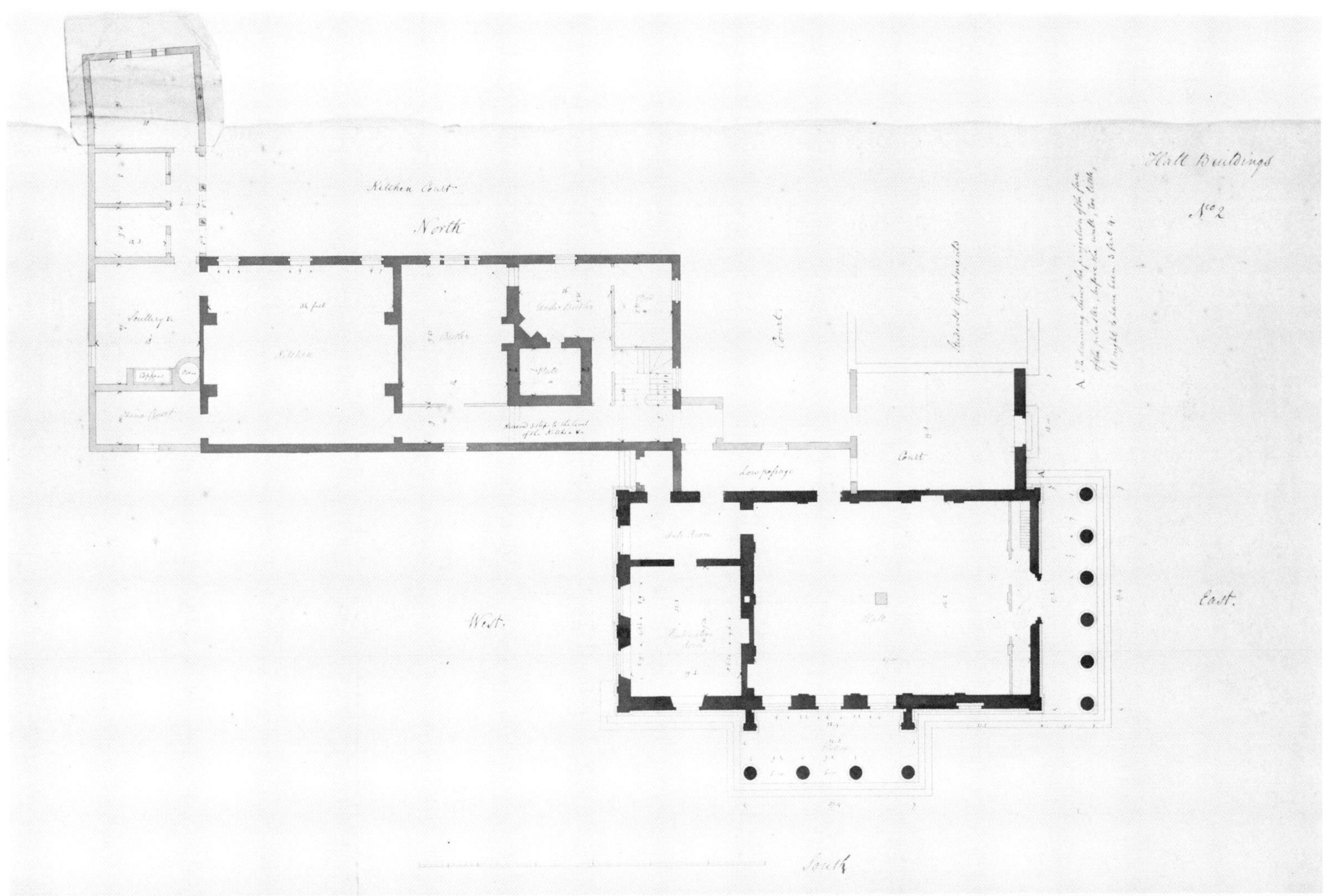

91

92. William **WILKINS**
Plan of the hall and kitchens.
Pen and ink with blue, grey and yellow washes; 46.1×92.3 cm. Inscribed in the upper right corner 'N.o 3'. *Location*: Downing College, Cambridge SWP42.

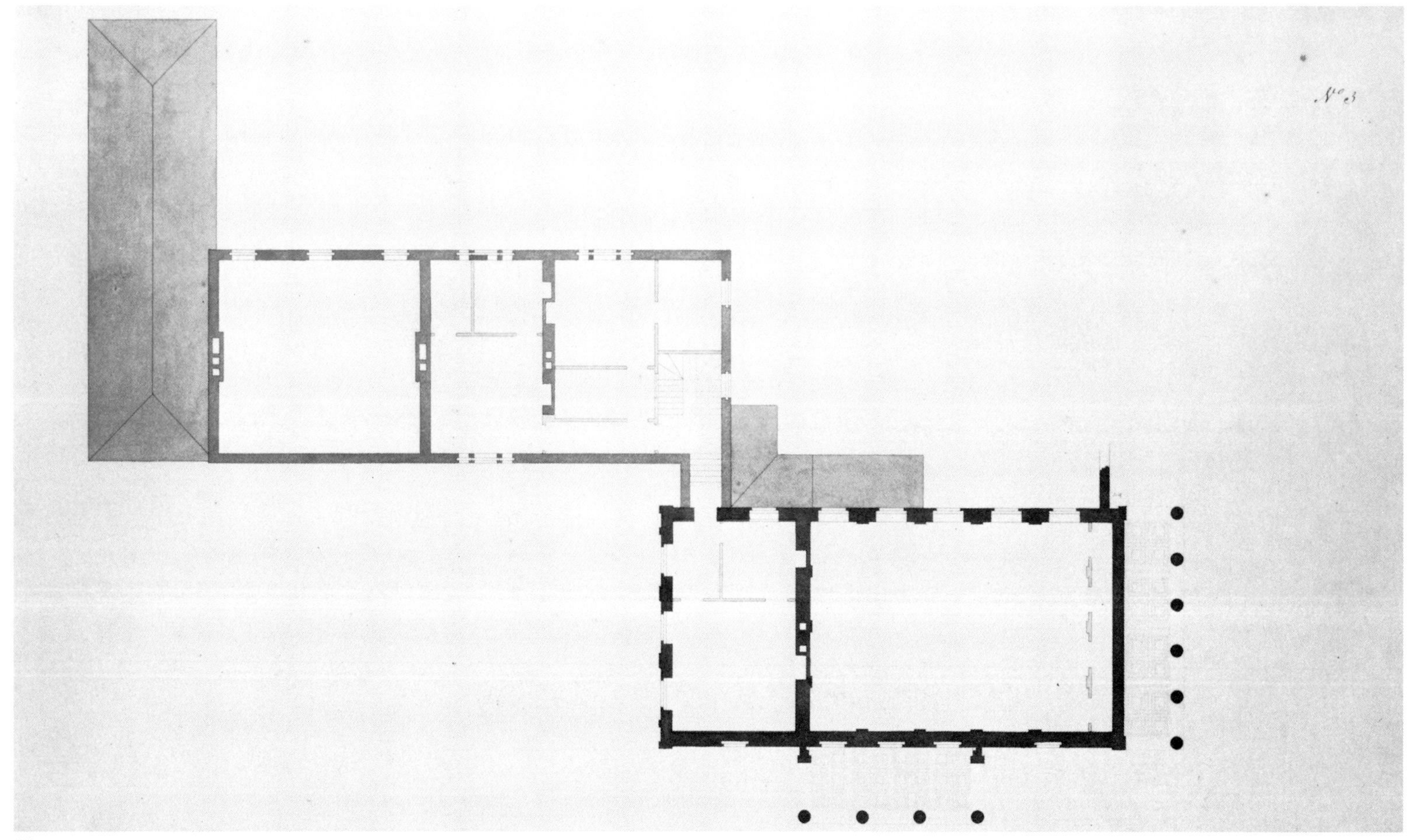

92

93. William **WILKINS**
Plan of the hall.
Pen and ink with red, black and grey washes; 45.9×91.7 cm. Inscribed with measurements; 'Hall Buildings N.o 3' (along the upper right margin). *Location*: Downing College, Cambridge SWP43.

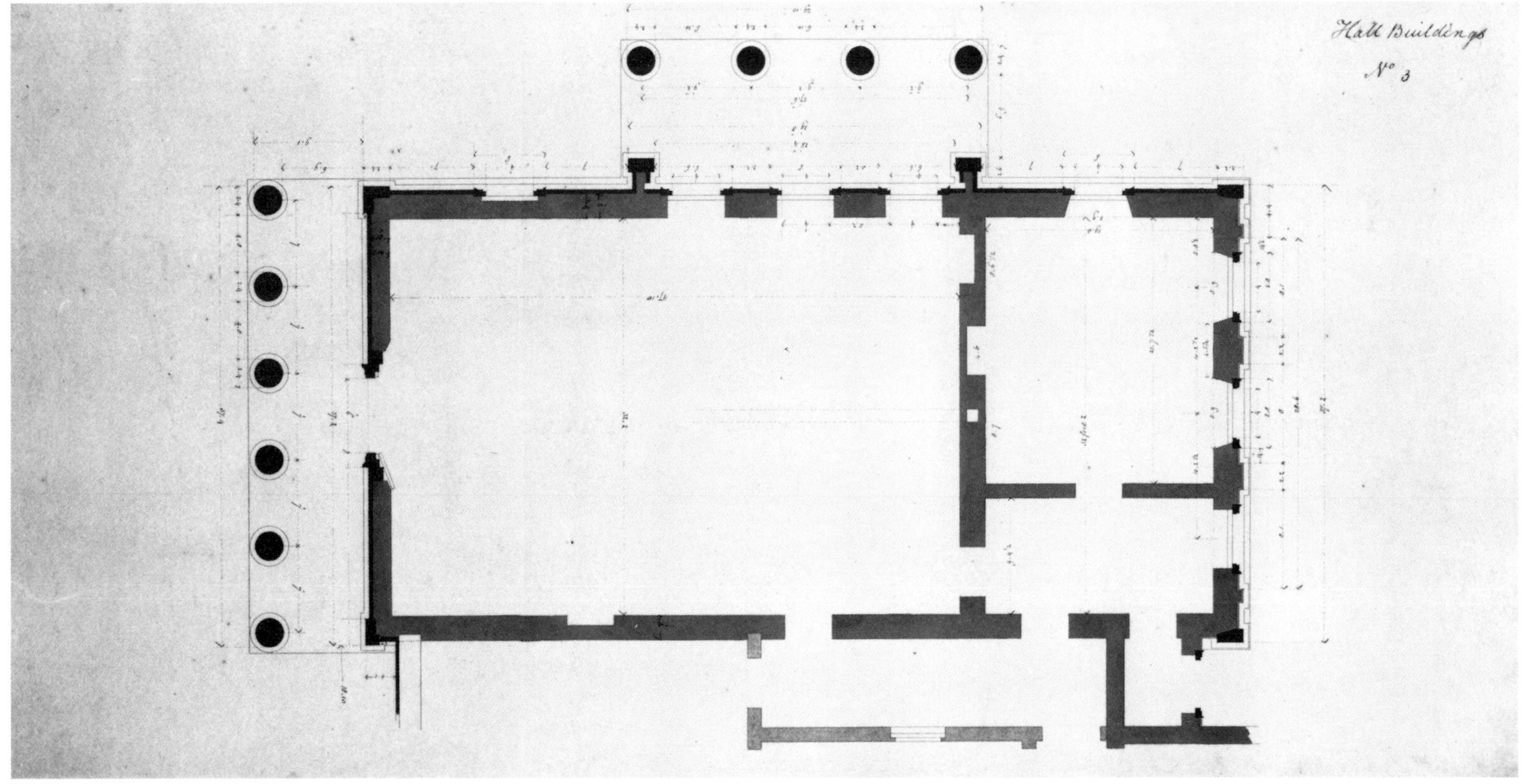

93

94. William **WILKINS**
Elevation of the south front of the hall.
Pen and ink; 46.2×59.5 cm. Scale 1/10 in. to 1 ft. Inscribed with measurements; 'Hall Buildings N.o 4 A'; 'The top bed of the Cornice must be in equal lengths. The lower bed in random lengths provided the joints be not below those of the upper bed'; 'The angular columns of both porticoes to have angular capitals, with two volutes in each front'; 'The Epystylia or Architraves above the Columns must extend from centre to centre of two Columns & be in one depth. The frize and lower bed of the Cornice in random lengths. The top bed of the Cornice must be in nearly equal lengths with a lions head sculptured in bold relief upon each length the joint nearly midway between each'; 'Elevation of the South Front of the Hall'; 'The lower course of the Columns must be 6 feet high, including the hollow & fillet. The Columns in four or not more than five courses, exclusive of the Capital. The lower Course of

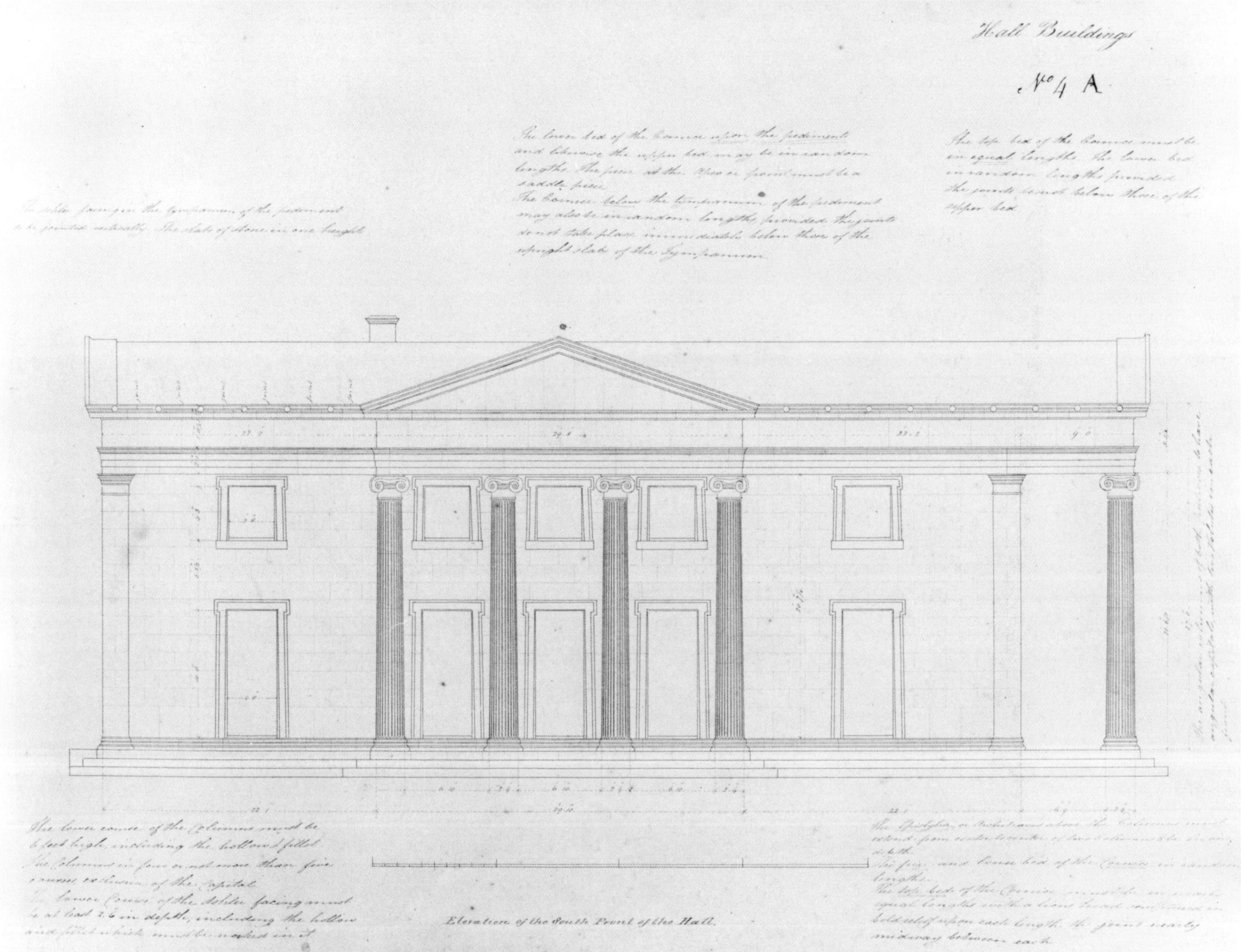

94

the Ashler facing must be at least 2.6″ in depth; including the hollow and fillet which must be worked in it'; 'The Ashler facing in the tympanum of the pediment to be jointed vertically. The slabs of stone in one height'; 'The lower bed of the Cornice upon the pediments and likewise the upper bed may be in random lenghts. The piece at the Apex or point must be a saddle piece. The Cornice below the tympanum of the pediment may also be in random lengths, provided the joints do not take place immediately below those of the upright slabs of the Tympanum'. *Location*: Downing College, Cambridge SWP44.

95. William **WILKINS**
Elevation of the east front of the hall.
Pen and ink over some pencil underdrawing; 46.3×59.8 cm. Scale 1/10 in. to 1 ft. Inscribed with some measurements; 'Hall Buildings N.o 5'; 'The upper member of this Cornice projects 9 inches before the face of the wall B'; 'The Capitals of the Columns at the angles of both porticoes, are angular, & are to be sculptured with four volutes in each'; 'Principal, or Eastern, portico'; 'East flank of the South portico'; 'The Ashler facing in the tympanum of the pediment to be jointed vertically in one height'. *Location*: Downing College, Cambridge SWP45.

96. William **WILKINS**
Elevation of the west front of the hall.
Pen and ink; 46×59.6 cm. Scale 1/10 in. to 1 ft. Inscribed with some measurements; 'Hall Buildings N.o 6'; 'The parts in the West front which are intended to be Stone are,/ 1 The Cornice upon the pediment/ 2 The Cornice below the pediment/ 3 The returns of the frize [sic], architrave and pilasters marked AA/ 4 The base molding and plinth/ 5 The window and door, architrave & sills/ The remainder to be in Roman Cement./ B. All the capitals of the pilasters in this front are to be ornamented like those on the South and East fronts, and all will be done in Cement'; 'Elevation of the West front of the Hall and Combination Room'; 'C. The lead of the flat behind the stone cornice must turn over and cover the top of the cornice which must drip towards the lead flat'. *Location*: Downing College, Cambridge SWP46.

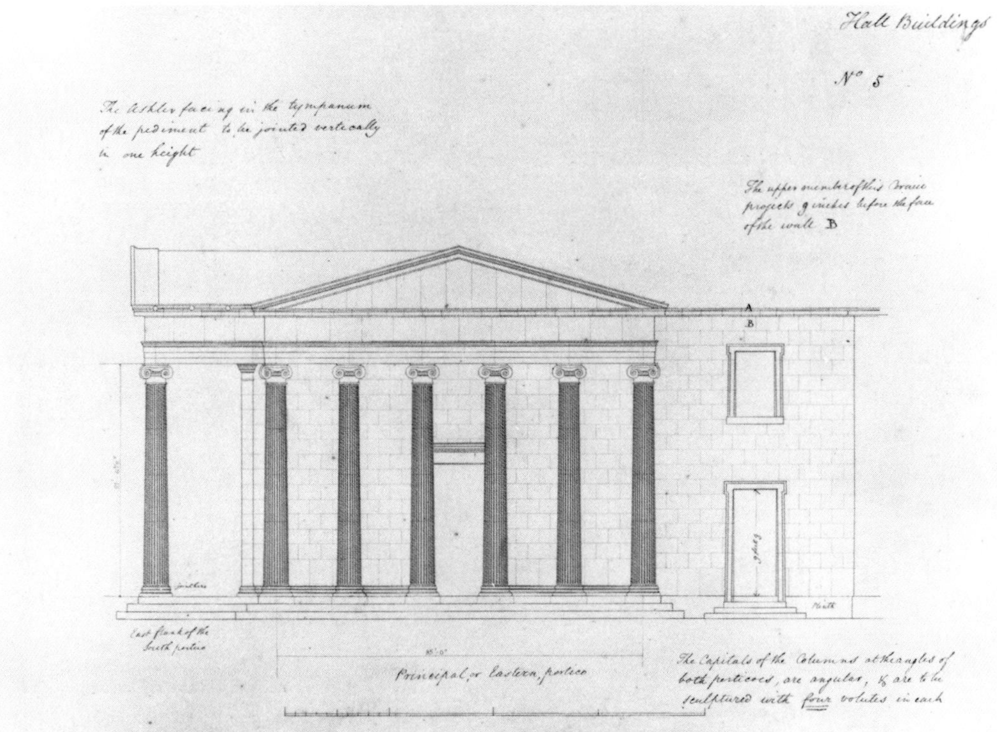

95

96

97. William **WILKINS**
Elevation of the principal door of the hall with profile and frontal views of the consoles supporting the architrave.
Pen and ink with grey washes over some pencil underdrawing; 46.5×59.8 cm. Inscribed with some measurements; 'Hall Buildings N.o 7'; 'Architrave half the Full size'; 'Width at the bottom of the door'; 'Width at the top of the door'; 'Stone facing'; 'projection of the Architrave'; 'Console half the Full size'; 'Cornice'; 'Section of the Hyperthyrum'; 'Door 12 feet high in the clear 6 feet wide in the clear'; 'Details of the Principal Entrance all of Stone'.
Location: Downing College, Cambridge SWP47.

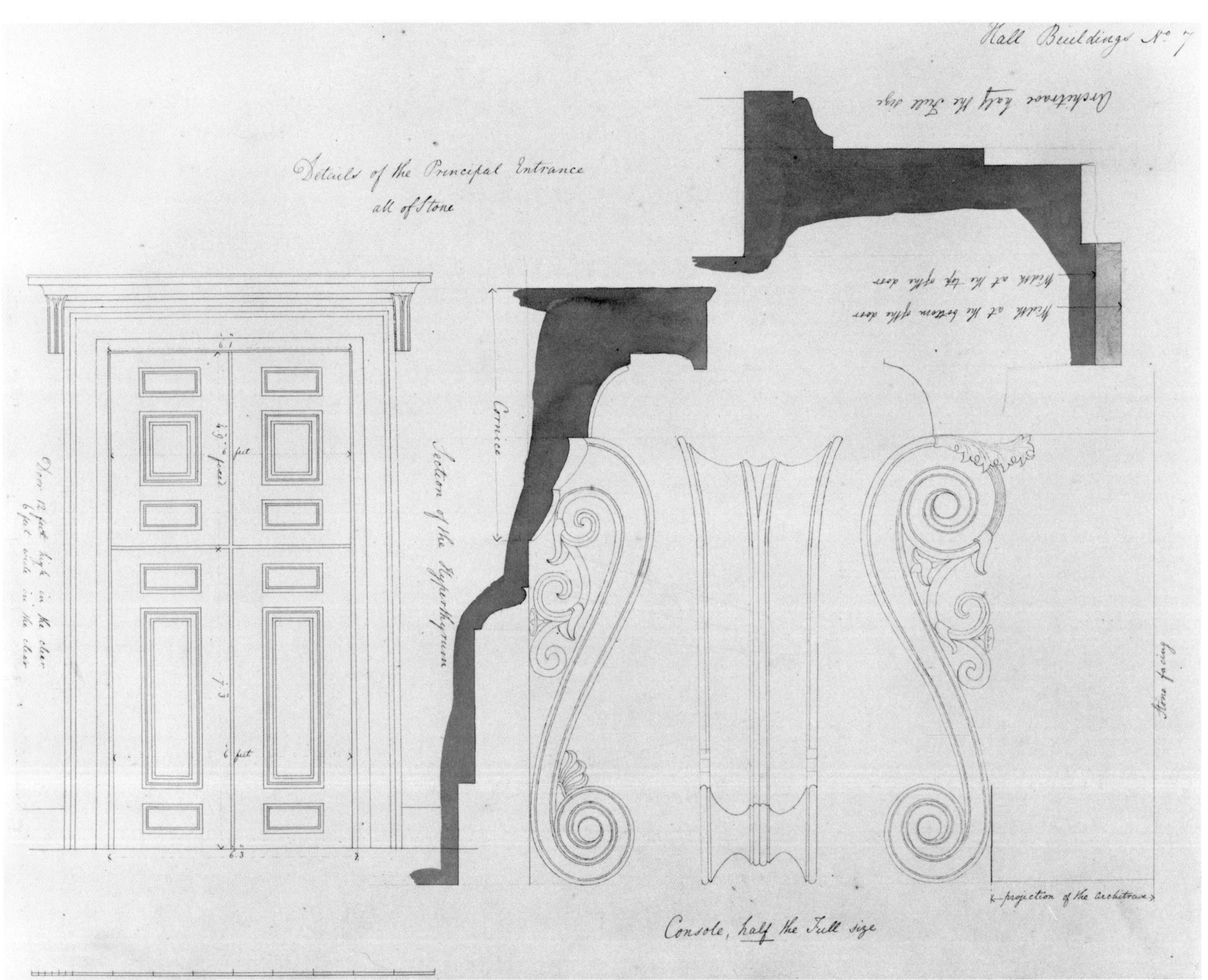

97

98. William **WILKINS**
Elevation of door and blank window inside the hall with details of the bracket supporting the architrave above the door.
Pen and ink with yellow and grey washes over some pencil underdrawing; 46.4 × 59.5 cm.

Scale 1/12 in. to 1 ft. Various measurements and inscriptions: 'Hall Buildings/ N. 18'; 'half the full size'; 'Wood Architrave'; 'Cornice over doors and windows in plaister'. *Location:* Downing College, Cambridge SWP48.

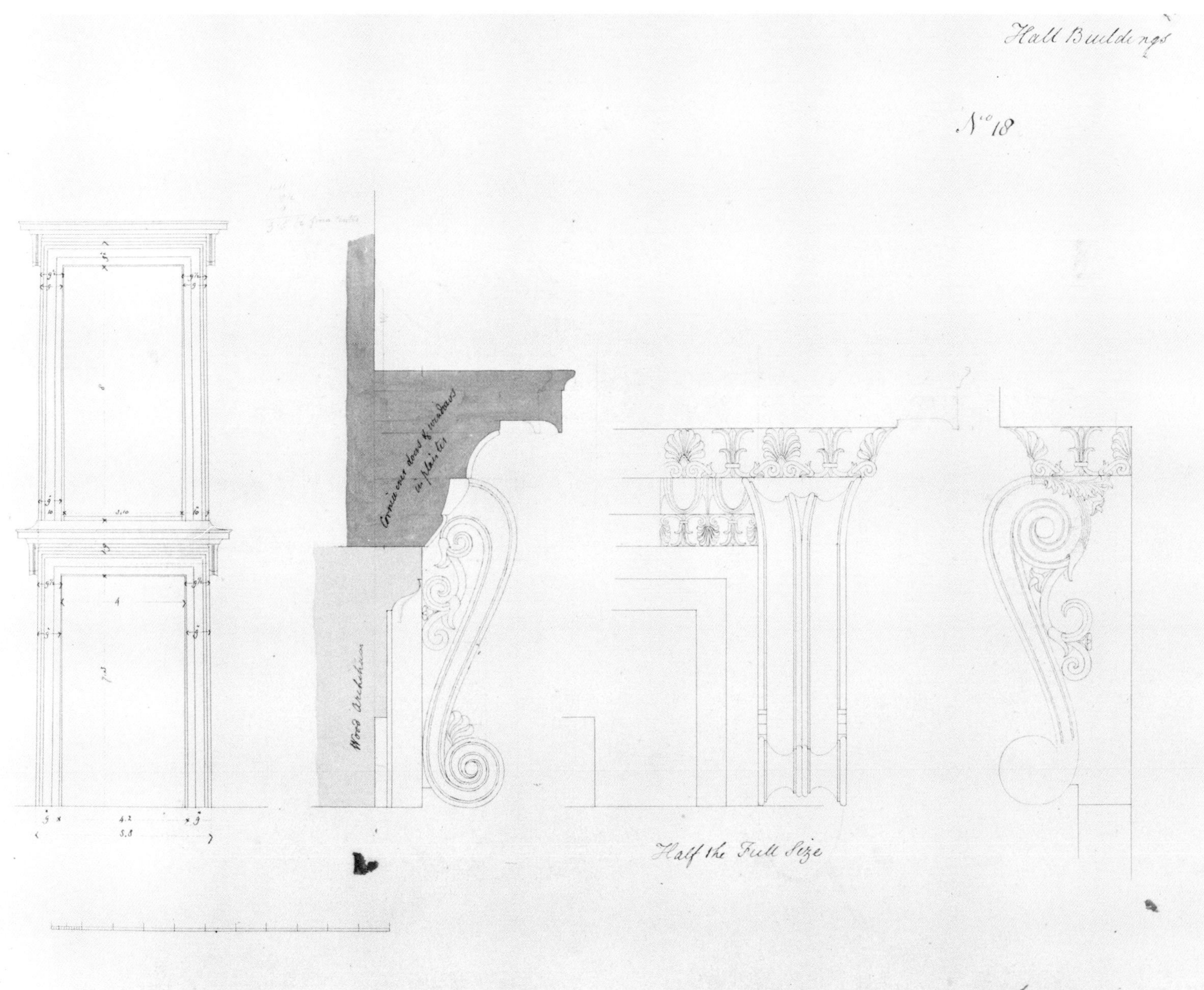

98

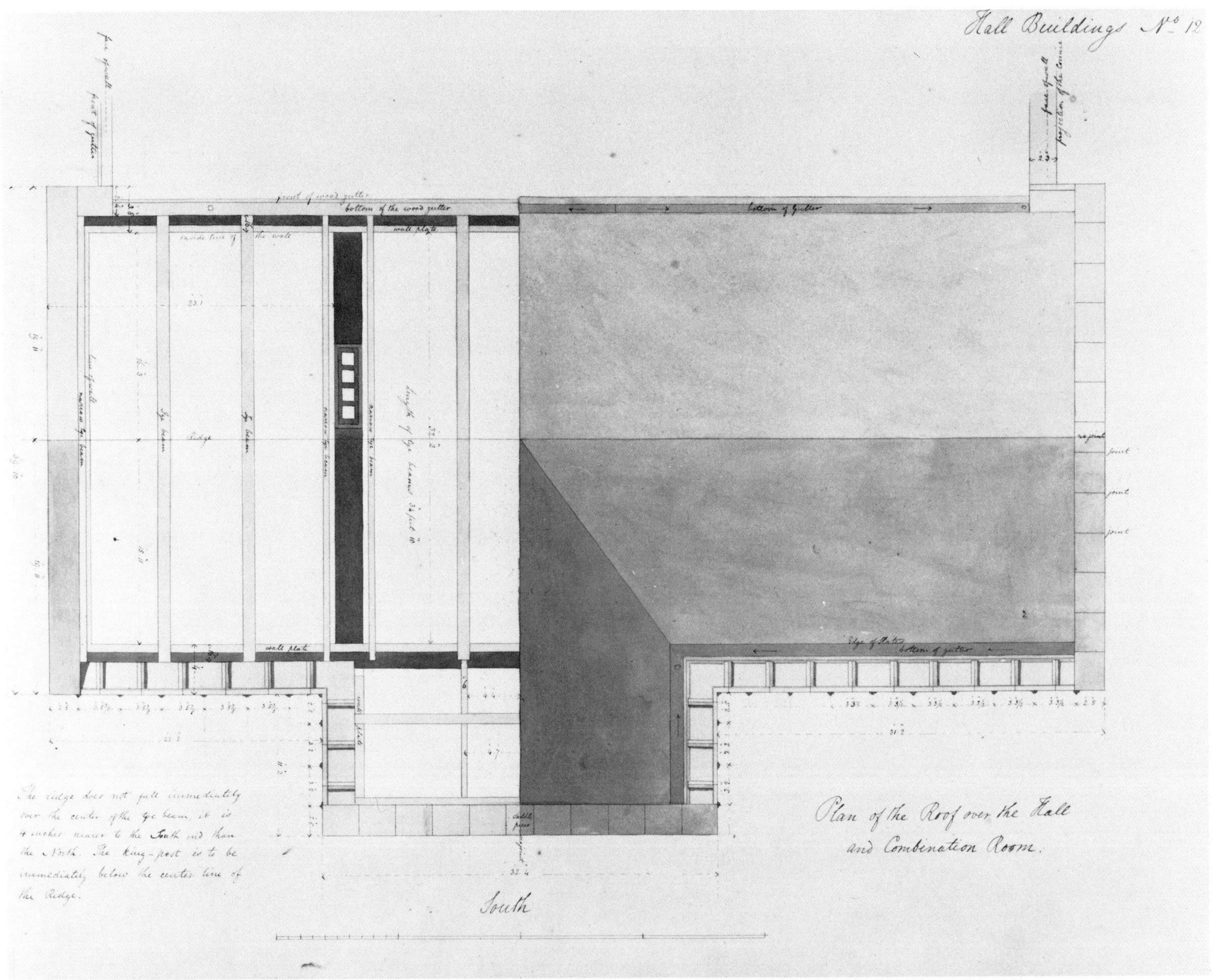
Hall Buildings No. 12
bottom of the wood gutter
bottom of gutter
wall plate
Ridge
wall plate
Edge of Slates
bottom of gutter
The ridge does not fall immediately
over the center of the tye beam, it is
4 inches nearer to the South end than
the North. The King-post is to be
immediately below the center line of
the Ridge.
Plan of the Roof over the Hall
and Combination Room.
South

101

99. William **WILKINS**
Section and part-plan of the hall. (see Pl. XII)
Pen and ink with black, brown, grey, red and yellow watercolours over some pencil underdrawing; 46.5×59.7 cm. Inscribed with measurements; 'N.o 8'; 'Elevation of the North side of the Hall, or Refectory'; 'Half pair of principals to stand clear from the face of the wall'. *Location*: Downing College, Cambridge SWP49.

100. William **WILKINS**
Transverse section of the hall. (see Pl.XI)
Pen and ink with black, brown, grey, red and yellow washes over some pencil underdrawing; 46.4×59.7 cm. Inscribed with measurements; 'Hall Buildings N.o 9'; 'south'; 'Transverse Section through the Hall'; 'A the floor of this passage must be kept up to the level of that of the Hall'; 'North'. *Location*: Downing College, Cambridge SWP50.

101. William **WILKINS**
Roof plan of the hall and combination room.
Pen and ink with blue, brown, grey and yellow washes; 46.2×59.8 cm. Scale 1/10 in. to 1 ft. Inscribed with measurements; 'Hall Buildings N.o 12'; 'face of wall projection of the cornice'; 'Edge of Slates bottom of gutter'; 'Plan of the Roof over Hall and Combination Room'; 'South'; 'Saddle piece no joint'; 'The ridge does not fall immediately over the centre of the tye beam, it is 4 inches nearer to the South end than the North. The King-post is to be immediately below the centre line of the Ridge'; 'West'; 'line of wall narrow tye beam'; 'face of wall; front of gutter'; 'front of wood gutter/ bottom of wood gutter wall plate'. *Location*: Downing College, Cambridge SWP51.

102. William **WILKINS**
Sections through the roof of the hall.
Pen and ink with black, blue, brown and yellow washes over some pencil underdrawing; 59.8×46.3 cm. Inscribed with some measurements; 'Hall Buildings N.o 13'; 'Roof over the Hall'; North'; 'Section looking West'; 'South'. *Location*: Downing College, Cambridge SWP52.

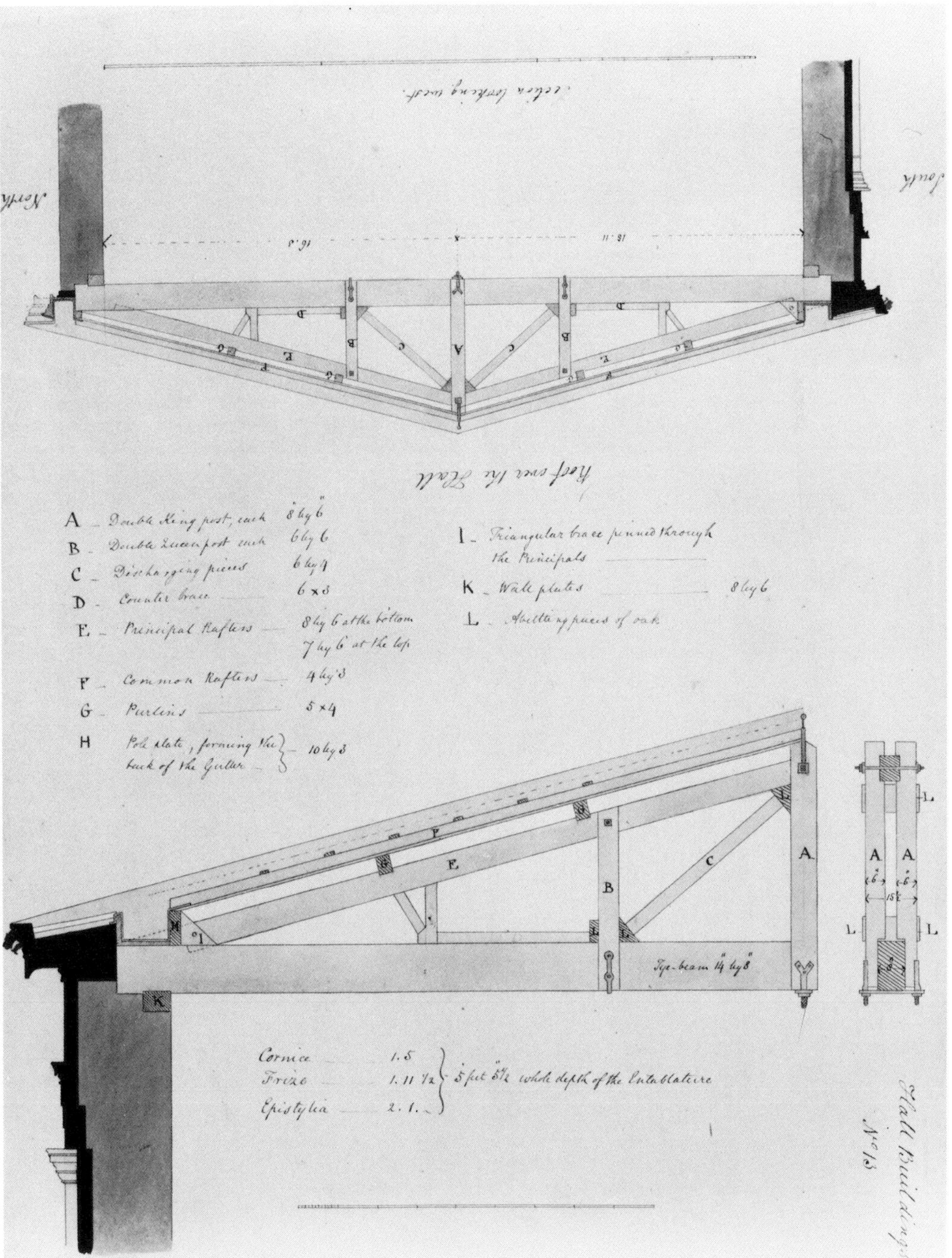

102

103. William **WILKINS**
Plan of the cornice and gutter of the hall's roof.
Pen and ink with blue, brown and grey washes over some pencil underdrawing; 45.8×59.6 cm. Scale 1/12 in. to 1 ft. Various inscriptions: 'Hall Buildings N.14 A'; 'Capping piece shown at AA half the full size'; 'top bed of the Cornice at the back'; 'Showing the joint when the capping piece is removed'; 'Upper face of the top-bed of the Cornice'; 'Line of the back of the Gutter'; 'Bottom of Gutter'; South-West Angle'; 'Top bed of the racking Cornice of the pediment'; 'Pediment at the West End'; 'B The courses of the top bed of the Cornice must be in equal lengths the joint taking place in the centre between two lions heads'. *Location*: Downing College, Cambridge SWP53.

104. William **WILKINS**
Constructional details of the pediment and cornice of the hall. (see Fig.27, p.60)
Pen and ink with grey and brown washes over some pencil underdrawing; 59.6×46.6 cm. Various inscriptions: 'Sheet lead to cover the top of the Cornice below the Pediment'; 'Throuting sunk in such side of the top bed. Line of top slates Rebated to cover the end of the slating. Side of the top bed. Pediment cornice'; 'Cornice, half the full size'; 'In the pediment the Cymatium projects as at a'; '16 inches projection'; 'The Lions heads perforated to let the water escape from the top bed of the Cornice'; 'depth of the top bed over the pediments'; 'Pediment Cornice'; 'joint of the under bed'; 'joint of the top bed, Lead run in to close the joint'. *Location*: Downing College, Cambridge SWP54.

105. William **WILKINS**
Constructional details of the roof of the hall.

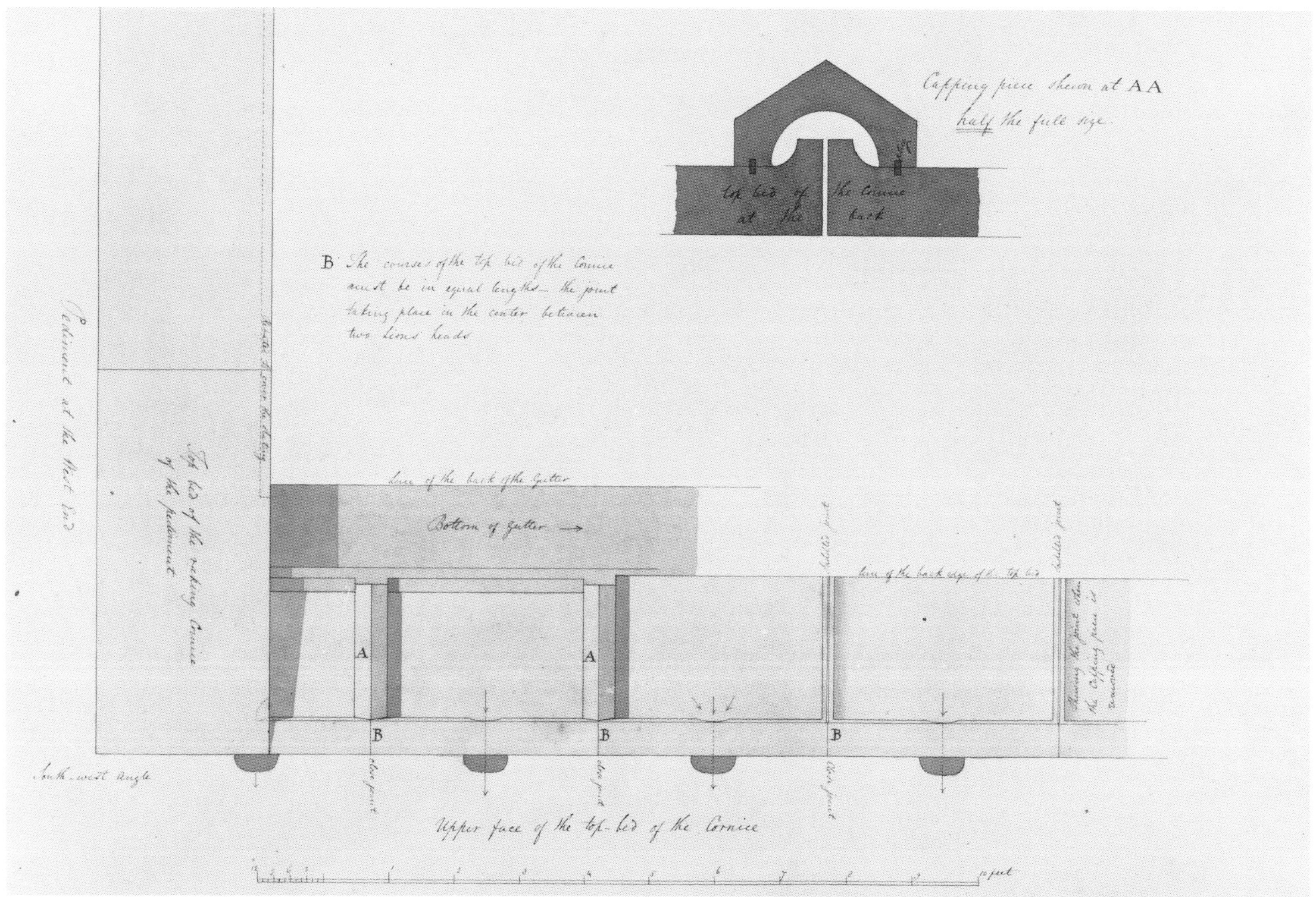

103

(see Pl. XIII)
Pen and ink with blue, brown, grey, red and yellow washes; 59.8×45.7 cm. Various measurements and inscriptions: 'Section of the Cornice in the South front of the Hall'; 'Back of the Cornice of the Western pediment'; 'Fillet mould upon the lower edge of the Rafter'. *Location*: Downing College, Cambridge SWP55.

106. William **WILKINS**
Constructional details of the soffit of the south and east porticoes of the hall.
Pen, black and red inks with grey wash; 46.1×59.6 cm. Scale 1/10 in. to 1 ft. Various measurements and inscriptions: 'N.16'; 'Section through the Lacunaria, or ceilings, of the porticoes/ Half the Full Size'; '2.2 in the four column portico'; '1.10' In the six column portico'; '10 inches & 8 inches'; 'soffit of beam'; 'A.A. Enriched ovals in plaister/ B Enriched ovals & bead of Do.'; 'East Portico'; 'South portico'; 'centre of tye beam'; 'line of frize [sic]'. *Location*: Downing College, Cambridge SWP56.

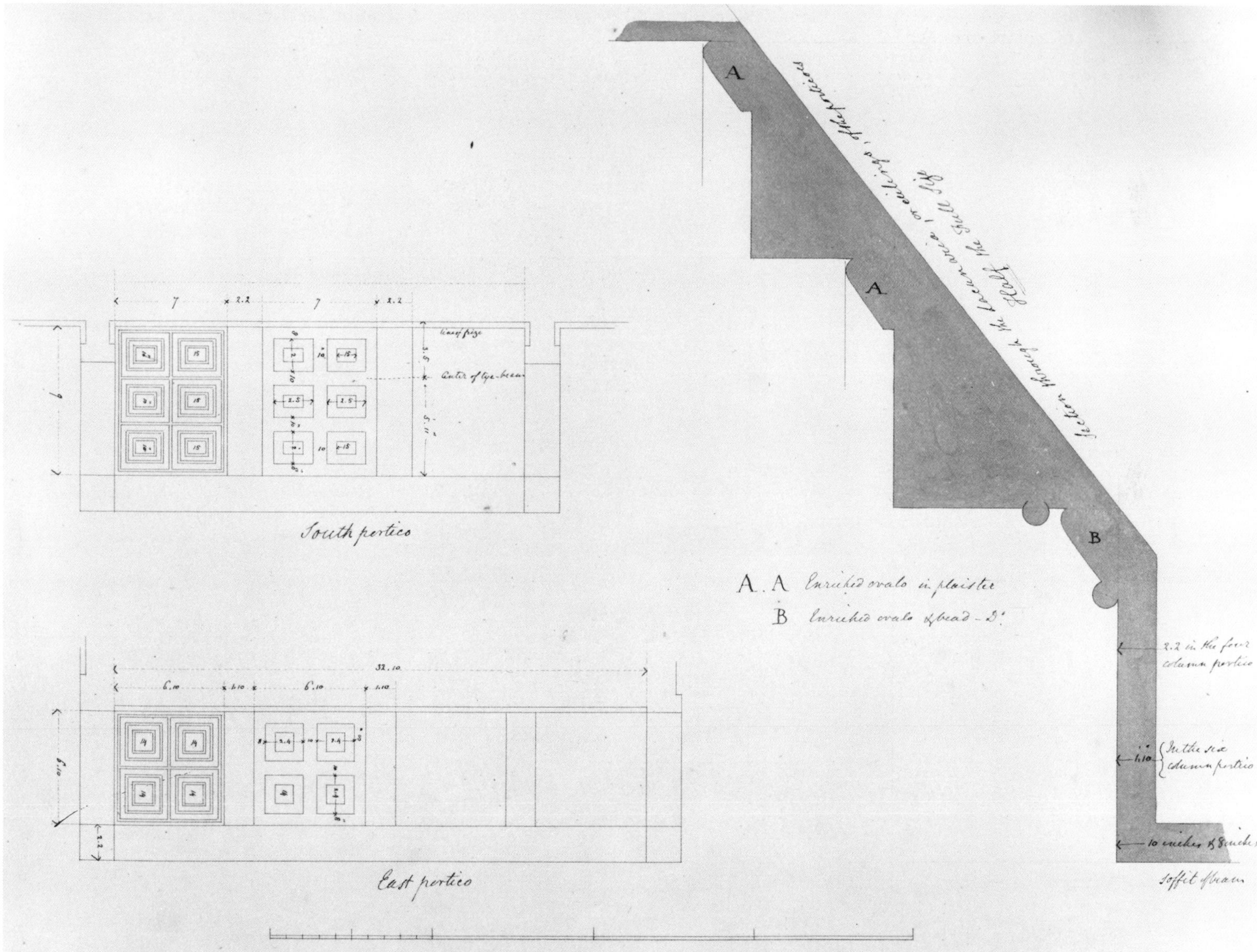

106

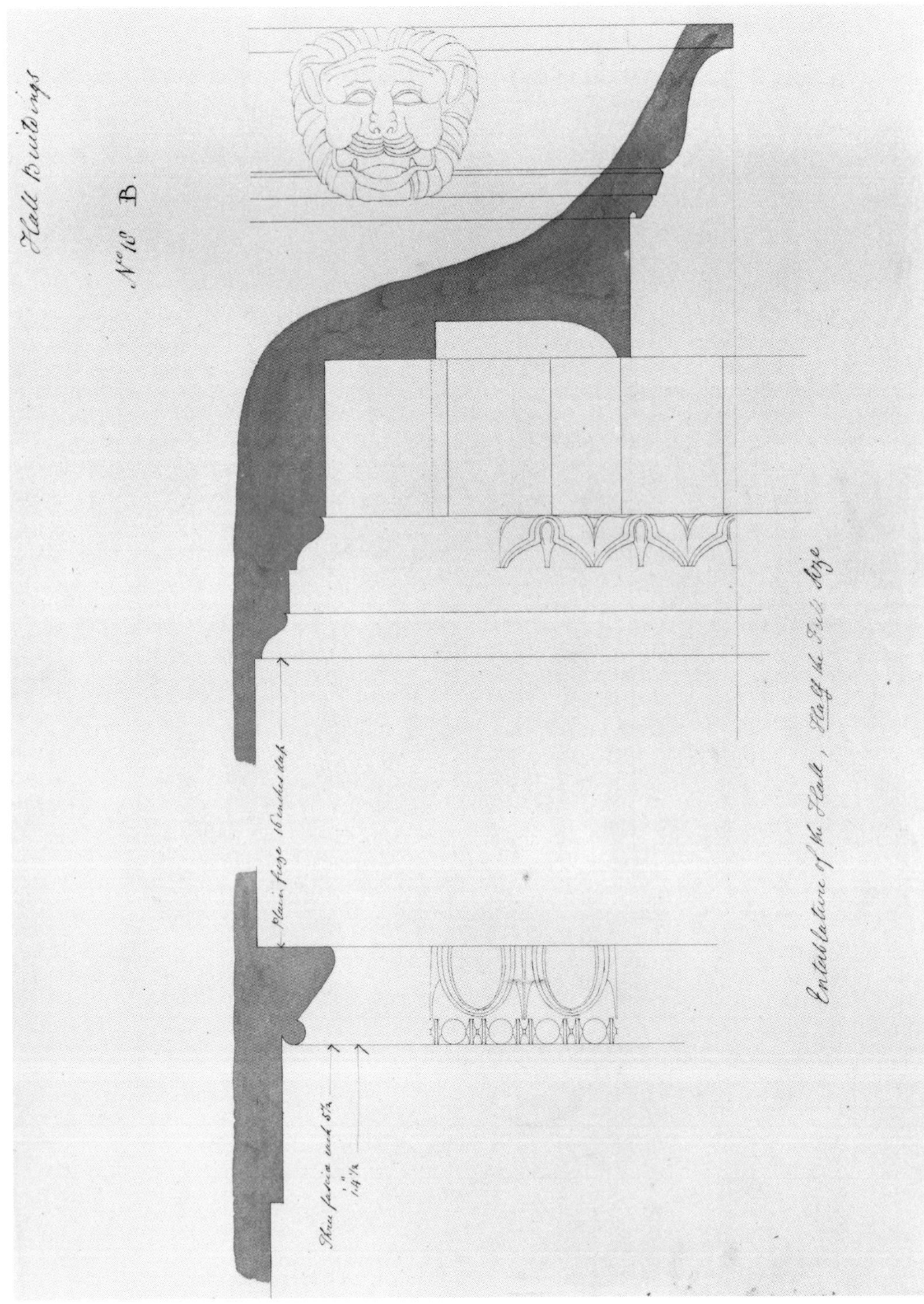

107

107. William **WILKINS**
Profile and details of the entablature in the hall.
Pen and ink with grey wash; 46.4×59.5 cm. Inscribed: 'Hall Buildings/ N. 18 B'; 'Entablature of the Hall, <u>Half</u> the Full Size'; 'Three fascia each 5½/ 1'4"½; 'Plain frize [sic] 16 inches deep'. *Location*: Downing College, Cambridge SWP57.

108. William **WILKINS**
Windows of the south front of the hall and combination room with profiles of their architraves.
Pen and ink with grey washes; 46.2×59.6 cm. Various measurements and inscriptions: 'Hall Buildings N. 21'; Architrave round the lower windows/ the <u>Full</u> size'; 'A This rebate diminishes from the bottom of the/ window to the top, where it shews ½ an inch / The rebate only diminishes the other moldings of the architrave are the same width both at the bottom and top'; 'Line of the upper face of/ the base the hollow/ and fillet are worked in the/ lower course of the Stone facing'; 'face of Stone work'; 'line of the sill'; 'Architrave round the/ upper windows/ <u>Full</u> size'; 'The extent of the window opening and the architraves at the bottom is/ 5 feet 7 and at the top of the lower window (B) it is 5 feet 5. The/ diminution is caused by the rebate A which at the top of the/ window is only ½ an inch'; 'Windows of the South front/ of the Hall and Combination/ Room'; 'top of base molding'; 'bottom of Epistylia'; 'Opening 3'8" in the clear' (repeated twice); 'Opening 4 feet in the clear' (repeated twice); 'face of the reveal at the top & head'; 'face of the reveal below'. *Location*: Downing College, Cambridge SWP58.

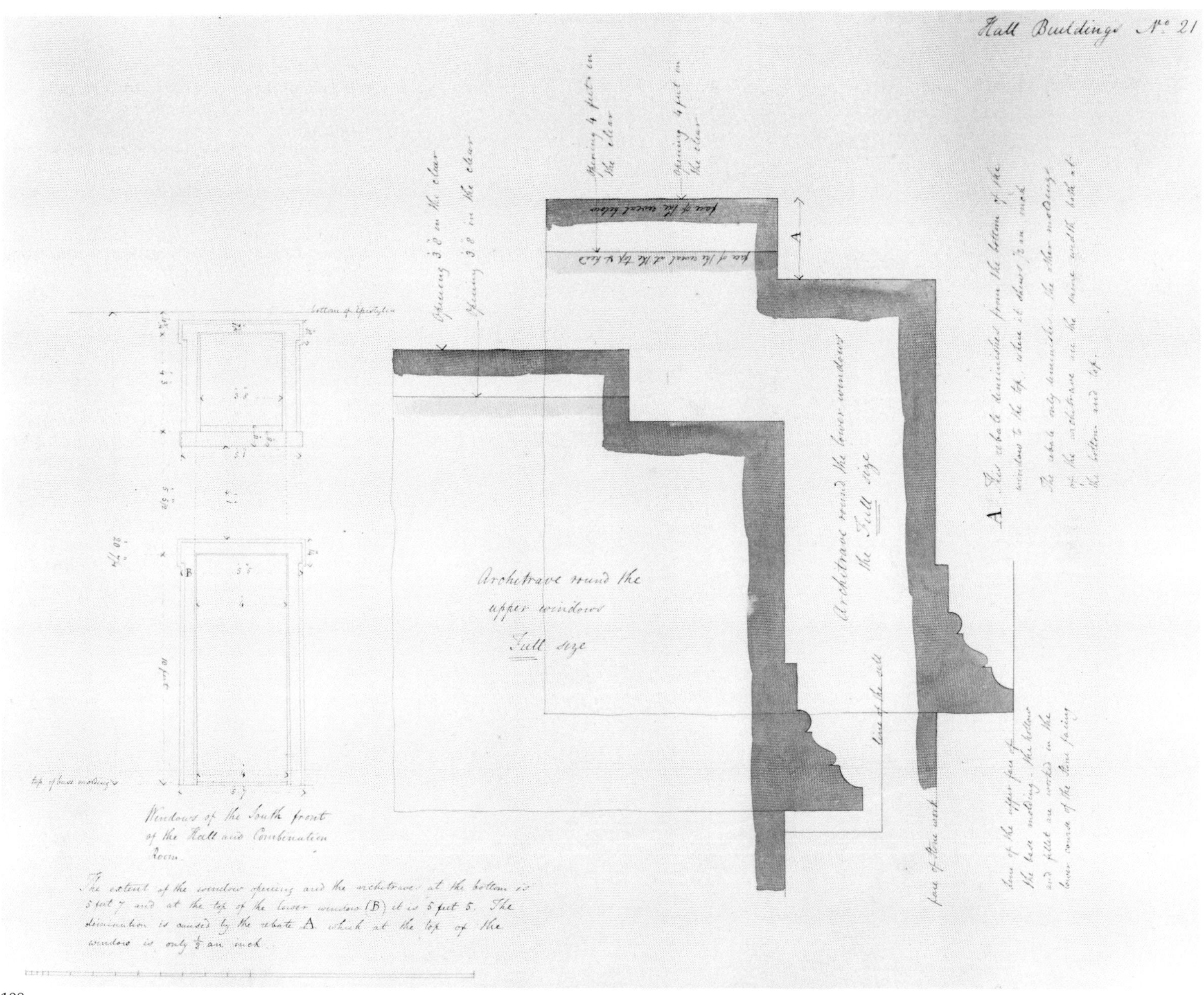
Hall Buildings No. 21
Architrave round the upper windows
Full size
Architrave round the lower windows
the Full size
Windows of the South front
of the Hall and Combination
Room.
The extent of the window opening and the architrave at the bottom is
5 feet 7 and at the top of the lower window (B) it is 5 feet 5. The
diminution is caused by the rebate A which at the top of the
window is only ½ an inch.

108

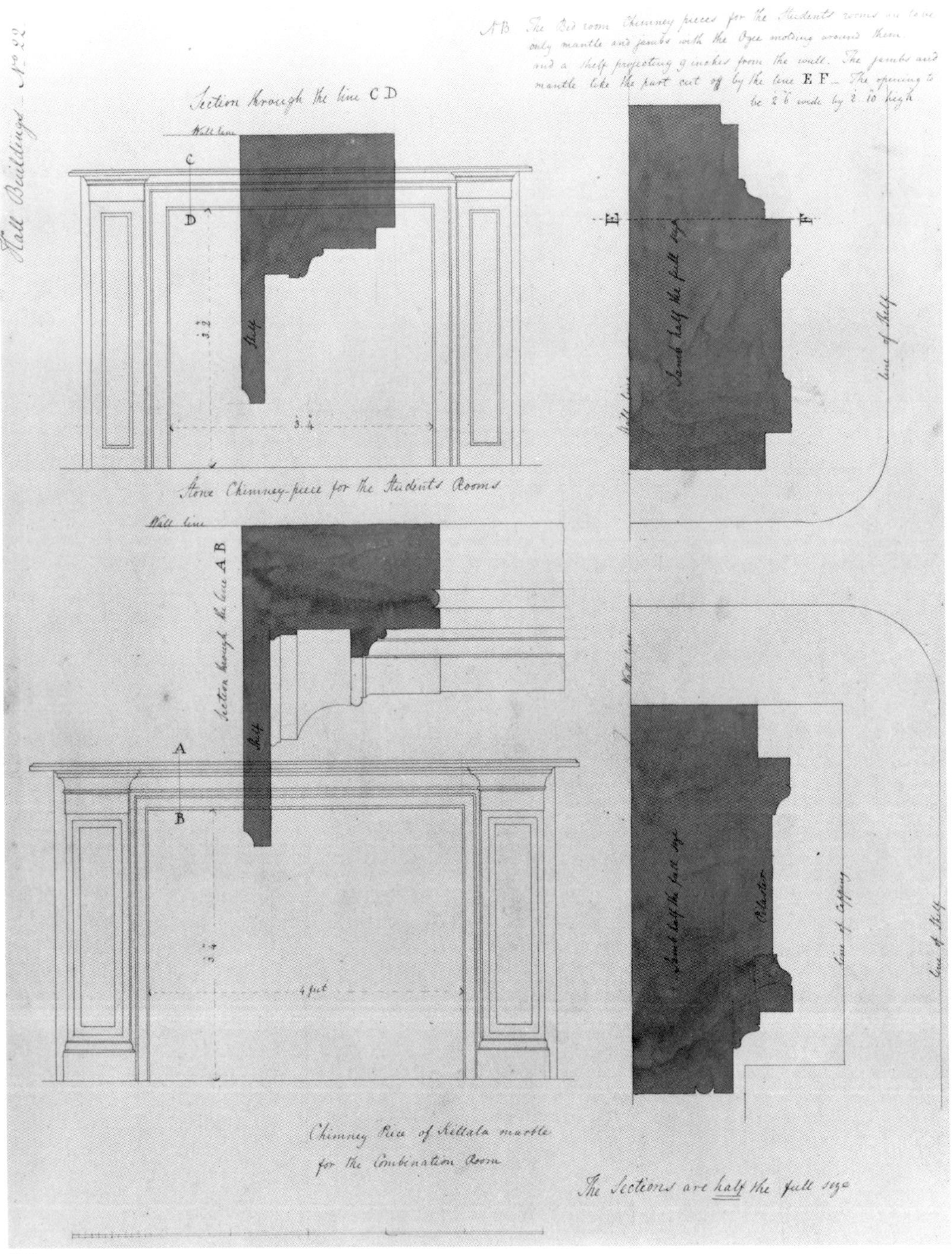

109

109. William **WILKINS**
Elevations and profiles of the fireplaces in the students' rooms and combination room.
Pen and ink with grey wash; 46.4×59.7 cm. Various measurements and inscriptions: 'Hall Buildings N. 22'; 'Section through the line CD/ Wall line'; 'N.N. The Bed room Chimney pieces for the Students rooms are to be/ only mantle and jambs with the Ogee molding around them/ and a shelf projecting 9 inches from the wall. The jambs and mantle like the part cut off by the line EF. The opening to/ be 2'6" wide by 2'10" high'; 'Jambs half the full size/ line of shelf'; 'Jamb half the full size/ Pilaster/ line of Capping'; 'The Sections are half the full size'; 'Chimney Piece of Killala marble/ for the Combination Room'; 'Section through the line A.B'; 'Stone Chimney-piece for the Students Rooms'. *Location*: Downing College, Cambridge SWP59.

110. William **WILKINS**
Section and profile of the base of the columns in the hall.
Pen and ink with grey and red washes over some pencil underdrawing; 46.3×59.8 cm. Inscribed: 'Hall Buildings N. 26'; 'plan of the flutings'; 'Worked in the lower course'; 'joint here'; 'Base-molding of the Antae/ or pilasters'; 'Half the Full Size'; 'Upper Step'; 'Base of the Columns'; 'Joint in this line'; 'Hollow and fillet to be worked in the lower course of the shaft'; 'Brick work/ One Fourth the/ Full Size'; 'top of the second step'; 'Addition to the/ base molding where it forms the/ Window Sill/ Base molding'; 'Ashler facing'; 'The hollow & fillet must be worked in the lower course of the Ashler facing'. *Location*: Downing College, Cambridge SWP60.

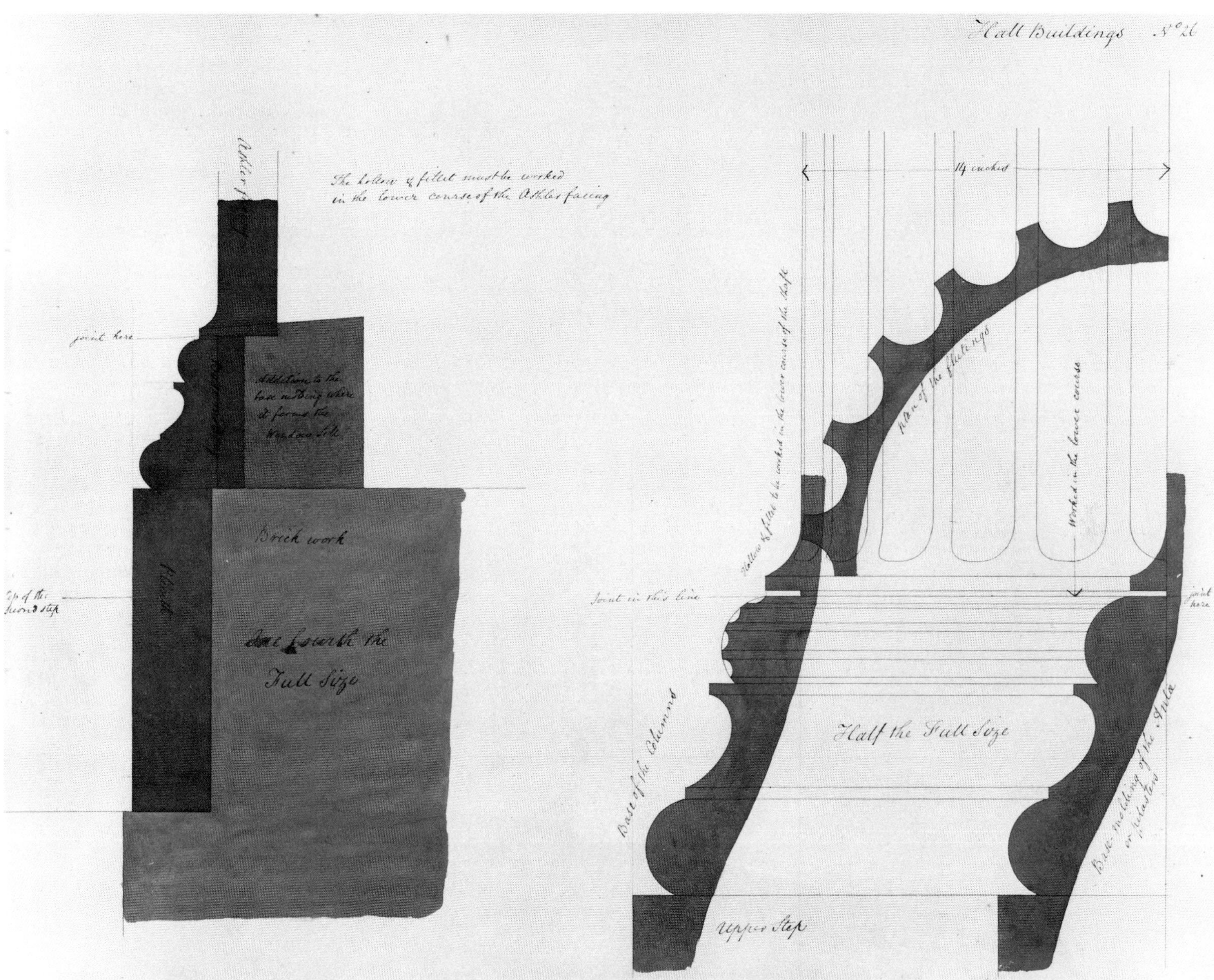
Hall Buildings No 26
The hollow & fillet must be worked
in the lower course of the Ashler facing
joint here
Addition to the base moulding where it forms the Window Sill
Brick work
Plinth
One fourth the Full Size
14 inches
Plan of the flutings
Worked in the lower course
Joint in this line
joint here
Half the Full Size
Base of the Columns
Base moulding of the Antae or pilasters
Upper Step

110

111. William **WILKINS**
Section of the first block of students' apartments adjoining the hall and kitchens. (see Pl. XIV)
Pen and ink with yellow, red and blue washes with some traces of pencil; 46.4×59.7 cm.
Location: Downing College, Cambridge SWP61.

112. William **WILKINS**
Plan of the ground storey of the first block of students' apartments adjoining the hall.
Pen and ink with yellow and grey washes; 46.5×59.6 cm. Scale ⅒ in. to 1 ft. Inscribed in the top right corner: 'No. / Students Apartments/ nex the Hall/ N. 1'. *Location*: Downing College, Cambridge SWP62.

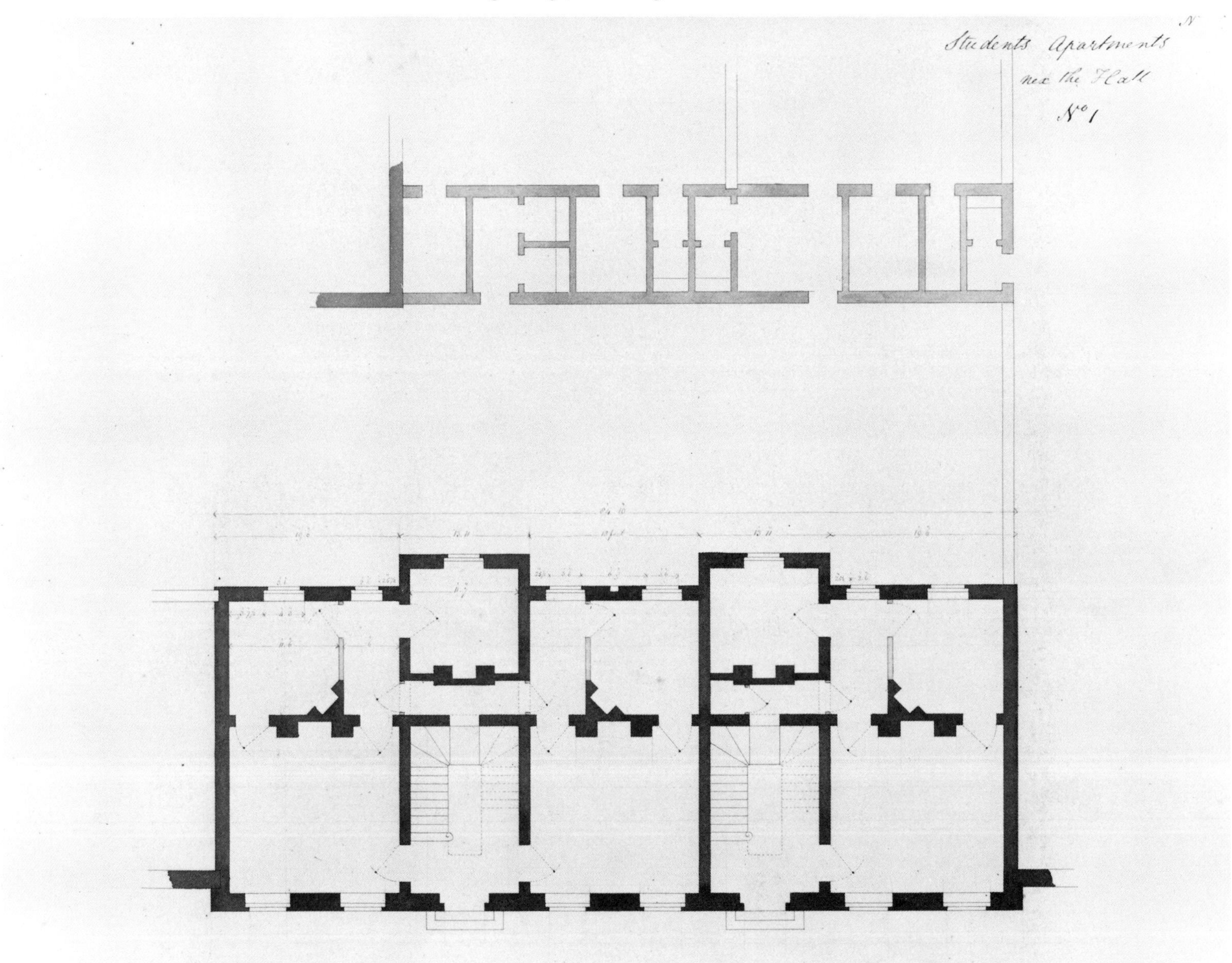

112

113. William **WILKINS**
Plan of the first floor of the first block of students' apartments adjoining the hall.
Pen and ink with grey and yellow washes; 46.2×59.6 cm. Scale 1/10 in. to 1 ft. Inscribed in the top right corner: 'Students Apartments/ next the Hall/ N.2'. *Location*: Downing College, Cambridge SWP63.

114. William **WILKINS**
Plan of the ground storey of the students' apartments in the west range. (see Fig.40, p.72)
Pen and ink with yellow and grey washes; 46. 4×59.6 cm. Inscribed: 'N. 1/ Students Apartments/ West'; 'Ground Plan'; 'Open Court'. *Location*: Downing College, Cambridge SWP64.

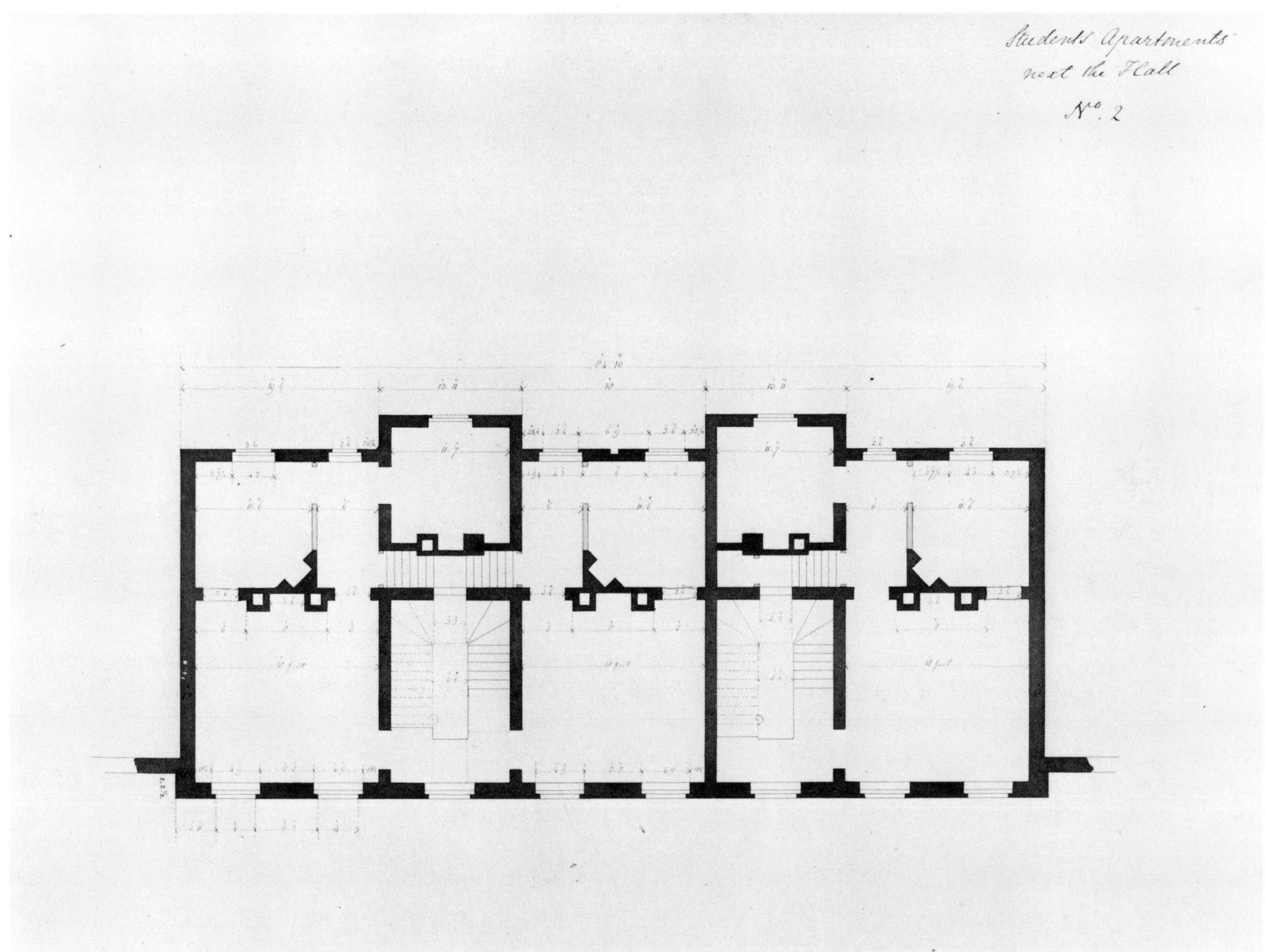

113

115. William **WILKINS**
Plan of the first floor of the students' apartments in the west range.
Pen and ink with yellow and grey washes; 45.7×59.6 cm. Scale 1/10 in. to 1 ft. Various measurements and inscriptions: 'N.2/ Students Apartments/ West'; 'Plan of the Upper floor'. *Location*: Downing College, Cambridge SWP65.

116. William **WILKINS**
Principal elevation of the students' apartments in the west range.
Pen and ink over some pencil underdrawing; 45.7×59.6 cm. Scale 1/10 in. to 1 ft. Measured and inscribed: 'N.3/ Students Apartments/ West'; 'Front next the Quadrangle'. *Location*: Downing College, Cambridge SWP66.

117. William **WILKINS**
Rear elevation of the students' apartments in the west range with detail of the window sash.
Pen and ink over some pencil underdrawing; 46.3×59.7 cm. Scale 1/10 in. to 1 ft. Inscribed: 'N.4/ Students Apartments/ West'; 'Iron frame/ fastened to/ the top of the/ upper sash'; 'Top sash alone to/ be hung/ Lower Sash to be/ fixed'; 'Front next the back Court'. *Location*: Downing College, Cambridge SWP67.

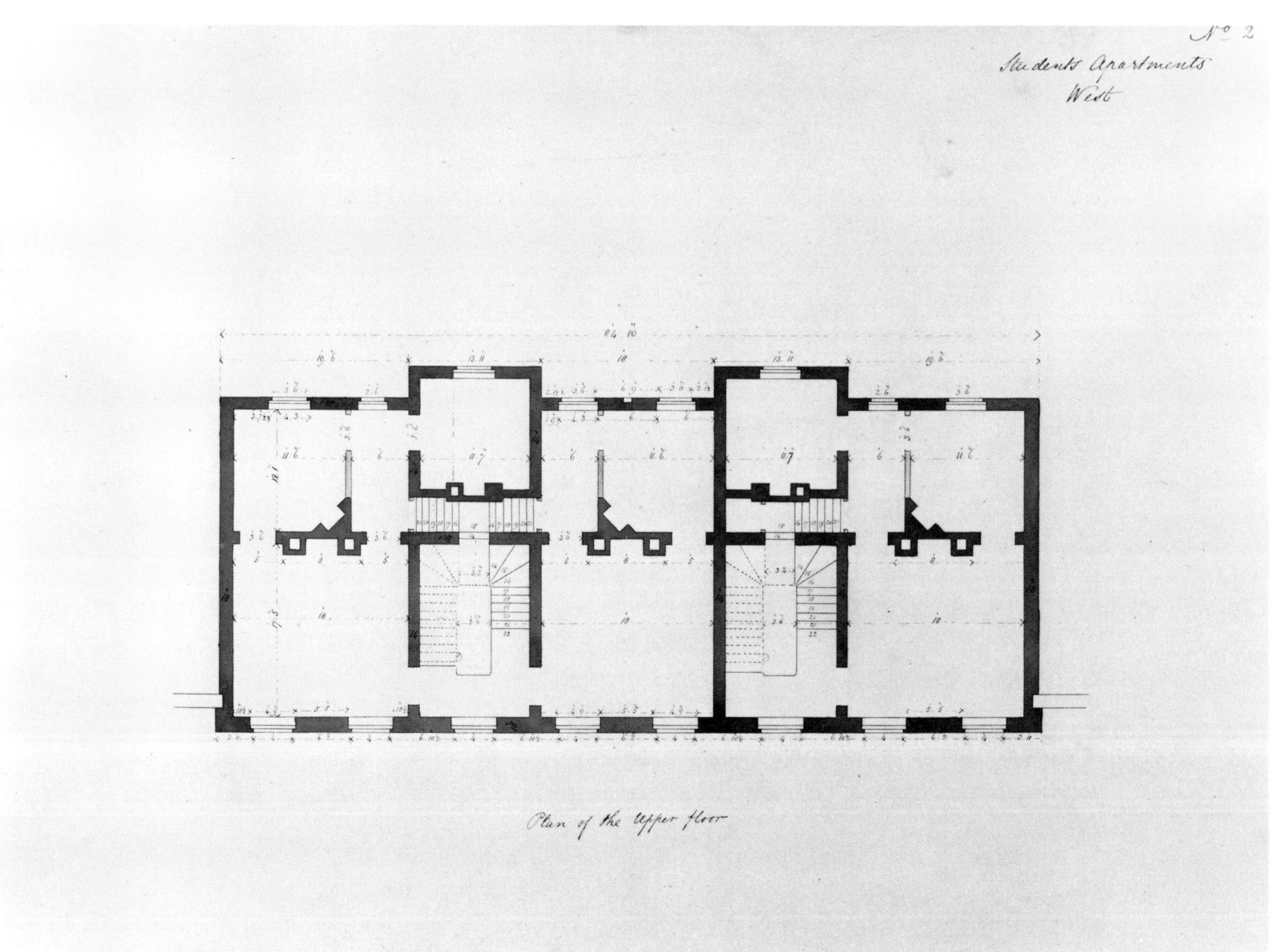

115

Front next the Quadrangle.

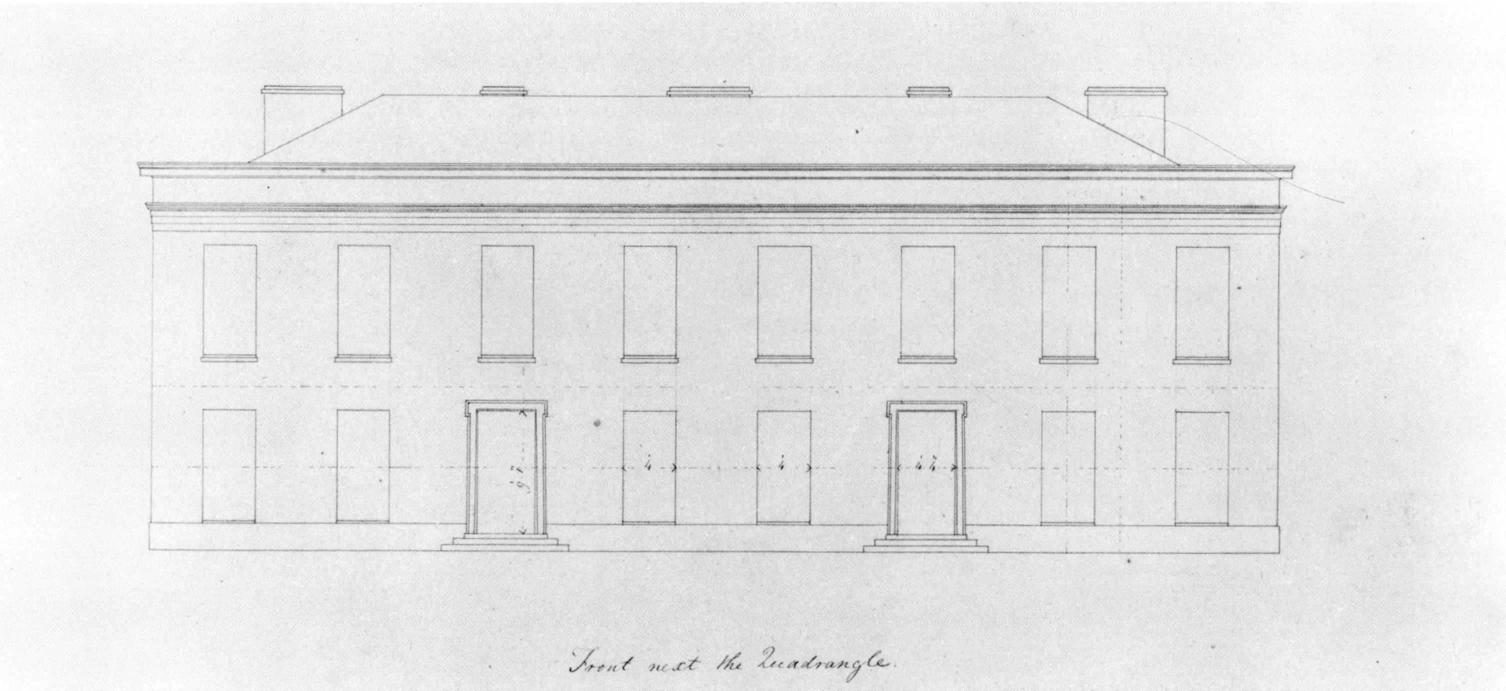

116

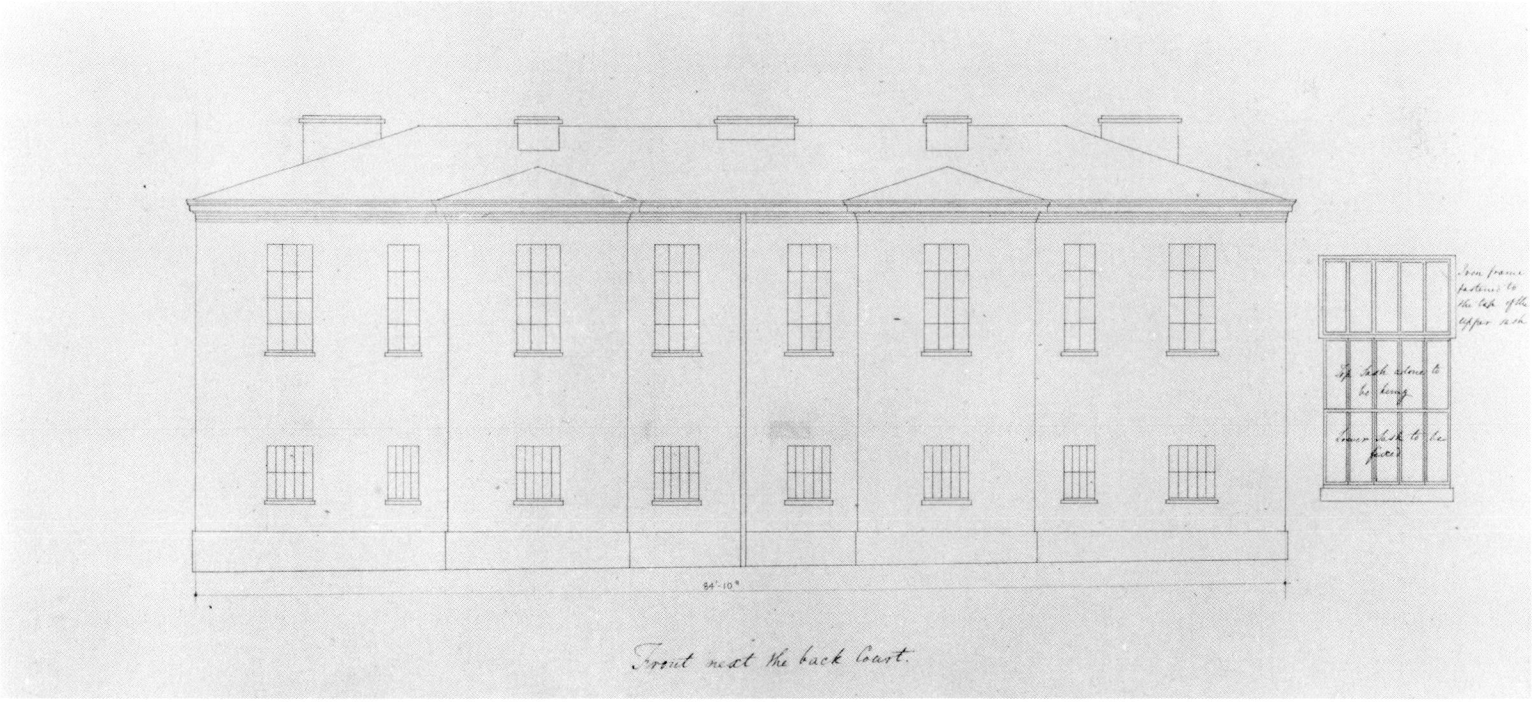
Iron frame fastened to the top of the upper sash
Top sash alone to be hung
Lower sash to be fixed
84'-10"
Front next the back Court.

117

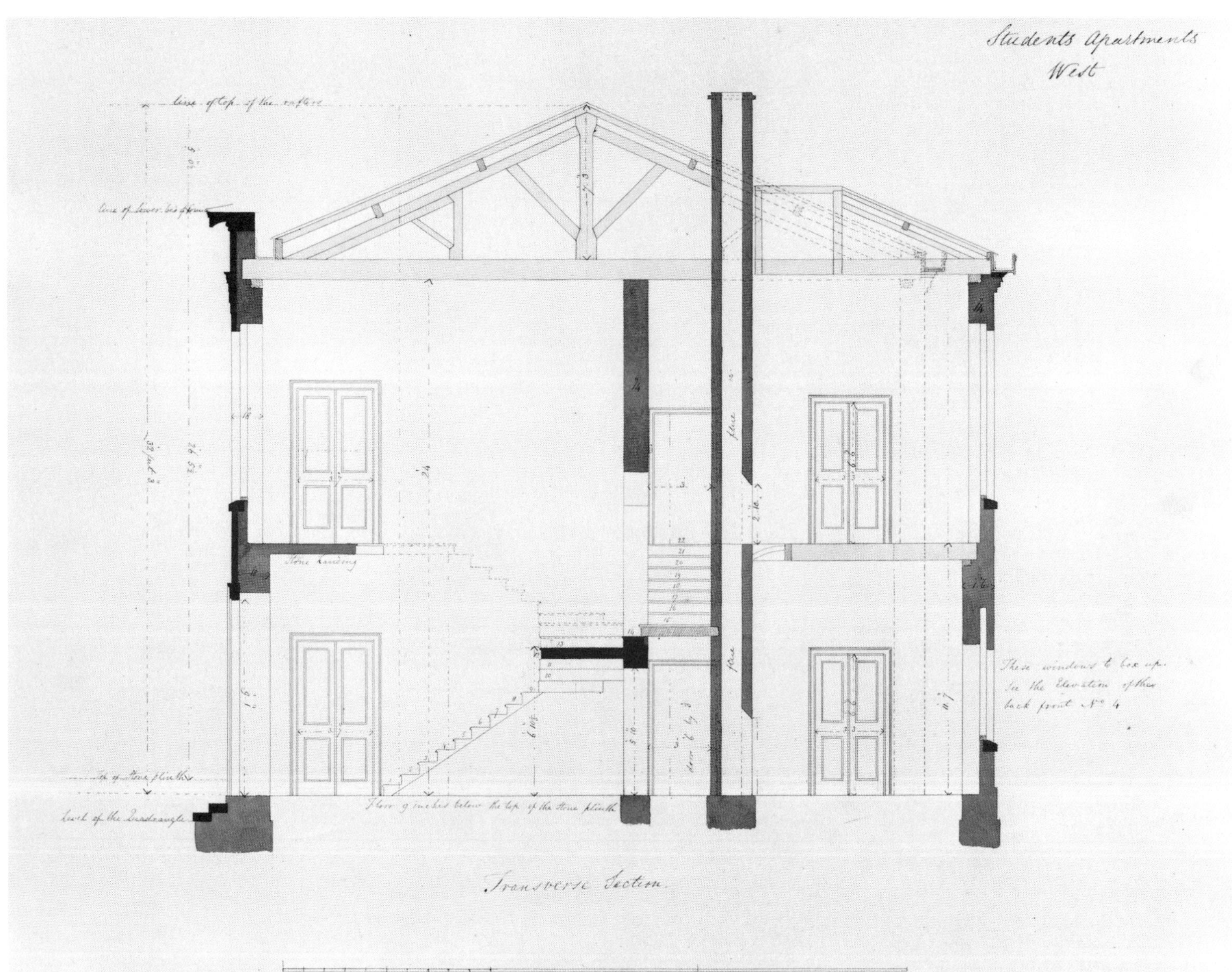
Students Apartments
West
line of top of the rafters
Stone Landing
flue
flue
These windows to box up.
See the Elevation of the
back front No 4
top of stone plinth
level of the Quadrangle
Floor 9 inches below the top of the stone plinth
Transverse Section

119

118. William **WILKINS**
Section through the students' apartments in the west range. (see Fig.41, p.72)
Pen and ink with yellow and grey washes; 46.2×59.8 cm. Various measurements and inscriptions: 'N.5/ Students Apartments/ West'; 'wood cornice/ North'; 'AA Stone Key Stones to the heads of these Arches 2'8" wide and 6 inches deep below the Stone Landing at the Crown/ BB The dotted steps shew the ascents to the back rooms/ CC Top of the wooden Landings leading to the back Stairs/ DD Entrance of the flues from the back Rooms into the main Stacks'; 'South/ wood cornice'. *Location*: Downing College, Cambridge SWP68.

119. William **WILKINS**
Transverse section of the students'apartments in the west range.
Pen and ink with yellow and grey washes; 46.4×59.7 cm. Scale 1⁄10 in. to 1 ft. Various measurements and inscriptions: 'N. 6/ Students Apartments/ West'; 'These windows to box up./ See the Elevation of the/ back front N. 4'; 'Floor 9 inches below the top of the stone plinth/ Transverse Section'; 'Top of the plinth/ Level of the Quadrangle'; 'line of lower bed of cornice'; 'line of top of the rafters'. *Location*: Downing College, Cambridge SWP69.

120. William **WILKINS**
Plan of the naked flooring in the students'apartments in the west range.
Pen and ink with yellow and grey washes; 46.2×59.6 cm. Scale 1⁄10 in. to 1 ft. Inscribed: 'N.7/ Students Apartments/ West'; 'AA Girders – 12" by 12"/ BB Bridging Joists/ CC Stout Joists/ DD Common Joists/ Plan of the Naked Flooring'. *Location*: Downing College, Cambridge SWP70.

121. William **WILKINS**
Plan of the roof covering the students' apartments in the west range.
Pen and ink with black and blue washes over some pencil underdrawing; 46.2×59.8 cm. Scale 1⁄10 in. to 1 ft. Inscribed: 'N.8/ Students Apartments/ West'; 'Stone cornice to be/ returned at this/ angle'; 'Gutter/ Top bed of the Cornice'; 'Plan of the Roof'; 'Stone cornice returned/ at this angle'. *Location*: Downing College, Cambridge SWP71.

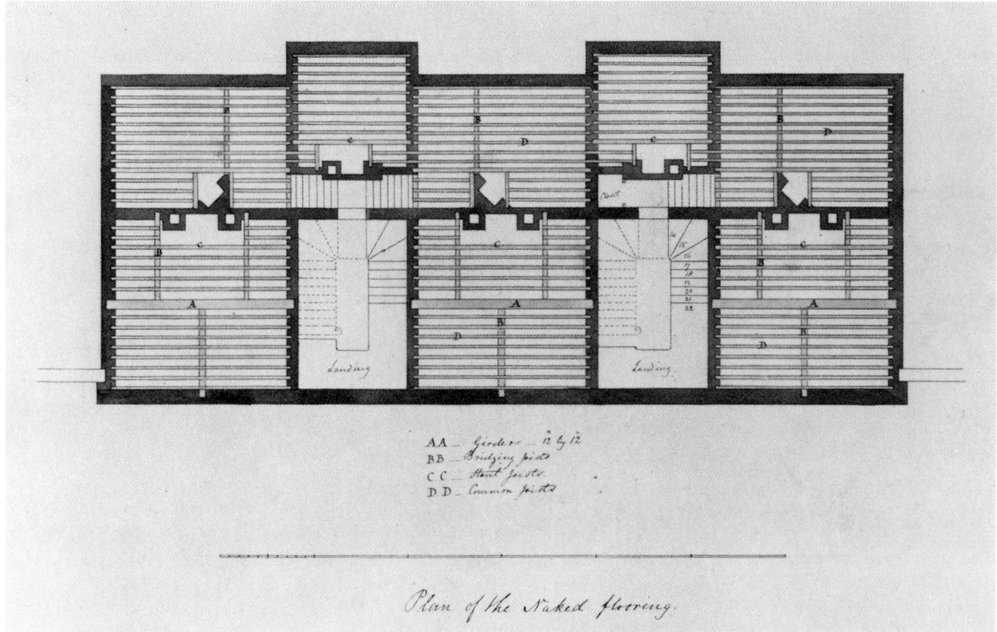

120

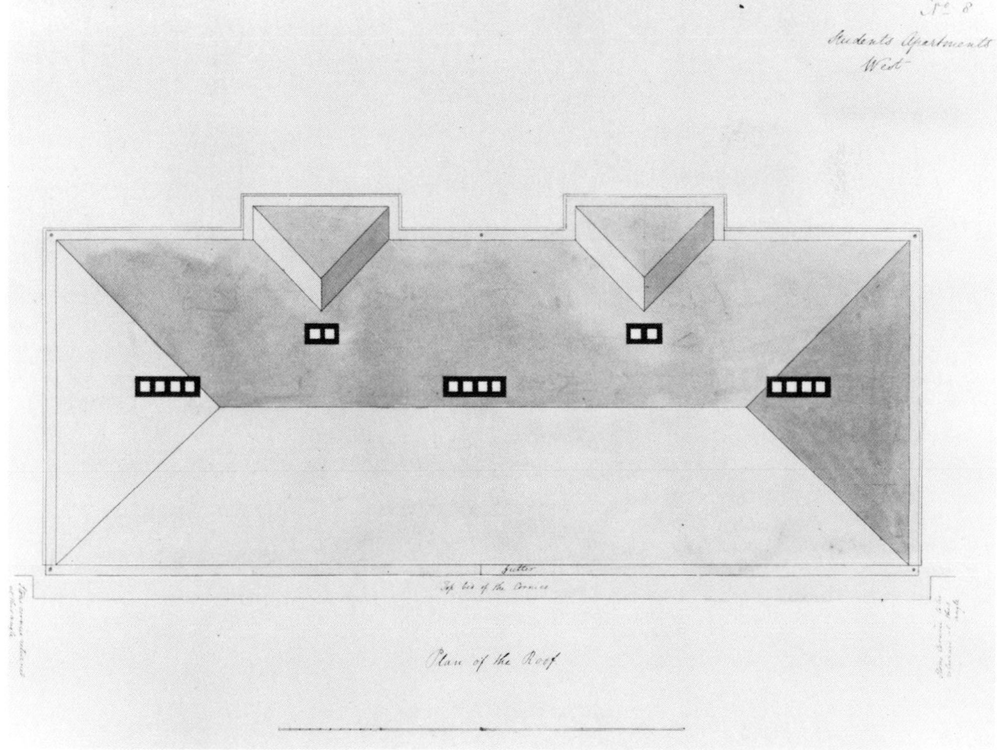

121

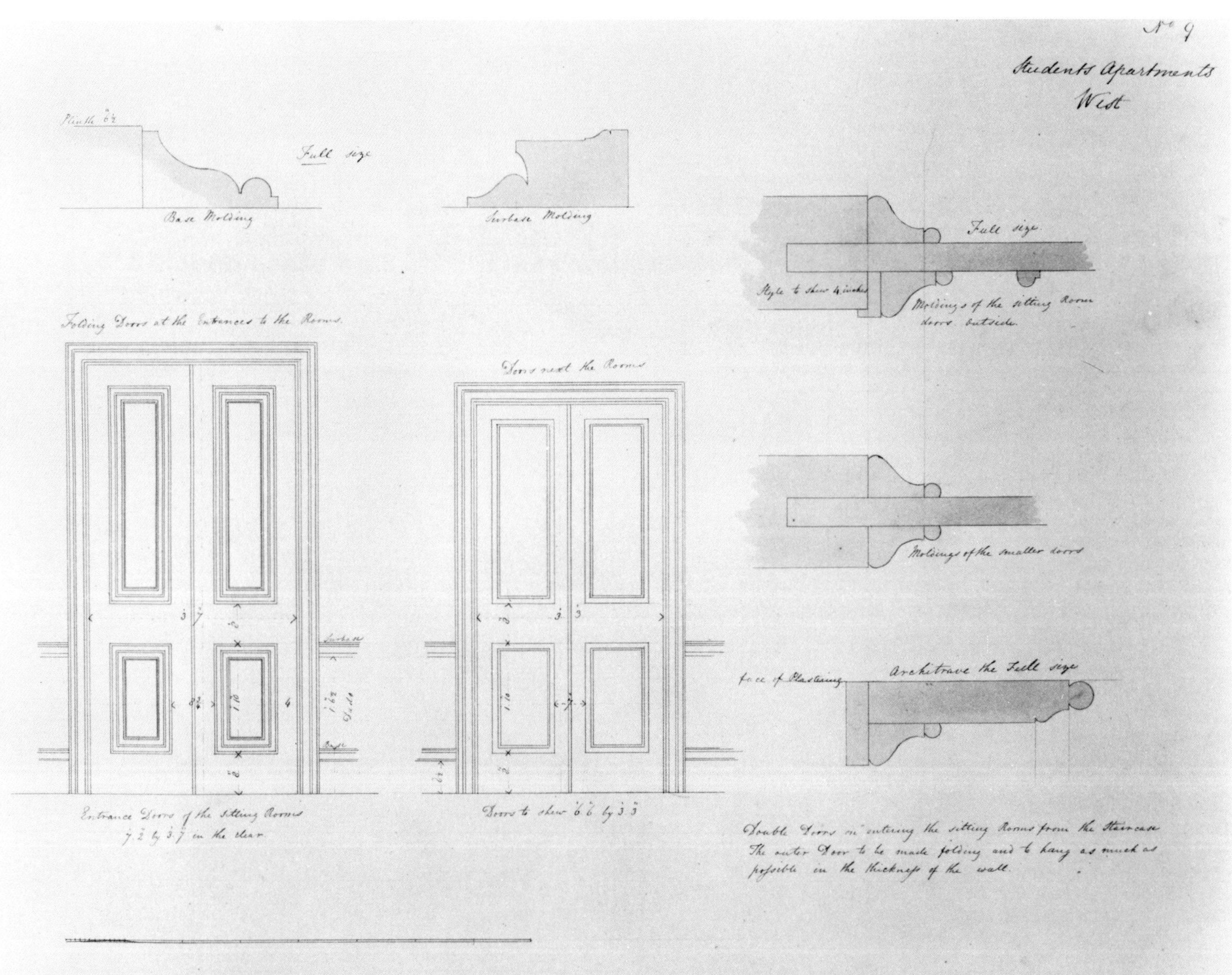
No 9
Students Apartments
West
Full size
Base Molding
Surbase Molding
Full size
Style to shew 4 inches
Moldings of the sitting Rooms
doors outside.
Folding Doors at the Entrances to the Rooms.
Doors next the Rooms
Molings of the smaller doors
Face of Plastering
Architrave the Full size
Entrance Doors of the sitting Rooms
7.2 by 3.7 in the clear
Doors to shew 6.6 by 3.3
Double Doors in entering the sitting Rooms from the Staircase
The outer Door to be made folding and to hang as much as
possible in the thickness of the wall.

122

122. William **WILKINS**
Elevations of the doors and profiles of the mouldings in the students'apartments in the west range.
Pen and ink with grey wash over some pencil underdrawing; 44.8×59.9 cm. Scale 1/12 in. to 1 ft. Inscribed: 'N.9/ Students Apartments/ West'; 'Full size/ Style to show 4 inches/ Moldings of the sitting Room/ doors outside'; 'Moldings of the smaller doors'; 'Face of Plastering/ Architrave the Full size'; 'Double Doors on entering the sitting Rooms from the Staircase/ The outer Door to be made folding and to hang as much as/ possible in the thickness of the wall'; 'Doors next the Rooms/ Doors to shew 6'6" by 3'3"'; 'Surbase/ Dado/ Base'; 'Folding Doors at the Entrances to the Rooms/ Entrance Doors of the Sitting Rooms/ 7'2" by 3'7" in the clear'; 'Plinth 6½"/ Base Molding'; 'Full Size'; 'Surbase Molding'; some measurements. *Location*: Downing College, Cambridge SWP72.

123. William **WILKINS**
Elevation of the window and sections of the sash including the folded shutters in the students'apartments.
Pen and ink with grey and yellow washes; 59.9×46.6 cm. Scale 1/12 in. to 1 ft. Inscribed: 'Sash bar the full size'; 'Students Apartments/ n.10'; 'wall line/ line of plastering'; 'Sashes in Shutters/ The Sashes to be double hung/ The two back flaps of the Shutters to/ be cut at the meeting rail'; 'face of wall/ face of plastering'; 'Shutters to be framed in one length'; 'Architrave/ Fascia for Window blinds'. *Location*: Downing College, Cambridge SWP73.

123

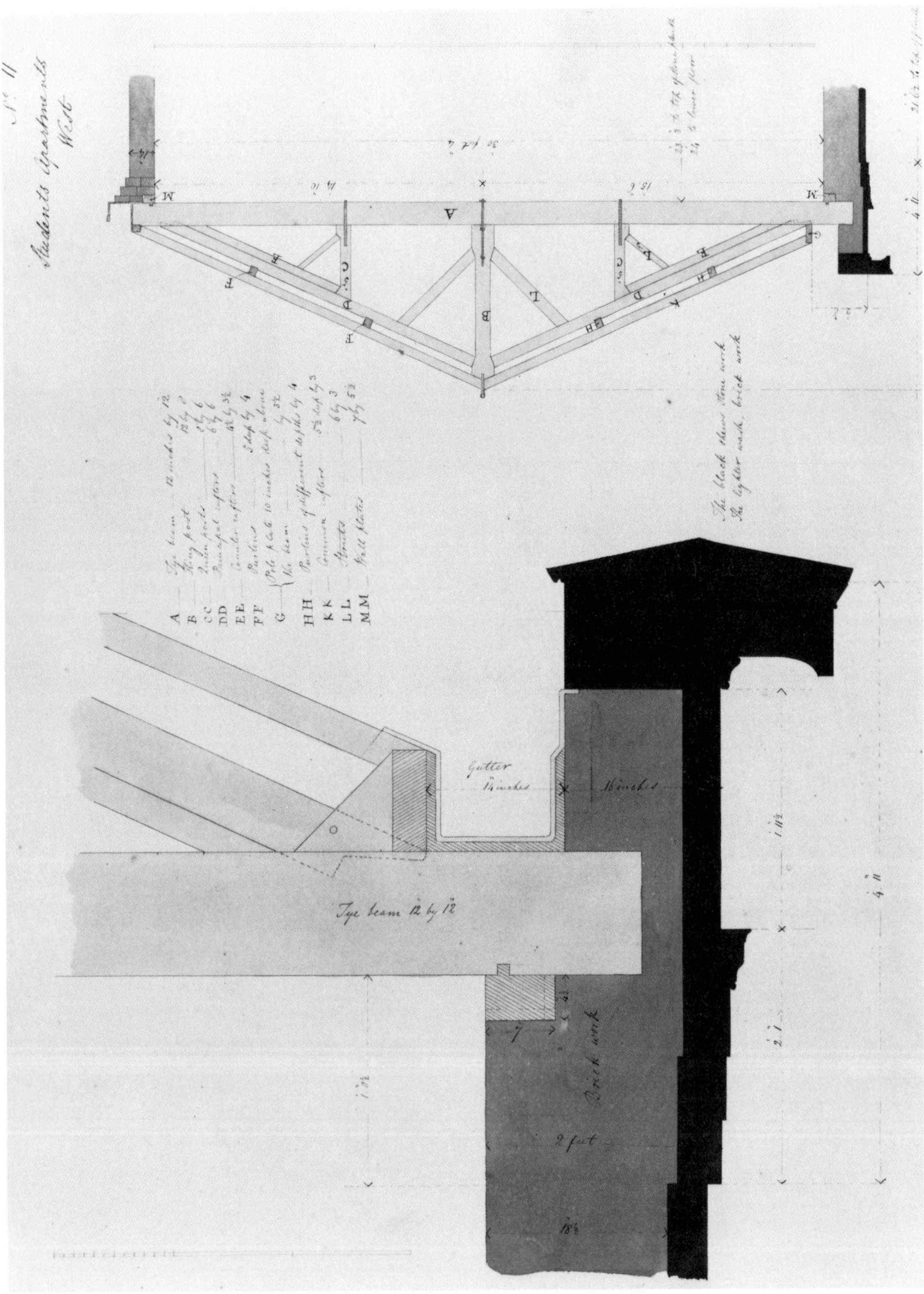

124

124. William **WILKINS**
Section through the roof and detail of the tye beam in the students'apartments.
Pen and ink with black, blue, grey and yellow washes; 45.9×60 cm. Scale 1⁄10 in. to 1 ft. Inscribed: 'N. 11/ Students Apartments/ West'; '23'3" to top of Stone plinth/ 24' to lower floor'; 'The black shews stone work./ The lighter wash, brick work'; 'tye beam 12" by 12"'; 'A. Tye beam 12 inches by 12"/ B. King post 12" by 8"/ CC. Queen posts 8 by 6/ DD. Principal rafters 6 by 6/ EE. Counter rafters 4½ by 3½ / FF. Purlins 5 deep by 4/ G. Pole plate 10 inches deep above the beam by 3½ / HH. Purlins of different depths by 4 / KK. Common rafters 5½ deep by 3 / LL. Struts 6 by 3 / MM. Wall plates 7 by 5½"'. *Location*: Downing College, Cambridge SWP74.

125. William **WILKINS**
Plans of connecting rooms in the Professor's lodge in the west range.
Pen and ink with yellow and grey washes; 46.5×59.8 cm. Scale 1⁄10 in. to 1 ft. Inscribed: 'N.1/ Professors Residence/ West' in the upper right corner. *Location*: Downing College, Cambridge SWP75.

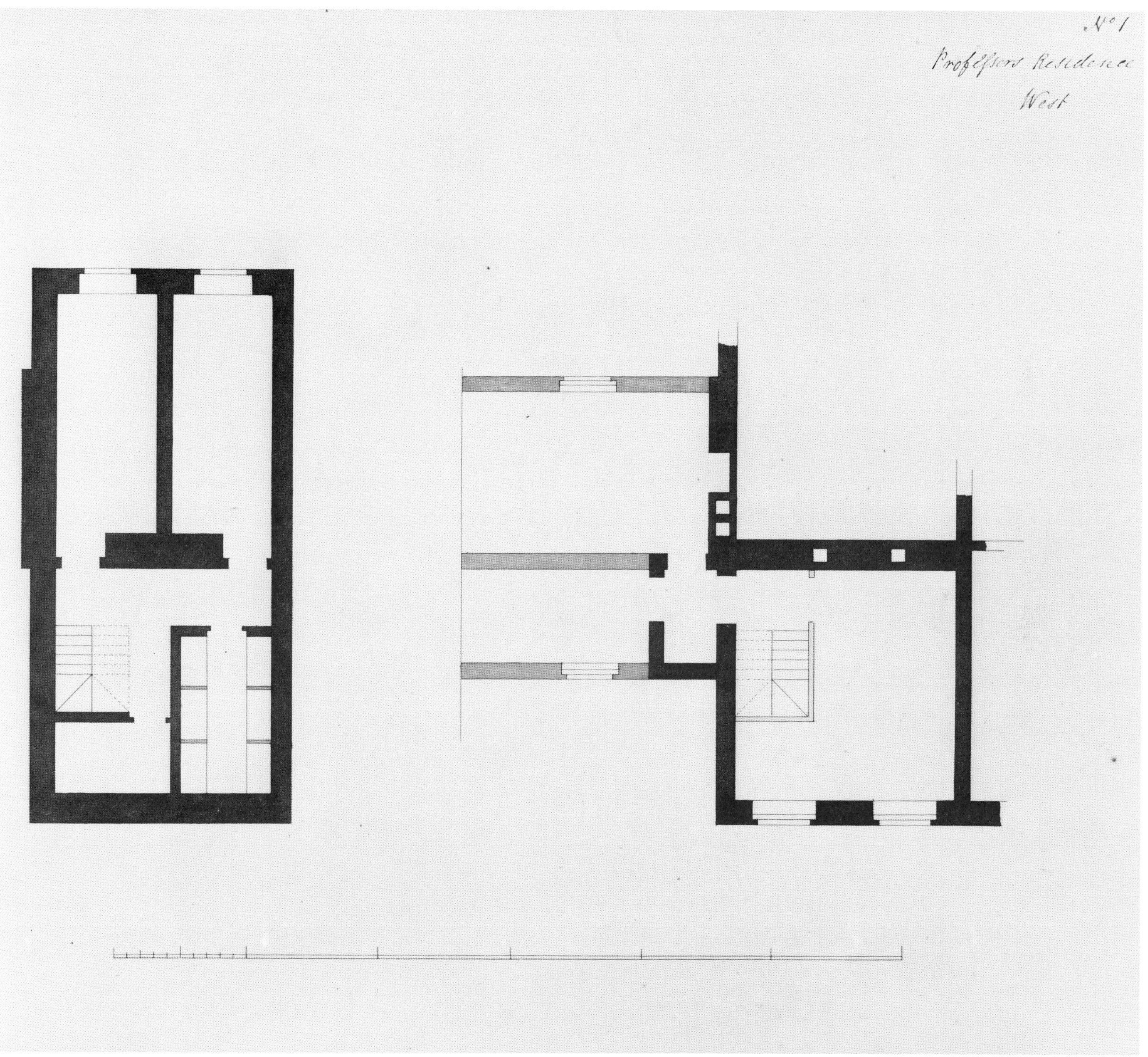

125

126. William **WILKINS**
Plan of the ground storey of the Professor's lodge in the west range.
Pen and ink with grey and yellow washes over some pencil underdrawing; 46.4×60 cm. Scale 1/10 in. to 1 ft. Inscribed: 'N.2/ Professors Residence/ West'; 'A. Square headed light over this door/ BB. To be raised to the level of the floor/ of the apartments/ C. A patent lifting pump to supply the/ three Water Closets/ F. A well to be sunk here/ N.B. N.3 Bramak's patent Water Closets/ and one upon the Chamber floor'; 'Ground plan/ The dimensions are marked above the plinth'; 'The Kitchen, Footmans pantry and Store Room are/ to be one foot below the level of the Dining Room/ and Study'; 'D. A patent lifting pump to/ supply the Water Closet above/ E. A well must be sunk/ here/ GG. Two steps here to descend/ one foot to the level of the/ Kitchen floor/ H. Ascend to Servants Rooms/ K. Descend to Cellars'; 'Open area for coals/ to be paved with bricks'; 'Open Court to be/ paved with pebbles'; 'An indent 4½ wide & 9 inches deep in/ the brick work, to be faced with bricks/ when the pipe is fixed'; various measurements.
Location: Downing College, Cambridge
SWP76.

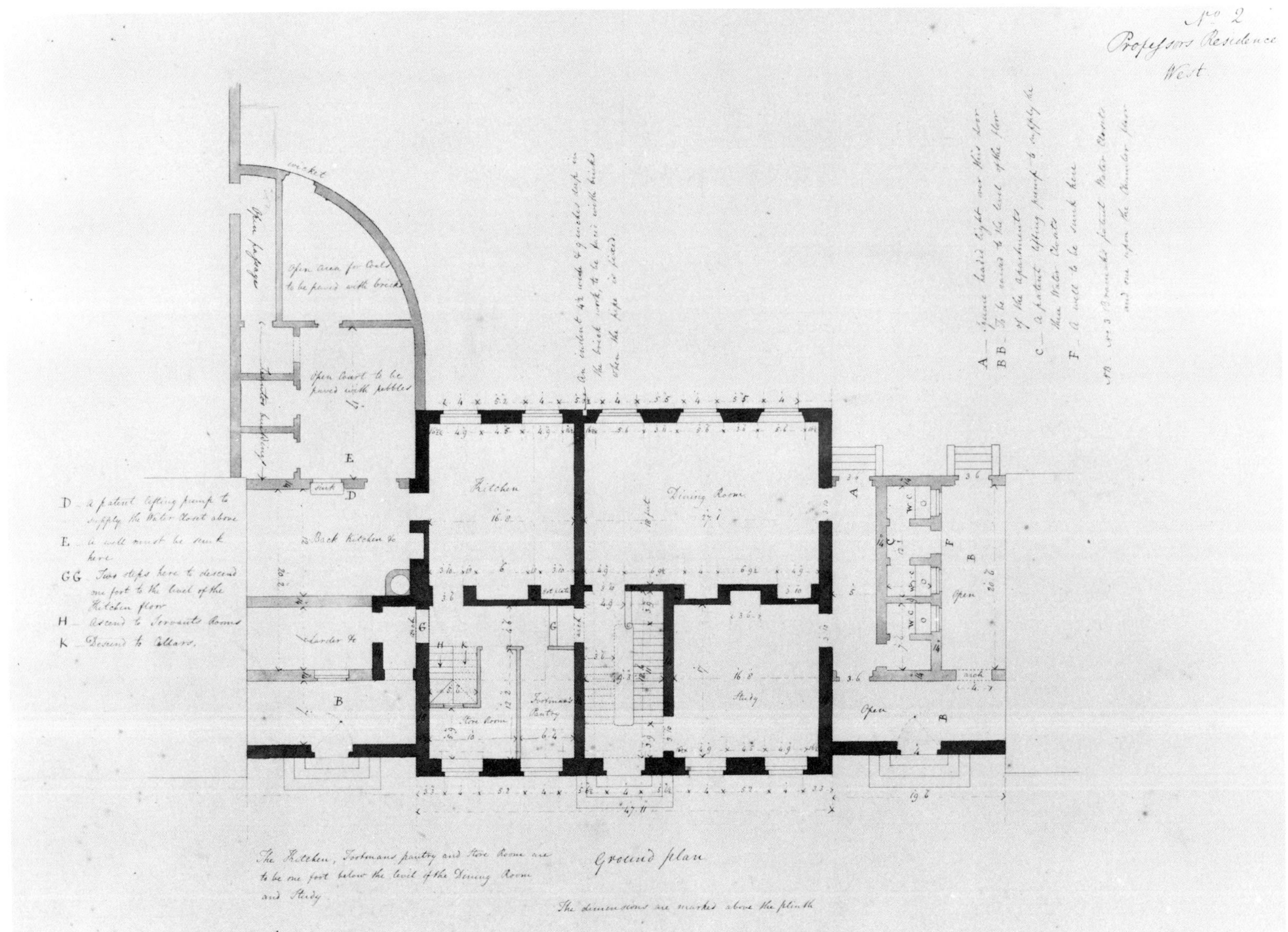

126

127. William **WILKINS**
Plan of the first storey of the Professor's lodge in the west range.
Pen and ink with blue, grey and yellow washes; 46.4×59.8 cm. Scale 1/10 in. to 1 ft. Inscribed: 'N.3/ Professors Residence/ West'; 'Chamber plan'; 'A. Ascend two steps to the passage here/ BB. Ascend one step from the passage/ to the single bed rooms/ C. Landing in one stone'; various measurements. *Location*: Downing College, Cambridge SWP77.

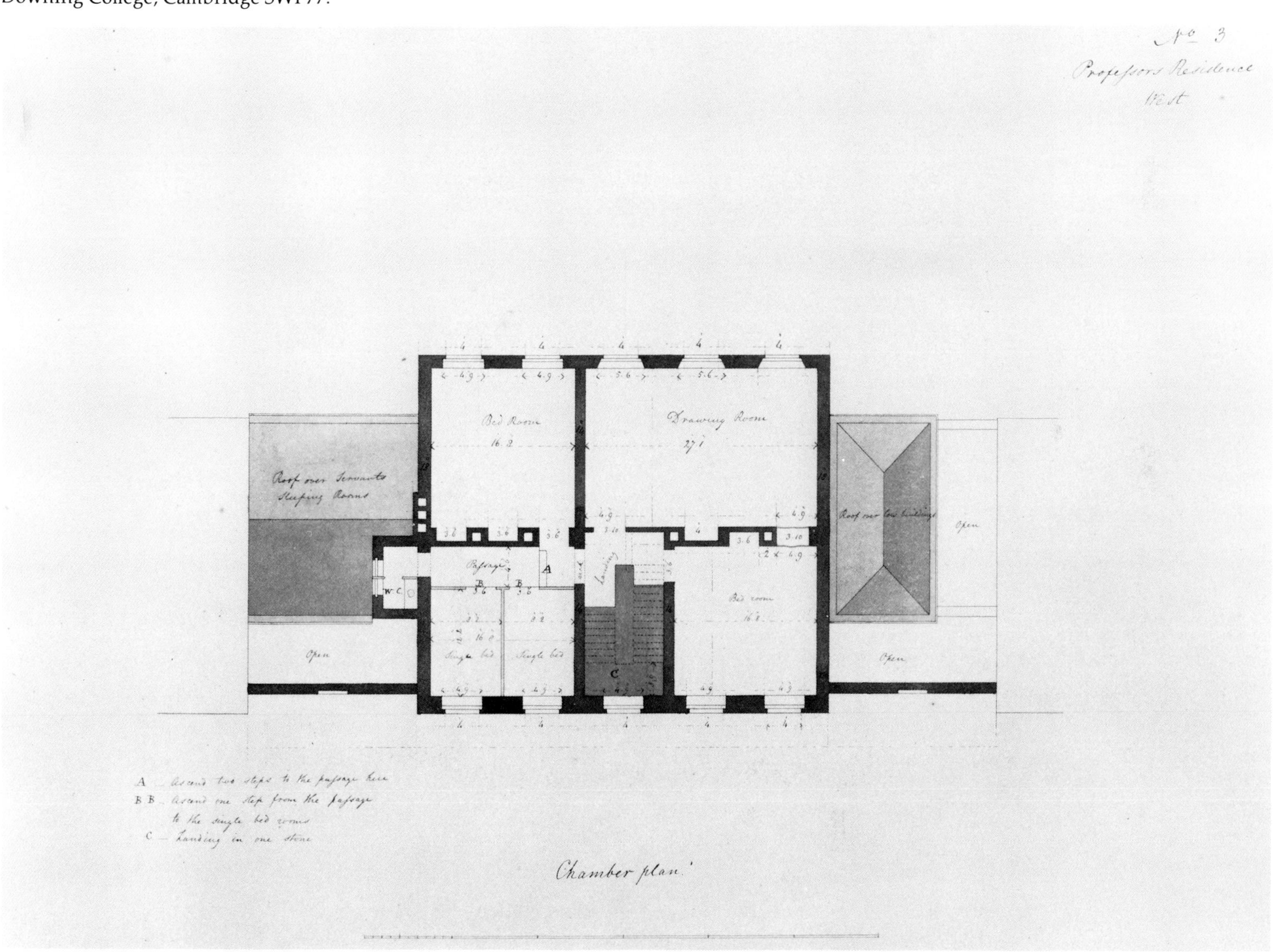

127

128. William **WILKINS**
Principal elevation of the Professor's lodge in the west range and section through the front rooms. Pen and ink over pencil underdrawing; 46.1×59.7 cm. Scale 1/10 in. to 1 ft. Inscribed: 'Professors Residence/ West N.4'; 'Elevation next the Quadrangle facing East/ The heights to be taken from the building already executed'; 'Level of plinth'; various measurements. *Location*: Downing College, Cambridge SWP78.

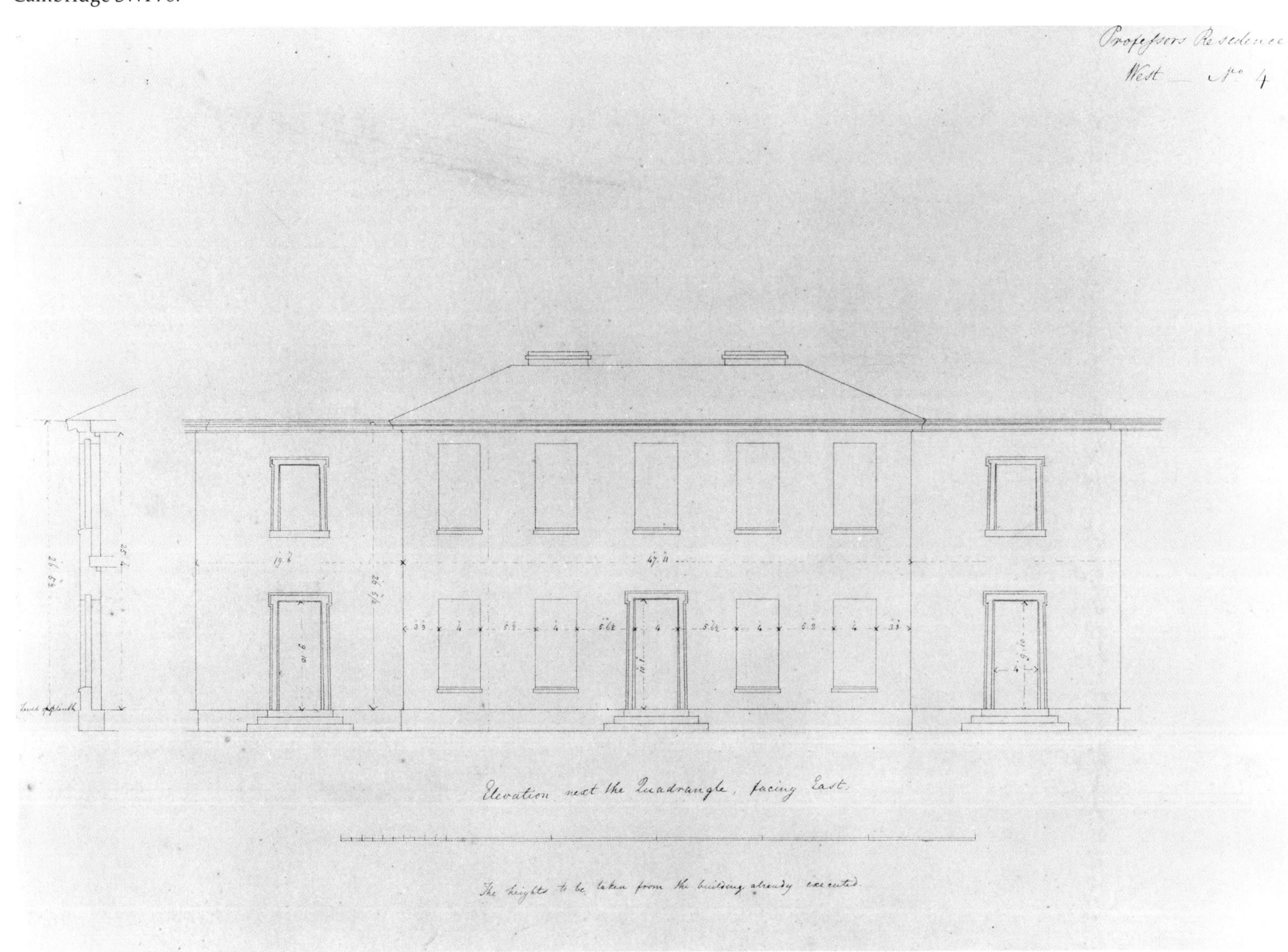

128

129. William **WILKINS**
Rear elevation of the Professor's lodge in the west range.
Pen and ink over pencil underdrawing; 46.2×59.9 cm. Scale 1/10 in. to 1 ft. Inscribed: 'Professors Residence/ West N.5'. *Location*: Downing College, Cambridge SWP79.

129

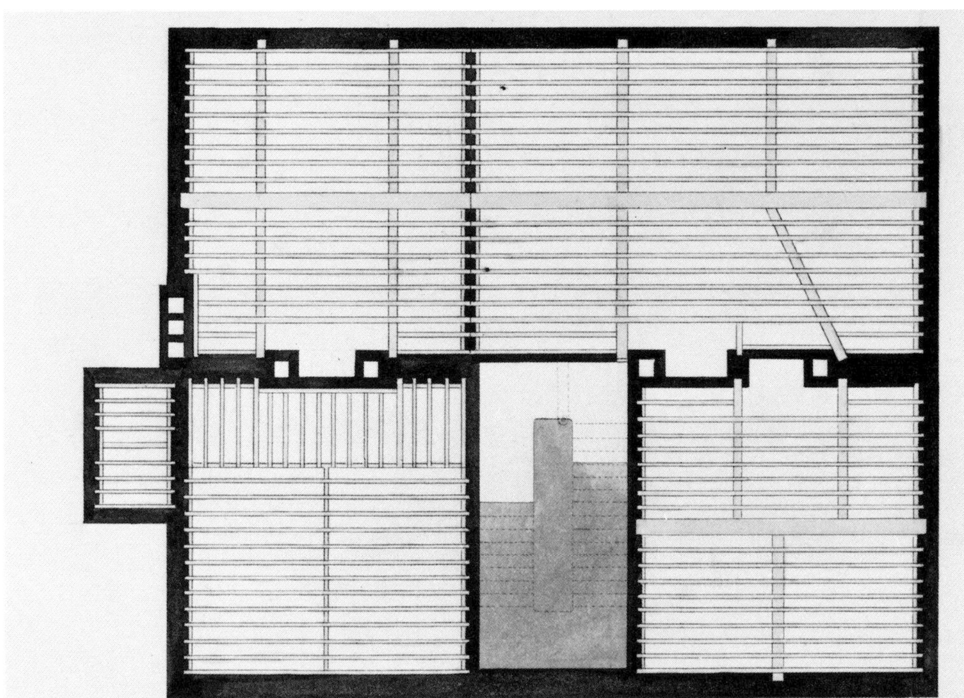

130

130. William **WILKINS**
Plan of the naked flooring of the Professor's lodge in the west range.
Pen and ink with grey and yellow washes over some traces of pencil; 46.3×59.9 cm. Scale 1/10 in. to 1 ft. Inscribed: 'Professors Residence/ West/ N.6'. *Location*: Downing College, Cambridge SWP80.

131. William **WILKINS**
Plan of the roofs of the Professor's lodge in the west range.
Pen and ink with black, blue and grey washes over some pencil underdrawing; 46.5×59.9 cm. Scale 1/10 in. to 1 ft. Inscribed: 'Professors Residence/ West/ N.7'; 'Coping'; 'Gutter/ Coping on top bed of the Cornice/ Plan of the Roofs'; 'Water pipe'; 'Roof over the/ Water Closet'; 'Covered through to carry the rain/ water through the roof'. *Location*: Downing College, Cambridge SWP81.

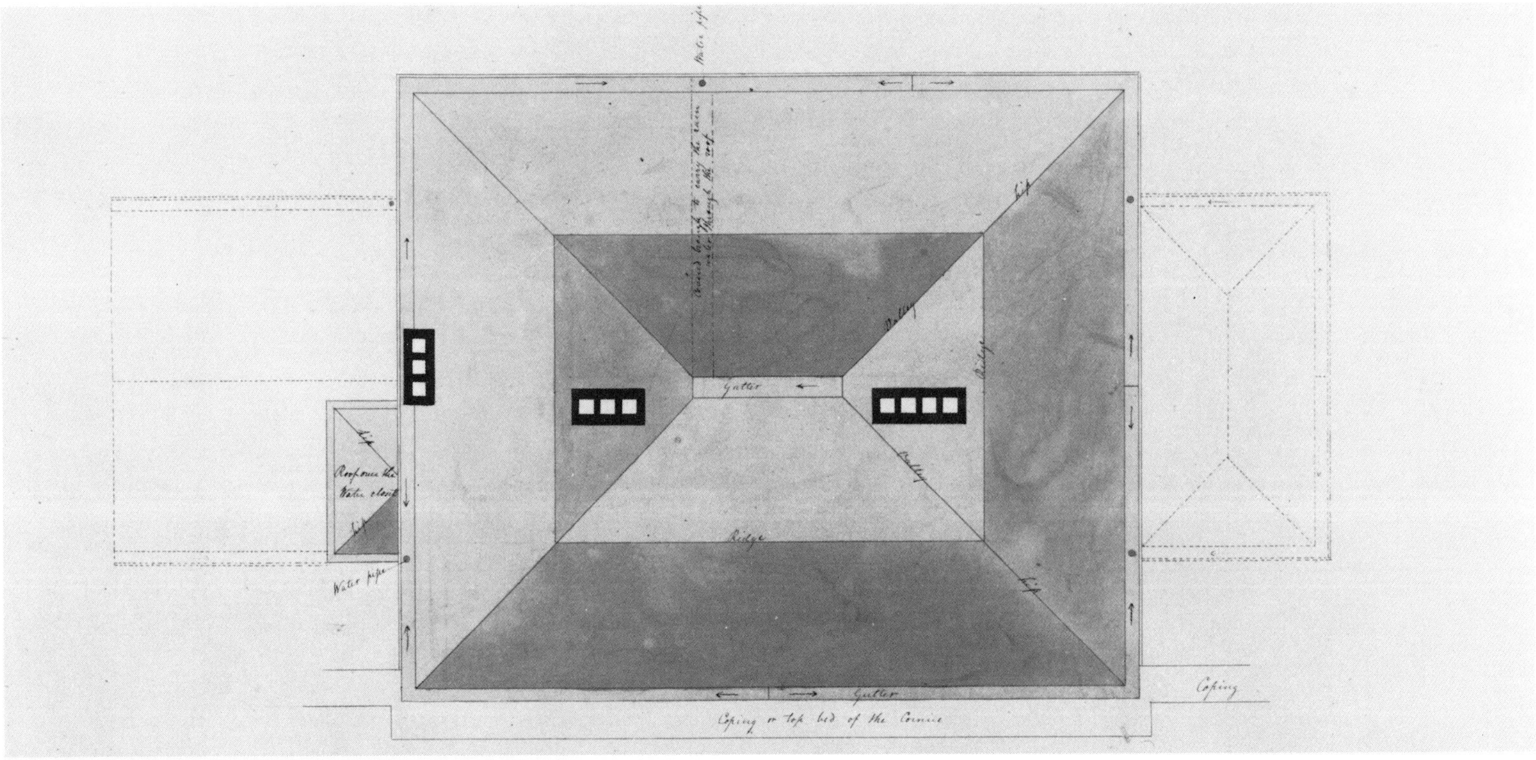

131

132. William **WILKINS**
Longitudinal section of the Professor's lodge in the west range.
Pen and ink with black, blue, brown, grey and yellow washes; 46.5×59.9 cm. Scale 1/10 in. to 1 ft. Inscribed: 'Professors Residence/ West N.8'; 'Hopper Roof/ A. Tye beam 12 inches by 12/ B. King post 12 by 8/ C. Principals 6 by 6/D. Purlins 5 by 4/ E. Pole plate 10 by 3/ F. Wall plates 7 by 5'; 'Section from East to West'; 'top of plinth'; 'Entrance doors to be double margin/ and hung upon the jamb E'. The/ upper part to be fixed'; 'A'. Level of the floor of the Footman's/ pantry & store room, one foot below/ the level of the top line of the Plinth/ B'. Level of the Mezzanine floor over/ the Footmans pantry & store room/ C'. Level of the floor of the bed rooms over/ the Mezzanine rooms./ D'. Window of Water-Closet at the/ end of the passage'; various measurements.
Location: Downing College, Cambridge SWP82.

133. William **WILKINS**
Section through the Professor's lodge in the west range. (see Fig.37, p.69)
Pen and ink with grey and yellow washes over some pencil underdrawing; 45.6×59.8 cm. Scale 1/10 in. to 1 ft. Inscribed: 'Professors Residence/ West N.9'; 'Level of ground – about 2'9" below the plinth of the/ principal front'; 'Depth of foundations here must be 4 feet below/ the Ground line'; 'depth 4 feet'; 'Floor of the cellars can only be 5'9"/ below the Ground'; 'The bottom of the drain is 7'6" below the surface of the Ground'; 'A. This wall must divide the Cellar/ equally if the drain, already costructed, is not in the way. If so the wall/ must be built close to one side of the/ drain'.
Location: Downing College, Cambridge SWP83.

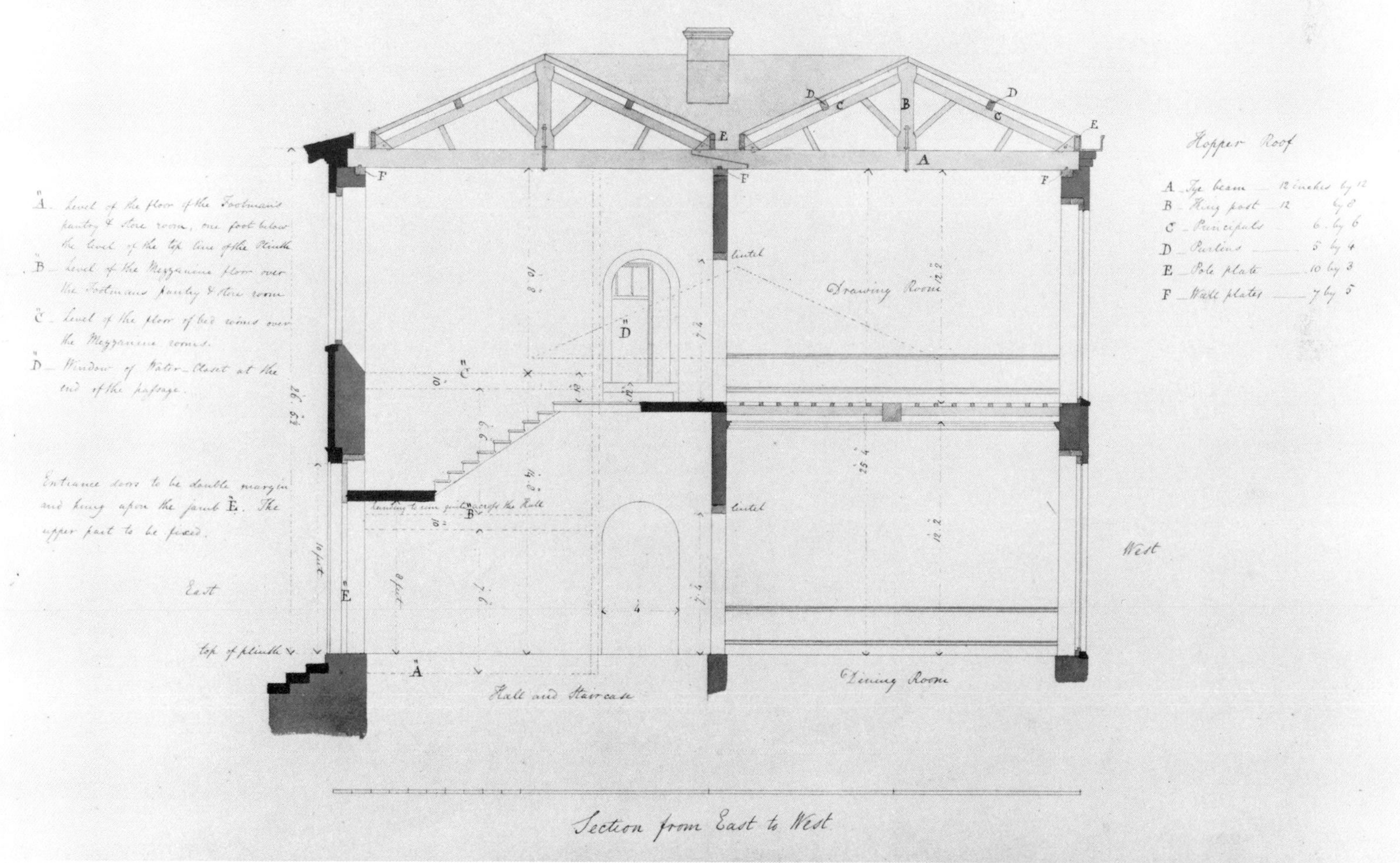

132

134. William **WILKINS**
Elevations of the doors and profiles of the mouldings in the Professor's lodge in the west range.
Pen and ink with yellow wash over some pencil underdrawing; 46.6×59.8 cm. Scale 1/12 in. to 1 ft. Inscribed: 'Professors Residence/ West/ N.10'; 'Drawings room &c. Door moldings'; 'Smaller doors'; 'Moldings the full size'; 'Architrave'; 'Bed Room Doors'; 'Drawing Room Dining Room/ and Study doors'; 'Surbase'; 'Base/ Plinth 6½ deep'; 'Surbase/ line of Stucco Dado'; some measurements. *Location*: Downing College, Cambridge SWP84.

135. William **WILKINS**
Elevations and profiles of the fireplaces in the Professor's lodge in the west range.
Pen and ink with grey wash over some pencil underdrawing; 46×60.1 cm. Scale 1/12 in. to 1 ft. Inscribed: 'Professors Residence/ West/ N.14'; 'Shelf/ Mantel/ Wall line'; 'The part A shews the/ jambs of the bed room Chimney/ pieces of which B is the line/ of the shelf'; 'The Bed room Chimney pieces/ to be of veined or Killala/ marble with stone slabs'; 'Jamb/ Half the full size'; 'Line of shelf'; 'Wall line'; 'Jamb/ Half the full size'; 'line of capping'; 'line of Shelf'; 'Dining and Drawing room Chimney pieces/ of veined marble with veined marble slabs'; 'Veined or Killala marble Chimney pieces for the / Study with stone slab'; some measurements. VERSO: inscribed in pencil 'This is the Last wanted'. *Location*: Downing College, Cambridge SWP85.

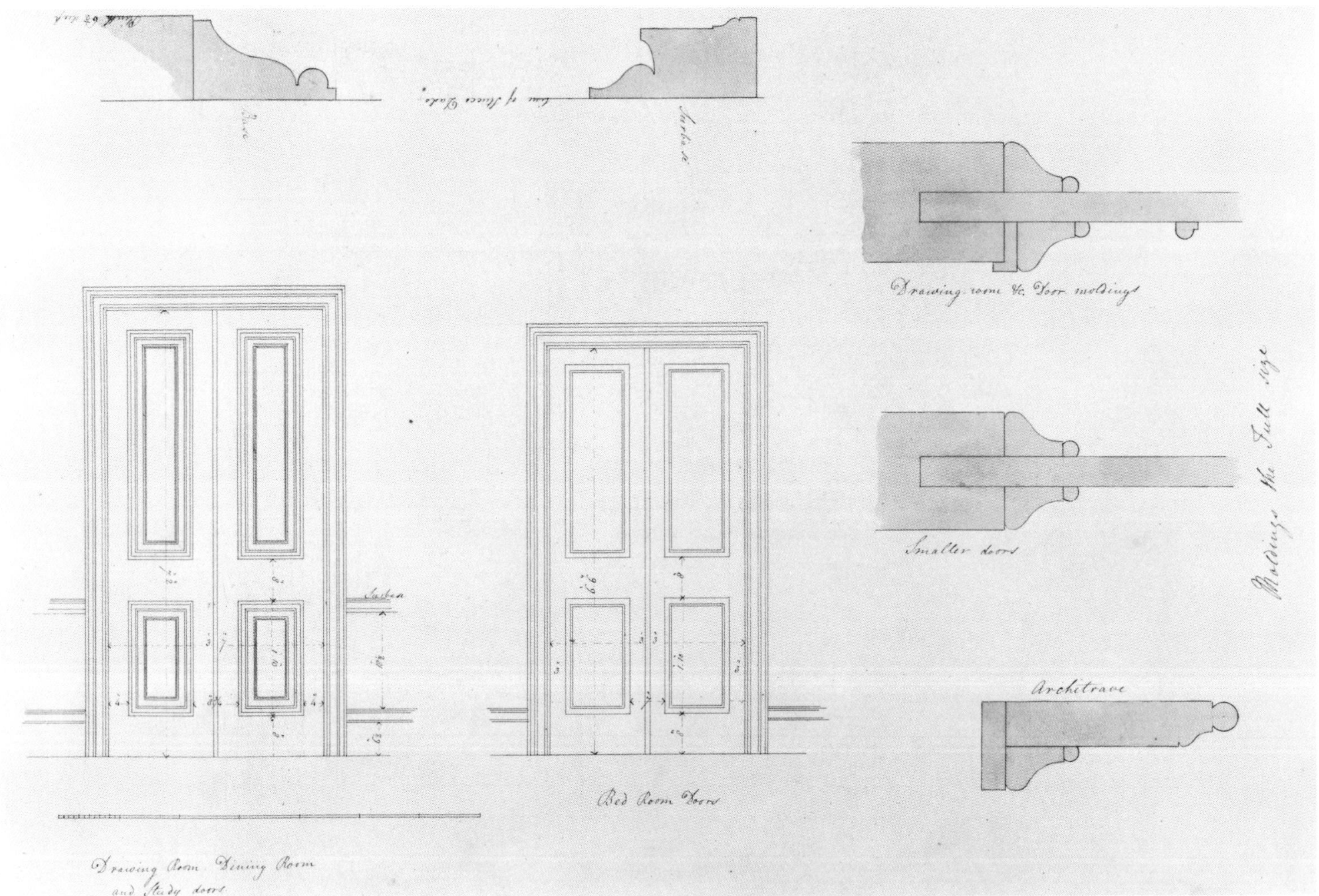

134

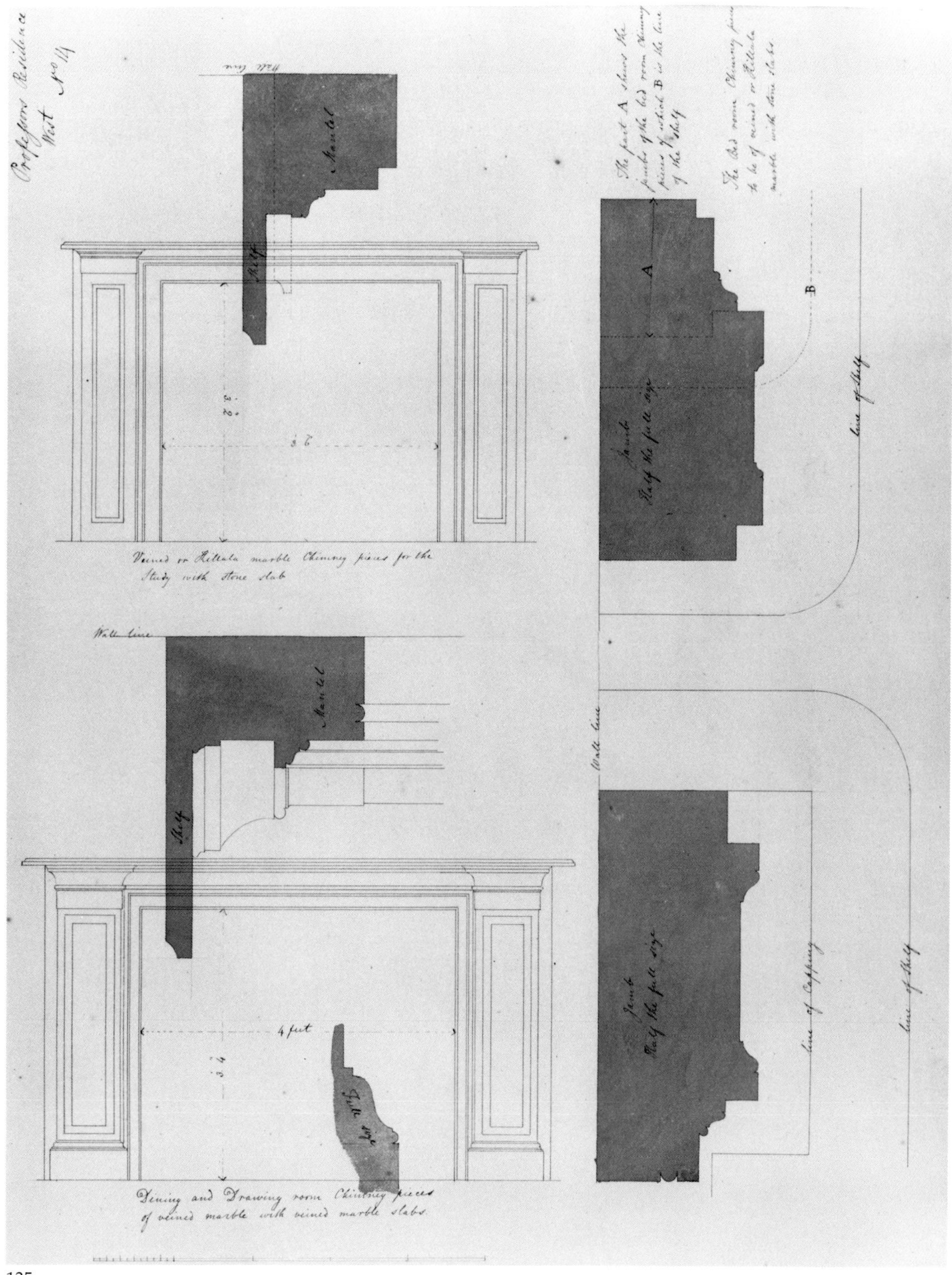

135

136

136. William **WILKINS**
Elevation of the window and sections of the sash including the folded shutters in the Professor's lodge in the west range.
Pen and ink with grey and yellow washes; 46.1×59.9 cm. Scale 1⁄12 in. to 1 ft. Inscribed: 'Professors Residence/ West/ N.11'; 'Wall line/ line of plastering'; 'Sashes and Shutters of the Rooms in the East front./ The sashes to be double hung. The two back/ flaps of the Shutters to be cut at the meeting-/ rail of the Sashes'; 'Stone sill'; 'Sash bar the full size'.
Location: Downing College, Cambridge SWP86.

137. William **WILKINS**
Elevation and constructional details of the windows in the dining and drawing rooms of the Professor's lodge in the west range.
Pen and ink with blue, grey and yellow washes over some traces of pencil; 46.5×59.8 cm. Scale 1⁄12 in. to 1 ft. Inscribed: 'Plan of the Window jamb & Shutters/ Half the Full size'; 'Professors Residence/ West/ N.12'; 'The back flap to be cut half way up the Shutter'; 'Meeting style/ Full size'; 'Floor line'; 'Dining and Drawing Room windows'; 'fascia for window blind'; 'A. Cast Iron throuted/ bar screwed into the/ Counter Sill'; 'Oak Counter Sill'; 'Lower rail'; various measurements.
Location: Downing College, Cambridge SWP87.

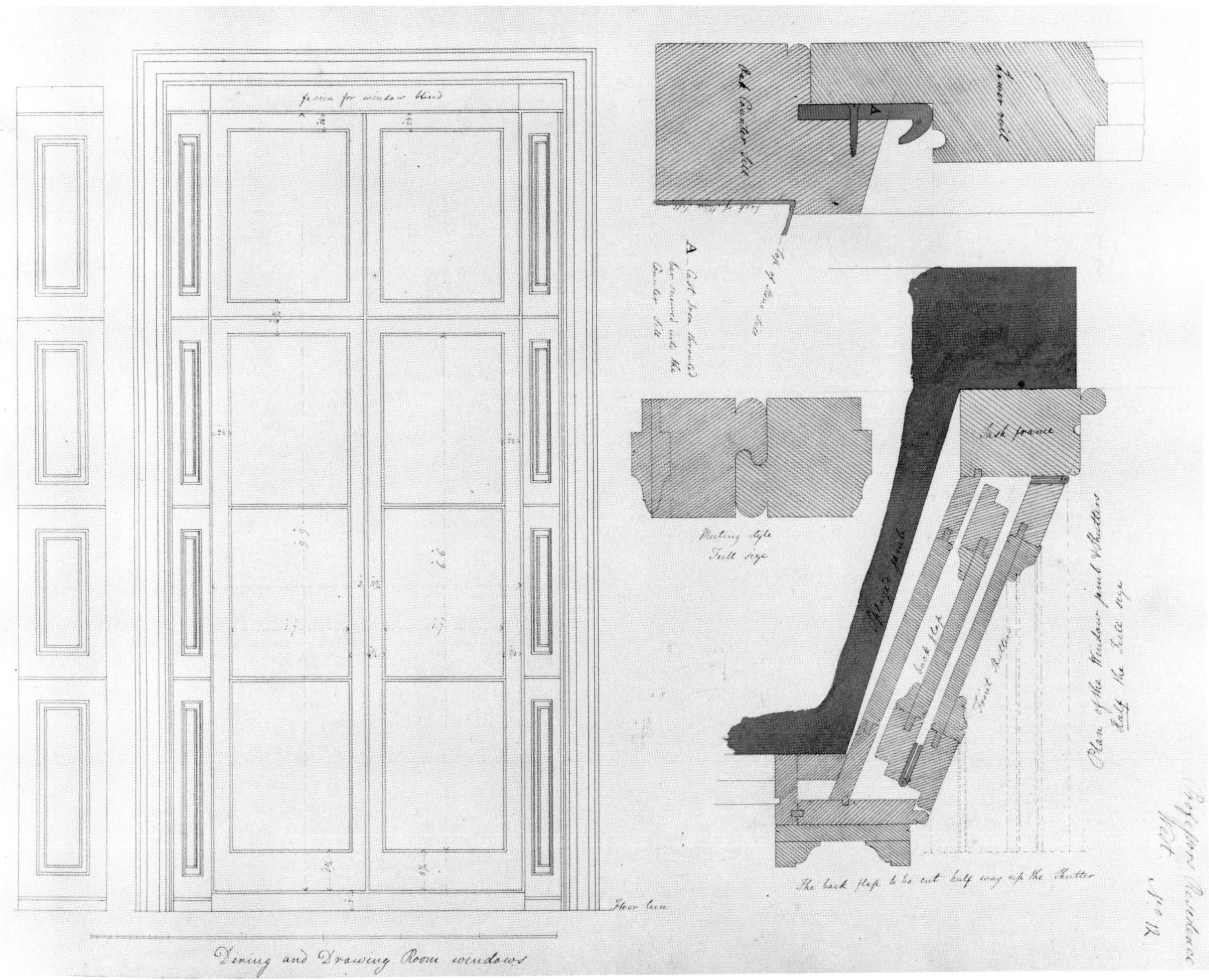
fascia for window blind
Floor line
Dining and Drawing Room windows
Meeting Style
Full size
Sash frame
back flap
Front Shutters
The back flap to be cut half way up the Shutter
Plan of the Window jamb & Shutters
Half the Full size

137

138. William **WILKINS**
General plan of the college at ground level.
(see Fig.46, p.77)
Pen and ink with black, grey, green and pink washes over some pencil underdrawing; 46.3×91.1 cm Scale 1/10 in. to 1 ft. Inscribed: 'General Ground Plan'. *Location*: Downing College, Cambridge SWP88.

139. William **WILKINS**
Southern half of the general plan of the college at ground level. (see Fig.22, p.56)
Pen and ink with grey and black washes over some pencil underdrawing; 46.7×92.3 cm. Scale 1/10 in. to 1 ft. Inscribed: 'The Southern half of the plan/ of Downing College/ as executed with the/ exception of the Centre/ building'; 'Professor's Garden/ East'; 'Lodge'; 'Chapel'; 'Ante Chapel'; 'Library'; 'Professor's Garden West'; various measurements. *Location*: Downing College, Cambridge SWP89.

140. William **WILKINS**
Northern half of the general plan of the college at ground level.
Pen and ink with grey, black and yellow washes over some pencil underdrawing; 46×92.2 cm. Scale 1/10 in. to 1 ft. Inscribed: 'North' and 'Propylea' in faint pencil; various measurements. *Location*: Downing College, Cambridge SWP90.

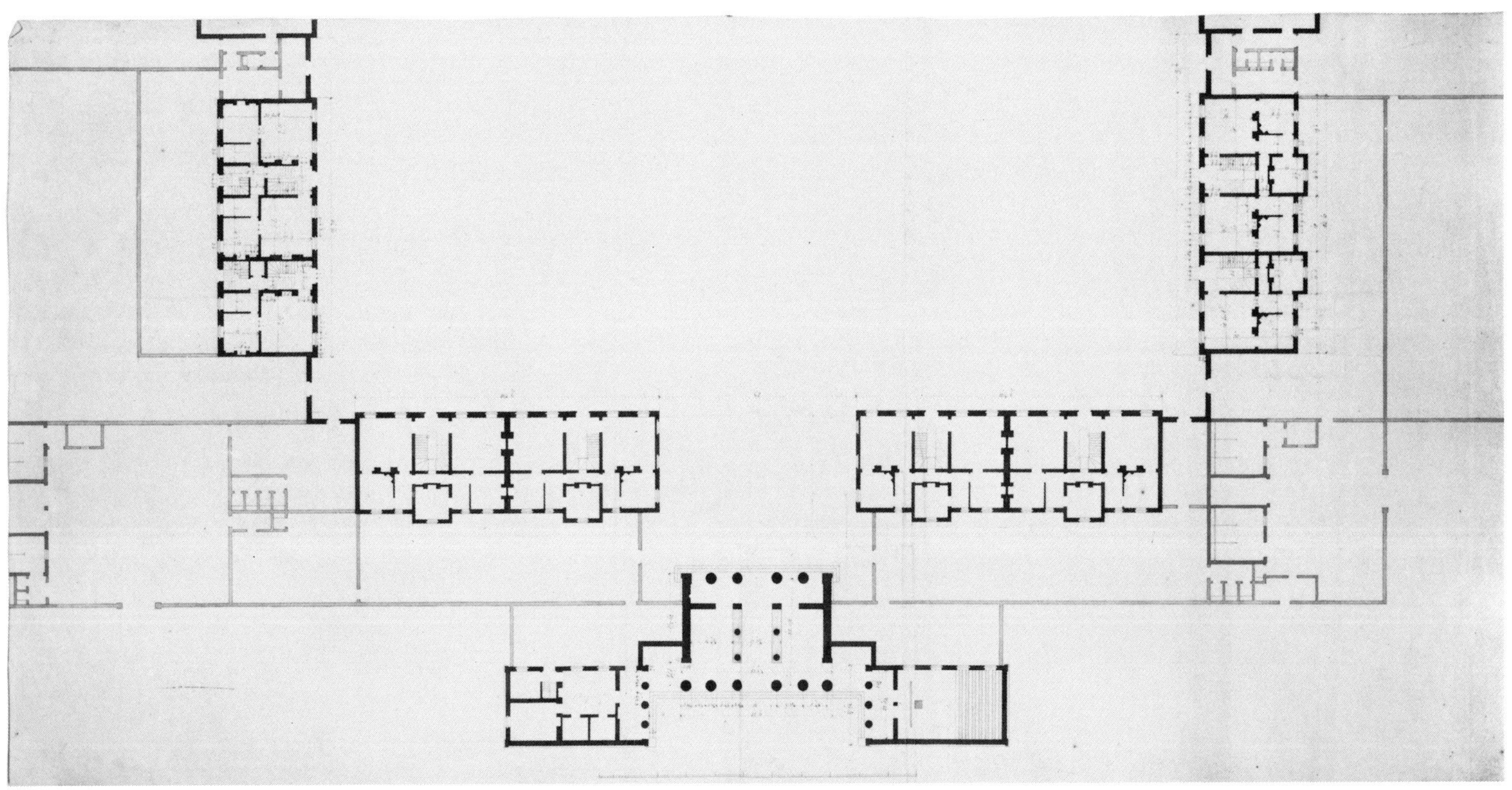

140

141. William **WILKINS**
Plan of the Propylea. (See Fig.44, p.76)
Pen and ink with grey wash; 46.5×59.7 cm. Scale 1/10 in. to 1 ft. Inscribed in pencil: 'Modified plan taking away two sets of rooms/ right and left of the North front'; 'Lecture Room'; '3 sets of Apartments/ like those on the East &/ West side of the Quadrangle'; 'Porters Lodge'. *Location*: Downing College, Cambridge SWP91.

142. William **WILKINS**
Plan of the Propylea showing reduced depth of the porticoes.
Pen and ink with grey and yellow washes over some pencil underdrawing; 46.2×59.6 cm. Scale 1/10 in. to 1 ft. Inscribed in faint pencil: 'here shewn too long'; various measurements. *Location*: Downing College, Cambridge SWP92.

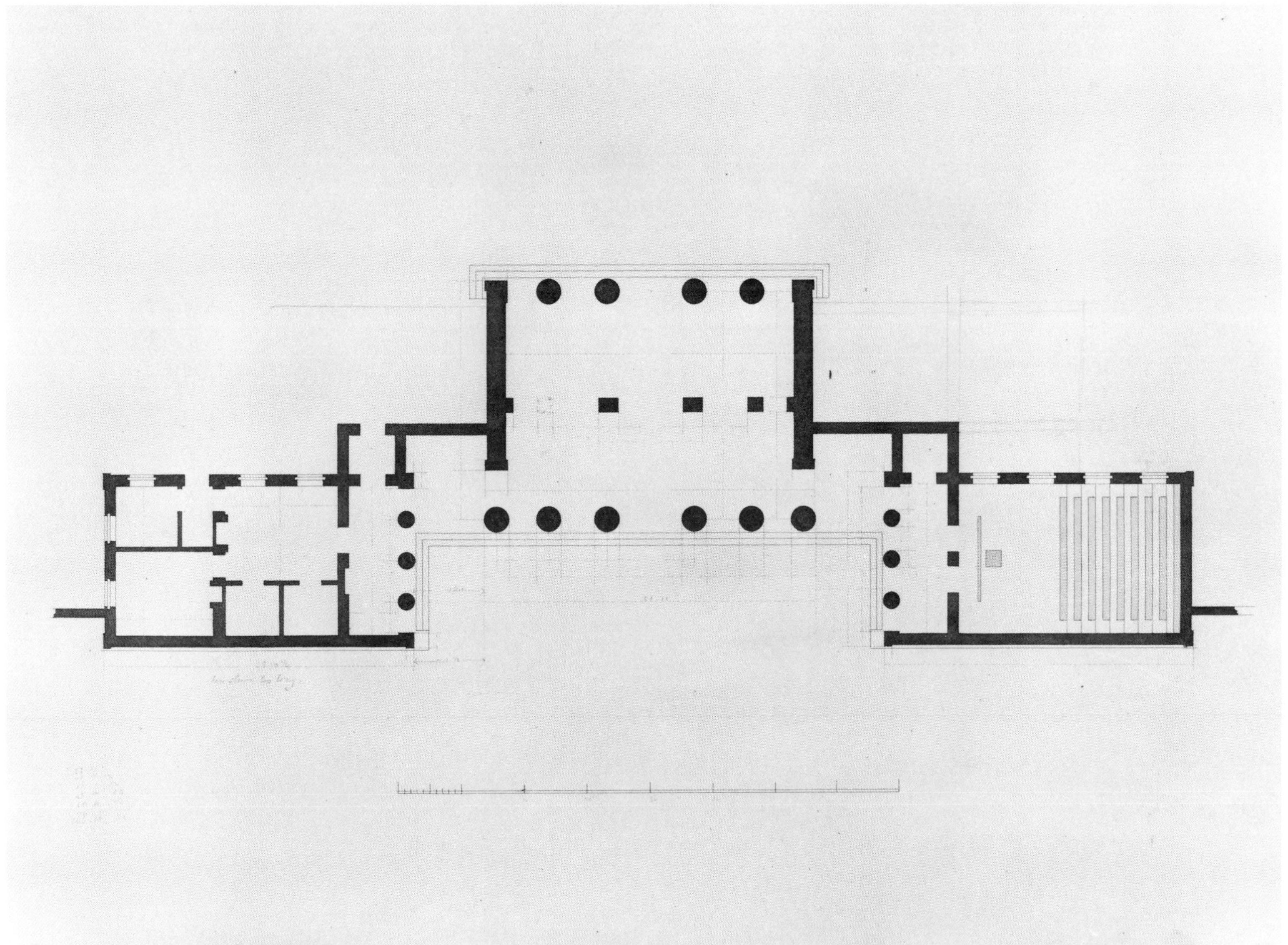

142

143. William **WILKINS**
Plan of the Propylea. (see Fig.45, p.76)
Pen and ink with grey wash over some pencil underdrawing; 46.2×58.6 cm. Scale 1/10 in. to 1 ft. Inscribed: 'Propylea'; 'North'; 'Plan of the Principal Portico'; 'South'; various measurements. *Location*: Downing College, Cambridge SWP93.

144. William **WILKINS**
Plan of the roof of the central building of the Propylea.
Pen and ink with black, grey, red and yellow washes; 46.2×59.6 cm. Scale 1/10 in. to 1 ft. Inscribed: 'Propylea/ Central building'; 'line of the frize [sic]/ Top bed of the Cornice'; 'The roof with the tiles off'; 'The roof with the tiles on'; 'Soffite of the/ Architrave'; 'Plan of the Ceiling'; 'backing behind the frize [sic]'; 'joint of the cornice' [repeated twice]; various measurements. *Location*: Downing College, Cambridge SWP94.

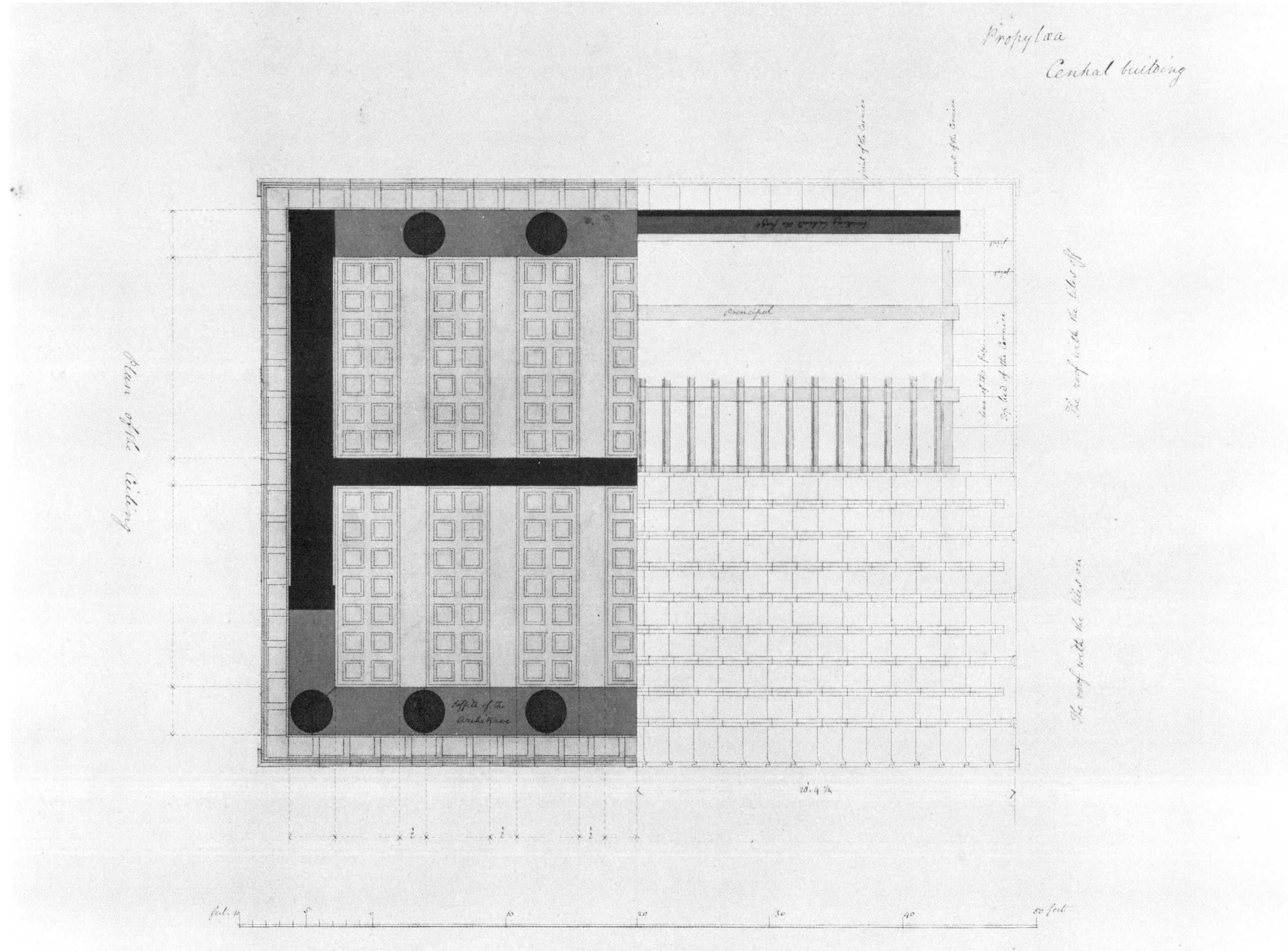

144

145. William **WILKINS**
Section of half of the roof of the central building of the Propylea.
Pen and ink with black, brown and yellow washes over some pencil underdrawing; 46.3×60 cm. Scale 1/12 in. to 1 ft. Inscribed: 'Propylea Central part'; 'Double King post'; 'Iron plate/ nut'; 'discharging piece'; 'smaller discharging piece'; 'upright'; 'Strut'; 'Tye 14 inches deep by 12 inches'; 'Brick work/ behind the metopa'; 'Section of Half the roof'; various measurements. *Location*: Downing College, Cambridge SWP95.

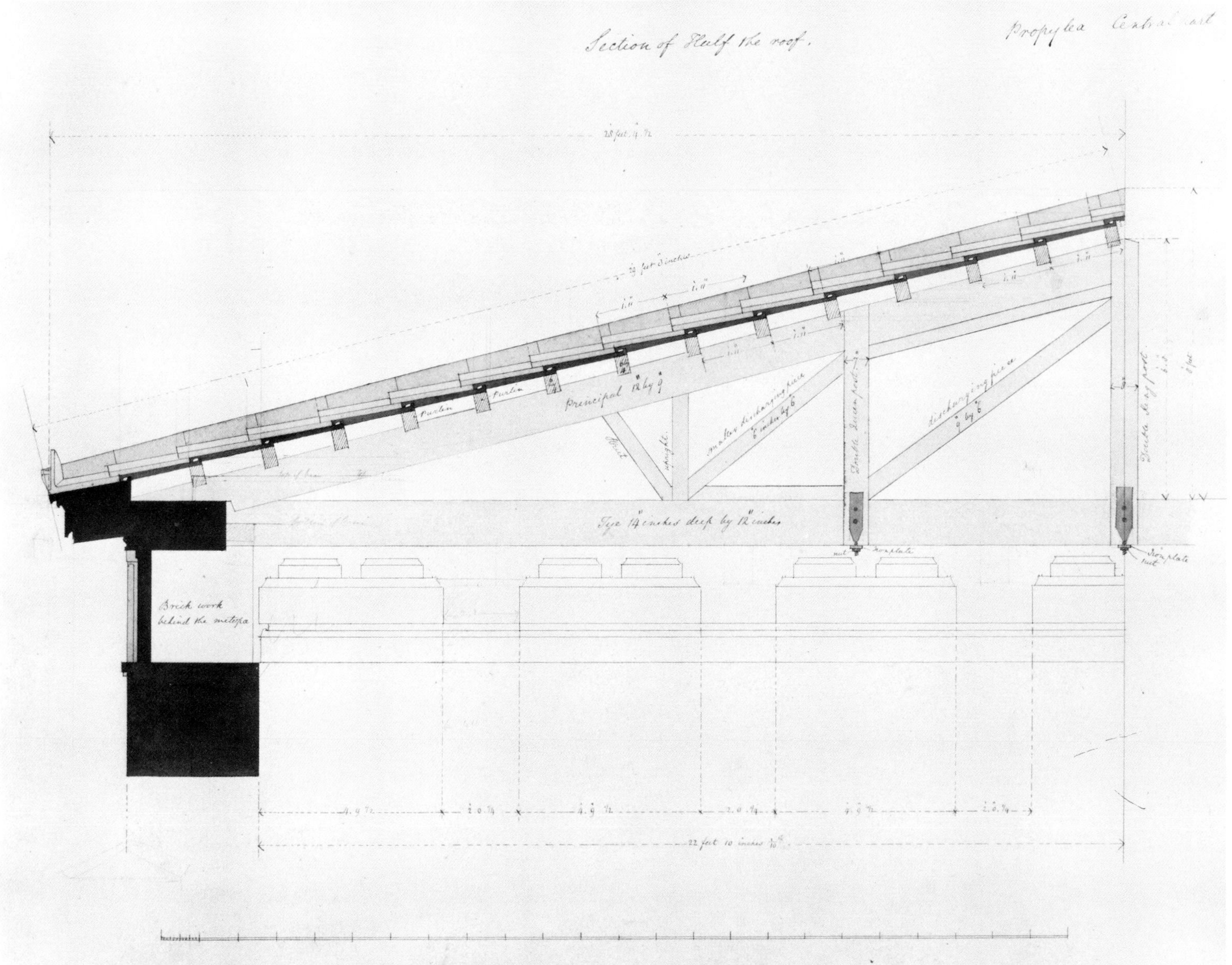

145

Buildings of the South front
Capital of the pilasters
for the Hall
Full Size

146

146. William **WILKINS**
Profile and half frontal view of the Corinthian capital to be used in the hall.
Pen and grey wash over some pencil underdrawing; 60×46.6 cm. Inscribed: 'Buildings of the South front'; 'Capital of the pilasters/ for the Hall/ Full Size'. *Location*: Downing College, Cambridge SWP96.

147. William **WILKINS**
Plan and section of the Corinthian pilaster to be used in the hall.
Pen and ink with grey wash over some pencil underdrawing; 46×59.7 cm. Inscribed: 'Buildings of the South front'; 'Plan of the pilasters for the Hall/ the Full size'. *Location*: Downing College, Cambridge SWP97.

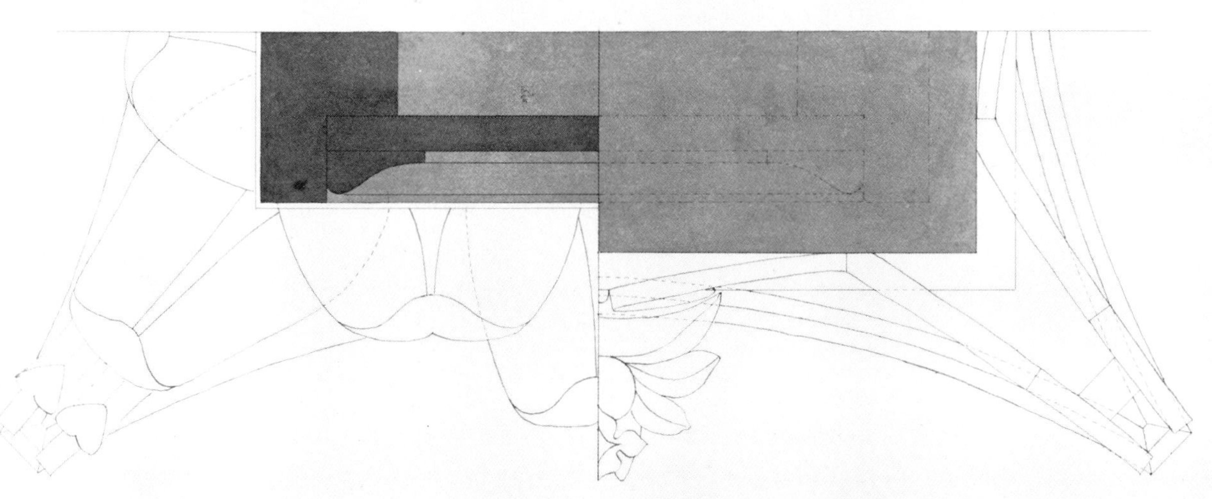

147

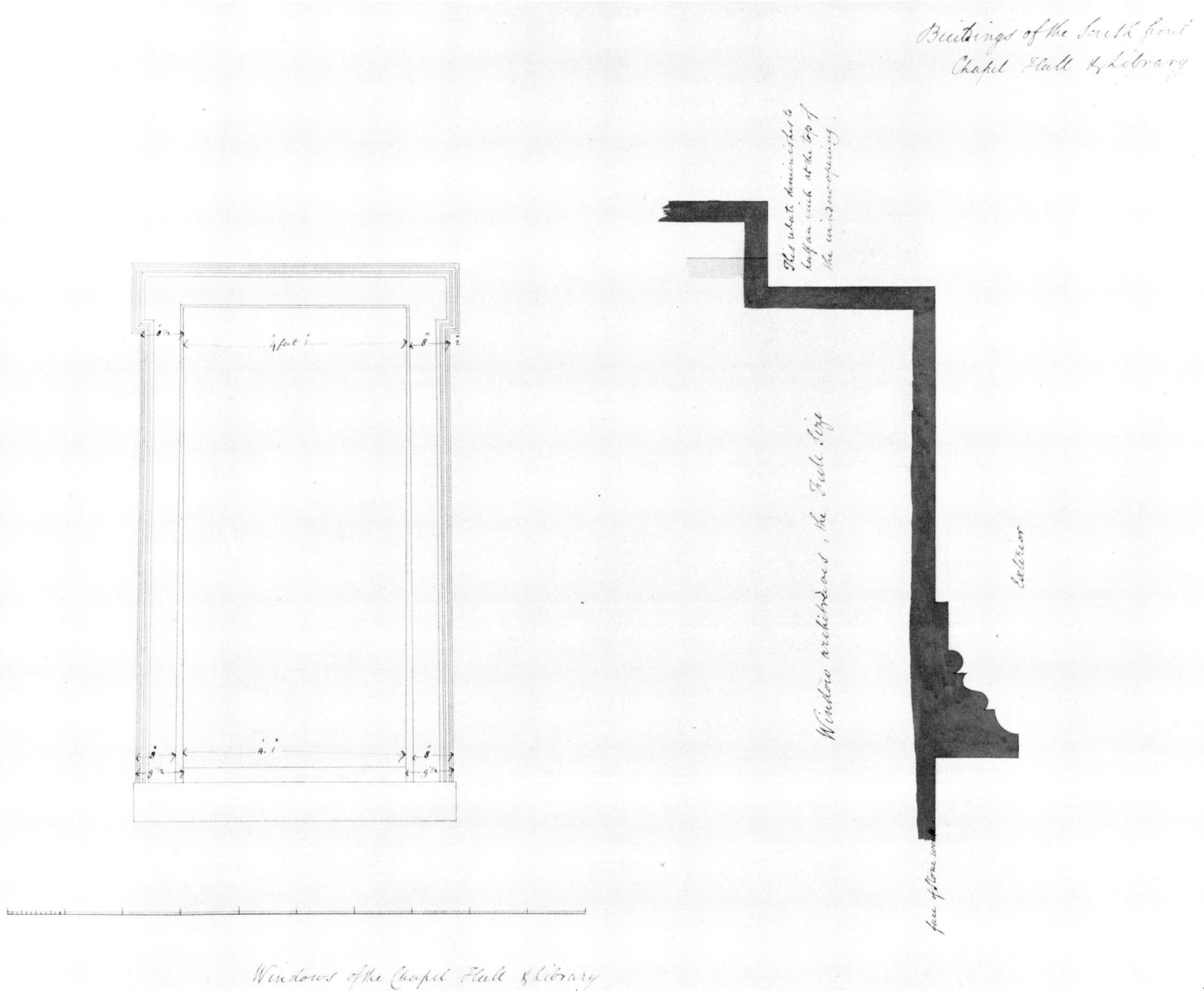
Buildings of the South front
Chapel Hall & Library
Window architraves, the Full Size
Exterior
4 feet 1
4.1
Windows of the Chapel Hall & Library

148

148. William **WILKINS**
Elevation and details of the windows in the chapel, hall and library.
Pen and ink with grey washes; 46.1×59.6 cm. Scale 1⁄12 in. to 1 ft. Inscribed: 'Buildings of the South front/ Chapel Hall & Library'; 'Window architraves, the Full Size'; 'face of stone work'; 'Exterior'; 'Windows of the Chapel Hall & Library'. *Location*: Downing College, Cambridge SWP98.

149. William **WILKINS**
Plans of the ground and first storeys of the Professor's lodge in the west range.
(see Fig.36, p.68)
Pen and ink with grey and yellow washes; 59.5×46.1 cm. Scale 1⁄10 in. to 1 ft. Inscribed: 'All the windows in the front, above and below, are to be 5 squares deep & bro't down to the floor'; 'Open passage to Professor's garden'; 'To Fellows' Garden'; 'Open Court'; 'Open Court'; 'Height of chimney openings 3′6″'; 'Professors Residence facing the East'; 'Stoves'; 'Jambs not splayed'; 'Dressing room'; 'Bed Room'; 'Bed Room'; 'Single bed'; 'Stud partition'. *Location*: Downing College, Cambridge SWP99.

150. William **WILKINS**
Elevation of the principal front of the students' and fellows' block on the north side of the quadrangle.
Pen and ink over some pencil underdrawing; 46×59.4 cm. Scale 1⁄10 in. to 1 ft. Inscribed: 'Students and Fellows apartments/ North side of the Quadrangle'. *Location*: Downing College, Cambridge SWP100.

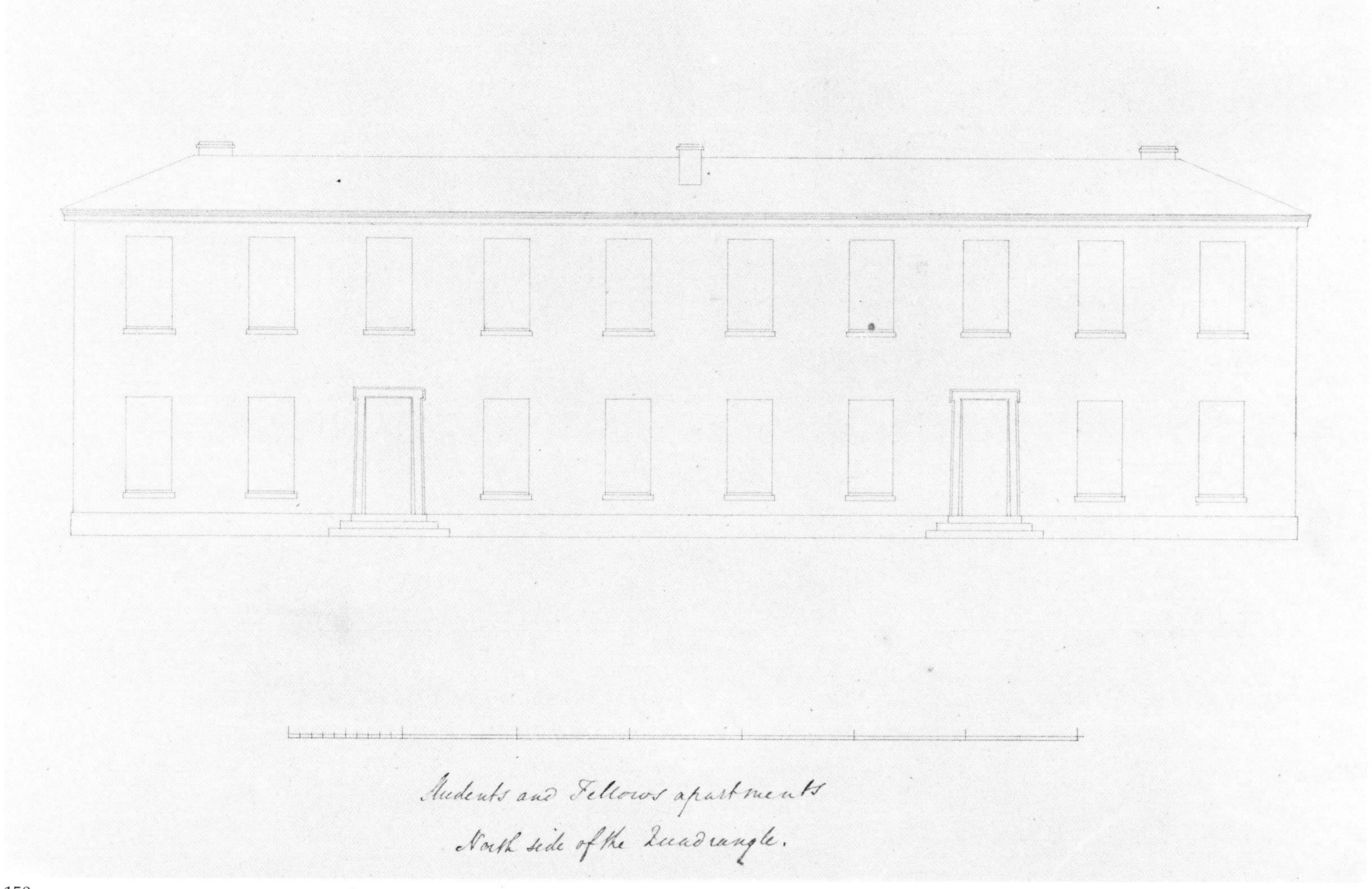

150

151. William **WILKINS**
Plans of the ground and first storeys of the students' and fellows' blocks on the north side of the quadrangle.
Pen and ink with grey wash over some pencil underdrawing; 45.8×91.5 cm. Scale 1/10 in. to 1 ft. Inscribed in faint pencil: 'Rooms on the/ North side of/ the Quadrangle'; 'Ground floor'; 'Upper floor'. *Location*: Downing College, Cambridge SWP101.

152. William **WILKINS**
Plans of the ground and first storey of one of the blocks on the north side of the quadrangle.
Pen and ink with grey and yellow washes; 59.2×46.3 cm. Scale 1/10 in. to 1 ft. Inscribed in faint pencil: 'Upper Plan'; 'Rooms forming North end of Quadrangle'. *Location*: Downing College, Cambridge SWP102.

153. William **WILKINS**
Two alternative plans for the improvement of the estate belonging to the college. (see Figs.42 and 43, pp.74 and 75)
Pen and ink with brown, grey, green and pink washes; 47×35 cm. Scale 1/10 in. to 1 ft. Signed and dated 'William Wilkins/ Arch.t 1817'. Inscribed: 'Plan for the Improvement of/ the Estate belonging to Downing/ College'; 'avenue of poplars to remain/ line of limes to remain'; 'new row of poplars/ new row of limes'. *Location*: Downing College, Cambridge SWP103.

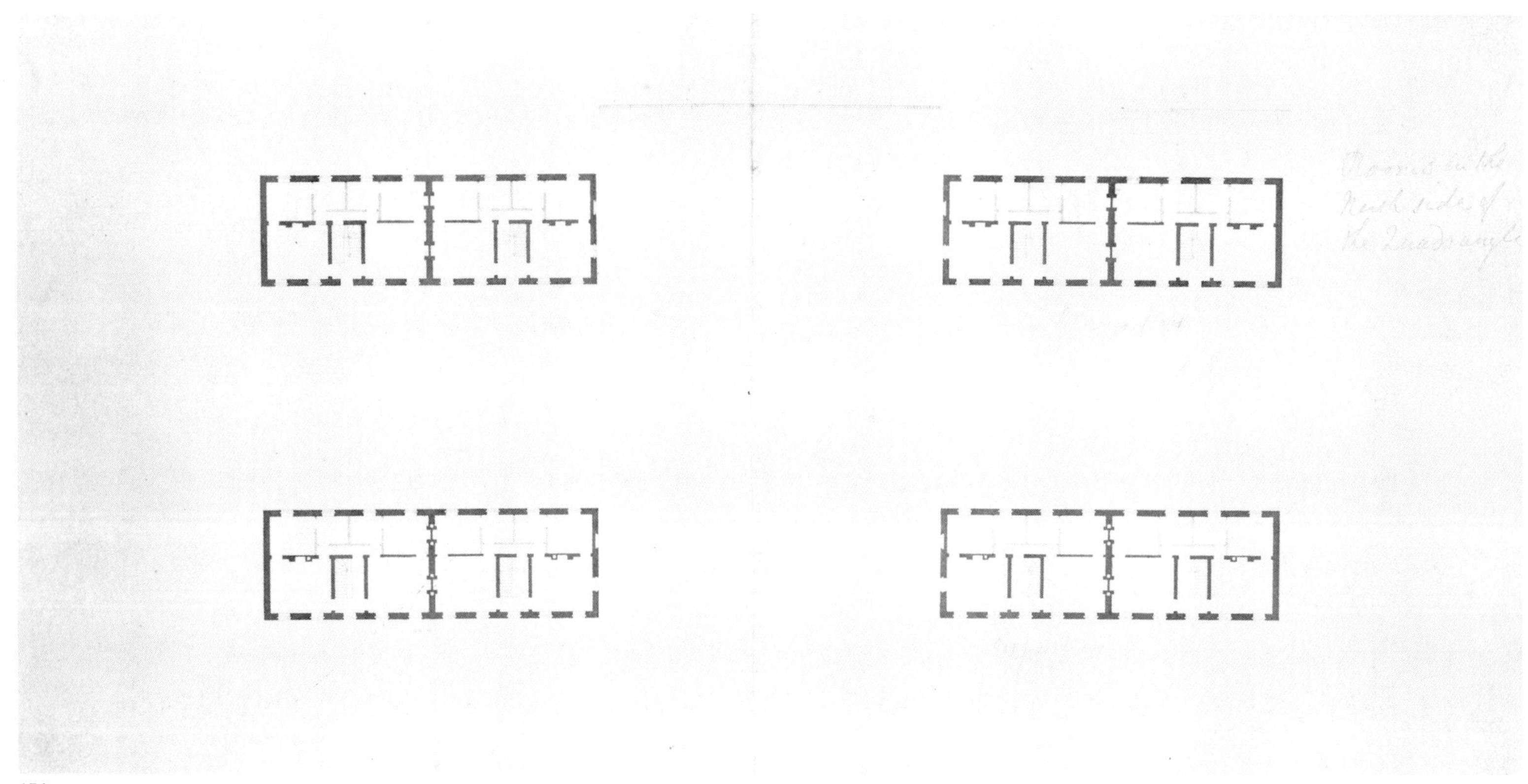

151

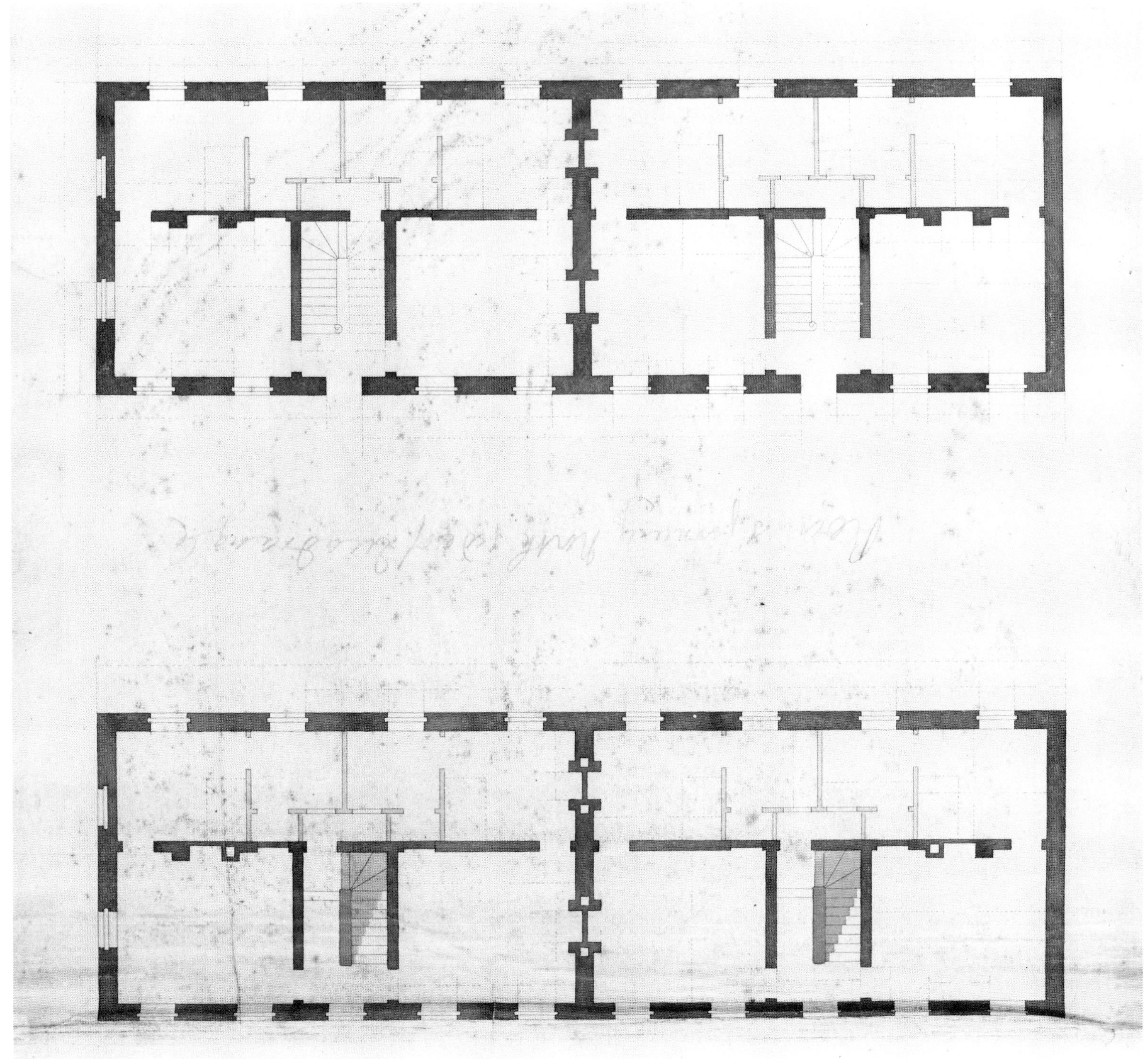

152

154

154. Perry **NISSY**
Proposed landscaping of the southern end of the college.
Pen and ink; 67.8×45.5 cm. Inscribed: 'View and section of Sunk/ fence for a College. 8 N. 1819'; 'Section of sunk fence'; 'Surface of Earth'; 'Slope to begin 18. or 20. feet from Return of Wall/ to begin with this sort of curve, and to be sunk 6 or 8 feet when it gets here/ If sunk 8 feet, with the 2 feet of wall or Blocking at the top, it will be in all 10 feet:/ 2 feet asunder each row, when up four or five feet high, and 6 or 8 feet in width, it would be impossible to get over it.'; 'face of building'; '12 feet Grass 16 feet Gravel 8 feet Grass & 4 feet flag stone/ Thought to be this width at least, and if made 10 or 15 feet wider, it will add/ much to the grandeur and consequence of the whole effect of the Buildings vz./ as the Buildings are low I have not raised the earth because it would/ hurt their appearance in the distance. The Earth that comes out/ would do famously to lay towards the North east Belt to add to/ that Plantation or any where you want to Plant.'; 'When you or Mrs Frere come to Grundisburgh Hall pray if you have one lend me a Catalogue or account of the Pictures & Prints in the Fitzwilliam Gallery. I forgot to mention about the Fence to keep Your Lodge distinct up to the Collonade. This can be surely managed with the sunk fence as I will point out to you. I have brought the sunk fence to terminate in a line with your Lodge to make it correspond with the other end but it may finish at the end of the Colonnade of the Chapel. I however think it will look best to come to the other point to make it uniform and then it will have a handsome appearance from your windows what you will see of it. As you have found the water you must bring the Fountain to the front, or the Centre of the Court.

Dear Sir, I intended some time back, to have done myself the pleasure to call at Grandisburgh Hall, and give you my opinion respecting the fence you are about to put up at Downing College. You mentioned an Iron Palisade to stand on the surface of the ground, but I am enclined [sic] to think that something which would not confine the Eye so much, would be more appropriate for such a situation, and more in harmony with the style of the Building. An Iron Fence is too meager and not massive enough for the front of such an Edifice.

The Trees you plant with the Intention of remaining as an ornament hereafter when the College is all built [i.e. the Elms] must now be regulated to the Proper Place from the face of the Building and supposing the width of the whole promenade to be 40 feet, which it must be at least, then the trees ought to be put in so as they stand about 10 feet from the sunk fence, and 30 from the face of the building. and if 10 feet more is added to the width, to place them at 40 feet, so much the better. The place where the two or three rows of spring are to be put under the wall, should be trenched and good earth put in from the surface soil. I think I shall see you set about the Front in it be long – as there can be no doubt the remaining ground towards Downing street if appropriated to a handsome arrangement of Houses would pay for it; and this might be managed so as to be perfectly distinct from the College and so as to get good stables and Gardens to each House and at the same time preserve a very handsome appearance. If this is not thought eligible, you have no good market in Cambridge a Capital one may be here got, and room for good Houses and Gardens too, and the Centre kept as a grand approach with an avenue, without injuring the Markets etc. When I have the pleasure of seeing you which I may do should I come to Cambridge about Easter I can then tell you the notions I have formed, and in the meantime remain your obliged & sincere friend Perry Nissy.' *Location*: Downing College, Cambridge.

Nothing is known about Perry Nissy except for what can be inferred from the letter attached to his plan for the landscaping of the college. He must have been a neighbour of William Frere in Suffolk, where the second Master of Downing had a family house. Nissy must have been a landscape designer of sorts, if not a professional one he was at least a competent amateur. The scheme for a commercial exploitation of the land north of the college, referred to in his letter, appears to be along the lines of the one proposed by Wilkins in 1817.

155. J. **BAILEY**
Perspective from the south west showing Wilkins' unexecuted southern block. (see Fig.35, p.66)
Pen and watercolour; 35.7×75 cm. Signed and dated 'J.Bailey 1830'. *Exhibited*: 'The Triumph of the Classical. Cambridge Architecture 1804–1834', Cambridge 1977. *Location:* Downing College, Cambridge.

156. C.G. **HARE** (1875–1932)
Perspective from the south west of the proposed new building. (see Fig.49, p.83)
Pen and watercolour; 37×55 cm. Signed and dated 'Geich Horsne 1924'. Inscribed: 'New Buildings DOWNING COLLEGE Cambridge' and on VERSO: 'C.G.Hare 1924'. *Location*: Downing College, Cambridge.

157. H. **BAKER** (1862–1946)
The proposed new east-west axis seen from the Porters' Lodge. (see Fig.50, p.86)
Pen and watercolour; 53×54 cm. Signed and dated 'H.L.G.Pilkington 1929'. *Location*: Downing College, Cambridge.

158. H. **BAKER**
Revised elevation of the Regent Street Gate and Porters' Lodge (1936). (see Fig.56, p.92)
Pen and watercolour; 47×74 cm. *Location*: Downing College, Cambridge.

159. A.T. **SCOTT** (1888–1962)
Elevation of the principal front of the north range including the chapel and students' rooms.
(see Pl.XXI)
Pen and watercolours; 50.5×70.8 cm. Signed and dated 'Arthur Betts 1950'. *Location*: Downing College, Cambridge.

160. A.T. **SCOTT**
Perspectival view of the chapel's interior looking north. (See Pl.XXIII)
Pen and watercolour; 65.7×40.5 cm. Signed and dated 'Arthur Betts 1950'. *Location*: Downing College, Cambridge.

161. A.T. **SCOTT**
View towards the south end of the Chapel.
(see Pl.XXIV)
Pen and watercolour; 65.7×40.5 cm. Signed and dated 'Arthur Betts 1950'. *Location*: Downing College, Cambridge.

Bibliography

Thomas HOPE, *Observations on the Plans and Elevations designed by James Wyatt Architect, for Downing College, Cambridge; in a Letter to Francis Annesley, Esq. M.P.*, (1804)

Robert WILLIS and John Willis CLARK, *The Architectural History of the University of Cambridge and of the Colleges of Cambridge and Eton* 3 vols., (Cambridge 1886)

L.CUST, *History of the Society of Dilettanti* ed. S.Colvin, (1898)

A.GRAVES, *The Royal Academy of Arts. A Complete dictionary of contributors and their work from its foundation in 1769 to 1904*, 8 vols., (1905)

G.WALKLEY, 'Designs for Downing College, Cambridge', *RIBA Journal*, XLV, 1938, p.1014

H. BAKER, *Architecture and Personalities*, (1944)

M.L.CLARKE, *Greek Studies in England 1700–1830*, (Cambridge 1945)

A.DALE, *James Wyatt*, (Oxford 1956)

E.KAUFMANN, 'Piranesi, Algarotti and Lodoli. A controversy in XVIIIth century Venice', *Essays in Honour of Hans Tietze*, (Paris 1958), pp.309–16

A.W.B.SIMPSON, *An Introduction to the History of the Land Law*, (Oxford, 1961)

W.HERRMANN, *Laugier and Eighteenth Century French Theory*, (1962)

J.MORDAUNT CROOK, 'Haileybury and the Greek Revival. The Architecture of William Wilkins, R.A.', *The Haileyburian and I.S.C. Chronicle*, (Hoddesdon 1964)

H.HONOUR, *Neo-Classicism*, (Harmondsworth 1968)

J.MORDAUNT CROOK, *The Greek Revival.* The RIBA drawings series, (Feltham 1968)

D.WATKIN, *Thomas Hope 1769–1831 and the Neo-Classical idea*, (1968)

D.WIEBENSON, *Sources of Greek Revival Architecture*, (1969)

B.LITTLE, 'Cambridge and the Campus', *Virginia Magazine of History and Biography*, LXXIX (April 1971), pp.190–201

ARTS COUNCIL OF GREAT BRITAIN, *The Age of Neo-Classicism*, (London and Harlow 1972)

J.MORDAUNT CROOK, *The Greek Revival. Neo-Classical Attitudes in British Architecture 1760–1870*, (1972)

D.LINSTRUM, *Catalogue of the Drawings Collection of the RIBA. The Wyatt Family*, (Farnborough 1973)

P. TUDOR-CRAIG, 'The Evolution of Ickworth', *Country Life*, 17 May 1973, pp.1362–65.

R.ROSENBLUM, *Transformations in late Eighteenth Century Art*, (Princeton 1974)

D.WATKIN, *The Triumph of the Classical. Cambridge Architecture 1804–1834*, (Cambridge 1977)

H.COLVIN, *A Biographical Dictionary of British Architects 1660–1840*, (1978)

S.FRENCH, *The History of Downing College*, (Cambridge 1978)

J.H.BAKER, *An Introduction to English Legal History*, (2nd ed. 1979)

K.GARLICK and A.MACINTYRE eds., *The Diary of Joseph Farington, vol.VI April 1803–December 1804*, (New Haven and London 1979)

A.BRAHAM, *The Architecture of the French Enlightenment*, (1980)

R.W.LISCOMBE, *William Wilkins 1778–1839*, (Cambridge 1980)

P.BICKNELL, 'The Development of the College Buildings', *Aspects of Downing History*, (Cambridge 1982), pp.2–18

K. CAVE ed., *The Diary of Joseph Farington, vol.VII January 1805–June 1806*, (New Haven and London 1982)

J.F.J.COLLETT-WHITE, *The Old House at Wrest*, (Bedford 1983)

Index